LATTER-DAY
PROPHETS
SPEAK

LATTER-DAY
PROPHETS
SPEAK

Selections from the
Sermons and Writings
of Church Presidents

Edited and Arranged
by
DANIEL H. LUDLOW

KEY TO ABBREVIATION OF TITLES:

BFRLS..................................Biography and Family Record of Lorenzo Snow
CR.......................................Conference Reports
DHC....................................Documentary History of the Church
DN......................................Deseret News
DNCS..................................Deseret News Church Section
DWN...................................Deseret Weekly News
GD......................................Gospel Doctrine
GG......................................The Government of God—*John Taylor*
IE..Improvement Era
IP...Items on Priesthood—*John Taylor*
JD..Journal of Discourses
JI...Juvenile Instructor *(now The Instructor)*
LEJ......................................Liahona, or Elders' Journal
MA......................................The Mediation and the Atonement—*John Taylor*
MS.......................................Millennial Star
OWTBS...............................The Only Way to Be Saved—*Lorenzo Snow*
RSM....................................Relief Society Magazine
TPJS....................................Teachings of the Prophet Joseph Smith
TS..Times and Seasons
YWJ.....................................Young Woman's Journal

The titles of all other books and materials used are written out in full.

In the abbreviated references the numbers refer to the volume and and page number, if separated by a colon. Thus, JD 12:240 refers to Journal of Discourses, volume 12 and page 240 of that volume. If numbers are not separated by a colon, they refer to page number only.

The date following the reference is usually the date when the discourse was given, except in the case of periodicals and written materials, when the date of publication is generally used.

The style of punctuation used in this volume followed, as closely as possible, that which appeared in the original sources. Thus, there is frequently a slight variance between the punctuation used in the text and popular usage.

All references are verbatim quotations, except where an ellipsis (. . . .) indicates that some material has been left out, or where brackets [ ] signify that the compiler has added words not in the original source.

Foreword

LATTER-DAY PROPHETS SPEAK, compiled and edited by Daniel H. Ludlow, is an outstanding contribution to Latter-day Saint Church literature. During recent years various writers have compiled and published in book form the most important doctrinal writings and teachings of six out of the eight Presidents who have presided over the Church of Jesus Christ. All of these books have been valuable additions to our writings, providing the Saints opportunities to gain a more comprehensive understanding of the Plan of Salvation. However, our people have had for many years a definite need for a one-volume work in which the principal doctrinal teachings of all the eight men who have presided over the Church of Jesus Christ are correlated and made available for church use. This task has now been accomplished in this book in a very commendable way by Brother Ludlow.

The author is one of the capable and faithful young men of the Church. He made an enviable record while attending the Utah State Agricultural College. For two years in succession he had the honor of being president of the student body. At the present time he is a teacher at his *Alma Mater*. His first interest, however, has always been the Church. With the hope in his heart of helping to proclaim the Gospel, he assigned himself the task of compiling this book, a work which consumed sixteen-months' time.

In preparing this volume pertinent teachings on definite Gospel subjects have been culled from the numerous sermons and writings of the Presidents of the Church and placed in their proper places under appropriate subject titles. Whenever it was possible, the compiler has presented a typical relevant statement under each subject head from each of the Latter-day Prophets, thereby giving the authoritative church viewpoint on each of those subjects. Furthermore, all superfluous and irrelevant statements have been omitted, thus avoiding confusion and waste of time of the reader. This factor in itself makes the book a convenient and excellent medium for the purpose of studying the Gospel.

Since this volume is entirely devoted to the religious teachings of God's mouthpieces on earth in the last dispensation of the Gospel—the dispensation of the fullness of times—and since the Saints have a high regard for modern revelation and the teachings of the Prophets of God, this book should take its place as one of the valuable and great works of the Church of Jesus Christ.

A glance at the table of contents shows how extensive the coverage of the Gospel doctrine is in this volume and how carefully the various topics have been outlined. The thirty-nine chapters are divided into five sections which Brother Ludlow calls "books." The first seven chapters present the theme of eternal progression from our pre-existent state to the time of our gaining exaltation. Then the author sets forth in ten chapters the principles and ordinances of the Gospel of Jesus Christ and the conditions necessary for men and women to come back into the presence of God. A section is devoted to Priesthood and church government. Book Four tells the story of the conditions and accomplishments during the last days, including the millennial reign of the Lord Jesus Christ. The last section is entitled "General Church Doctrines and Practices." In twelve excellent chapters such basic doctrines as "The Godhead," "Prophecy and Revelation," Temple Marriage," "The Word of Wisdom," Missionary Work," Education," and other pertinent doctrines are discussed.

This book presents such a complete coverage of the Gospel of Jesus Christ as taught by the Presidents of the Church in the latter days and is so logically and conveniently compiled and outlined that it could serve well as an excellent course of study for church groups. This volume will continue for many years to hold a high place among other volumes of church literature as one of the principal Latter-day Saint reference books on church doctrine.

MILTON R. HUNTER
Of the First Council of the Seventy

Preface

Continuous revelation from God to the President of the Church is one of the basic beliefs of members of the Church of Jesus Christ of Latter-day Saints. If this belief is true, and the compiler knows that it is, then the statements of the Presidents of the Church should stand next to the Scriptures as authoritative sources on the various gospel doctrines.

It has been the aim of the compiler of this work to choose those statements of the several Presidents which would most clearly portray their beliefs on gospel questions. In order to gain this end, the compiler has carefully searched through over a thousand volumes of Church periodicals, newspapers, histories and general books on Church doctrines and has selected from these voluminous sources several thousand statements from the recorded discourses and writings of the eight Presidents of the Church who have served in this dispensation. This collection of material has, in turn, been sorted and re-sorted until those statements which best deal on the various areas chosen, in the humble opinion of the compiler, have been included in this compilation. Needless to say, thousands of priceless gems of thought have, of necessity, been discarded to keep this volume from becoming too large.

The compiler has tried, as far as possible, to avoid duplication from the previous books printed on the statements and writings of the Presidents of the Church. However, the thorough methods used by the previous compilers along these lines have made the complete lack of repetition impossible. Appreciation is extended to these authors and compilers for their inspiration and excellent example.

The compiler expresses sincere thanks to Dr. Milton R. Hunter, of the First Council of the Seventy, for his guidance, inspiration and help in seeing this book on the press. Gratitude is also expressed to Dr. Hunter for writing the foreword of this volume. Humble appreciation is extended to President David O. McKay for his encouragement and aid, and to Elder John A. Widtsoe and Bryant S. Hinckley for reading the manuscript and making helpful suggestions.

Acknowledgment is also hereby made to those considerate workers at the libraries of the Brigham Young University, the University of Utah, the Utah State Agricultural College, the Church Historian's Office, and the Logan L.D.S. Institute of Religion for their helpful suggestions and assistance.

Sincere thanks also to my wife, Luene Ludlow, for her untiring and uncomplaining aid throughout the months of preparation and work on this compilation.

And, most important of all, thanks to Him above, without whose help no accomplishment is possible. If this volume will help to disseminate some of those divine truths which originate from God our Father, the humble hopes of the compiler will have been realized.

—DANIEL H. LUDLOW

Logan, Utah
June 10, 1947

Table of Contents

BOOK ONE

THE ETERNAL PLAN OF PROGRESSION

BOOK THREE

THE PRIESTHOOD

BOOK FOUR

THE LAST DAYS

BOOK FIVE

GENERAL CHURCH DOCTRINES AND PRACTICES

BOOK ONE

The Eternal Plan of Progression

Knowest thou whence thou camest?
Thine Origin? Who thou art? What?
and whither Thou art bound? A
chrysalis of yesterday: Today a gaudy
fluttering butterfly—A moth; tomorrow crushed, and then an end of thee.
Is this so? And must thou perish
Thus, and die ingloriously without a
Hope?

—JOHN TAYLOR
MS 8:178
September 5, 1846

CHAPTER I

The Pre-Existent State

THE SPIRIT OF MAN IS ETERNAL

THE MIND or the intelligence which man possesses is co-equal with God Himself . . .

I am dwelling on the immortality of the spirit of man. Is it logical to say that the intelligence of spirits is immortal and yet that it had a beginning? The intelligence of spirits had no beginning, neither will it have an end. That is good logic. That which has a beginning may have an end. There never was a time when there were not spirits; for they are co-equal (co-eternal) with our Father in heaven . . .

Intelligence is eternal and exists upon a self-existent principle. It is a spirit from age to age, and there is no creation about it.
—*Joseph Smith, Jr.,* TPJS, p. 353-354, April, 1844

The spirit of man is not a created being; it existed from eternity and will exist to eternity. Anything created cannot be eternal; and earth, water, etc., had their existence in an elementary state, from eternity.
—*Joseph Smith, Jr.,* DHC 3:387, July 2, 1839

Mankind are organized of element designed to endure to all eternity; it never had a beginning and never can have an end. There never was a time when this matter, of which you and I are composed, was not in existence, and there never can be a time when it will pass out of existence; it cannot be annihilated.
—*Brigham Young,* JD 3:356, June 15, 1856

Spirit is a substance, . . . it is material, but . . . it is more pure, elastic and refined matter than the body; . . . it existed before the body, can exist in the body; and will exist separate from body, when the body will be mouldering in the dust; and will, in the resurrection, be again united with it.
—*Joseph Smith, Jr.,* DHC 4:575, April, 1842

ALL SPIRITS ARE THE CHILDREN OF GOD

The doctrine of pre-existence pours a wonderful flood of light upon the otherwise mysterious problem of man's origin. It shows that man, as a spirit, was begotten and born of heavenly parents and reared to maturity in the eternal mansions of the Father, prior to coming upon the earth in a temporal body to undergo an experience in mortality.

—Heber J. Grant, IE 28:1090, September, 1925

We believe that we are the offspring of our Father in heaven, and that we possess in our spiritual organizations the same capabilities, powers and faculties that our Father possesses, although in an infantile state, requiring to pass through a certain course or ordeal by which they will be developed and improved according to the heed we give to the principles we have received . . .

We are born in the image of God our Father; He begot us like unto Himself. There is the nature of deity in the composition of our spiritual organization; in our spiritual birth our Father transmitted to us the capabilities, powers and faculties which He Himself possessed, as much so as the child on its mother's bosom possesses, although in an undeveloped state, the faculties, powers and susceptibilities of its parent.

—Lorenzo Snow, JD 14:300;302, January 14, 1872

Every spirit that comes to this earth to take upon it a tabernacle is a son or a daughter of God and possesses all the intelligence and all the attributes that any son or daughter can enjoy, either in the spirit world or in this world, except that in the spirit, and separated from the body, they lacked just the tabernacle of being like God the Father.

—Joseph F. Smith, YWJ 6:371-372, March 12, 1895

Our Father in heaven begat all the spirits that ever were, or ever will be, upon this earth; and they were born spirits in the eternal world. Then the Lord by His power and wisdom organized the mortal tabernacle of man. We were made first spiritual and afterwards temporal.   *—Brigham Young,* JD 1:50, April 9, 1852

With regard to our position before we came here, I will say that we dwelt with the Father and with the Son, as expressed

in the hymn, "O my Father." . . . We dwelt in the presence of
God before we came here.

—*Wilford Woodruff*, MS 56:229, October 8, 1893

I am grateful that in the midst of the confusion of our
Father's children there has been given to the members of this
great organization a sure knowledge of the origin of man, that
we came from the spirit world where our spirits were begotten
by our Father in heaven, that He formed our first parents from
the dust of the earth, and that their spirits were placed in their
bodies, and that man came, not as some have believed, not as
some have preferred to believe, from some of the lower walks
of life, but our ancestors were those beings who lived in the
courts of heaven. We came not from some menial order of life,
but our ancestor is God our Heavenly Father.

—*George Albert Smith*, CR, p. 33, October, 1925

Children are the offspring of God, their spirits were begotten
in the holy heavens of our Father, and they are given to us for
our blessing. We, as stewards, are permitted to receive them in
their infancy, to educate and prepare them, not alone that they
may become great in this world and bring honor to us here,
but, by observing the laws of God, that they might live again
with us in the presence of our Father throughout the endless
ages of eternity.   —*George Albert Smith*, CR, p. 36, October, 1907

It does seem strange that so many people doubt our divine
ancestry, and that God is the Father of our spirits; yet from the
very beginning, from the very earliest period of which we have
any record in this world, He has been teaching men and women
this fact . . .

When God created the earth and placed our first parents
upon it, He did not leave them without knowledge concerning
Himself. It is true that there had been taken from them the
remembrance of their pre-existent life, but in His tender mercy
He talked with them and later He sent His choice servants to
instruct them in the things pertaining to eternal life.

—*George Albert Smith*, CR, p. 90-91, October, 1928

THE GREAT COUNCIL IN HEAVEN

Where did we come from? From God. Our spirits existed
before they came to this world. They were in the councils of

the heavens before the foundations of the earth were laid . . .
We sang together with the heavenly hosts for joy when the
foundations of the earth were laid and when the plan of our
existence upon this earth and redemption were mapped out . . .
We were unquestionably present in those councils when that
wonderful circumstance occurred . . . when Satan offered himself
as a savior of the world if he could but receive the honor and
glory of the Father for doing it. . . . We were, no doubt, there
and took part in all those scenes, we were vitally concerned in
the carrying out of these great plans and purposes, we understood
them, and it was for our sakes they were decreed and are to be
consummated.   —*Joseph F. Smith,* JD 25:57, February 17, 1884

I dare say that in the spirit world, when it was proposed to
us to come into this probation and pass through the experience
that we are now receiving, it was not altogether pleasant and
agreeable; the prospects were not so delightful in all respects
as might have been desired. Yet there is no doubt that we saw
and understood clearly there, that, in order to accomplish our
exaltation and glory, this was a necessary experience; and however disagreeable it might have appeared to us, we were willing
to conform to the will of God, and consequently we are here.
              —*Lorenzo Snow,* MS 56:49, October 6, 1893

At the first organization in heaven we were all present and
saw the Savior chosen and appointed and the plan of salvation
made, and we sanctioned it.
              —*Joseph Smith, Jr.,* TPJS, p. 181, January, 1841

In regard to the battle in heaven . . . I cannot relate the
principal circumstances, it is so long since it happened: but I
do not think it lasted very long; for when Lucifer, the Son of
the Morning, claimed the privilege of having the control of this
earth and redeeming it a contention rose; but I do not think it
took long to cast down one-third of the hosts of heaven, as it
is written in the Bible. But let me tell you that it was one-third
part of the spirits who were prepared to take tabernacles upon
this earth, and who rebelled against the other two-thirds of the
heavenly host; and they were cast down to this world.
              —*Brigham Young,* JD 5:54-55, July 19, 1857

THE GLORIOUS PLAN

The glorious plan which God has given
To bring a ruined world to heaven,
Was framed in Christ ere time had birth,
Was sealed in heaven ere known on earth.
—*John Taylor,* Gospel Kingdom, p. 383

ALL MORTAL BEINGS KEPT THEIR FIRST ESTATE

We have been placed upon this earth because of our faithfulness in having kept our first estate. The labors that we performed in the sphere that we left before we came here have had a certain effect upon our lives here, and to a certain extent they govern and control the lives that we lead here, just the same as the labors that we do here will control and govern our lives when we pass from this stage of existence.
—*Heber J. Grant,* IE 46:75, February, 1943

A knowledge of pre-existence has been given to the Latter-day Saints; a knowledge that we are here because we kept our first estate . . .

We ascertain that not only was the Savior in the beginning with the Father, but also that you and I were there. We dwelt there, and by reason of faithfulness, having kept our first estate, we have been permitted to come into this world and receive tabernacles of flesh. The fact that we are living in the flesh is evidence that we did keep our first estate.
—*George Albert Smith,* CR, p. 47-48, October, 1906

We have learned that we existed with God in eternity before we came into this life, and that we kept our estate. Had we not kept what is called our first estate and observed the laws that governed there, you and I would not be here today. We are here because we are worthy to be here, and that arises, to a great extent at least, from the fact that we kept our first estate.
—*Lorenzo Snow,* MS 56:450, April 7, 1894

THE ETERNAL PLAN

The Latter-day Saints have often been ridiculed on account of their belief in the pre-existence of spirits and for marrying for time and all eternity, both being Bible doctrines. We have often been requested to give our views in relation to these principles, but considered the things of the kingdom belonged to the children of the kingdom, therefore not meet to give them to those without. But being very politely requested by a lady a few days ago (a member of the Church) to answer the following questions, we could not consistently refuse—viz:

"Where did I come from? What am I doing here? Whither am I going? And what is my destiny after having obeyed the truth, if faithful to the end?"

For her benefit and all others concerned, we will endeavor to answer the questions in brief, as we understand them. The reason will be apparent for our belief in the pre-existence of spirits and in marrying for time and all eternity.

Lady, whence comest thou? Thine origin? What art thou doing here? Whither art thou going, and what is thy destiny? Declare unto me if thou hast understanding. Knowest thou not that thou art a spark of Deity, struck from the fire of His eternal blaze, and brought forth in the midst of eternal burning?

Knowest thou not that eternities ago thy spirit, pure and holy, dwelt in thy Heavenly Father's bosom and in His presence, and with thy mother, one of the queens of heaven, surrounded by thy brother and sister spirits in the spirit world, among the Gods? That as thy spirit beheld the scenes transpiring there, and thou grewest in intelligence, thou sawest worlds upon worlds organized and peopled with kindred spirits who took upon them tabernacles, died, were resurrected, and received their exaltation on the redeemed worlds they once dwelt upon. Thou being willing and anxious to imitate them, waiting and desirous to obtain a body, a resurrection, and exaltation also, and having obtained permission, madest a covenant with one of thy kindred spirits to be thy guardian angel while in mortality, also with two others, male and female spirits, that thou wouldst come and take a tabernacle through their lineage, and become one of their offspring. You also chose a kindred spirit whom you loved in the spirit world (and who had permission to come to this planet and take a tabernacle), to be your head, stay, husband, and protector on the earth and to exalt you in eternal worlds. All these were arranged, likewise the spirits who should tabernacle through your lineage. Thou longed, thou sighed, and thou prayed to thy Father in heaven for the time to arrive when thou couldst come to this earth, which had fled and fallen from where it was first organized, near the planet Kolob. Leaving thy Father's and

Mother's bosom and all thy kindred spirits, thou camest to earth, took a tabernacle, and imitated the deeds of those who had been exalted before you.

At length the time arrived, and thou heard the voice of thy Father saying, go, daughter, to yonder lower world, and take upon thee a tabernacle, and work out thy probation with fear and trembling, and rise to exaltation. But, daughter, remember you go on this condition, that is, you are to forget all things you ever saw, or knew to be transacted in the spirit world; you are not to know or remember anything concerning the same that you have beheld transpire here; but you must go and become one of the most helpless of all beings that I have created, while in your infancy; subject to sickness, pain, tears, mourning, sorrow, and death. But when truth shall touch the cords of your heart, they will vibrate; then intelligence shall illuminate your mind, and shed its lustre in your soul, and you shall begin to understand the things you once knew, but which had gone from you. You shall then begin to understand and know the object of your creation. Daughter, go and be faithful as thou hast been in thy first estate.

Thy spirit, filled with joy and thanksgiving, rejoiced in thy Father and rendered praise to His holy name, and the spirit world resounded in anthems of praise to the Father of spirits. Thou bade Father, Mother, and all farewell, and, along with thy guardian angel, thou came on this terraqueous globe. The spirits thou hast chosen to come and tabernacle through their lineage, and your head having left the spirit world some years previous, thou came a spirit pure and holy. Thou hast obeyed the truth, and thy guardian angel ministers unto thee and watches over thee. Thou hast chosen him you loved in the spirit world to be thy companion. Now, crowns, thrones, exaltations, and dominions are in reserve for thee in the eternal worlds, and the way is opened for thee to return to the presence of thy Heavenly Father, if thou wilt only abide by and walk in a celestial law, fulfill the designs of thy Creator and hold out to the end that when mortality is laid in the tomb, you may go down to your grave in peace, arise in glory, and receive your everlasting reward in the resurrection of the just, along with thy head and husband. Thou wilt be permitted to pass by the Gods and angels who guard the gates, and onward, upward to thy exaltation in a celestial world among the Gods, to be a priestess queen upon thy

Heavenly Father's throne, and a glory to thy husband and off-spring, to bear the souls of men, to people other worlds (as thou didst bear their tabernacles in mortality) while eternity goes and eternity comes; and if you will receive it, lady, this is eternal life. And herein is the saying of the Apostle Paul fulfilled, that the man is not without the woman, neither is the woman without the man, in the Lord; that man is the head of the woman, and the glory of the man is the woman. Hence, thine origin, the object of thy ultimate destiny. If faithful, lady, the cup is within thy reach; drink then the heavenly draught and live.

—*John Taylor,* "The Mormon," August 29, 1857

CHAPTER II

The Mortal Probation

A. PURPOSE OF THE MORTAL PROBATION

THE OBJECT of our being placed upon this earth is that we may work out an exaltation, that we may prepare ourselves to go back and dwell with our Heavenly Father; and our Father, knowing the faults and failings of men, has given us certain commandments to obey, and if we will examine those requirements and the things that devolve upon us we will find that they are all for our individual benefit and advancement. The school of life in which we are placed and the lessons that are given to us by our Father will make of us exactly what He desires, so that we may be prepared to dwell with Him.

—Heber J. Grant, IE 48:123, March, 1945

We have come to sojourn in the flesh, to obtain tabernacles for our immortal spirits. . . . The object of our earthly existence is that we might have a fullness of joy and that we may become the sons and daughters of God, in the fullest sense of the word, being heirs of God and joint heirs with Jesus Christ, to be kings and priests unto God, to inherit glory, dominion, exaltation, thrones, and every power and attribute developed and possessed by our Heavenly Father. This is the object of our being on this earth. *—Joseph F. Smith, JD 19:259, April 11, 1878*

I sometimes wonder if people realize the purpose of their existence, and the importance of the labor that men and women are expected to perform while on the earth. . . .

We have been placed here for a purpose. That purpose is that we may overcome the evil temptations that are placed in our way, that we may learn to be charitable to one another, that we may overcome the passions with which we are beset, so that when the time comes for us to go to the other side we may be worthy, by reason of the effort we have put forth, to enjoy the blessings that our Father has in store for the faithful . . .

We are not here to while away the hours of this life and then pass to a sphere of exaltation; but we are here to qualify ourselves day by day for the positions that our Father expects us to fill hereafter.
                                    —*George Albert Smith*, CR, p. 59; 61-62, April, 1905

The object of our being here is to do the will of the Father as it is done in heaven, to work righteousness in the earth, to subdue wickedness and put it under our feet, to conquer sin and the adversary of our souls, to rise above the imperfections and weaknesses of poor, fallen humanity, by the inspiration of Almighty God and His power made manifest, and thus become indeed the Saints and servants of the Lord in the earth.
                                    —*Joseph F. Smith*, CR, p. 85, April, 1902

We are here to cooperate with God in the salvation of the living, in the redemption of the dead, in the blessings of our ancestors, in the pouring out (of) blessings upon our children; we are here for the purpose of redeeming and regenerating the earth on which we live, and God has placed His authority and His counsels here upon the earth for that purpose, that men may learn to do the will of God on the earth as it is done in heaven. This is the object of our existence.
                                    —*John Taylor*, JD 21:94, April 13, 1879

The Lord designs to bring us up into the celestial kingdom. He has made known, through direct revelation, that we are His offspring, begotten in the eternal worlds, that we have come to this earth for the special purpose of preparing ourselves to receive a fullness of our Father's glory when we shall return into His presence. Therefore, we must seek the ability to keep this law, to sanctify our motives, desires, feelings and affections, that they may be pure and holy, and our will in all things be subservient to the will of God, and have no will of our own except to do the will of our Father . . . One of the chief difficulties that many suffer from is that we are too apt to forget the great object of life, the motive of our Heavenly Father in sending us here to put on mortality, as well as the holy calling with which we have been called; and hence, instead of rising above the little transitory things of time, we too often allow ourselves to come down to the level of the world without availing ourselves of the divine help which God has instituted, which alone can enable us to overcome them. We are no better than the rest of the world if we do not cultivate the feeling to be perfect, even as our Father in heaven is perfect.

—Lorenzo Snow, JD 20:189; 191, April 7, 1879

It is the wish of our Heavenly Father to bring all His children back into His presence. The spirits of all the human family dwelt with Him before they took tabernacles of flesh and became subject to the fall and to sin. He is their spiritual Father and has sent them here to be clothed with flesh and to be subject, with their tabernacles, to the ills that afflict fallen humanity. When they have proved themselves faithful in all things, and worthy before Him, they can then have the privilege of returning again to His presence, with their bodies, to dwell in the abodes of the blessed. If man could have been made perfect, in his double capacity of body and spirit, without passing through the ordeals of mortality, there would have been no necessity of our coming into this state of trial and suffering. Could the Lord have glorified His children in spirit, without a body like His own, He no doubt would have done so.

—Brigham Young, JD 11:43, January 8, 1865

IMPORTANCE OF OBTAINING A MORTAL BODY

We came to this earth that we might have a body and present it pure before God in the celestial kingdom. The great principle of happiness consists in having a body. The devil has no body, and herein is his punishment. He is pleased when he can obtain the tabernacle of man, and when cast out by the Savior he asked to go into the herd of swine, showing that he would prefer a swine's body to having none.

All beings who have bodies have power over those who have not. The devil has no power over us only as we permit him.

—Joseph Smith, Jr., TPJS, p. 181, January, 1841

Our mortal bodies are all important to us; without them we never can be glorified in the eternities that will be. We are in this state of being for the express purpose of obtaining habitations for our spirits to dwell in, that they may become personages of tabernacle.   *—Brigham Young,* JD 9:286, February 23, 1862

It is absolutely necessary that we should come to the earth and take upon us tabernacles; because if we did not have taber-

nacles we could not be like God nor like Jesus Christ. God has a tabernacle of flesh and bone. He is an organized being just as we are, who are now in the flesh. Jesus Christ . . . had a fleshly tabernacle; He was crucified on the cross; and His body was raised from the dead . . . We are precisely in the same condition and under the same circumstances that God our Heavenly Father was when He was passing through this or a similar ordeal. We are destined to come forth out of the grave as Jesus did, and to obtain immortal bodies as He did . . . This is the object of our existence in the world.
                    —*Joseph F. Smith*, JD 25:58-59, February 17, 1884

Man was created in the image of God, and he was the offspring of Deity Himself and consequently made in His likeness; and being made in that likeness, he was a Son of God, and the very object of his being planted upon the earth was that he might multiply. Why? That the spirits which had existed with their Heavenly Father might have tabernacles to inhabit and become mortal, and, through the possession of these tabernacles and the plan of salvation, that they might be raised to greater dignity, glory and exaltation than it would be possible for them to enjoy without these . . . God had a purpose, therefore, in the organization of this earth, and in the placing of man upon it, and He has never deviated one hair to the right or to the left in regard to man and his destiny from that time until the present.
                    —*John Taylor*, JD 17:370, April 8, 1875

The object of man's taking a body is that through the redemption of Jesus Christ both soul and body may be exalted in the eternal world, when the earth shall be celestial, and obtain a higher exaltation than he could be capable of doing without a body. For when man was first made, he was made "a little lower than the angels." But through the atonement and resurrection of Jesus Christ he is placed in a position to obtain an exaltation higher than angels. For, says the Apostle, "know ye not that we shall judge angels." . . .
Another object that we came here for and took bodies was to propagate our species. For if it is for our benefit to come here, it is also for the benefit of others.
Hence the first commandment given to man was to "Be fruitful and multiply, and replenish the earth." (Genesis 1:28)
                    —*John Taylor*, MS 13:81, March 15, 1851

There were certain great principles involved in the organization of this earth, and one was that there might be a place provided whereon the children of our Heavenly Father could live and propagate their species and have bodies formed for the spirits to inhabit who were the children of God; for we are told that He is the God and Father of the spirits of all flesh. It was requisite, therefore, that an earth should be organized; it was requisite that man should be placed upon it; it was requisite that bodies should be prepared for those spirits to inhabit, in order that the purposes of God pertaining to His progeny might be accomplished, and that those spirits might be enabled, through the medium of the everlasting gospel, to return unto the presence of their Heavenly Father, as Gods among the Gods.
—John Taylor, JD 25:303-304, October, 1884

MORTALITY IS A STATE OF TRIAL FOR MAN

The whole mortal existence of man is neither more nor less than a preparatory state given to finite beings, a space wherein they may improve themselves for a higher state of being.
—Brigham Young, JD 1:334, December 5, 1853

Yours, as well as my eternal destiny, our future position throughout the ages of eternity, depend upon the few hours, the few days, the few weeks we spend in the flesh.
—Wilford Woodruff, JD 19:362, June 30, 1878

The trials and temptations have been very great to many of our people and more or less, perhaps, to all of us. The Lord seems to require some proof on our part, something to show that He can depend upon us when He wants us to accomplish certain things in His interest. The reason is that the condition in which we will be placed in the future, as time passes along, as eternity approaches, and as we move forward in eternity and along the line of our existence, we shall be placed in certain conditions that require very great sacrifice in the interests of humanity, in the interests of the Spirit of God, in the interest of His children and our own children, in generations to come, in eternity.
—Lorenzo Snow, CR, p. 2, October, 1900

We are placed on this earth to prove whether we are worthy to go into the celestial world, the terrestrial, or the telestial, or

to hell, or to any other kingdom, or place, and we have enough
of life given us to do this.
                            —*Brigham Young*, JD 4:269, March 8, 1857

I heard the Prophet Joseph say, in speaking to the Twelve
on one occasion: "You will have all kinds of trials to pass through.
And it is quite as necessary for you to be tried as it was for
Abraham and other men of God, and (said he) God will feel
after you, and He will take hold of you and wrench your very
heart strings, and if you cannot stand it you will not be fit for
an inheritance in the celestial kingdom of God."
                            —*John Taylor*, JD 24:197, June 18, 1883

We have been called to pass through trials many times, and
I do not think we should complain, because if we had no trials
we should hardly feel at home in the other world in the company
of the prophets and apostles who were sawn asunder, crucified,
etc., for the word of God and testimony of Jesus Christ.
                            —*Wilford Woodruff*, JD 23:328, December 10, 1882

We are here that we may be educated in a school of suffering and of fiery trials, which school was necessary for Jesus our
Elder Brother, who, the Scriptures tell us, was made perfect
through suffering. It is necessary we suffer in all things, that we
may be qualified and worthy to rule and govern all things, even
as our Father in heaven and His Eldest Son Jesus.
                            —*Lorenzo Snow*, MS 13:363, December 1, 1851

It has been decreed by the Almighty that spirits, upon taking
bodies, shall forget all they had known previously, or they could
not have a day of trial—could not have an opportunity for proving
themselves in darkness and temptation, in unbelief and wickedness, to prove themselves worthy of eternal existence.
                            —*Brigham Young*, JD 6:333, June 19, 1859

There is not a single condition of life that is entirely unnecessary; there is not one hour's experience but what is beneficial to all those who make it their study and aim to improve
upon the experience they gain. What becomes a trial to one
person is not noticed by another.
                            —*Brigham Young*, JD 9:292, May 25, 1862

"WHAT IS MAN, THAT THOU ART MINDFUL OF HIM?"

What is he? He had his being in the eternal worlds; he existed before he came here. He is not only the son of man, but he is the Son of God also. He is a God in embryo and possesses within him a spark of that eternal flame which was struck from the blaze of God's eternal fire in the eternal world, and he is placed here upon the earth that he may possess true intelligence, true light, true knowledge,—that he may know himself—that he may know God—that he may know something about what he was before he came here—that he may know something about what he is destined to enjoy in the eternal worlds—that he may be fully acquainted with his origin, with his present existence, and with his future destiny—that he may know something about the strength and weakness of human nature—that he may understand the Divine law, and learn to conquer his passions, and bring into subjection every principle that is at variance with the law of God—that he may understand his true relationship to God; and finally, that he may learn how to subdue, to conquer, subject all wrong, seek after, obtain, and possess every true, holy, virtuous, and heavenly principle; and, as he is only a sojourner, that he may fulfill the measure of his creation, help himself and family, be a benefit to the present and future generations, and go back to God, having accomplished the work he came here to perform. —*John Taylor*, JD 8:3-4, February 19, 1860

OUR IDENTITY WILL NEVER CHANGE

We will progress and develop and grow in wisdom and understanding, but our identity can never change. We did not spring from spawn. Our spirits existed from the beginning, have existed always, and will continue forever. We did not pass through the ordeals of embodiment in the lesser animals in order to reach the perfection to which we have attained in manhood and womanhood, in the image and likeness of God. God was and is our Father, and His children were begotten in the flesh of His own image and likeness, male and female . . .

They change from worse to better; they may change from evil to good, from unrighteousness to righteousness, from humanity to immortality, from death to life everlasting. They may progress in the manner in which God has progressed; they may grow

and advance, but their identity can never be changed, worlds
without end—remember that God has revealed these principles,
and I know they are true.

—*Joseph F. Smith*, IE 12:595;598, June, 1909

THE SOUL IS COMPOSED OF SPIRIT AND BODY

We are called mortal beings because in us are seeds of
death, but in reality we are immortal beings because there is
also within us the germ of eternal life. Man is a dual being,
composed of the spirit which gives life, force, intelligence and
capacity to man, and the body which is the tenement of the spirit
and is suited to its form, adapted to its necessities, and acts in
harmony with and to its utmost capacity yields obedience to
the will of the spirit. The two combined constitute the soul. The
body is dependent upon the spirit, and the spirit during its
natural occupancy of the body is subject to the laws which apply
to and govern it in the mortal state.

—*Joseph F. Smith*, JD 23:169, June 18, 1882

All spirits came from God, and they came pure from His
presence, and were put into earthly tabernacles, which were
organized for that express purpose; and so the spirit and the body
became a living soul. If these souls should live, according to
the law of heaven, God ordained that they should become temples prepared to inherit all things.

—*Brigham Young*, JD 6:291, August 15, 1852

What is the body without the spirit? It is lifeless clay.
What is it that affects this lifeless clay? It is the spirit, it is the
immortal part, the eternal being, that existed before it came
here, that exists within us, and that will continue to exist, and
that by and by will redeem these tabernacles and bring them
forth out of the grave.   —*Joseph F. Smith*, JD 25:250, July 18, 1884

THE BLESSINGS OF LIVING A WORTHY LIFE

A man or a woman who places the wealth of this world and
the things of time in the scales against the things of God and
the wisdom of eternity, has no eyes to see, no ears to hear, no
heart to understand.   —*Brigham Young*, JD 15:18, April 28, 1872

Upon our lives here is predicated the degree of perfection in which we shall arise, as well as the time when that event shall take place. A man will not awake on the resurrection morning to find that all that he neglected to do in mortal life has been put to the credit side of his account and that the debit side of his ledger shows a clean page. That is not the teaching of the gospel. "Whatsoever a man soweth, that shall he also reap. For he that soweth to his flesh shall of the flesh reap corruption; but he that soweth to the Spirit shall of the Spirit reap life everlasting." He whose every act has fitted him for the enjoyment of eternity will be far in advance of the man whose all has been centered on the things of this life.

—*Heber J. Grant, MS 56:201, March 31, 1904*

All intelligent beings who are crowned with crowns of glory, immortality, and eternal lives must pass through every ordeal appointed for intelligent beings to pass through, to gain their glory and exaltation. Every calamity that can come upon mortal beings will be suffered to come upon the few, to prepare them to enjoy the presence of the Lord. If we obtain the glory that Abraham obtained, we must do so by the same means that he did . . . we must pass through the same experience and gain the knowledge, intelligence, and endowments that will prepare us to enter into the celestial kingdom of our Father and God . . . Every trial and experience you have passed through is necessary for your salvation. —*Brigham Young, JD 8:150, August 26, 1860*

Will you spend the time of your probation for naught and fool away your existence and being? You were organized and brought into being for the purpose of enduring forever, if you fulfill the measure of your creation, pursue the right path, observe the requirements of the celestial law, and obey the commandments of our God. It is then, and then only, you may expect the blessing of eternal lives will be conferred upon you. It can be obtained upon no other principle.

—*Brigham Young, JD 1:113-114, February 27, 1853*

B. THE POWERS OF EVIL

One-third part of the spirits that were prepared for this earth rebelled against Jesus Christ and were cast down to the earth, and they have been opposed to Him from that day to this,

with Lucifer at their head. He is their great General—Lucifer, the Son of the Morning. He was once a brilliant and influential character in heaven, and we will know more about him hereafter.
—*Brigham Young*, JD 5:55, July 19, 1857

Who is Satan? He is a being of God's own make, under His control, subject to His will, cast out of heaven for rebellion; and when his services can be dispensed with, an angel will cast him into the bottomless pit. Can he fight against and overcome God? verily, No! Can he alter the designs of God? verily, No! Satan may rage; but the Lord can confine him within proper limits. He may instigate rebellion against God, but the Lord can bind him in chains.   —*John Taylor*, GG, p. 81, Published August, 1852

This arch enemy of God and man, called the devil, the "Son of the Morning," who dwells here on the earth, is a personage of great power; he has great influence and knowledge. He understands that if this kingdom, which he rebelled against in heaven, prevails on the earth, there will be no dominion here for him . . . There is a vast number of fallen spirits, cast out with him, here on the earth. They do not die and disappear; they have not bodies only as they enter the tabernacles of men. They have not organized bodies and are not to be seen with the sight of the eye. But there are many evil spirits amongst us, and they labor to overthrow the Church and kingdom of God.
—*Wilford Woodruff*, JD 13:163, December 12, 1869

Every person who desires and strives to be a Saint is closely watched by fallen spirits that came here when Lucifer fell, and by the spirits of wicked persons who have been here in tabernacles and departed from them, but who are still under the control of the prince of the power of the air. Those spirits are never idle; they are watching every person who wishes to do right and are continually prompting them to do wrong.
—*Brigham Young*, JD 7:239, September 1, 1859

THE POWER OF LUCIFER AND HIS FOLLOWERS

Let it not be forgotten that the evil one has great power in the earth and that by every possible means he seeks to darken the minds of men and then offers them falsehood and deception in the guise of truth. Satan is a skillful imitator, and as genuine gospel truth is given the world in ever-increasing abundance, so he spreads the counterfeit coin of false doctrine. Beware of his spurious currency, it will purchase for you nothing but disappointment, misery and spiritual death. The "father of lies" he has been called, and such an adept has he become, through the ages of practice in his nefarious work, that were it possible he would deceive the very elect.

—Joseph F. Smith, JI 37:562, September, 1902

Every spirit, or vision, or singing, is not of God. The devil is an orator; he is powerful; he took our Savior on to a pinnacle of the temple and kept Him in the wilderness for forty days . . . The devil can speak in tongues ; . . . he can tempt all classes.

—Joseph Smith, Jr., DHC 3:392, July 2, 1839

You are aware that many think that the devil has rule and power over both body and spirit. Now, I want to tell you that he does not hold any power over man, only so far as the body overcomes the spirit that is in a man, through yielding to the spirit of evil. The spirit that the Lord puts into the tabernacle of flesh is under the dictation of the Lord Almighty; but the spirit and body are united in order that the spirit may have a tabernacle, and be exalted; and the spirit is influenced by the body and the body by the spirit.

In the first place the spirit is pure and under the special control and influence of the Lord, but the body is of the earth and is subject to the power of the devil and is under the mighty influence of that fallen nature that is of the earth. If the spirit yields to the body, the devil then has power to overcome both the body and spirit of that man and he loses both.

—Brigham Young, JD 2:255-256, April 6, 1855

When the devil got possession of the earth, his power extended to that which pertains to the earth. He obtained influence over the children of men in their present organization, because the spirits of men yielded to the temptations of the evil principle that the flesh or body is subjected to.

—Brigham Young, JD 3:208, February 17, 1856

You never felt a pain or ache, or felt disagreeable, or uncomfortable in your bodies and minds, but what an evil spirit was present causing it. Do you realize that the ague, the fever,

the chills, the severe pain in the head, the pleurisy, or any pain in the system, from the crown of the head to the soles of the feet, is put there by the devil? You do not realize this, do you?
—*Brigham Young*, JD 4:133, December 4, 1856

It is not every revelation that is of God, for Satan has the power to transform himself into an angel of light; he can give visions and revelations as well as spiritual manifestations and table-rappings.   —*John Taylor*, MS 19:197, November 2, 1856

KNOWLEDGE OF GOOD AND EVIL NECESSARY FOR EXALTATION

There is not, has not been, and never can be any method, scheme, or plan devised by any being in this world for intelligence to eternally exist and obtain an exaltation, without knowing the good and the evil—without tasting the bitter and the sweet. Can the people understand that it is actually necessary for opposite principles to be placed before them, or this state of being would be no probation, and we should have no opportunity for exercising the agency given us? Can they understand that we cannot obtain eternal life unless we actually know and comprehend by our experience the principle of good and the principle of evil, the light and the darkness, truth, virtue, and holiness, —also vice, wickedness, and corruption.
—*Brigham Young*, JD 7:237, August 28, 1859

You cannot give any person their exaltation, unless they know what evil is, what sin, sorrow, and misery are, for no person could comprehend, appreciate, and enjoy an exaltation upon any other principle.—*Brigham Young*, JD 3:369, June 22, 1856

It was necessary and proper that there should be good and evil, light and darkness, sin and righteousness, one principle of right opposed to another of wrong, that man might have his free agency to receive the good and reject the evil, and by receiving the good (through the atonement of Jesus Christ and the principles of the gospel), they might be saved and exalted to the eternal Godhead, and go back to their Father and God, while the disobedient would have to meet the consequences of their own acts.
—*John Taylor*, JD 22:301, August 28, 1881

I find in tracing out the Scriptures, that from the beginning there have existed two powers—the powers of light and the powers of darkness; that both these things existed in the heavens before they came here, that the powers of darkness were cast out, and thus became the devil and his angels. This antagonism, then, existed before, and it is necessary it should exist. It is necessary men should be tried and purged and purified and made perfect through suffering.

—*John Taylor*, JD 20:305, July 6, 1879

Darkness and sin were permitted to come on this earth. Man partook of the forbidden fruit in accordance with a plan devised from eternity, that mankind might be brought in contact with the principles and powers of darkness, that they might know the bitter and the sweet, the good and the evil, and be able to discern between light and darkness, to enable them to receive light continually. —*Brigham Young*, JD 7:158, May 29, 1859

Sin is in the world, but it is not necessary that we should sin, because sin is in the world; but, to the contrary, it is necessary that we should resist sin, and for this purpose is sin necessary. Sin exists in all the eternities. Sin is co-eternal with righteousness, for it must needs be that there is an opposition in all things.

—*Brigham Young*, JD 10:2-3, September 28, 1862

The principles of truth and goodness, and of eternal lives and the power of God are from eternity to eternity. The principle of falsehood and wickedness, the power of the devil and the power of death are also from eternity to eternity. These two powers have ever existed and always will exist in all the eternities that are yet to come. —*Brigham Young*, JD 11:234-235, June 3, 1866

Sin is upon every earth that ever was created, and if it was not so, I would like some philosophers to let us know how people can be exalted to become Sons of God and enjoy a fullness of glory with the Redeemer. Consequently every earth has its redeemer, and every earth has its tempter; and every earth and the people thereof, in their turn and time, receive all that we receive and pass through all the ordeals that we are passing through. —*Brigham Young*, JD 14:71-72, July 10, 1870

We have learned many things through suffering, we call it
suffering; I call it a school of experience . . . Why is it that good
men should be tried? Why is it, in fact, that we should have a
devil? Why did not the Lord kill him long ago? Because He
could not do without him. He needed the devil and a great
many of those who do his bidding just to keep men straight,
that we may learn to place our dependence upon God and trust
in Him, and to observe His laws and keep His commandments.
                        —John Taylor, JD 23:336, October 29, 1882

Well, do you think that persecution has done us good?
Yes. I sit and laugh and rejoice exceedingly when I see persecution. I care no more about it than I do about the whistling of
the north wind, the croaking of the crane that flies over my
head, or the crackling of the thorns under the pot. The Lord
has all things in His hand; therefore let it come, for it will give
me experience.   *—Brigham Young*, JD 2:8, October 23, 1853

Now, we are thankful to the Lord that we are counted
worthy to be taken notice of by the devil. I would fear very
much for our safety if we had fallen into a condition where the
devil ceased to be concerned about us.
                        —Joseph F. Smith, CR, p. 5, October, 1905

HOW TO DISTINGUISH BETWEEN GOOD AND EVIL

People are liable in many ways to be led astray by the power
of the adversary, for they do not fully understand that it is
a hard matter for them to always distinguish the things of God
from the things of the devil. There is but one way by which they
can know the difference, and that is by the light of the spirit of
revelation, even the spirit of our Lord Jesus Christ. Without
this we are all liable to be led astray and forsake our brethren,
forsake our covenants and the Church and kingdom of God on
earth . . . Consequently, it becomes us, as Saints, to cleave to the
Lord with all our hearts and seek unto Him until we do enjoy
the light of His Spirit, that we may discern between the righteous
and the wicked, and understand the difference between false
spirits and true.   *—Brigham Young*, JD 3:43-44, October 6, 1855

There are many spirits in the world, and it needs the power
of discerning them, and the Holy Priesthood, to detect the wrong
and adhere to the right. *—John Taylor*, MS 19:197, November 2, 1856

The difference between God and the devil is that God creates and organizes, while the whole study of the devil is to destroy.   —*Brigham Young*, JD 13:4, April 7, 1869

The devil delights in the work of destruction—to burn and lay waste and destroy the whole earth. He delights to convulse and throw into confusion the affairs of men, politically, religiously and morally, introducing war with its long train of dreadful consequences. It is evil which causeth all these miseries and all deformity to come upon the inhabitants of the earth. But that which is of God is pure, lovely, holy and full of all excellency and truth, no matter where it is found, in hell, in heaven, upon the earth, or in the planets.
                    —*Brigham Young*, JD 11:240, June 3, 1866

There are two influences in the world today and have been from the beginning. One is an influence that is constructive, that radiates happiness and builds character. The other influence is one that destroys, turns men into demons, tears down and discourages. We are all susceptible to both. The one comes from our Heavenly Father and the other comes from the source of evil that has been in the world from the beginning seeking to bring about the destruction of the human family.
                    —*George Albert Smith*, DNCS, June 17, 1944

CHAPTER III

The Spirit World

WHERE IS THE SPIRIT WORLD?

WHEN YOU lay down this tabernacle, where are you going? Into the spiritual world . . . Where is the spirit world? It is right here. Do the good and evil spirits go together? Yes, they do. Do they both inhabit one kingdom? Yes, they do. Do they go to the sun? No. Do they go beyond the boundaries of the organized earth? No, they do not. They are brought forth upon this earth, for the express purpose of inhabiting it to all eternity. Where else are you going? No where else, only as you may be permitted. —*Brigham Young, JD 3:369, June 22, 1856*

Is the spirit world here? It is not beyond the sun, but is on this earth that was organized for the people that have lived and that do and will live upon it. No other people can have it, and we can have no other kingdom until we are prepared to inhabit this eternally. —*Brigham Young, JD 3:372, June 22, 1856*

It reads that the spirit goes to God who gave it. Let me render this Scripture a little plainer; when the spirits leave their bodies they are in the presence of our Father and God; they are prepared then to see, hear and understand spiritual things. But where is the spirit world? It is incorporated within this celestial system. Can you see it with your natural eyes? No. Can you see spirits in this room? No. Suppose the Lord should touch your eyes that you might see, could you then see the spirits? Yes, as plainly as you now see bodies, as did the servant of Elijah. If the Lord would permit it, and it was His will that it should be done, you could see the spirits that have departed from this world as plainly as you now see bodies with your natural eyes. —*Brigham Young, JD 3:368, June 22, 1856*

WHAT BEINGS EXIST IN THE SPIRIT WORLD?

The righteous and the wicked all go to the same world of spirits until the resurrection . . .

The great misery of departed spirits in the world of spirits, where they go after death, is to know that they came short of the glory that others enjoy and that they might have enjoyed themselves, and they are their own accusers.
—*Joseph Smith, Jr.*, DHC 5:425, June 11, 1843

There is a place called "Paradise," to which the spirits of the dead go, awaiting the resurrection, and their reunion with the body . . . This Paradise, however, is not the place for resurrected bodies, but for departed spirits.
—*John Taylor*, GG, p. 39, Published August, 1852

No spirit of Saint or sinner, of the Prophet or him that kills the Prophet, is prepared for their final state: all pass through the veil from this state and go into the world of spirits; and there they dwell, waiting for their final destiny.
—*Brigham Young*, JD 6:294, August 15, 1852

The spirits of all men, as soon as they depart from this mortal body, whether they are good or evil . . . are taken home to that God who gave them life, where there is a separation, a partial judgment, and the spirits of those who are righteous are received into a state of happiness which is called Paradise, a state of rest, a state of peace, where they expand in wisdom, where they have respite from all their troubles, and where care and sorrow do not annoy. The wicked, on the contrary, have no part nor portion in the Spirit of the Lord, and they are cast into outer darkness, being led captive, because of their own iniquity, by the evil one. And in this space between death and the resurrection of the body, the two classes of souls remain, in happiness or in misery, until the time which is appointed of God that the dead shall come forth and be reunited, both soul and body, and be brought to stand before God, and be judged according to their works. This is the final judgment.
—*Joseph F. Smith*, IE 7:621-622, June, 1904

Flesh and blood cannot go there [the spirit world]; but flesh and bones, quickened by the Spirit of God, can.
—*Joseph Smith, Jr.*, DHC 6:52, October 9, 1843

The spirits in the eternal world are like the spirits in this world. When those who have come into this world and received tabernacles, then died and again have risen and received glorified bodies, they will have an ascendency over the spirits who have received no bodies, or kept not their first estate, like the devil.   —*Joseph Smith, Jr.*, DHC 5:403, May 21, 1843

THE TRANSITION FROM DEATH INTO
THE SPIRIT WORLD

We shall turn round and look upon it (the valley of death) and think, when we have crossed it, why this is the greatest advantage of my whole existence, for I have passed from a state of sorrow, grief, mourning, woe, misery, pain, anguish and disappointment into a state of existence, where I can enjoy life to the fullest extent as far as that can be done without a body. My spirit is set free, I thirst no more, I want to sleep no more, I hunger no more, I tire no more, I run, I walk, I labor, I go, I come, I do this, I do that, whatever is required of me, nothing like pain or weariness, I am full of life, full of vigor, and I enjoy the presence of my Heavenly Father, by the power of His Spirit . . . The spirits of the living that depart this life go into the world of spirits, and if the Lord withdraws the veil it is much easier for us then to behold the face of our Father who is in heaven than when we are clothed upon with this mortality.
          —*Brigham Young*, JD 17:142, July 19, 1874

I cannot help but think that in every death there is a birth; the spirit leaves the body dead to us and passes to the other side of the veil alive to that great and noble company that are also working for the accomplishment of the purposes of God, in the redemption and salvation of a fallen world.
          —*Wilford Woodruff*, JD 22:348, January 29, 1882

Whether the spirit remains in the body a minute, an hour, a day, a year, or lives there until the body has reached a good old age, it is certain that the time will come when they [the spirit and the body] will be separated, and the body will return to mother earth, there to sleep upon that mother's bosom. That is all there is about death.
          —*Brigham Young*, JD 17:143, July 19, 1874

CONDITIONS OF THE SPIRIT WORLD

The brightness and glory of the next apartment is inexpressible. It is not encumbered . . . so that when we advance in years we have to be stubbing along and be careful lest we fall down. We see our youth, even, frequently stubbing their toes and falling down. But yonder, how different! They move with ease and like lightning. If we want to visit Jerusalem, or this, that, or the other place—and I presume we will be permitted if we desire—there we are, looking at its streets. If we want to behold Jerusalem as it was in the days of the Savior; or if we want to see the Garden of Eden as it was when created, there we are, and we see it as it existed spiritually, for it was created first spiritually and then temporally, and spiritually it still remains. And when there we may behold the earth as at the dawn of creation, or we may visit any city we please that exists upon its surface. If we wish to understand how they are living here on these western islands, or in China, we are there; in fact, we are like the light of the morning . . .

Here, we are continually troubled with ills and ailments of various kinds, . . . but in the spirit world we are free from all this and enjoy life, glory, and intelligence; and we have the Father to speak to us, Jesus to speak to us, and angels to speak to us, and we shall enjoy the society of the just and the pure who are in the spirit world until the resurrection.
—*Brigham Young*, JD 14:231, September 16, 1871

If we are faithful to our religion when we go into the spirit world, the fallen spirits—Lucifer and the third part of the heavenly hosts that came with him, and the spirits of wicked men who have dwelt upon this earth, the whole of them combined will have no influence over our spirits. Is not that an advantage? Yes. All the rest of the children of men are more or less subject to them, and they are subject to them as they were while here in the flesh.   —*Brigham Young*, JD 7:240, September 1, 1859

Suppose that a man is evil in his heart—wholly given up to wickedness and in that condition dies, his spirit will enter the spirit world intent upon evil. On the other hand, if we are striving with all the powers and faculties God has given us to improve upon our talents, to prepare ourselves to dwell in eternal

life, and the grave receives our bodies while we are thus engaged, with what disposition will our spirits enter their next
state? They will be still striving to do the things of God, only
in a much greater degree—learning, increasing, growing in grace
and in the knowledge of the truth.
                              —*Brigham Young,* JD 7:333, October 8, 1859

Some people dream, you know, and think and teach that all
the glory they ever expect to have in the world to come is to
sit in the light and glory of the Son of God and sing praises
and songs of joy and gratitude all their immortal lives. We
do not believe in any such thing. We believe that every man
will have his work to do in the other world, just as surely as
he had it to do here, and a greater work than he can do here.
We believe that we are on the road of advancement, of development in knowledge, in understanding, and in every good thing,
and that we will continue to grow, advance and develop throughout the eternities that are before us.
                              —*Joseph F. Smith,* CR, p. 8, April, 1912

If the veil could be taken from our eyes and we could see
into the spirit world, we would see that Joseph Smith, Brigham
Young and John Taylor had gathered together every spirit that
ever dwelt in the flesh in this Church since its organization. We
would also see the faithful apostles and elders of the Nephites
who dwelt in the flesh in the days of Jesus Christ. In that assembly we would also see Isaiah and every prophet and apostle
that ever prophesied of the great work of the Lord. In the midst
of those spirits we would see the Son of God, the Savior, who
presides and guides and controls the preparing of the kingdom
of God on the earth and in heaven . . . The Son of God stands
in the midst of that body of celestial spirits and teaches them
their duties concerning the day in which we live and instructs
them what they must do to prepare and qualify themselves to
go with Him to the earth when He comes to judge every man
according to the deeds done in the body.
                    —*Wilford Woodruff,* "The Vision" by Lundwall, p. 96, April 7, 1893

Spirits are just as familiar with spirits as bodies are with
bodies, though spirits are composed of matter so refined as not
to be tangible to this coarser organization.
                              —*Brigham Young,* JD 3:371-372, June 22, 1856

You may ask if they are baptized there? No. Can they have hands laid upon them for the gift of the Holy Ghost? No. None of the outward ordinances that pertain to the flesh are administered there, but the light, glory, and power of the Holy Ghost are enjoyed just as freely as upon this earth; and there are laws which govern and control the spirit world, and to which they are subject. —*Brigham Young,* JD 2:138, December 3, 1854

SPIRIT BEINGS WATCH OVER MORTALS

Our fathers and mothers, brothers, sisters and friends who have passed away from this earth, having been faithful and worthy to enjoy these rights and privileges, may have a mission given them to visit their relatives and friends upon the earth again, bringing from the divine Presence messages of love, of warning, of reproof and instruction to those whom they had learned to love in the flesh.
—*Joseph F. Smith,* JD 22:351, January 29, 1882

Spirits can only be revealed in flaming fire or glory. Angels have advanced further, their light and glory being tabernacled; and hence they appear in bodily shape.
—*Joseph Smith, Jr.,* DHC 6:51, October 9, 1843

I believe that those who have been chosen in this dispensation and in former dispensations, to lay the foundation of God's work in the midst of the children of men, for their salvation and exaltation, will not be deprived in the spirit world from looking down upon the results of their own labors, efforts and mission assigned them by the wisdom and purpose of God, to help to redeem and to reclaim the children of the Father from their sins. So I feel quite confident that the eye of Joseph, the Prophet, and of the martyrs of this dispensation, and of Brigham, and John, and Wilford, and those faithful men who were associated with them in their ministry upon the earth, are carefully guarding the interests of the kingdom of God in which they labored and for which they strove during their mortal lives. I believe they are as deeply interested in our welfare today, if not with greater capacity, with far more interest, behind the veil, than they were in the flesh . . . they see us, they are solicitous for our welfare, they love us now more than ever.
—*Joseph F. Smith,* CR, p. 2-3, April, 1916

The spirits of the just are . . . blessed in their departure to
the world of spirits. Enveloped in flaming fire, they are not far
from us, and know and understand our thoughts, feelings, and
motions, and are often pained therewith.

—*Joseph Smith, Jr.,* DHC 6:52, October 9, 1843

THE VISION OF THE REDEMPTION OF THE DEAD

As I pondered over these things which are written (1 Peter
3:18-20; 1 Peter 4:6) the eyes of my understanding were opened,
and the Spirit of the Lord rested upon me, and I saw the hosts
of the dead, both small and great. And there were gathered
together in one place an innumerable company of the spirits of
the just, who had been faithful in the testimony of Jesus while
they lived in mortality, and who had offered sacrifice in the
similitude of the great sacrifice of the Son of God, and had suffered tribulation in their Redeemer's name. All these had departed the mortal life, firm in the hope of a glorious resurrection,
through the grace of God the Father and His Only Begotten
Son, Jesus Christ.

I beheld that they were filled with joy and gladness, and
were rejoicing together because the day of their deliverance
was at hand. They were assembled awaiting the advent of the
Son of God into the spirit world, to declare their redemption
from the bands of death. Their sleeping dust was to be restored
unto its perfect frame, bone to his bone, and the sinews and
the flesh upon them, the spirit and the body to be united never
again to be divided, that they might receive a fullness of joy.

While this vast multitude waited and conversed, rejoicing
in the hour of their deliverance from the chains of death, the
Son of God appeared, declaring liberty to the captives who had
been faithful, and there He preached to them the everlasting
gospel, the doctrine of the resurrection and the redemption of
mankind from the fall, and from individual sins on conditions of
repentance. But unto the wicked He did not go, and among the
ungodly and the unrepentant who had defiled themselves while
in the flesh, His voice was not raised, neither did the rebellious
who rejected the testimonies and the warnings of the ancient
prophets behold His presence, nor look upon His face. Where
these were, darkness reigned, but among the righteous there
was peace, and the Saints rejoiced in their redemption, and

bowed the knee and acknowledged the Son of God as their Redeemer and Deliverer from death and the chains of hell. Their countenances shone and the radiance from the presence of the Lord rested upon them and they sang praises unto His Holy Name.

I marveled, for I understood that the Savior spent about three years in His ministry among the Jews and those of the House of Israel, endeavoring to teach them the everlasting gospel and call them unto repentance; and yet, notwithstanding His mighty works and miracles and proclamation of the truth in great power and authority, there were but few who hearkened to His voice and rejoiced in His presence and received salvation at His hands. But His ministry among those who were dead was limited to the brief time intervening between the crucifixion and His resurrection; and I wondered at the words of Peter wherein he said that the Son of God preached unto the spirits in prison who sometime were disobedient, when once the long-suffering of God waited in the days of Noah, and how it was possible for Him to preach to those spirits and perform the necessary labor among them in so short a time.

And as I wondered, my eyes were opened, and my understanding quickened, and I perceived that the Lord went not in person among the wicked and the disobedient who had rejected the truth, to teach them; but behold, from among the righteous He organized His forces and appointed messengers, clothed with power and authority, and commissioned them to go forth and carry the light of the gospel to them that were in darkness, even to all the spirits of men. And thus was the gospel preached to the dead. And the chosen messengers went forth to declare the acceptable day of the Lord, and proclaim liberty to the captives who were bound; even unto all who would repent of their sins and receive the gospel. Thus was the gospel preached to those who had died in their sins, without a knowledge of the truth, or in transgression, having rejected the prophets. These were taught faith in God, repentance from sin, vicarious baptism for the remission of sins, the gift of the Holy Ghost by the laying on of hands, and all other principles of the gospel that were necessary for them to know in order to qualify themselves that they might be judged according to men in the flesh, but live according to God in the spirit.

And so it was made known among the dead, both small and great, the unrighteous as well as the faithful, that redemption had been wrought through the sacrifice of the Son of God upon the cross. Thus was it made known that our Redeemer spent His time during His sojourn in the world of spirits, instructing and preparing the faithful spirits of the prophets who had testified of Him in the flesh, that they might carry the message of redemption unto all the dead unto whom He could not go personally because of their rebellion and transgression, that they through the ministration of His servants might also hear His words . . .

I beheld that the faithful elders of this dispensation, when they depart from mortal life, continue their labors in the preaching of the gospel of repentance and redemption, through the sacrifice of the Only Begotten Son of God, among those who are in darkness and under the bondage of sin in the great world of the spirits of the dead. The dead who repent will be redeemed, through obedience to the ordinances of the house of God, and after they have paid the penalty of their transgressions, and are washed clean, shall receive a reward according to their works, for they are heirs of salvation.

Thus was the vision of the redemption of the dead revealed to me, and I bear record, and I know that this record is true, through the blessing of our Lord and Savior, Jesus Christ, even so. Amen.   —Joseph F. Smith, IE 22:166-170, December, 1918

This *Vision of the Redemption of the Dead* was submitted October 31, 1918 to the Counselors in the First Presidency, the Council of the Twelve and the Patriarch, and by them unanimously accepted.

MISSIONARY WORK IN THE SPIRIT WORLD

Compare those inhabitants on the earth who have heard the gospel in our day, with the millions who have never heard it, or had the keys of salvation presented to them, and you will conclude at once as I do, that there is a mighty work to perform in the spirit world.   —Brigham Young, JD 4:285, March 15, 1857

Jesus was the first man that ever went to preach to the spirits in prison, holding the keys of the gospel of salvation to them. Those keys were delivered to Him in the day and hour

that He went into the spirit world, and with them He opened the door of salvation to the spirits in prison.
                                        —*Brigham Young*, JD 4:285, March 15, 1857

Jesus Christ became a ministering spirit (while His body was lying in the sepulchre) to the spirits in prison, to fulfill an important part of His mission, without which He could not have perfected His work, or entered into His rest.
                                        —*Joseph Smith, Jr.*, DHC 4:425, October 3, 1841

If the elders of Israel in these latter times go and preach to the spirits in prison, they associate with them, precisely as our elders associate with the wicked in the flesh, when they go to preach to them.   —*Brigham Young*, JD 2:137, December 3, 1854

I believe . . . that when the gospel is preached to the spirits in prison, the success attending that preaching will be far greater than that attending the preaching of our elders in this life. I believe there will be very few indeed of those spirits who will not gladly receive the gospel when it is carried to them. The circumstances there will be a thousand times more favorable.
                                        —*Lorenzo Snow*, MS 56:50, October 6, 1893

Now, among all these millions and thousands of millions of spirits that have lived in the earth and have passed away, from generation to generation, since the beginning of the world, without the knowledge of the gospel,—among them you may count that at least one-half are women. Who is going to preach the gospel to the women? Who is going to carry the testimony of Jesus Christ to the hearts of the women who have passed away without a knowledge of the gospel? Well, to my mind, it is a simple thing. These good sisters that have been set apart, ordained to the work, called to it, authorized by the authority of the Holy Priesthood to minister, for their sex, in the House of God for the living and for the dead, will be fully authorized and empowered to preach the gospel and minister to the women while the elders and prophets are preaching it to the men. The things we experience here are typical of the things of God and the life beyond us.   —*Joseph F. Smith*, YWJ 23:130, January, 1912

The Resurrection

LATTER-DAY SAINT BELIEF IN THE RESURRECTION

IF IN THIS LIFE we receive our all; if when we crumble back to dust we are no more, from what source did we emanate, and what was the purpose of our existence?
—*Joseph Smith, Jr.*, DHC 2:14, January 22, 1834

We believe that we are immortal beings. We believe in the resurrection of the dead, and that as Jesus came forth from the grave to everlasting life, His spirit and body uniting again never more to be separated, so has He opened the way for every son and daughter of Adam, whether living or dead, to come forth from the grave to a newness of life, to become immortal souls, body and spirit united, never to be severed any more.
—*Joseph F. Smith*, IE 6:505, May, 1903

There will be no more mystery in the resurrection from the dead to life and everlasting light than there is in the birth of man into the world, when we understand the truth, as we will some day, as the Lord of glory instituted it.
—*Joseph F. Smith*, GD, p. 216, November 25, 1917

The whole structure of "Mormonism" is based on individuality beyond the grave. What an absurdity for us to go to the temples, day after day, to perform ordinances for people, if there were no identity, no personality beyond the grave!
—*Heber J. Grant*, MS 92:684, August 24, 1930

Man is an eternal being; his body is eternal. It may die and slumber, but it will burst the barriers of the tomb and come forth in the resurrection of the just.
—*John Taylor*, JD 13:230, May 6, 1870

I do not regard my own life. I am ready to be offered a sacrifice for this people; for what can our enemies do? Only kill the body, and their power is then at an end. Stand firm, my friends; never flinch. Do not seek to save your lives, for he that is afraid to die for the truth will lose eternal life. Hold out to the end, and we shall be resurrected and become like Gods, and reign in celestial kingdoms, principalities, and eternal dominions.   —*Joseph Smith, Jr.,* DHC 6:500, June 18, 1844

It is written that the greatest gift God can bestow upon man is the gift of eternal life. The greatest attainment that we can reach is to preserve our identity to an eternal duration in the midst of the heavenly hosts. We have the words of eternal life given to us through the gospel, which, if we obey, will secure unto us that precious gift. —*Brigham Young,* JD 8:7, March 4, 1860

We distinctly believe that Jesus Christ Himself is the true, and only true type of the resurrection of men from death unto life. We believe there is no other form of resurrection from death to life; that as He rose, and as He preserved His identity, even to the scars of the wounds in His hands and feet and side, . . . so it will be with you and with every son and daughter of Adam, born into the world. You will not lose your identity any more than Christ did.   —*Joseph F. Smith,* CR, p. 135, April, 1912

A VISION OF THE FIRST AND SECOND RESURRECTION

While I was upon my knees praying, my room was filled with light. I looked up and a messenger stood by my side. I arose, and this personage told me he had come to instruct me. He presented before me a panorama. He told me he wanted me to see with my eyes and understand with my mind what was coming to pass in the earth before the coming of the Son of Man. He commenced with what the revelations say about the sun being turned to darkness, the moon to blood, and the stars falling from heaven. These things were all presented to me one after another, as they will be, I suppose, when they are manifest before the coming of the Son of Man.

Then he showed me the resurrection of the dead—what is termed the first and second resurrection. In the first resurrection I saw no graves, nor anyone raised from the grave. I saw legions of celestial beings, men and women who had received the gospel, all clothed in white robes. In the form they were presented to me, they had already been raised from the grave. After this, he showed me what is termed the second resurrection. Vast fields of graves were before me, and the Spirit of God rested upon the earth like a shower of gentle rain, and when that fell upon the graves they were opened, and an immense host of human beings came forth. They were just as diversified in their dress as we are here, or as they were laid down. This personage taught me with regard to these things. Among other things he showed me were seven lions like burnished brass placed in the heavens. I asked the messenger what they were for. He said they were representatives of the different dispensations of the gospel of Christ to men, and they would all be seen in the heaven among the signs that would be shown. After this passed by me, he disappeared.   —*Wilford Woodruff,* MS 67:612, October 19, 1896

JESUS CHRIST IS THE PATTERN OF THE RESURRECTION

Jesus is the first begotten from the dead, as you will understand. Neither Enoch, Elijah, Moses, nor any other man that ever lived on earth, no matter how strictly he lived, ever obtained a resurrection until after Jesus Christ's body was called from the tomb by the angel. He was the first begotten from the dead. He is the Master of the resurrection—the first flesh that lived here after receiving the glory of the resurrection.
            —*Brigham Young,* JD 8:260, April 1, 1860

We believe that Christ . . . was crucified upon the cross, that He died, His spirit leaving His body, and was buried and was on the third day resurrected, His spirit and body re-uniting, . . . that He is a resurrected being, and that in His pattern every man, woman, and child that ever lived shall come forth from the grave a resurrected being, even as Christ is a resurrected being.   —*Heber J. Grant,* MS 99:395;396, May 30, 1937

I believe . . . that we will come up in the resurrection from death to life again, as literally ourselves as did Christ, the Son of God, rise from the dead . . . His body . . . rose when the spirit returned into it again, with the wounds of the nails in His hands and in His feet, and of the spear in His side, so literally, so actually the same identical body that it bore the marks that it received upon the cross. And I believe that He is the first fruits of the resurrection from death to life and that He is the true type of the resurrection; that every man, woman and child will rise from the dead, will come up precisely as He did, because there is no other name given under heaven by which we will be saved, neither is there any other way provided by which man can be raised again from death to life, but by the way instituted by the Son of God.

—*Joseph F. Smith,* MS 74:803, November 20, 1912

After Jesus was crucified of man, He went in the spirit to the spirits that were in prison . . . When Jesus had done this He again took up the body of flesh and bones which had been hung upon the cross and pierced unto death and laid away in the tomb; that body which had passed through the portal of death and the ordeal of the grave, He again brought forth from death unto life. Thus He conquered death and gained the victory over the grave and brought about the resurrection from the dead through the power of the gospel and the Holy Priesthood.

—*Joseph F. Smith,* JD 22:43, February 6, 1881

Jesus, the Only Begotten of the Father . . . had power to lay down His life and take it up again, and if we keep inviolate the covenants of the gospel, remaining faithful and true to the end, we too, in His name and through His redeeming blood, will have power in due time to resurrect these our bodies after they shall have been committed to the earth.

—*Joseph F. Smith,* JD 18:277, April 8, 1876

WHO WILL BE RESURRECTED?

Every creature that is born in the image of God will be resurrected from the dead . . . just as sure as we go down into the grave, through the transgression of our first parents, by whom death came into the world, so sure will we be resurrected from the dead by the power of Jesus Christ. It matters not whether we have done well or ill, whether we have been intelligent or ignorant, or whether we have been bondsmen or slaves or freemen, all men will be raised from the dead.

—*Joseph F. Smith,* MS 58:162, January 20, 1895

What, will everybody be resurrected? Yes, every living being; "but every man in his own order, Christ the first fruits;

afterward they that are Christ's at His coming. Then cometh the end." That is, the Saints shall live and reign with Christ a thousand years. One of the apostles says, "But the rest of the dead live not again until the thousand years are expired." But all must come forth from the grave, some time or other.

—John Taylor, JD 18:333, December 31, 1876

As Jesus was born of woman, lived and grew to manhood, was put to death and raised from the dead to immortality and eternal life, so it was decreed in the beginning that man should be, and will be, through the atonement of Jesus, in spite of himself, resurrected from the dead. Death came upon us without the exercise of our agency; we had no hand in bringing it originally upon ourselves; it came because of the transgression of our first parents. Therefore, man, who had no hand in bringing death upon himself, shall have no hand in bringing again life unto himself; for as he dies in consequence of the sin of Adam, so shall he live again, whether he will or not, by the righteousness of Jesus Christ, and the power of His resurrection.

—Joseph F. Smith, IE 11:385, March 16, 1902

You are entities; you have living souls within you; and you will be raised from the dead just as sure as Jesus Christ was raised from the dead. As sure as by Adam you die, so sure by Christ will you be raised from the dead. This is inevitable. It is according to God's plan. He has decreed it, and you cannot help yourselves. Do what you may, you cannot dodge that. It will come just as surely as birth and death come. The resurrection will come to all the children of men; but the resurrection of the righteous will come only to those who obey the commandments of the Lord.

—Joseph F. Smith, MS 68:164-165, December 24, 1905

All who have lived on the earth according to the best light they had, and [who] would have received the fullness of the gospel had it been preached to them, are worthy of a glorious resurrection and will attain to this by being administered for, in the flesh, by those who have the authority. All others will have a resurrection and receive a glory, except those who have sinned against the Holy Ghost.

—Brigham Young, JD 15:136, August 24, 1872

THE SPIRIT AND THE BODY TO BE REUNITED

It is a very great blessing that in the providences of the Lord and in the revelations that have been given by our Father in heaven we have the assurance that the spirit and the body, in due time, will be reunited. . . . we have assurance through the revelations that have been given by the Lord our God that that is the purpose of God, that the body and the spirit shall be eternally united and that there will come a time, through the blessing and mercy of God, when we will no more have sorrow, but when we shall have conquered all of these things that are of a trying and distressing character and shall stand up in the presence of the living God, filled with joy and peace and satisfaction.   —*Heber J. Grant, IE* 43:330, June, 1940

Man is an eternal being, composed of body and spirit: his spirit existed before he came here; his body exists with the spirit in time, and after death the spirit exists without the body. In the resurrection, both body and spirit will finally be reunited; and it requires both body and spirit to make a perfect man, whether in time or eternity.
    —*John Taylor, GG,* p. 27, Published August, 1852

The body is not perfect without the spirit, nor the spirit without the body; it takes the two to make a perfect man, for the spirit requires a tabernacle to give it power to develop itself and to exalt it in the scale of intelligence, both in time and eternity.   —*John Taylor, GG,* p. 32, Published August, 1852

After the body and spirit are separated by death, what, pertaining to this earth, shall we receive first? The body; that is the first object of a divine affection beyond the grave. We first come in possession of the body. The spirit has overcome the body, and the body is made subject in every respect to that divine principle God has planted in the person. The spirit within is pure and holy and goes back pure and holy to God, dwells in the spirit world pure and holy, and, by-and-by, will have the privilege of coming and taking the body again. Some person holding the keys of the resurrection, having previously passed through that ordeal, will be delegated to resurrect our bodies, and our spirits will be there and prepared to enter into their bodies.   —*Brigham Young, JD* 9:139, July 28, 1861

THE RESURRECTION OF THE BODY

When the angel who holds the keys of the resurrection shall sound his trumpet, the peculiar fundamental particles that organized our bodies here, if we do honor to them,—though they be deposited in the depths of the sea, and though one particle is in the north, another in the south, another in the east, and another in the west,—will be brought together again in the twinkling of an eye, and our spirits will take possession of them. We shall then be prepared to dwell with the Father and the Son, and we never can be prepared to dwell with them until then.
—*Brigham Young,* JD 8:28, March 25, 1860

The elements which compose this temporal body will not perish, will not cease to exist, but in the day of the resurrection these elements will come together again, bone to bone, and flesh to flesh.   —*Joseph F. Smith,* IE 7:623, June, 1904

The question may be asked, do not the particles that compose man's body, when returned to mother earth, go to make or compose other bodies? No, they do not . . . Neither can the particles which have comprised the body of man become parts of the bodies of other men, or of beasts, fouls, fish, insect, or vegetables. They are governed by divine law and though they may pass from the knowledge of the scientific world, that divine law still holds, governs and controls them. Man's body may be buried in the ocean, it may be eaten by wild beasts, or it may be burned to ashes, they may be scattered to the four winds, yet the particles of which it is composed will not be incorporated into any form of vegetable or animal life, to become a component part of their structure. . . . at the sound of the trumpet of God every particle of our physical structures necessary to make our tabernacles perfect will be assembled, to be rejoined with the spirit, every man in his order. Not one particle will be lost.   —*Brigham Young,* LEJ 1:153, 1875

The very particles that compose our bodies will be brought forth in the morning of the resurrection, and our spirits will then have tabernacles to be clothed with, as they have now, only they will be immortal tabernacles—spiritual tabernacles.
—*Brigham Young,* JD 8:28, March 25, 1860

All must come forth from the grave, some time or other, in the selfsame tabernacles that they possessed while living on the earth. It will be just as Ezekiel has described it—bone will come to its bone, and flesh and sinew will cover the skeleton, and at the Lord's bidding breath will enter the body, and we shall appear, many of us, a marvel to ourselves . . .

I know that some people of very limited comprehension will say that all the parts of the body cannot be brought together, for, say they, the fish probably have eaten them up, or the whole may have been blown to the four winds of heaven, etc. It is true the body, or the organization, may be destroyed in various ways, but it is not true that the particles out of which it was created can be destroyed. They are eternal; they never were created. This is not only a principle associated with our religion, or in other words, with the great science of life, but it is in accordance with acknowledged science. You may take, for instance, a handful of fine gold, and scatter it in the street among the dust; again, gather together the materials among which you have thrown the gold, and you can separate one from the other so thoroughly, that your handful of gold can be returned to you; yes, every grain of it. You may take particles of silver, iron, copper, lead, etc., and mix them together with any other ingredients, and there are certain principles connected with them by which these different materials can be eliminated, every particle cleaving to that of its own element.

—*John Taylor,* JD 18:333-334, December 31, 1876

What a glorious thought it is . . . that those from whom we have to part here, we will meet again and see as they are. We will meet the same identical being that we associated with here in the flesh—not some other soul, some other being, or the same being in some other form, but the same identity and the same form and likeness, the same person we knew and were associated with in our mortal existence, even to the wounds in the flesh. Not that a person will always be marred by scars, wounds, deformities, defects or infirmities, for these will be removed in their course, in their proper time, according to the merciful providence of God. Deformity will be removed; defects will be eliminated, and men and women shall attain to that perfection of their spirits, to the perfection that God designed in the beginning. It is His purpose that men and women, His children,

born to become heirs of God, and joint heirs with Jesus Christ, shall be made perfect, physically as well as spiritually, through obedience to the law by which He has provided the means that perfection shall come to all His children.
—*Joseph F. Smith*, IE 12:592, June, 1909

BLOOD TO BE REPLACED BY SPIRITUAL MATTER

The blood He [Christ] spilled upon Mount Calvary He did not receive again into His veins. That was poured out, and when He was resurrected another element took the place of the blood. It will be so with every person who receives a resurrection; the blood will not be resurrected with the body, being designed only to sustain the life of the present organization. When this is dissolved, and we again obtain our bodies by the power of the resurrection, that which we now call the life of the body, and which is formed from the food we eat and the water we drink, will be supplanted by another element; for flesh and blood cannot inherit the kingdom of God. —*Brigham Young*, JD 7:163, June 5, 1859

When the resurrection and exaltation of man shall be consummated, although more pure, refined and glorious, yet will he still be in the same image, and have the same likeness, without variation or change in any of his parts or faculties, except the substitution of spirit for blood.
—*John Taylor*, MA, p. 166, Published in 1892

God Almighty Himself dwells in eternal fire; flesh and blood cannot go there for all corruption is devoured by the fire. "Our God is a consuming fire." When our flesh is quickened by the Spirit, there will be no blood in this tabernacle.
—*Joseph Smith, Jr.*, DHC 6:366, May 12, 1844

THE RESURRECTION OF CHILDREN

In the resurrection of the dead the child that was buried in its infancy will come up in the form of the child that it was when it was laid down; then it will begin to develop. From the day of the resurrection, the body will develop until it reaches the full measure of the stature of its spirit, whether it be male or female.   —*Joseph F. Smith*, IE 12:594, June, 1909

The body will come forth as it is laid to rest, for there is no growth or development in the grave. As it is laid down, so will it arise, and changes to perfection will come by the law of restitution. But the spirit will continue to expand and develop, and the body after the resurrection will develop to the full stature of man.

—*Joseph F. Smith, IE 7:623-624, June, 1904*

As concerning the resurrection, I will merely say that all men will come from the grave as they lie down, whether old or young; there will not be "added unto their stature one cubit," neither taken from it; all will be raised by the power of God, having spirit in their bodies, and not blood. Children will be enthroned in the presence of God and the Lamb with bodies of the same stature that they had on earth, having been redeemed by the blood of the Lamb; they will there enjoy the fullness of that light, glory and intelligence, which is prepared in the celestial kingdom.

—*Joseph Smith, Jr., DHC 4:555-556, March 20, 1842*

The spirits of our children are immortal before they come to us, and their spirits, after bodily death, are like they were before they came. They are as they would have appeared if they had lived in the flesh, to grow to maturity or to develop their physical bodies to the full stature of their spirits. If you see one of your children that has passed away it may appear to you in the form in which you would recognize it, the form of childhood; but if it came to you as a messenger bearing some important truth, it would perhaps come . . . in the stature of full-grown manhood . . .

The spirit of Jesus Christ was full-grown before He was born into the world; and so our children were full-grown and possessed their full stature in the spirit before they entered mortality, the same stature that they will possess after they have passed away from mortality, and as they will also appear after the resurrection, when they shall have completed their mission.

—*Joseph F. Smith, IE 21:570-571, February, 1918*

Little children who are taken away in infancy and innocence before they have reached the years of accountability . . . are redeemed by the blood of Christ, and they are saved just as surely as death has come into the world through the fall of our first parents. It is further written that Satan has no power over men or women, except that power which he gains over them in this world. In other words, none of the children of the Father who are redeemed through obedience, faith, repentance, and baptism for the remission of sins, and who live in that redeemed condition, and die in that condition are subject to Satan. Thereafter he has no power over them. They are absolutely beyond his reach, just as little children are who die without sin.

Joseph F. Smith, YWJ 6:370, March 12, 1895

MARRIAGE RELATIONSHIPS TO CONTINUE AFTER THE RESURRECTION

It is the gospel that teaches a woman that she has a claim upon a man, and a man that he has a claim upon a woman in the resurrection; it is the gospel that teaches them that, when they rise from the tombs in the resurrection, they will again clasp hands, be reunited, and again participate in that glory for which God designed them before the world was.

—*John Taylor,* JD 16:376, February 1, 1874

There is no Latter-day Saint in all the world but knows as truly and as fully as God can impart that knowledge to the soul of man, that he shall live again after death, and that men and women shall be associated together as God has ordained and they have been united by His power, to dwell together forever and forever; and they shall know as they are known, they shall see as they are seen, and they shall understand as God understands; for they are His children.

—*Joseph F. Smith,* CR, p. 39, April, 1907

I think it has been taught by some that as we lay our bodies down they will so rise again in the resurrection with all the impediments and imperfections that they had here; and that if a wife does not love her husband in this state she cannot love him in the next. This is not so. Those who attain to the blessing of the first or celestial resurrection will be pure and holy, and perfect in body. Every man and woman that reaches to this unspeakable attainment will be as beautiful as the angels that surround the throne of God. If you can, by faithfulness in this life, obtain the right to come up in the morning of the resurrection, you need entertain no fears that the wife will be dissatisfied with her husband, or the husband with the wife; for those of the first resurrection will be free from sin and from the consequences and power of sin.

—*Brigham Young,* JD 10:24, October 6, 1862

In the next life we will have our bodies glorified and free from sickness and death. Nothing is so beautiful as a person in a resurrected and glorified condition. There is nothing more lovely than to be in this condition and have our wives and children and friends with us. —*Lorenzo Snow,* CR, p. 63, October, 1900

DISTINCTION BETWEEN TRANSLATED AND RESURRECTED BODIES

Translated bodies cannot enter into rest until they have undergone a change equivalent to death. Translated bodies are designed for future missions.

The angel that appeared to John on the Isle of Patmos was a translated or resurrected body (i.e. personage); Jesus Christ went in body after His resurrection to minister to resurrected bodies. —*Joseph Smith, Jr.,* DHC 4:425, October 3, 1841

Now the doctrine of translation is a power which belongs to this priesthood. There are many things which belong to the powers of the priesthood and the keys thereof, that have been kept hid from before the foundation of the world; they are hid from the wise and prudent to be revealed in the last times.

Many have supposed that the doctrine of translation was a doctrine whereby men were taken immediately into the presence of God and into an eternal fullness, but this is a mistaken idea. Their place of habitation is that of the terrestrial order, and a place prepared for such characters He held in reserve to be ministering angels unto many planets, and who as yet have not entered unto so great a fullness as those who are resurrected from the dead. "Others were tortured, not accepting deliverance, that they might obtain a better resurrection." (Hebrews 11:35)

—*Joseph Smith, Jr.,* DHC 4:209-210, October, 1840

When a person passes beyond the veil, he can only officiate in the spirit world; but when he is resurrected he officiates as a resurrected being, and not as a mortal being.

—*Brigham Young,* JD 9:88-89, May 7, 1861

ON DEATH AND BURIAL

That which we call death is merely the slumber and rest of this mortal clay, and that only for a little season, while the spirit, the life, has gone to enjoy again the presence and society of those from whence it came, and to whom it is joy again to return. And this will be the condition of the righteous until the morning of the resurrection when the spirit will have power to call forth the lifeless frame to be united again, and they both become a living soul, an immortal being, filled with the light and power of God.

—Joseph F. Smith, JD 21:263, April 11, 1878

What is commonly called death does not destroy the body, it only causes a separation of spirit and body, but the principle of life, inherent in the native elements, of which the body is composed, still continues with the particles of that body and causes it to decay, to dissolve itself into the elements of which it was composed, and all of which continue to have life.

—Brigham Young, JD 3:276, March 23, 1856

The Lord takes many away, even in infancy, that they may escape the envy of man and the sorrows and evils of this present world; they were too pure, too lovely, to live on earth; therefore, if rightly considered, instead of mourning we have reason to rejoice as they are delivered from evil, and we shall soon have them again.   *—Joseph Smith, Jr., DHC 4:553, March 20, 1842*

When Jesus was resurrected they found the linen, but the body was not there. When Joseph is resurrected, you may find the linen that enshrouded his body, but you will not find his body in the grave, no more than the disciples found the body of Jesus when they looked where it was lain.

—Brigham Young, JD 4:286, March 15, 1857

I would esteem it one of the greatest blessings, if I am to be afflicted in this world, to have my lot cast where I can find brothers and friends all around me. But this is not the thing I referred to: it is to have the privilege of having our dead buried on the land where God has appointed to gather His Saints together and where there will be none but Saints, where they may have the privilege of laying their bodies where the Son of Man will make His appearance, and where they may hear the sound of the trump that shall call them forth to behold Him, that in the morn of the resurrection they may come forth in a body and come up out of their graves and strike hands immediately in eternal glory and felicity, rather than be scattered thousands of miles apart. There is something good and sacred to me in this thing. The place where a man is buried is sacred to me . . .

I will tell you what I want. If tomorrow I shall be called to lie in yonder tomb, in the morning of the resurrection let me strike hands with my father, and cry, "My Father," and he will say, "My son, my son," as soon as the rock rends and before we come out of our graves . . .

God has revealed His Son from the heavens and the doctrine of the resurrection also; and we have a knowledge that those we bury here God will bring up again, clothed upon and quickened by the Spirit of the great God; and what mattereth it whether we lay them down or we lay down with them, when we can keep them no longer?

—Joseph Smith, Jr., DHC 5:361-362, April 16, 1843

CHAPTER V

The Judgment

THE JUDGMENT EXTENDS TO ALL

EVERY MAN will have to render an account of his stewardship, and every one will be held responsible for his own works, whether good or evil. We will be judged for the deeds done in the flesh; if they have been evil we will have to pay the penalty and satisfy justice and the demands of a broken law. Those that have sinned against the Holy Ghost will have no redemption. All will be saved with this exception, and come out of the "prison" and be exalted and receive a reward and an inheritance in the mansions prepared for them in the house of God. God does not judge men as we do, nor look upon them in the same light that we do. He knows our imperfections—all the causes, the "whys and wherefores" are made manifest unto Him. He judges us by our acts and the intents of our hearts. His judgments will be true, just and righteous; ours are obscured by the imperfections of man.

—Joseph F. Smith, JD 24:78, February 2, 1883

Of what good is our faith, our repentance, our baptism, and and all the sacred ordinances of the gospel by which we have been made ready to receive the blessings of the Lord if we fail, on our part, to keep the commandments? All that we expect, or all that we are promised, is predicated on our own actions, and if we fail to act, or to do the work which God has required of us, we are little better than those who have not received the principles and ordinances of the gospel. We have only started, and when we rest there, we are not following our faith by our works and are under condemnation; our salvation is not attained.

—Heber J. Grant, IE 24:259, January, 1921

Some men who think they are doing pretty well and doing, according to their own expression, "as they darned please," will wake up to find they have not been doing the will of God. They may have thought that they had wives and children, but they

will wake up to find that they have not got them, and that they are deprived of many of those great blessings they anticipated enjoying. With all of our mercy, kindness, and tender feeling towards our brethren and sisters, and towards all people, we cannot violate the law of God, nor transgress those principles which He has laid down with impunity. He expects us to do those things that are acceptable before Him, and if we don't we must pay the penalty of our departure from correct principle.
—John Taylor, JD 25:163, June 15, 1884

There is not a man or woman, who violates the covenants made with their God, that will not be required to pay the debt. The blood of Christ will never wipe that out, your own blood must atone for it; and the judgments of the Almighty will come, sooner or later, and every man and woman will have to atone for breaking their covenants.
—Brigham Young, JD 3:247, March 16, 1856

If there is any man in this Church that does wrong, that breaks the law of God, it mattereth not what his standing may be, whether among the Twelve, the high priests, seventies, or elders, or in any other standing, there is a tribunal that will reach their case in process of time, there is authority before whom they can be tried. Therefore let no one turn against the cause of God and stop in the road to destruction, on the plea that somebody has done wrong: it is no excuse for you or I to do wrong because another does: the soul that sins, alone must bear it. Should I step aside from the path of duty it would not destroy the gospel of Jesus Christ, or even one principle of eternal truth, they would remain the same. Neither would it be any excuse for you to commit sin! but I should have to bear my own sins, and not the sins of others—so with all men.
—Wilford Woodruff, MS 5:111, December, 1844

THE JUDGMENT TO BE FAIR AND JUST

He [God] holds the reins of judgment in His hands; He is a wise Lawgiver and will judge all men, not according to the narrow, contracted notions of men, but, "according to the deeds done in the body whether they be good or evil," or whether these deeds were done in England, America, Spain, Turkey, or India. He will judge them, "not according to what they have

not, but according to what they have," those who have lived
without law will be judged without law, and those who have a
law will be judged by that law. We need not doubt the wisdom
and intelligence of the Great Jehovah; He will award judgment
or mercy to all nations according to their several deserts, their
means of obtaining intelligence, the laws by which they are
governed, the facilities afforded them of obtaining correct information, and His inscrutable designs in relation to the human
family; and when the designs of God shall be made manifest, and
the curtain of futurity be withdrawn, we shall all of us eventually
have to confess that the Judge of all the earth has done right . . .

The idea that some men form of the justice, judgment, and
mercy of God is too foolish for an intelligent man to think of:
for instance, it is common for many of our orthodox preachers
to suppose that if a man is not what they call converted, if he
dies in that state, he must remain eternally in hell without any
hope . . . The plans of Jehovah are not so unjust, the statements
of holy writ so visionary, nor the plan of salvation for the human
family so incompatible with common sense; at such proceedings
God would frown with indignance, angels would hide their heads
in shame, and every virtuous, intelligent man would recoil.

If human laws award to each man his deserts and punish
all delinquents according to their several crimes, surely the Lord
will not be more cruel than man, for He is a wise legislator, and
His laws are more equitable, His enactments more just, and
His decisions more perfect than those of man; and as man judges
his fellow man by law and punishes him according to the penalty
of the law, so does God of heaven judge "according to the deeds
done in the body."

—*Joseph Smith, Jr.*, DHC 4:595-596; 597; 598, April, 1842

The punishment of God is Godlike. It endures forever,
because there never will be a time when people ought not to
be damned, and there must always be a hell to send them to.
How long the damned remain in hell, I know not, nor what
degree of suffering they endure. If we could by any means
compute how much wickedness they are guilty of, it might be
possible to ascertain the amount of suffering they will receive.
They will receive according as their deeds have been while in
the body. God's punishment is eternal, but that does not prove
that a wicked person will remain eternally in a state of punishment.   —*Brigham Young*, JD 9:147-148, January 12, 1862

JUDGMENT BASED ON THOUGHTS AND ACTIONS

We may succeed in hiding our affairs from men; but it is written that for every word and every secret thought we shall have to give an account in the day when accounts have to be rendered before God, when hypocrisy and fraud of any kind will not avail us; for by our words and by our works we shall be justified, or by them we shall be condemned.

—John Taylor, JD 24:232, a. June, 1883

We may deceive one another in some circumstances, as counterfeit coin passes for that which is considered true and valuable among men. But God searches the hearts and tries the reins of the children of men. He knows our thoughts and comprehends our desires and feelings; He knows our acts and the motives which prompt us to perform them. He is acquainted with all the doings and operations of the human family, and all the secret thoughts and acts of the children of men are open and naked before Him, and for them He will bring them to judgment.

—John Taylor, JD 16:301-302, November 16, 1873

If for every word and secret act all men shall be brought to judgment, how much more will the public acts of public men be brought into account before God and before the Holy Priesthood.

—John Taylor, JD 20:42-43, August 4, 1878

Every man that dies shall live again and shall stand before the bar of God, to be judged according to his works, whether they be good or evil. It is then that all will have to give an account for their stewardship in this mortal life.

—Joseph F. Smith, GD, p. 69, March 16, 1902

Thank God for that noble, that just, that Godlike principle of the gospel of Jesus Christ, that every one of us will have to give an account for the deeds we do in the flesh, and that every man will be rewarded according to his works, whether they be good or evil. Thank God for that principle; for it is a just principle; it is Godlike. For such a principle to be omitted from the work of the Lord would be an omission too serious to contemplate. It could not be. The only thing is for us to find out that it is so, and that it will be so, and that you and I and every one of us will have to answer for the deeds we do and will be rewarded according to our works, whether they be good or evil.

—Joseph F. Smith, IE 21:10-11, September 13, 1917

Each and every intelligent being will be judged according to the deeds done in the body, according to his works, faith, desires, and honesty or dishonesty before God; every trait of his character will receive its just merit or demerit, and he will be judged according to the law of heaven.

—*Brigham Young,* JD 8:154, August 26, 1860

We are living eternal life, and our position hereafter will be the result of our lives here. Every man will be judged according to his works, and he will receive only that degree of glory that he has earned.

—*George Albert Smith,* CR, p. 139, April, 1945

We judge a man not always by his looks or appearance; not always by hearing him preach a sermon; but we judge him by what he has done or failed to do in the past. That is just the way the Lord intends to do with you or me exactly. We will be judged according to what we have done or what we have failed to [do] all along the line of our experiences.

—*Lorenzo Snow,* CR, p. 3, October, 1900

Every person will receive his just reward for the good he may do and for his every act. But let it be remembered that all blessings which we shall receive, either here or hereafter, must come to us as a result of our obedience to the laws of God upon which these blessings are predicated.

—*Joseph F. Smith,* IE 16:71, November, 1912

The walk of man is made up of acts performed from day to day. It is the aggregate of the acts which I perform through life that makes up the conduct that will be exhibited in the day of judgment, and when the books are opened there will be the life which I have lived for me to look upon, and there also will be the acts of your lives for you to look upon . . . It is the moments and the little acts that make the sum of the life of man.

—*Brigham Young,* JD 3:342, June 15, 1856

The sectarian doctrine of final rewards and punishments is as strange to me as their bodiless, partless, and passionless God. Every man will receive according to the deeds done in the body, whether they be good or bad. All men, excepting those who sin against the Holy Ghost, who shed innocent blood

or who consent thereto, will be saved in some kingdom; for in my Father's house, says Jesus, are many mansions.
                    —*Brigham Young*, JD 11:125-126, June 18, 1865

MAN HELD ACCOUNTABLE FOR HIS INFLUENCE AND CONDUCT

I believe in obeying the commandments of God or else get out of the way. We ought not to be stumbling blocks to those who are trying to enter in at the door. God will hold us responsible for this. If there is a man on earth that has done wrong because I have set him the example, I am in some measure responsible for that wrong, and I will have to pay the debt in some way.   —*Joseph F. Smith*, MS 56:820, October 5, 1894

Remember that the Lord holds all of us responsible for our conduct here. He held our father Adam responsible for his conduct, but no more than He does us, in proportion to the station we hold. The kings of the earth will have to give an account to God, for their conduct in a kingly capacity. Kings are heads of nations, governors are heads of provinces; so are fathers or husbands governors of their own houses, and should act accordingly.   —*Brigham Young*, DHC 4:309, March 10, 1841

We know that every man will be judged according to the deeds done in the body; and whether our sin be against our own peace and happiness alone or whether it affects that of others, as the Lord lives we will have to make satisfaction or atonement; God requires it, and it is according to His providences, and we cannot escape it.   —*Joseph F. Smith*, JD 21:13, December 7, 1879

God will bless no king, no emperor and no president who will not give unto his subjects the rights and privileges in their relationship to God which the Father Himself has given unto them. Whenever these subjects are deprived of their rights, those who preside over them are held responsible.
                    —*Wilford Woodruff*, DWN 40:561, April 6, 1890

I will say that this nation and all nations, together with presidents, kings, emperors, judges, and all men, righteous and wicked, have got to go into the spirit world and stand before the bar of God. They have got to give an account of the deeds done in the body.   —*Wilford Woodruff*, MS 52:741, October 6, 1890

WHO WILL JUDGE?

When we reflect upon the statement of creatures being judged without law, the question arises as to who are to be their judges. We may here state that Christ is called the judge of the quick and the dead, the judge of all the earth . . . It is also further stated that the Saints shall judge the world. Thus Christ is at the head, His apostles and disciples seem to take the next prominent part; then comes the action of the Saints, or other branches of the priesthood, who it is stated shall judge the world. This combined priesthood, it would appear, will hold the destiny of the human family in their hands and adjudicate in all matters pertaining to their affairs; and it would seem to be quite reasonable, if the Twelve Apostles in Jerusalem are to be the judges of the Twelve Tribes, and the Twelve Disciples on this continent are to be the judges of the descendants of Nephi, that the brother of Jared and Jared should be the judges of the Jaredites, their descendants; and, further, that the First Presidency and Twelve who have officiated in our age, should operate in regard to mankind in this dispensation.
—*John Taylor,* MA, p. 155;156-157, Published in 1892

And you men of the Holy Priesthood—you apostles, presidents, bishops, and high priests in Zion—will be called upon to be the judges of the people . . . You shall record their tithings, and give them credit for that which they do; and the Lord will determine the difference between the credit which they make for themselves and the credit which they should make. The Lord will judge between us in that respect; but we shall judge the people, first requiring them to do their duty.
—*Joseph F. Smith,* CR, p. 72, April, 1901

MAN WILL HELP TO JUDGE HIMSELF

In reality a man cannot forget anything. He may have a lapse of memory; he may not be able to recall at the moment a thing that he knows or words that he has spoken; he may not have the power at his will to call up these events and words; but let God Almighty touch the mainspring of the memory and awaken recollection, and you will find then that you have not even forgotten a single idle word that you have spoken! I believe the word of God to be true, and, therefore, I warn the

youth of Zion, as well as those who are advanced in years, to beware of saying wicked things, of speaking evil, and taking in vain the name of sacred things and sacred beings. Guard your words, that you may not offend even man, much less offend God.
—Joseph F. Smith, IE 6:503-504, May, 1903

Man sleeps the sleep of death, but the spirit lives where the record of his deeds is kept—that does not die—man cannot kill it; there is no decay associated with it, and it still retains in all its vividness the remembrance of that which transpired before the separation by death of the body and the ever-living spirit. Man sleeps for a time in the grave, and by-and-by he rises again from the dead and goes to judgment; and then the secret thoughts of all men are revealed before Him with whom we have to do; we cannot hide them; it would be in vain for a man to say then, I did not do so-and-so; the command would be, Unravel and read the record which he has made of himself, and let it testify in relation to these things, and all could gaze upon it. If a man has acted fraudulently against his neighbor—has committed murder, or adultery, or anything else, and wants to cover it up, that record will stare him in the face. He tells the story himself, and bears witness against himself. It is written that Jesus will judge not after the sight of the eye, or after the hearing of the ear, but with righteousness shall He judge the poor, and reprove with equity the meek of the earth. It is not because somebody has seen things or heard anything by which a man will be judged and condemned, but it is because that record that is written by the man himself in the tablets of his own mind—that record that cannot lie—will in that day be unfolded before God and angels, and those who shall sit as judges.
—John Taylor, JD 11:78-79, February 5, 1865

If I had time to enter into this subject alone I could show you upon scientific principles that man himself is a self-registering machine, his eyes, his ears, his nose, the touch, the taste, and all the various senses of the body are so many media whereby man lays up for himself a record which perhaps nobody else is acquainted with but himself; and when the time comes for that record to be unfolded all men that have eyes to see, and ears to hear will be able to read all things as God Himself reads them and comprehends them, and all things, we are told, are naked and open before Him with whom we have to do.
—John Taylor, JD 26:31, December 14, 1884

We read something like this, "But I say unto you, that every idle word that men shall speak, they shall give account thereof in the day of judgment." Now, this is a remarkable declaration. Look at the millions of human beings that inhabit this earth, and that have inhabited it from the creation up to the present time . . . Then, if we could discover the thoughts and reflections of these numerous millions of human beings, look at the wisdom, the intelligence, the folly, the nonsense, the good and the evil that is connected with every one of them, it is so vast and complicated that the human mind could not receive it, and it seems as if it would be almost a thing impossible for God to gaze upon the whole of them,—to comprehend the whole, and judge of the whole correctly. How shall this be done? My understanding of the thing is that God has made each man a register within himself, and each man can read his own register, so far as he enjoys his perfect faculties. This can be easily comprehended.

Let your memories run back, and you can remember the time when you did a good action; you can remember the time when you did a bad action; the thing is printed there . . . It is written in your own record, and you there read it . . . Now, if you are in possession of a spirit or intellectuality of that kind, whereby you are enabled to read your own acts, do you not think that that being who has placed that spirit and that intelligence within you holds the keys of that intelligence and can read it whenever He pleases? Is not that philosophical, reasonable, and scriptural? I think it is . . . Well, then, upon this principle we can readily perceive how the Lord will bring into judgment the actions of men when He shall call them forth at the last day.   —*John Taylor*, JD 11:77-78, February 5, 1865

JUDGE NOT YOUR FELLOW MORTALS!

A person who would say another is not a Latter-day Saint, for some trifling affair in human life, proves that he does not possess the Spirit of God. Think of this, brethren and sisters; write it down, that you may refresh your memories with it; carry it with you, and look at it often. If I judge my brethren and sisters, unless I judge them by the revelations of Jesus Christ, I have not the Spirit of Christ; if I had, I should judge no man.
                    —*Brigham Young*, JD 1:339, December 5, 1853

Let us be patient with one another. I do not altogether look at things as you do. My judgment is not in all things like yours, nor yours like mine. When you judge a man or woman, judge the intentions of the heart. It is not by words, particularly, nor by actions, that men will be judged in the great day of the Lord; but, in connection with words and actions, the sentiments and intentions of the heart will be taken, and by these will men be judged. —*Brigham Young,* JD 8:10, March 4, 1860

I am very thankful that it is not our province, in our present condition, to judge the world; if it were, we would ruin everything. We have not sufficient wisdom, our minds are not filled with the knowledge and power of God; the spirit needs to contend with the flesh a little more until it shall be successful in subduing its passions, until the whole soul is brought into perfect harmony with the mind and will of God. And we must also acquire the discretion that God exercises in being able to look into futurity and to ascertain and know the results of our acts away in the future, even in eternity, before we will be capable of judging. —*Brigham Young,* JD 19:7-8, April 29, 1877

Our acts are recorded, and at a future day they will be laid before us, and if we should fail to judge right and injure our fellow beings, they may there, perhaps, condemn us.
—*Joseph Smith, Jr.,* DHC 2:26, February 9, 1834

WHERE MUCH IS GIVEN, MUCH IS EXPECTED

Those who do not profess to know anything of the Lord are far better off than we are, unless we live our religion, for we who know our Master's will and do it not will be beaten with many stripes; while they who do not know the Master's will and do it not will be beaten with few stripes. This is perfectly reasonable. We cannot chastise a child for doing that which is contrary to our wills, if he knows no better; but when our children are taught better and know what is required of them, if they then rebel, of course, they expect to be chastised, and it is perfectly right that they should be.
—*Brigham Young,* JD 16:111, June 27, 1873

We will not be judged as our brothers and sisters of the world are judged; but according to the greater opportunities placed in our keeping. We will be among those who have received the word of the Lord, who have heard His sayings, and if we do them it will be to us eternal life, but if we fail condemnation will result.

—George Albert Smith, CR, p. 47, October, 1906

We shall not be cast off . . . for those sins which we ignorantly commit, which are the results of misunderstanding in all honesty before the Lord. The difficulty does not lie here; the danger lies in our failing to live up to that which we know to be right and proper. For this we will be held responsible before the Lord; for this we will be judged and condemned unless we repent.   *—Joseph F. Smith,* JD 20:26, July 7, 1878

In some instances you will find examples of people out in the world who do not know as much as you do of the gospel of Jesus Christ, who have not the testimony of the Spirit in their hearts as you have, of the divinity of Christ and of Joseph Smith, who are just as devout, just as humble, just as contrite in spirit, and as devoted to what they know, as some of us are, and they will be rewarded according to their works, every one of them, and will receive a reward far surpassing anything that they dream of.   *—Joseph F. Smith,* CR, p. 8, April, 1912

CHAPTER VI

The Three Degrees of Glory

THE THREE HEAVENS

W E READ in the Bible that there is one glory of the sun, another glory of the moon, and another glory of the stars. In the book of Doctrine and Covenants these glories are called telestial, terrestrial, and celestial, which is the highest. These are worlds, different departments, or mansions, in our Father's house. —*Brigham Young, JD 1:312, February 20, 1853*

St. Paul informs us of three glories and three heavens. He knew a man that was caught up to the third heavens. Now, if the doctrine of the sectarian world, that there is but one heaven, is true, Paul, what do you tell that lie for, and say there are three? Jesus said unto His disciples, "In my Father's house are many mansions, if it were not so, I would have told you. I go to prepare a place for you, and I will come and receive you to myself, that where I am ye may be also." —*Joseph Smith, Jr., DHC 5:426, June 11, 1843*

The God of heaven, who created this earth and placed His children upon it, gave unto them a law whereby they might be exalted and saved in a kingdom of glory. For there is a law given unto all kingdoms, and all things are governed by law throughout the whole universe. Whatever law anyone keeps he is preserved by that law, and he receives whatever reward that law guarantees unto him. It is the will of God that all His children should obey the highest law, that they may receive the highest glory that is ordained for all immortal beings. —*Wilford Woodruff, MS 48:801, October 26, 1886*

As eternal beings we all have to stand before Him [God] to be judged; and He has provided different degrees of glory— the celestial, the terrestrial, and the telestial glories—which are provided according to certain unchangeable laws which cannot be controverted . . .

For those who are ready to listen to Him and be brought under the influence of the Spirit of God and be led by the principles of revelation and the light of heaven, and who are willing to yield obedience to His commands at all times and carry out His purposes upon the earth, and who are willing to abide a celestial law, He has prepared for them a celestial glory, that they may be with Him for ever and ever.

And what about the others? They are not prepared to go there any more than lead is prepared to stand the same test as gold or silver; and there they cannot go. And there is a great gulf between them. But He [God] will do with them just as well as He can. A great many of these people in the world, thousands and hundreds of millions of them, will be a great deal better off through the interposition of the Almighty than they have any idea of. But they cannot enter into the celestial kingdom of God; where God and Christ are they cannot come.
                              —*John Taylor*, JD 20:116, January 6, 1879

No man will receive a celestial glory unless he abides a celestial law; no man will receive a terrestrial glory unless he abides a terrestrial law, and no man will receive a telestial glory unless he abides a telestial law. There is a great difference between the light of the sun at noonday and the glimmer of the stars at night, but that difference is no greater than the difference of the glory in the several portions of the kingdom of God.
                              —*Wilford Woodruff*, JD 17:250, October 9, 1874

The glory of the telestial world no man knows, except he partakes of it; and yet, in that world they differ in glory as the stars in the firmament differ one from the other. The terrestrial glory is greater still, and the celestial is the greatest of all; that is the glory of God the Father, where our Lord Jesus Christ reigns.   —*Brigham Young*, JD 6:293, August 15, 1852

We are told that if we cannot abide the law of the celestial kingdom we cannot inherit a celestial glory. Is not that doctrine? Yes. "But," says one, "are not we all going into the celestial kingdom?" I think not, unless we turn round and mend our ways very materially. It is only those who can abide a celestial glory and obey a celestial law that will be prepared to enter a celestial kingdom. "Well," says another, "are the others going to be burned up?" No. "Do you expect everybody to walk according to this higher law?" No, I do not. And do I expect those that do not are going into the celestial kingdom? No, I do not. "Well, where will they go?" If they are tolerably good men and do not do anything very bad, they will get into a terrestrial kingdom, and if there are some that cannot abide a terrestrial law, they may get into a telestial kingdom, or otherwise, as the case may be. —*John Taylor*, JD 26:133, October 6, 1883

Paul ascended into the third heaven, and he could understand the three principal rounds of Jacob's ladder—the telestial, the terrestrial, and the celestial glories or kingdoms, where Paul saw and heard things which were not lawful for him to utter. I could explain a hundred fold more than I ever have of the glories of the kingdoms manifested to me in the vision, were I permitted, and were the people prepared to receive them. —*Joseph Smith, Jr.*, DHC 5:402, May 21, 1843

ENTRANCE REQUIREMENTS OF THE CELESTIAL KINGDOM

God has in reserve a time, or period appointed in His own bosom, when He will bring all His subjects, who have obeyed His voice and kept His commandments, into His celestial rest. This rest is of such perfection and glory that man has need of a preparation before he can, according to the laws of that kingdom, enter it and enjoy its blessings. This being the fact, God has given certain laws to the human family, which, if observed, are sufficient to prepare them to inherit this rest. —*Joseph Smith, Jr.*, DHC 2:12, January 22, 1834

If you and I ever get into the celestial kingdom, we have got to keep the law of that kingdom. *Show me the law that a man keeps and I will tell you where he is going.* —*Wilford Woodruff*, MS 51:596, July 29, 1889

I always have said and believed, and I believe today, that it will pay you and me and all the sons and all the daughters of Adam to abide the celestial law, for celestial glory is worth all we possess; if it calls for every dollar we own and our lives into the bargain, if we obtain an entrance into the celestial kingdom of God it will amply repay us. The Latter-day Saints have started out for celestial glory, and if we can only manage to be faithful enough to obtain an inheritance in the kingdom, where God and Christ dwell, we shall rejoice through the endless ages of eternity.   —*Wilford Woodruff*, JD 17:250, October 9, 1874

Those men, or those women, who know no more about the power of God and the influences of the Holy Spirit than to be led entirely by another person, suspending their own understanding, and pinning their faith upon another's sleeve, will never be capable of entering into the celestial glory, to be crowned as they anticipate; they will never be capable of becoming Gods. They cannot rule themselves, to say nothing of ruling others, but they must be dictated to in every trifle, like a child . . . They never can hold sceptres of glory, majesty, and power in the celestial kingdom. Who will? Those who are valiant and inspired with the true independence of heaven, who will go forth boldly in the service of their God, leaving others to do as they please, determined to do right, though all mankind besides should take the opposite course.   —*Brigham Young*, JD 1:312, February 20, 1853

The man who drinks with the drunken, and who lives an immoral life, and who gives himself up to evil things should not hope to go into the celestial kingdom of our Heavenly Father, for the Lord has said he cannot go there.
                    —*George Albert Smith*, CR, p. 71, October, 1923

A man may be saved, after the judgment, in the terrestrial kingdom, or in the telestial kingdom, but he can never see the celestial kingdom of God without being born of the water and the Spirit. He may receive a glory like unto the moon (i.e of which the light of the moon is typical), or a star (i.e. of which the light of the stars is typical), but he can never come unto Mount Zion, and unto the city of the living God . . . unless he becomes as a little child and is taught by the Spirit of God.
                    —*Joseph Smith, Jr.*, DHC 1:283, August, 1832

How few there are on the earth today, or in any dispensation, who have been able to abide the celestial law of God. It brings down the hatred of the whole generation in which we live. No man can live the celestial law without bringing upon his head persecution.
                    —*Wilford Woodruff*, JD 22:209, January 9, 1881

One of the beautiful things to me in the gospel of Jesus Christ is that it brings us all to a common level. It is not necessary for a man to be a president of a stake, or a member of the Quorum of the Twelve, in order to attain a high place in the celestial kingdom. The humblest member of the Church, if he keeps the commandments of God, will obtain an exaltation just as much as any other man in the celestial kingdom. The beauty of the gospel of Jesus Christ is that it makes us all equal in as far as we keep the commandments of the Lord. In as far as we observe to keep the laws of the Church we have equal opportunities for exaltation.

—George Albert Smith, CR, p. 25, October, 1933

We must have faith in God, we must repent of our sins, because while we are in a sinful condition we are in no way prepared to enter into the celestial kingdom, and we are informed that if we cannot keep the celestial law we cannot abide a celestial glory. The gospel has been restored in these latter days to prepare men for the celestial kingdom. This gospel has not been given to qualify men for any other kingdom, but has been given to us to prepare us that we may dwell upon this earth when it has been celestialized, when our Redeemer will dwell here and He will be our Lawgiver and our King.

—George Albert Smith, CR, p. 102-103, October, 1926

Jesus offered up one of the most essential prayers that could possibly be offered up by a human or heavenly being—no matter who, pertaining to the salvation of the people, and embodying a principle without which none can be saved, when He prayed the Father to make His disciples one, as He and His Father were one. He knew that if they did not become one, they could not be saved in the celestial kingdom of God. If persons do not see as He did while in the flesh, hear as He heard, understand as He understood, and become precisely as He was, according to their several capacities and callings, they can never dwell with Him and His Father.

—Brigham Young, JD 6:96, November 29, 1857

I know that there is no man on this earth who can call around him property, be he a merchant, tradesman, or farmer, with his mind continually occupied with: "How shall I get this or that; how rich can I get; or, how much can I get out of this brother or from that brother?" and dicker and work, and take advantage here and there—no such man ever can magnify the priesthood nor enter the celestial kingdom. Now, remember, they will not enter that kingdom; and if they happen to go there, it will be because somebody takes them by the hand, saying, "I want you for a servant;" or, "Master, will you let this man pass in my service?" "Yes, he may go into your service; but he is not fit for a lord, nor a master, nor fit to be crowned;" and if such men get there, it will be because somebody takes them in as servants.   —*Brigham Young,* JD 11:297, February 3, 1867

No man or woman in this dispensation will ever enter into the celestial kingdom of God without the consent of Joseph Smith.   —*Brigham Young,* JD 7:289, October 9, 1859

There are a few individuals in this dispensation who will inherit celestial glory, and a few in other dispensations; but before they receive their exaltation they will have to pass through and submit to whatever dispensation God may decree. But for all this they will receive their reward—they will become Gods, they will inherit thrones, kingdoms, principalities, and powers through the endless ages of eternity, and to their increase there will be no end, and the heart of man has never conceived of the glory that is in store for the sons and daughters of God who keep the celestial law.
                        —*Wilford Woodruff,* JD 18:39, June 27, 1875

No organized beings are prepared to become associated with or crowned heirs in the celestial kingdom, until they have passed through these ordeals and have drunk of the bitter cup to the dregs, so that they know and understand good from evil.
                        —*Brigham Young,* JD 6:144, December 27, 1857

No man can enter the celestial kingdom and be crowned with a celestial glory, until he gets his resurrected body.
                        —*Brigham Young,* JD 3:371, June 22, 1856

CONDITIONS OF THE CELESTIAL GLORY

The heavens were opened upon us, and I beheld the celestial kingdom of God, and the glory thereof, whether in the body or out I cannot tell. I saw the transcendent beauty of the gate through which the heirs of that kingdom will enter, which was like unto circling flames of fire; also the blazing throne of God, whereon was seated the Father and the Son. I saw the beautiful streets of that kingdom, which had the appearance of being paved with gold. I saw Father Adam and Abraham, and my father and my mother, my brother, Alvin, that has long since slept, and marvelled how it was that he had obtained an inheritance in that kingdom, seeing that he had departed this life before the Lord had set His hand to gather Israel the second time and had not been baptized for the remission of sins.

Thus came the voice of the Lord unto me, saying—

"All who have died without a knowledge of this gospel, who would have received it if they had been permitted to tarry, shall be heirs of the celestial kingdom of God; also all that shall die henceforth without a knowledge of it, who would have received it with all their hearts, shall be heirs of that kingdom, for I, the Lord, will judge all men according to their works, according to the desire of their hearts."

And I also beheld that all children who die before they arrive at the years of accountability are saved in the celestial kingdom of heaven.

—Joseph Smith, Jr., DHC 2:380-381, January 21, 1836

When we arrive in the celestial kingdom of God, we shall find the most perfect order and harmony existing, because there is the perfect pattern, the most perfect order of government carried out. *—John Taylor,* MS 9:321, May 7, 1847

A man who has had his mind opened to the operation of the priesthood of the Son of God—who understands anything of the government of heaven, must understand that finite beings are not capable of receiving and abiding the celestial law in its fullness. When can you abide a celestial law? When you become a celestial being, and never until then. When you hear men and women talk about living a celestial law, you may know that they are ignorant of the fact that no finite being is living in its fullness, or can. *—Brigham Young,* JD 7:143, May 22, 1859

While we are here we are surrounded by temptations because we are where devils dwell. They are around us and have power to tempt us; and here is the place they work. But there is no man or woman who has been true and faithful here until death, that will ever be disturbed or annoyed by them after death, for the reason that when faithful Saints receive their resurrected bodies they will occupy a place in the celestial kingdom, and there devils do not dwell. In that kingdom there will be no one to tempt you or lead you astray. If you are true and faithful here you will be true and faithful there, and be so throughout all eternity.   —*Wilford Woodruff*, "Wilford Woodruff" by Cowley, p. 618-619, November 16, 1897

In the celestial kingdom of God there is oneness—there is union.   —*Wilford Woodruff*, MS 52:577, August 3, 1890

If we live for it, our Heavenly Father will give to us eternal life in the celestial kingdom—and that celestial kingdom will be this earth which we dwell upon, when it is cleansed and purified, and when it becomes the kingdom that will be presided over by Jesus Christ our Lord. —*George Albert Smith*, DNCS, May 26, 1945

All Christians are looking for celestial glory, but can they abide it? They cannot; it would consume them, for "our God is a consuming fire." They think they could abide a celestial kingdom; but they could not.   —*John Taylor*, JD 14:151, June 25, 1871

Some might suppose that it would be a great blessing to be taken and carried directly into heaven and there set down, but in reality that would be no blessing to such persons; they could not reap a full reward, could not enjoy the glory of the kingdom, and could not comprehend and abide the light thereof, but it would be to them a hell intolerable, and I suppose would consume them much quicker than would hell fire. It would be no blessing to you to be carried into the celestial kingdom, and obliged to stay therein, unless you were prepared to dwell there.
—*Brigham Young*, JD 3:221, March 2, 1856

When you see celestial beings, you will see men and women, but you will see those beings clothed upon with robes of celestial purity. We cannot bear the presence of our Father now; and we are placed at a distance to prove whether we will honor these tabernacles, whether we will be obedient and prepare ourselves to live in the glory of the light, privileges, and blessings of celestial beings. We could not have the glory and the light without first knowing the contrast. Do you comprehend that we could have no exaltation, without first learning by contrast?
—*Brigham Young*, JD 4:54, September 21, 1856

THE FAMILY UNIT IN THE CELESTIAL KINGDOM

Who are there besides the Latter-day Saints who contemplate the thought that beyond the grave we will continue in the family organization? the father, the mother, the children recognizing each other in the relations which they owe to each other and in which they stand to each other? this family organization being a unit in the great and perfect organization of God's work, and all destined to continue throughout time and eternity.
—*Joseph F. Smith*, RSM 4:316, June, 1917

Children are taken away in their infancy, and they go to the spirit world. They come here and fulfill the object of their coming, that is, they tabernacle in the flesh. They come to receive a probation and inheritance on the earth; they obtain a body or tabernacle, and that tabernacle will be preserved for them, and in the morning of the resurrection the Spirits and bodies will be reunited, and as here we find children of various ages in a family, from the infant at the mother's breast to manhood, so will it be in the family organization in the celestial world. Our children will be restored to us as they are laid down if we, their parents, keep the faith and prove ourselves worthy to obtain eternal life; and if we do not so prove ourselves our children will still be preserved, and will inherit celestial glory. This is my view in regard to all infants who die, whether they are born to Jew or Gentile, righteous or wicked.
—*Wilford Woodruff*, JD 18:32, June 27, 1875

The ultimatum of our travel in this path of exaltation will bring to us the fullness of our Lord Jesus Christ, to stand in the presence of our Father, to receive of His fullness, to have the pleasure of increasing in our posterity worlds without end, to enjoy those pleasant associations that we have had in this life, to have our sons and our daughters, our husbands and our wives, surrounded with all the enjoyment that heaven can bestow, our bodies glorified like unto the Savior's, free from disease and all the ills of life, and free from the disappointments and vexations and the unpleasant sacrifices that we are making here.
—*Lorenzo Snow*, MS 61:530, May 8, 1899

You who are seated here will have opportunities of standing in the presence of multitudes, and I can easily imagine, yonder in the next life, after we have passed along perhaps a thousand years or more, that many of you who are here today will have an audience before you of your own posterity. I am as sure of it as I am that I am talking to you; I know it just as well as I know anything. Now we are starting in. Most of us, no doubt, have sons and daughters who will continue faithful to your counsels, and in the other life they will be with you and increase with you.   —*Lorenzo Snow,* CR, p. 55, October, 1898

THE GLORIES OTHER THAN THE CELESTIAL

There are some people who have supposed that if we are quickened telestial bodies that eventually, throughout the ages of eternity, we will continue to progress until we will find our place in the celestial kingdom, but the Scriptures and revelations of God have said that those who are quickened telestial bodies cannot come where God and Christ dwell, worlds without end.   —*George Albert Smith,* CR, p. 172, October, 1945

If a man cannot abide a celestial law, he cannot receive a celestial glory, if a man cannot abide a terrestrial law he cannot receive a terrestrial glory; and if he cannot abide a telestial law he cannot receive a telestial glory, but will have to dwell in a kingdom which is not a kingdom of glory. This is according to the revelations of God to us.
          —*Wilford Woodruff,* JD 12:278, July 19, 1868

Any person knowing and understanding the Scriptures as they are, and understanding the mind and will of God, can understand at once that when he is shut out from the presence of the Lord, when he does not hear His voice, sees not His face, receives not the ministering of His angels or ministering spirits, and has no messenger from the heavens to visit him, he must surely be in hell.   —*Brigham Young,* JD 2:137, December 3, 1854

Those who have not attained to . . . [the celestial kingdom], but can obey a terrestrial law, will receive a terrestrial glory, and enjoy a terrestrial kingdom, and so on. But I believe, furthermore, that there are eternal grades of progression, which will continue worlds without end, and to an infinity of enjoyment, expansion, glory, progression, and of everything calculated to ennoble and exalt mankind.
          —*John Taylor,* JD 1:159, June 12, 1853

CHAPTER VII

Godhood: Men Shall Become Gods

MAN'S DESTINY

As man now is, God once was:
As God now is, man may be.
—*Lorenzo Snow, BFRLS, p. 46, Spring, 1840*

M AN IS MADE an agent to himself before his God; he is organized for the express purpose that he may become like his Master. . . .

The Lord created you and me for the purpose of becoming Gods like Himself; when we have been proved in our present capacity and have been faithful with all things He puts into our possession. We are created, we are born for the express purpose of growing up from the low estate of manhood, to become Gods like unto our Father in heaven. That is the truth about it, just as it is. The Lord has organized mankind for the express purpose of increasing in that intelligence and truth, which is with God, until he is capable of creating worlds on worlds, and becoming Gods, even the sons of God.

—*Brigham Young, JD 3:93, August 8, 1852*

MAN'S DESTINY

"Let this mind be in you, which was also in Christ Jesus, who, being in the form of God, thought it not robbery to be equal with God." (Philippians 2:5,6)

Dear Brother:

Hast thou not been unwisely bold,
Man's destiny to thus unfold?
To raise, promote such high desire,
Such vast ambition thus inspire?

Still, 'tis no phantom that we trace
Man's ultimatum in life's race;
This royal path has long been trod
By righteous men, each now a God:

As Abra'm, Isaac, Jacob, too,
First babes, then men—to gods they grew.
As man now is, our God once was;
As now God is, so man may be,—
Which doth unfold man's destiny.

*   •   •   •*

The boy, like to his father grown,
Has but attained unto his own;
To grow to sire from state of son,
Is not 'gainst Nature's course to run.

A son of God, like God to be,
Would not be robbing Deity;
And he who has this hope within,
Will purify himself from sin.

You're right, St. John, supremely right:
Whoe'er essays to climb this height,
Will cleanse himself of sin entire—
Or else 'twere needless to aspire.
                            —*Lorenzo Snow*, IE 22:660, June, 1919
                                    Written January 11, 1892

We are destined and foreordained to become like God, and unless we do become like Him we will never be permitted to dwell with Him. When we become like Him you will find that we will be presented before Him in the form in which we were created, male and female.
                            —*Joseph F. Smith*, GD, p. 276, June 12, 1898

The fact that we receive the Holy Ghost is proof that the Spirit in warring with the flesh has overcome, and by continuing in this state of victory over our sinful bodies we become the sons and daughters of God, Christ having made us free, and whoever the Son makes free is free indeed. Having fought the good fight we then shall be prepared to lay our bodies down to rest to await the morning of the resurrection when they will come forth and be reunited with the spirits, the faithful, as it is said, receiving crowns, glory, immortality and eternal lives, even a fullness with the Father, when Jesus shall present His work to the Father, saying, "Father, here is the work thou gavest me to do." Then will they become gods, even the sons of God; then will they become eternal fathers, eternal mothers, eternal sons and eternal daughters; being eternal in their organization, they go from glory to glory, from power to power; they will never cease to increase and to multiply, worlds without end. When they receive their crowns, their dominions, they then will be prepared to frame earths like unto ours and to people them in the same manner as we have been brought forth by our parents, by our Father and God.

—Brigham Young, JD 18:259, October 8, 1876

As man now is, God once was—even the babe of Bethlehem, advancing to childhood—thence to boyhood, manhood, then to the Godhead. This, then, is the "mark of the prize of man's high calling in Christ Jesus."

We are the offspring of God, begotten by Him in the spirit world, where we partook of His nature as children here partake of the likeness of their parents. Our trials and sufferings give us experience, and establish within us principles of godliness.

—Lorenzo Snow, JD 26:368, January 10, 1886

It is for the exaltation of man to a state of superior intelligence and Godhead that the mediation and atonement of Jesus Christ is instituted; and that noble being, man, made in the image of God, is rendered capable not only of being a son of man, but also a son of God, through adoption, and is rendered capable of becoming a God, possessing the power, the majesty, the exaltation and the position of a God.

—John Taylor, MA, p. 140-141, Published in 1892

MEN ARE GODS IN EMBRYO!

Man is the child of God, formed in the divine image and endowed with divine attributes, and even as the infant son of our earthly father and mother is capable in due time of becoming a man, so the undeveloped offspring of celestial parentage is capable, by experience through ages of aeons, of evolving into a God.   *—Joseph F. Smith,* IE 13:81, November, 1909

We are the offspring of God, born with the same faculties and powers as He possesses, capable of enlargement through the experience that we are now passing through in our second

estate . . . He has begotten us in His own image. He has given us faculties and powers that are capable of enlargement until His fullness is reached which He has promised—until we shall sit upon thrones, governing and controlling our posterity from eternity to eternity, and increasing eternally.
                    —*Lorenzo Snow*, MS 56:772, October 5, 1894

If we take man, he is said to have been made in the image of God, for the simple reason that he is a son of God, and being His son, he is, of course, His offspring, an emanation from God, in whose likeness, we are told, he is made. He did not originate from a chaotic mass of matter, moving or inert, but came forth possessing, in an embryonic state, all the faculties and powers of a God. And when he shall be perfected, and have progressed to maturity, he will be like his Father—a God, being indeed His offspring. As the horse, the ox, the sheep, and every living creature, including man, propagates its own species and perpetuates its own kind, so does God perpetuate His.
                    —*John Taylor*, MA, p. 164-165, Published in 1892

God, the Father, is like His Son . . . it would be inconsistent and impossible for a spirit to beget a man like Christ, and therefore the Father and the Son are the exact resemblance of each other.   —*Joseph F. Smith*, CR, p. 5, October 6, 1911

We were born in the image of God our Father; He begat us like unto Himself. There is the nature of Deity in the composition of our spiritual organization. In our spiritual birth, our Father transmitted to us the capabilities, powers and faculties which He possessed, as much so as the child on its mother's bosom possesses, although in an undeveloped state, the faculties, powers and susceptibilities of its parent.
                    —*Lorenzo Snow*, DWN 20:597, January 14, 1872

Let me read that prayer a little more: "Our Father, who art in heaven." What, is He indeed my Father? Yes. Is He our Father? Yes, . . . we are the children of God; that is the relationship that we sustain to Him. Being born of the Spirit, we become the sons of God . . . . And what else? The heirs of God, and joint heirs with Jesus Christ our Lord. Is this the position we occupy? So say the Scriptures. And what is the difference between those who have been born of the water and the Spirit, and those who know not the gospel, and who possess none of the gifts thereof? Let us stop and inquire. You have sons, have you not? Yes. What will the boys be when they are grown up? They will be men, will they not? They are now the sons of men. If a man be inducted into the family of God, and becomes a son of God, what will he become when he gets his growth? You can figure that out yourselves. —*John Taylor*, JD 24:2-3, February 11, 1883

This [Godhood of man] will not detract anything from the glory and might of our Heavenly Father, for He will still remain our Father, and we shall still be subject to Him, and as we progress in glory and power, the more it enhances the glory and power of our Heavenly Father. This principle holds good in either state, whether mortal or immortal.

—*Brigham Young*, JD 10:5, September 28, 1862

ETERNAL INCREASE PROMISED TO THE FAITHFUL

The Lord has blessed us with the ability to enjoy an eternal life with the Gods, and this is pronounced the greatest gift of God. The gift of eternal life, without a posterity, to become an angel, is one of the greatest gifts that can be bestowed; yet the Lord has bestowed on us the privilege of becoming father of lives. What is a father of lives as mentioned in the Scriptures? A man who has a posterity to an eternal continuance. That is the blessing Abraham received, and it perfectly satisfied his soul. He obtained the promise that he should be the father of lives.

—*Brigham Young*, JD 8:63, May 20, 1860

We understand that we are to be made kings and priests unto God; now if I be made the king and lawgiver to my family, and if I have many sons, I shall become the father of many fathers, for they will have sons, and their sons will have sons, and so on, from generation to generation, and, in this way, I may become the father of many fathers, or the king of many kings. This will constitute every man a prince, king, lord, or whatever the Father sees fit to confer upon us.

In this way we can become King of kings, the Lord of lords, or, Father of fathers, or Prince of princes, and this is the only course, for another man is not going to raise up a kingdom for you.

—*Brigham Young*, JD 3:265-266, July 14, 1855

So far as the stages of eternal progression and attainment have been made known through divine revelation, we are to understand that only resurrected and glorified beings can become parents of spirit offspring. Only such exalted souls have reached maturity in the appointed course of eternal life; and the spirits born to them in the eternal worlds will pass in due sequence through the several stages or estates by which the glorified parents have attained exaltation.

—*Joseph F. Smith,* IE 19:942, June 30, 1916

MEN, AS GODS, SHALL ORGANIZE NEW WORLDS

I expect, if . . . faithful, . . . that we shall see the time . . . that we shall know how to prepare to organize an earth like this—know how to prepare that earth, how to redeem it, how to sanctify it, and how to glorify it, with those who live upon it who hearken to our counsels.

The Father and the Son have attained to this point already; I am on the way, and so are you, and every faithful servant of God . . .

After men have got their exaltations and their crowns—have become Gods, even the sons of God—are made Kings of kings and Lords of lords, they have the power then of propagating their species in spirit; and that is the first of their operations with regard to organizing a world. Power is then given to them to organize the elements, and then commence the organization of tabernacles. How can they do it? Have they to go to that earth? Yes, an Adam will have to go there, and he cannot do without Eve; he must have Eve to commence the work of generation, and they will go into the garden, and continue to eat and drink of the fruits of the corporeal world, until this grosser matter is diffused sufficiently through their celestial bodies to enable them, according to the established laws, to produce mortal tabernacles for their spiritual children.

This is the key for you. The faithful will become Gods, even the sons of God.   —*Brigham Young,* JD 6:274-275, August 28, 1852

If men are faithful, the time will come when they will possess the power and the knowledge to obtain, organize, bring into existence, and own. "What, of themselves, independent of their Creator?" No. But they and their Creator will always be one, they will always be of one heart and of one mind, working and operating together; for whatsoever the Father doeth so doeth the son, and so they continue throughout all their operations to all eternity. —*Brigham Young*, JD 2:304, June 3, 1855

It [matter] is brought together, organized, and capacitated to receive knowledge and intelligence, to be enthroned in glory, to be made angels, Gods—beings who will hold control over the elements, and have power by their word to command the creation and redemption of worlds, or to extinguish suns by their breath and disorganize worlds, hurling them back into their chaotic state. This is what you and I are created for. —*Brigham Young*, JD 3:356, June 15, 1856

We shall go on from one step to another, reaching forth into the eternities until we become like the Gods, and shall be able to frame for ourselves, by the behest and command of the Almighty. All those who are counted worthy to be exalted and to become Gods, even the sons of God, will go forth and have earths and worlds like those who framed this and millions on millions of others. —*Brigham Young*, JD 17:143, July 19, 1874

DISTINCTION BETWEEN ANGELS AND GODS

Gods have an ascendency over the angels, who are ministering servants. In the resurrection, some are raised to be angels; others are raised to become Gods.
Joseph Smith, Jr., DHC 5:426-427, June 11, 1843

Angels are those beings who have been on an earth like this and have passed through the same ordeals that we are now passing through. They have kept their first estate far enough to preserve themselves in the priesthood. They did not so violate the law of the priesthood and condemn themselves to the sin against the Holy Ghost as to be finally lost. They are not crowned with the celestial ones. They are persons who have lived upon an earth, but did not magnify the priesthood in that high degree that many others have done who have become Gods, even the sons of God . . . . They are single, without families or kingdoms to reign over. —*Brigham Young*, JD 9:102, January 5, 1816

The man who passes through this probation, and is faithful, being redeemed from sin by the blood of Christ, through the ordinances of the gospel, and attains to exaltation in the kingdom of God, is not less but greater than the angels . . . . And why? Because the resurrected, righteous man has progressed beyond the pre-existent or disembodied spirits, and has risen above them, having both spirit and body as Christ has, having gained the victory over death and the grave, and having power over sin and Satan, in fact, having passed from the condition of the angel to that of a God. He possesses keys of power, dominion and glory that the angel does not possess—and cannot possess without gaining them in the same way that he gained them, which will be by passing through the same ordeals and proving equally faithful. . . . Man in his pre-existent condition is not perfect, neither is he in the disembodied estate. There is no perfect estate but that of the risen Redeemer, which is God's estate, and no man can become perfect except he become *like them* [the Gods].

—*Joseph F. Smith*, JD 23:172-173, June 18, 1882

ETERNAL PROGRESSION IS THE LAW OF HEAVEN

If there was a point where man in his progression could not proceed any further, the very idea would throw a gloom over every intelligent and reflecting mind. God Himself is increasing and progressing in knowledge, power, and dominion, and will do so, worlds without end. It is just so with us.

—*Wilford Woodruff*, JD 6:120, December 6, 1857

Man is a dual being, possessed of body and spirit, made in the image of God and connected with Him and with eternity. He is a God in embryo and will live and progress throughout the eternal ages, if obedient to the laws of the Godhead, as the Gods progress throughout the eternal ages.

—*John Taylor*, JD 23:65, April 9, 1882

We are immortal beings. That which dwells in this body of ours is immortal, and will always exist. Our individuality will always continue. Eternities may begin, eternities may end, and still we shall have our individuality. Our identity is insured. We will be ourselves, and nobody else. Whatever changes may arise, whatever worlds may be made or pass away, our identity will always remain the same; and we will continue on improving, advancing and increasing in wisdom, intelligence, power and dominion, worlds without end.

—Lorenzo Snow, CR, p. 2, April, 1901

I rejoice to know that whatever degree of intelligence we attain unto in this life shall rise with us in the life to come, and we shall have just that much the advantage of those who have not gained intelligence, because of their failure to study diligently.

—Heber J. Grant, CR, p. 24, October, 1907

If I improve upon what the Lord has given me, and continue to improve, I shall become like those who have gone before me; I shall be exalted in the celestial kingdom and be filled to overflowing with all the power I can wield; and all the keys of knowledge I can manage will be committed unto me. What do we want more? I shall be just like every other man—have all that I can, in my capacity, comprehend and manage.

—Brigham Young, JD 6:276, August 28, 1852

You have got to learn how to be Gods yourselves, and to be kings and priests to God, the same as all Gods have done before you, namely, by going from one small degree to another, and from a small capacity to a great one; from grace to grace, from exaltation to exaltation.

—Joseph Smith, Jr., TS August 15, 1844, Delivered April, 1844

BOOK TWO

The Gospel Plan of Salvation

*The gospel of the Son of God . . .
embraces all morality, all virtue, all
light, all intelligence, all greatness,
and all goodness. It introduces a
system of laws and ordinances, and a
code of moral rectitude which, if
obeyed by the human family, will lead
them back to the presence of God.*
—BRIGHAM YOUNG
JD 11:235
June 3, 1866

CHAPTER VIII

Definition and Nature of the Gospel

THE GOSPEL PLAN

T HE GOSPEL OF JESUS CHRIST is perhaps one of the most comprehensive subjects that mankind can reflect upon. It not only embraces things as they now exist, associated with the human family, but it takes us back to days that are past and gone, to the organizations of this world and of other worlds and, by the principle of revelation it develops, unfolds and makes manifest unto the human family the great purposes of God as they shall transpire throughout every succeeding age. There are thousands of details or minutiae mixed up with these great projects, purposes, and designs; some of them we comprehend correctly, or think we do; others are not so clear and comprehensible to our minds.   —*John Taylor*, JD 10:123, March 1, 1863

For me, the plan of salvation must be a system that is pure and holy in all its points; it must reveal things that no other Church or kingdom can reveal; it must circumscribe the knowledge that is upon the face of the earth, or it is not from God. Such a plan incorporates every system of true doctrine on the earth, whether it be ecclesiastical, moral, philosophical, or civil; it incorporates all good laws that have been made from the days of Adam until now; it swallows up the laws of nations, for it exceeds them all in knowledge and purity; it circumscribes the doctrines of the day, it takes from the right and the left, it brings all truth together in one system and leaves the chaff to be scattered hither and thither.

—*Brigham Young*, JD 7:148, May 22, 1859

The gospel is the greatest thing in all the world. There is nothing to compare with it. The possessions of this earth are of no consequence when compared with the blessings of the gospel. Naked we came into the world, and naked we will go out of the world, so far as earthly things are concerned; for we must leave them behind; but the eternal possessions which are ours through

obedience to the gospel of Jesus Christ do not perish—the ties that God has created between me and those whom He has given to me, and the divine authority which I enjoy through the Holy Priesthood, these are mine throughout all eternity.
                              —*Joseph F. Smith*, IE 21:102-103, December, 1917

The gospel of Christ is one of the greatest blessings that can be bestowed upon man. Eternal life, the Lord says, is the greatest gift of God. We can obtain that, only through obedience to this gospel.   —*Wilford Woodruff*, JD 12:280, July 19, 1868

The principles of the gospel, to the unbeliever, have neither worth nor efficacy; but with us, who believe them, they comprehend everything pertaining to the well-being of man in time and eternity; with us the gospel is the Alpha and Omega, the beginning and the end.   —*John Taylor*, JD 14:186, March 20, 1870

WHAT IS THE GOSPEL?

The gospel of our Lord Jesus Christ embraces all the laws and ordinances necessary for the salvation of man . . . . No man can be saved in opposition to its saving ordinances, but must receive each one in the spirit of humility and faith. Technically, the term "Gospel" signifies "good news" and is said to be taken from, or founded on, the annunciation of the angel who appeared to the shepherds at the time of the Savior's birth declaring, "Behold, I bring you good tidings of great joy, which shall be to all people."
In the theological sense, the gospel means more than just the tidings of good news . . . for it embraces every principle of eternal truth. There is no fundamental principle, or truth, anywhere in the universe, that is not embraced in the gospel of Jesus Christ.   —*Joseph F. Smith*, JI 51:164, March, 1916

The everlasting gospel made known in the last days is nothing more nor less than the ancient religion restored. It is the commencement of the "restitution of all things, spoken of by all the holy prophets since the world was." It is the bringing back of ancient, eternal principles, whereby men can know God as they knew Him formerly; not a vague fantasy, not a simple form, but a living reality. Its doctrines, its ordinances, its prin-

ciples, its priesthood are from above, revealed from the heavens, and yet strictly in conformity with all former revelations. It has not been, it cannot be successfully controverted, either in its divine authenticity, its doctrines, ordinances, or priesthood. It is adapted to the wants of the human family, to the world morally, socially, religiously and politically. It is not a sickly, sentimental, effeminate plaything; nor a ghostly, spiritual, sing-song, ethereal dream, but a living, sober, matter-of-fact reality adapted to body and spirit, to earth and heaven, to time and eternity. It enters into all the ramifications of life. It does not adapt itself to the philosophy, politics, creeds, and opinions of men, but fashions them in its divine mold. It cannot be twisted into the multitudinous latitudinarian principles of a degenerate world; but lifts all that are in the world who will be subject to its precepts, to its own ennobling, exalted and dignified standard. It searches all truth, and grasps at all intelligence. It is the revealed living and abiding will of God to man; a connection between the heavens and the earth. It is nature, philosophy, heavens and earth, time and eternity united. It is the philosophy of the heavens and the earth, of God, and angels, and saints.
—*John Taylor,* "The Mormon " Vol. 1, No. 23, July 28, 1855

The gospel of the Son of God that has been revealed is a plan or system of laws and ordinances, by strict obedience to which the people who inhabit this earth are assured that they may return again into the presence of the Father and the Son.
—*Brigham Young,* JD 13:233, February 20, 1870

What is this gospel to which we refer? It is the only power of God unto salvation, it is the only plan that will enable man to go back into the presence of his Maker and enjoy the celestial kingdom. It is the only plan that will bring peace and happiness to all the children of men, of every race and creed.
—*George Albert Smith,* CR, p. 93, October, 1928

The gospel of Jesus Christ is the opening avenue—the open gate in the road or way from earth to heaven, through which direct revelation comes to the children of men in their various capacities, according to their callings and standing in the society in which they live. The gospel of salvation is a portion of the law that pertains to the kingdom where God resides.
—*Brigham Young,* JD 8:159, September 2, 1860

The gospel itself is a principle of revelation, and without revelation we can have no gospel. . . . The gospel is a living, abiding, eternal principle, . . . the medium through which God conveys intelligence to the human mind; the principle by which Gods are governed and all nations controlled.
—*John Taylor*, JD 20:300-301, July 6, 1879

The gospel in its fullness . . . is simply a code of laws, ordinances, gifts and graces which are the power of God unto salvation. The laws and ordinances which the Lord has revealed in these latter days are calculated to save all the sons and daughters of Adam and Eve who have not sinned against the Holy Ghost.
—*Brigham Young*, JD 15:122, August 11, 1872

The gospel is a fountain of truth, and truth is what we are after. We have embraced the truth—namely, the gospel of the Son of God.   —*Brigham Young*, JD 12:68, June 23, 1867

The gospel is a code of laws which originated in the heavens, and which is given to men on the earth to enable them to assimilate themselves to those who are in heaven, that in the observance of the laws and principles which they are governed by we may be like unto them and become fitted to dwell with them when we shall have done with the things of time. The principles of the gospel are not only perfect in themselves, but the organization of the Church is also perfect in itself, and the order of government which God has instituted for His people as a pattern of that which is in the heavens.
—*Joseph F. Smith*, MS 54:641, July 4, 1892

THE PURPOSE OF THE GOSPEL

The purpose of the gospel of Jesus Christ is to prepare us for the celestial kingdom. The Lord has revealed to us that there are other kingdoms of glory and other kingdoms not of glory; but in order that men might be prepared for the celestial kingdom He sent His Only Begotten Son into the world. He overcame death and found the way of the resurrection, and delivered the message of life and salvation to the children of men . . . .

The only plan that will prepare men for the celestial kingdom is the plan that has been given by Jesus Christ, our Lord.
—*George Albert Smith*, CR, p. 28:30, April, 1934

God has restored the gospel for the purpose of bringing life and immortality to light; and without the knowledge of the gospel there is no knowledge of life and immortality; for men cannot comprehend these principles only as they are made known unto them, and they cannot be revealed only through the medium of the gospel, and through obedience to the laws of salvation associated therewith.

—John Taylor, JD 22:218, June 27, 1881

It is conceded by all who have taken the time to study in any degree whatever, the plan of life and salvation and the principles of the gospel of Jesus Christ, on which life and salvation are based, that their object is to develop man so that he will become sufficiently perfected to be worthy to dwell in the presence of our Father in heaven. . . . Every principle of the gospel has been revealed to us for our individual advancement and for our individual perfection.

—Heber J. Grant, MS 66:168-169, March 17, 1904

We have got the gospel of life and salvation. I do not say that we have *a* gospel, but I say that we have *the* definite and only gospel that ever was or ever will be that will save the children of men. *—Brigham Young,* JD 12:313, November 29, 1868

No man, in time or in eternity, will ever be saved in the celestial kingdom of God without the gospel of Christ.

—Wilford Woodruff, MS 56:660, September 2, 1894

CHARACTERISTICS OF THE GOSPEL PLAN

The gospel embraces principles that dive deeper, spread wider, and extend further than anything else that we can conceive. The gospel teaches us in regard to the being and attributes of God; it also teaches us our relationship to that God and the various responsibilities we are under to Him as His offspring; it teaches us the various duties and responsibilities that we are under to our families and friends, to the community, to the living and the dead; it unfolds to us principles pertaining to futurity. In fact, according to the saying of one of the old disciples, it "brings life and immortality to light," brings us into relationship with God, and prepares us for an exaltation in the eternal world. There is something grand, profound and intellectual associated with the principles of the gospel as it stands connected with the salvation and exaltation of man.

—*John Taylor*, JD 16:369, February 1, 1874

My standing in the Church is worth to me more than this life—ten thousand thousand times. For in this I have life everlasting. In this I have the glorious promise of the associations of my loved ones throughout all eternity. In obedience to this work, in the gospel of Jesus Christ, I shall gather around me my family, my children, my children's children, until they become as numerous as the seed of Abraham, or as countless as the sands upon the seashore. For this is my right and privilege and the right and privilege of every member of the Church of Jesus Christ of Latter-day Saints who holds the priesthood and will magnify it in the sight of God. Without it there is death and desolation—disintegration and disinheritance; without it there may be a chance to become a ministering spirit, a servant unto servants throughout the endless ages; but in this gospel there is a chance to become a Son of God, in the image and likeness of the Father and of His Only Begotten Son in the flesh. I would rather take my boys and my girls to the grave, while they are innocent, than to see them . . . led away from the gospel of salvation.

—*Joseph F. Smith*, CR, p. 137, April, 1912

Happy is the man, indeed, who can . . . be at rest and seek for no other road to peace than by the doctrines of Jesus Christ. His gospel teaches us to love our fellowmen, to do to others as we would have others do to us, to be just, to be merciful, to be forgiving, and to perform every good act calculated to enlarge the soul of man. His perfected philosophy teaches also that it is better to suffer wrong than to do wrong, and to pray for our enemies and for those who despitefully use us. There are no other gospels or systems of philosophy that bear these marks of divinity and immortality. You may hunt the philosophies of the world in vain for any code of ethics that insures the peace and rest that may be found in His comprehensive, yet simple gospel.   —*Joseph F. Smith*, IE 7:717, July, 1904

The gospel is like a little leaven put into a certain portion of meal, and it is working and operating, and the ultimate result will be that the whole lump will be leavened.

—*John Taylor*, JD 24:124, April 8, 1883

I feel it is only a question of time, if we do our part, until most of our Father's children who are in the world and do not now understand will learn of the truth and will be glad to be identified with the Church of Jesus Christ of Latter-day Saints.

In order to do that they will not have to give up any good thing they have learned in the Methodist Church, they will not have to surrender anything that is good that they have learned in the Catholic Church, they will not have to give away or lose sight of any blessing that has come to them from any quarter in order to belong to the Church of Jesus Christ. That is the beauty of this work. To me it is all-comprehensive; when it comes to that which is good there is not a virtue, there is not a desirable attribute that a human being may attain to that he is not able to enjoy to its fullest extent as a member of the Church of Jesus Christ of Latter-day Saints.

—*George Albert Smith,* CR, p. 26, October, 1933

The gospel is very simple when we understand it properly. It is plain and easily understood. It is always right, good, uplifting, comforting and enlightening. It prompts men and women to do that which is acceptable before God, who is just, righteous, all-wise, all-good, and all-merciful.

The gospel teaches us to forgive, to overcome selfishness, covetousness; to abjure anger, wrath, faultfinding, complaining and the spirit of contention and strife. The gospel warns and forewarns the children of men against the evils which bring disunion and contention and shut out honesty and love from among the children of men; which mislead people to acts of injustice, selfishness, covetousness, wickedness and sin, things which the gospel of Jesus Christ teaches us to eschew and avoid as we would the gates of hell. There is nothing intricate or incomprehensible in the gospel of Jesus Christ to those who possess the Spirit of the Lord.

—*Joseph F. Smith,* GD, p. 213, November 25, 1917

THE ETERNAL NATURE OF THE GOSPEL

As the gospel is a principle that emanates from God, like its Author, it is "the same yesterday, today, and for ever,"— eternal and unchangeable. God ordained it before the morning

stars sang together for joy, or ere this world rolled into existence,
for the salvation of the human race. It has been in the mind of
God, and as often as developed it has been manifested as an
eternal, unchangeable, undeviating plan by which to save, bless,
exalt, and dignify man, and to accomplish this end by one
certain, unalterable method of salvation, according to its degree
of manifestation . . .

The gospel is a certain living, abiding, eternal principle.
That which is written in the New Testament is like a chart of
a country, if you please; but the gospel is the country itself. A
man having the map of the United States in his possession would
be considered foolish if he supposed he possessed the United
States; and because a man may have the Old and New Testament in his possession, it does not argue that he has the gospel . . .

Well, but the gospel is contained in the Old and New Testament. It is not, nor in the Book of Mormon, nor in the revelations we have received. These are simple records, histories, commandments, etc. The gospel is a living, abiding, eternal, and
unchangeable principle that has existed co-equal with God and
always will exist, while time and eternity endure, wherever it
is developed and made manifest.
    —*John Taylor*, JD 7:361-362, January 15, 1860

There is not a principle associated with the gospel of the
Son of God but what is eternal in its nature and consequences,
and we cannot with impunity trample upon any principle that
is correct without having to suffer the penalty thereof before
God and the holy angels, and in many instances before men. The
principles of the gospel being eternal, they were framed and
originated with the Almighty in eternity before the world was,
according to certain eternal laws, and hence the gospel is called
the everlasting gospel. —*John Taylor*, JD 21:112, November 28, 1879

We are not connected with a something that will exist only
for a few years, some of the peculiar ideas and dogmas of men,
some nice theory of their forming; the principles that we believe
in reach back into eternity, they originated with the Gods in
the eternal worlds, and they reach forward to the eternities
that are to come. We feel that we are operating with God in
connection with those who were, with those who are, and with
those who are to come. —*John Taylor*, JD 17:206, October 7, 1874

We are safe in saying that from the day that Adam was created and placed in the Garden of Eden to this day, the plan of salvation and the revelations of the will of God to man are unchanged, although mankind have not for many ages been favored therewith, in consequence of apostasy and wickedness. There is no evidence to be found in the Bible that the gospel should be one thing in the days of the Israelites, another in the days of Christ and His Apostles, and another in the 19th century, but, on the contrary, we are instructed that God is the same in every age, and that His plan of saving His children is the same . . . The plan of salvation is one, from the beginning of the world to the end thereof.

—Brigham Young, JD 10:324, July 31, 1864

There is a very foolish idea prevailing in the world that there was no such thing as the gospel until Jesus came. It is the greatest folly in creation . . . They always had the gospel whenever men had a knowledge of God. It is the gospel that brings life and immortality to light; it is the gospel that places man in a position to obtain a just knowledge of God and of the eternities to come, of their position on the earth, and of their position as it will be hereafter . . . And if you trace out the records of either the Book of Mormon or the Bible or those of any people that have lived upon the earth and find anywhere a people that had a knowledge of life and immortality, then I will point out a people that had the gospel.

—John Taylor, JD 20:223, December 15, 1878

Mormonism, a nickname for the real religion of the Latter-day Saints, does not profess to be a new thing, except to this generation. It proclaims itself as the original plan of salvation, instituted in the heavens before the world was, and revealed from God to man in different ages. That Adam, Enoch, Noah, Abraham, Moses, and other ancient worthies had this religion successively, in a series of dispensations, we, as a people, verily believe. To us, the gospel taught by the Redeemer in the meridian of time was a restored gospel, of which, however, He was the author, in His pre-existent state. Mormonism, in short, is the primitive Christian faith restored, the ancient gospel brought back again—this time to usher in the last dispensation, introduce the Millennium, and wind up the work of redemption as pertaining to this planet. *—Lorenzo Snow,* MS 64:1, October, 1901

Now, here is one principle that I wish to impress upon the minds of every Saint of God who dwells upon the earth—and I want our reporters to write it down—I want to impress it upon the rulers of our nation and upon all the inhabitants of this nation and every other nation namely, that the love of God, faith, hope and charity, and the gospel of Jesus Christ, with all the ordinances thereof, with the Holy Priesthood, which has power both in heaven and on the earth, and the principles which have been revealed for the salvation and exaltation of the children of men—that these are principles you cannot annihilate. They are principles that no combination of men can destroy. They are principles that can never die . . . The inhabitants of the earth have tried for generations to destroy these principles. Yet it matters not what may take place on the earth. Republics may be destroyed, kingdoms overthrown, empires broken up, thrones cast down, the sun may be turned to darkness, the moon to blood, the stars may fall from heaven, and heaven and earth itself may pass away, but not one jot or tittle of these principles will ever be destroyed. I would to God the world could understand this.

—*Wilford Woodruff*, JD 22:342, October 23, 1881

THE GOSPEL IS ALWAYS THE SAME

Now, any man acquainted with the Scriptures can clearly understand that there is but one true gospel. There never was but one gospel. Whenever that gospel has been upon the earth it has been the same in every dispensation. The ordinances of the gospel have never been changed from the days of Adam to the present time and never will be to the end of time.

—*Wilford Woodruff*, JD 24:239, July 20, 1883

Now taking it for granted that the Scriptures say what they mean and mean what they say, we have sufficient grounds to go on and prove from the Bible that the gospel has always been the same; the ordinances to fulfill its requirements, the same, and the officers to officiate, the same; and the signs and fruits resulting from the promises, the same.

—*Joseph Smith, Jr.*, TS 3:904, September 1, 1842

The Lord has not one gospel for the living and another for the dead, any more than He has one gospel for the Savior and another for His brethren. The same gospel that saved those before us saves us, and will save those who come after us, adapting itself to the circumstances of all.
—Joseph F. Smith, MS 36:348, May 17, 1874

All the teachings of the patriarchs and prophets have shown us but one gospel. There is but one gospel, there never was but one and there never will be. The gospel revealed for the salvation of man is the same in every age of the world.
—Wilford Woodruff, JD 16:263-264, October 8, 1873

There is but one gospel, neither will there be any other for the salvation of this, nor of any other world that we know of; but this we do know that this gospel preached in any age of the world will produce the same effect.
—Wilford Woodruff, JD 10:12, July 27, 1862

Science and philosophy through all the ages have undergone change after change . . . These things may undergo continuous changes, but the word of God is always true, is always right. The principles of the gospel are always true, the principles of faith in God, repentance from sin, baptism for the remission of sins by authority of God, and the laying on of hands for the gift of the Holy Ghost—these principles are always true and are always absolutely necessary for the salvation of the children of men, no matter who they are or where they are.
—Joseph F. Smith, IE 14:641, May, 1911

We are informed by the revelation of St. John that in the last days there would be something like six hundred three score and six different religious sects and parties in the earth. Of course, there could be but one of them right; for there is but one right way. There is but one gospel; there never was but one and never will be. That gospel never deviates from one generation to another.
—Wilford Woodruff, MS 56:659, September 2, 1894

THE GOSPEL WILL BE PRESENTED TO EVERYONE

All that have lived or will live on this earth will have the privilege of receiving the gospel. They will have apostles, pro-

phets and ministers there, as we have here, to guide them in
the ways of truth and righteousness and lead them back to God.
All will have a chance for salvation and eternal life. What do
you think of that gospel? No one will be denied the privilege
of having it. Where is there a sectarian that can tell you anything about the power of the gospel?
                    —*Brigham Young*, "The Contributor" 10:321, July, 1889

It will be the privilege of every son and daughter of Adam,
sometime in their life, either in the body or in the spirit, to hear
the glad tidings of great joy proclaimed to them, for God is
just and is no respecter of persons.
                    —*Wilford Woodruff*, JD 19:227, September 16, 1877

CHAPTER IX

The First Principles of the Gospel

A. FAITH

WHEN YOU climb up a ladder you must begin at the bottom and ascend step by step, until you arrive at the top; and so it is with the principles of the gospel—you must begin with the first and go on until you learn all the principles of exaltation. But it will be a great while after you have passed through the veil before you will have learned them. It is not all to be comprehended in this world; it will be a great work to learn our salvation and exaltation even beyond the grave.

—Joseph Smith, Jr., TS August 15, 1844, Delivered April, 1844

Faith is the first principle of revealed religion. It is written that without faith it is impossible to please God. It is also written that the just shall live by faith. Therefore I say it is necessary for all men to have faith in God, the Maker and Creator of all things, the Ruler of heaven and earth. Without faith worlds could not have been made; without it they could not be held in their positions; but by faith all things are possible with God and with man.

—Joseph F. Smith, MS 57:609, May 13, 1894

What the world needs today more than anything else is an implicit faith in God, our Father, and in Jesus Christ, His Son, as the Redeemer of the world.

—Heber J. Grant, CR, p. 9, April, 1935

Faith in God is an irrevocable principle, just as much as "thou shalt not kill;" "thou shalt not steal;" "thou shalt not commit adultery."   *—Joseph F. Smith*, CR, p. 11, October, 1912

The gospel that we preach is the power of God unto salvation; and the first principle of that gospel is . . . faith in God, and faith in Jesus Christ His Son, our Savior. We must believe that He is the character He is represented to be in the holy Scriptures. Believe that He told the truth when He said to His

disciples, "Go ye forth and preach the gospel to every creature; he that believeth and is baptized shall be saved, but he that believeth not shall be damned." We must believe that this same Jesus was crucified for the sins of the world.
                            —*Brigham Young*, JD 13:143, July 11, 1869

We . . . should seek with all our souls to grow in grace, light, and truth, that in due time we may receive a fullness. The Lord has a great many principles in store for us; and the greatest principles which He has for us are the most simple and plain. The first principles of the gospel which lead us unto eternal life are the simplest, and yet none are more glorious or important unto us.   —*Wilford Woodruff*, JD 5:50, March 22, 1857

HOW FAITH MAY BE ACQUIRED

Faith is a gift of God; it is the fruitage of righteous living. It does not come to us by our command but is the result of doing the will of our Heavenly Father.
                    —*George Albert Smith*, CR, p. 103, October, 1913

Faith comes by hearing the word of God, through the testimony of the servants of God; that testimony is always attended by the Spirit of prophecy and revelation.
                        —*Joseph Smith, Jr.*, DHC 3:379, June 27, 1839

A moral life is one of the means by which we cultivate faith but it is not the only means. We may not see any moral virtue in the ordinance of baptism, in the laying on of hands, or in any other rite or ceremony of the Church, but our obedience to these rites and ordinances may be quite as helpful in developing our faith as any act of charity we may perform. Faith is always a gift of God to man, which is obtained by obedience, as all other blessings are.
                        —*Joseph F. Smith*, JI 38:657, November 1, 1903

The Savior told His apostles on one occasion when they had not faith sufficient to cast out devils that that kind by which He accomplished it came only by fasting and prayer. How does the faith required as the first principle in the plan of salvation or gospel come? Let Paul answer: "So then faith cometh by hearing, and hearing by the word of God." (Romans 10:17)

It is not the letter then that bringeth faith but hearing the word of God dispensed by a living oracle or minister of God clothed upon with power from on high. It is not a recorded gospel but the preached word which emanates with power from a man of God inspired by the Holy Ghost.

Faith without works being dead, it is evident that living faith and that which is acceptable to God, is that which not only believes in God, but acts upon that belief. It is not only the cause of action, but includes both cause and action. Or in other words it is belief or faith made perfect by works.
—*John Taylor,* "The Mormon" Vol. 1, No. 27, August 25, 1855

Faith is a gift of God, and when people have faith to live the gospel, and to listen to the counsel of those who preside in the wards and stakes and of the General Authorities of the Church, it has been my experience that they have been abundantly blessed of the Lord, and that many of them have come out of great financial and other difficulties in a most miraculous and wonderful way. "Obedience is better than sacrifice, and to hearken than the fat of rams."
—*Heber J. Grant,* IE 39:332, June, 1936

Faith is a gift of God, and faith comes to each and all of us who serve God and supplicate Him for the guidance of His Spirit. There is no danger of any man or woman losing his or her faith in this Church if he or she is humble and prayerful and obedient to duty. I have never known of such an individual losing his faith. By doing our duty faith increases until it becomes perfect knowledge.
—*Heber J. Grant,* CR, p. 131, April, 1934

THE POWER OF FAITH

Because faith is wanting, the fruits are. No man since the world was had faith without having something along with it. The ancients quenched the violence of fire, escaped the edge of the sword, women received their dead, etc. By faith the worlds were made. A man who has none of the gifts has no faith; and he deceives himself, if he supposes he has. Faith has been wanting, not only among the heathen, but in professed

Christendom also, so that tongues, healings, prophecy, and prophets and apostles, and all the gifts and blessings have been
wanting.   —*Joseph Smith, Jr.,* DHC 5:218, January 2, 1843

Faith comes by hearing the word of God. If a man has not
faith enough to do one thing, he may have faith to do another:
if he cannot remove a mountain, he may heal the sick. Where
faith is, there will be some of the fruits: all gifts and powers
which were sent from heaven were poured out on the heads of
those who had faith.
            —*Joseph Smith, Jr.,* DHC 5:355, April 13, 1843

If the Latter-day Saints will walk up to their privileges and
exercise faith in the name of Jesus Christ and live in the enjoyment of the fullness of the Holy Ghost constantly day by day,
there is nothing on the face of the earth that they could ask for
that would not be given to them. The Lord is waiting to be very
gracious unto this people and to pour out upon them riches,
honor, glory, and power, even that they may possess all things
according to the promises He has made through His apostles
and prophets.
                —*Brigham Young,* JD 11:114, June, 1865

DISTINCTION BETWEEN FAITH AND BELIEF

Faith is an eternal principle; belief is an admission of the
fact. Faith, to us, is the gift of God; belief is inherent in the
children of men and is the foundation for the reception of
faith . . . Belief and unbelief are independent in men, the same
as other attributes. Men can acknowledge or reject, turn to
the right or to the left, rise up or remain seated, you can say
that the Lord and His gospel are not worthy of notice, or you can
bow to them. . . .
Faith is an eternal principle—one of the attributes of the
Deity by which the worlds are and were created. Belief is the
admission of either truth or falsehood.
                —*Brigham Young,* JD 8:16-17, March 5, 1860

If we speak of faith in the abstract, it is the power of God
. . . to those who believe and obey His commandments. On
the other hand, no living, intelligent being, whether serving God
or not, acts without belief. He might as well undertake to live

without breathing as to live without the principle of belief. But he must believe the truth, obey the truth, and practice the truth, to obtain the power of God called faith.

—Brigham Young, JD 8:259, April 1, 1860

B. REPENTANCE

You may deceive the bishop and you may deceive the president of the stake, and you may deceive the General Authorities of the Church, but you can not deceive the Lord Jesus Christ nor the Holy Ghost. You know yourselves better than anybody else and if there is anything wrong in you, now is the time to repent and make yourselves square with the Lord; and if you do not repent, the time will come when you will be humbled, and the higher up you get the greater will be your fall.

—John Taylor, "Temples of the Most High" by Lundwall, p. 105, May, 1884

If you have sinned against the people, confess to them. If you have sinned against a family or a neighborhood, go to them and confess. If you have sinned against your ward, confess to your ward. If you have sinned against one individual, take that person by yourselves and make your confession to him. And if you have sinned against your God, or against yourselves, confess to God, and keep the matter to yourselves, for I do not want to know anything about it.

—Brigham Young, JD 8:362, March 10, 1860

Ever keep in exercise the principle of mercy and be ready to forgive our brother on the first intimations of repentance, and asking forgiveness; and should we even forgive our brother, or even our enemy, before he repent or ask forgiveness, our Heavenly Father would be equally as merciful unto us.

—Joseph Smith, Jr., DHC 3:383, July 2, 1839

Repentance of sin is an eternal principle and is as essential in its place and is as much an integral part of the gospel of Jesus Christ as is: "Thou shalt not kill," or, "Thou shalt have no other gods before Me."

—Joseph F. Smith, CR, p. 11, October, 1912

All sins shall be forgiven, except the sin against the Holy Ghost; for Jesus will save all except the sons of perdition. What must a man do to commit the unpardonable sin? He must receive the Holy Ghost, have the heavens opened unto Him, and know God, and then sin against Him. After a man has sinned against the Holy Ghost, there is no repentance for him.
—*Joseph Smith, Jr.*, TS August 15, 1844, Delivered April, 1844

WHAT IS TRUE REPENTANCE?

True repentance is not only sorrow for sins and humble penitence and contrition before God, but it involves the necessity of turning away from them, a discontinuance of all evil practices and deeds, a thorough reformation of life, a vital change from evil to good, from vice to virtue, from darkness to light. Not only so, but to make restitution, so far as it is possible, for all the wrongs we have done, to pay our debts, and restore to God and man their rights—that which is due to them from us. This is true repentance, and the exercise of the will and all the powers of body and mind is demanded to complete this glorious work of repentance; then God will accept it.
—*Joseph F. Smith*, JD 19:190, September 30, 1877

The second principle of the gospel of salvation is repentance. It is a sincere and godly sorrow for and a forsaking of sin, combined with full purpose of heart to keep God's commandments.
—*John Taylor*, MA, p. 182, Published in 1892

When men truly and heartily repent, and make manifest to the heavens that their repentance is genuine by obedience to the requirements made known to them through the laws of the gospel, then are they entitled to the administration of salvation, and no power can withhold the good Spirit from them.
—*Brigham Young*, JD 10:18, October 6, 1862

There is nothing in the world that is more splendid than to have in our hearts a desire to forgive the sinner if he only repents, but I want to say, do not forgive a sinner if he does not repent. "By this ye shall know that a man has repented, that he confesses his sin and forsakes it, and is guilty no more." It is up to the Lord, however, and unless they confess their sins we are not obligated to forgive, but when they really and truly repent it is one of the obligations that rest upon us to forgive those who have sinned. —*Heber J. Grant*, RSM 23:341, April 3, 1936

And what is repentance? The forsaking of sin. The man who repents, if he be a swearer, swears no more; or a thief, steals no more; he turns away from all former sins and commits them no more. It is not repentance to say, I repent today, and then steal tomorrow; that is the repentance of the world, which is displeasing in the sight of God. Repentance is the second principle. —*Wilford Woodruff*, JD 23:127, May 14, 1882

REPENTANCE NECESSARY FOR EXALTATION

No man can be saved in the kingdom of God in sin. No man will ever be forgiven of his sins by the just Judge, except he repent of his sins . . . Men can only be saved and exalted in the kingdom of God in righteousness, therefore we must repent of our sins and walk in the light as Christ is in the light, that His blood may cleanse us from all sins, and that we may have fellowship with God and receive of His glory and exaltation. —*Joseph F. Smith*, CR, p. 4, October, 1907

You cannot take a murderer, a suicide, an adulterer, a liar, or one who was or is thoroughly abominable in his life here, and simply by the performance of an ordinance of the gospel cleanse him from sin and usher him into the presence of God. God has not instituted a plan of that kind, and it cannot be done. He has said you shall repent of your sins. The wicked will have to repent of their wickedness . . . Do not forget that. Do not forget it . . . when you seek to save either the living or the dead. . . . you can only do it on the principle of their repentance and acceptance of the plan of life. —*Joseph F. Smith*, CR, p. 6;7, October, 1907

Now, my brethren, you who have sinned, repent of your sins. I can say to you in regard to Jesus and the atonement (it is so written, and I firmly believe it), that Christ has died for all. He has paid the full debt, whether you receive the gift or not. But if we continue to sin, to lie, steal, bear false witness, we must repent of and forsake that sin to have the full efficacy of the blood of Christ. Without this it will be of no effect; repentance must come, in order that the atonement may prove a benefit to us. Let all who are doing wrong cease doing wrong; live no longer in transgression, no matter of what kind; but live every day of your lives according to the revelations given, and so that your examples may be worthy of imitation. Let us remember that we never get beyond the purview of our religion—never, never!   *—Brigham Young,* JD 11:375, April 8, 1867

We believe in preaching the doctrine of repentance in all the world . . . but in order to be benefited by the doctrine of repentance, we must believe in obtaining the remission of sins. And in order to obtain the remission of sins, we must believe in the doctrine of baptism in the name of the Lord Jesus Christ. And if we believe in baptism for the remission of sins, we may expect a fulfillment of the promise of the Holy Ghost, for the promise extends to all whom the Lord our God shall call.
                    —Joseph Smith, Jr., DHC 2:256, September 1, 1835

DEATHBED REPENTANCE IS NOT SCRIPTURAL

I do not believe in the ideas that we hear sometimes advanced in the world, that it matters but little what men do in this life, if they will but confess Christ at the end of their journey in life, that that is all-sufficient, and that by so doing they will receive their passport into heaven. I denounce this doctrine. It is unscriptural, it is unreasonable, it is untrue, and it will not avail any man, no matter by whom this idea may be advocated; it will prove an utter failure unto men.
                    —Joseph F. Smith, CR, p. 3, October, 1907

We should take warning and not wait for the deathbed to repent, as we see the infant taken away by death, so may the youth and middle-aged as well as the infant be suddenly called into eternity. Let this, then, prove as a warning to all not to procrastinate repentance, or wait till a deathbed, for it is the will of God that man should repent and serve Him in health, and in the strength and power of his mind in order to secure His blessing, and not wait until he is called to die.
                    —Joseph Smith, Jr., DHC 4:554, March 20, 1842

If a person has determined that sin can easily be wiped out, and hence, that he will enjoy unlawful pleasures in youth, repenting in later life with an idea in his mind that repentance will blot out completely the results of his sin and debauchery, and place him on a level with his fellow who has kept in virtue the commandments from the beginning—time will wake him up to his serious and great mistake. He may and will be forgiven, if he repents; the blood of Christ will make him free and will wash him clean, though his sins be as scarlet; but all this will not return to him any loss sustained, nor place him on an equal footing with his neighbor who has kept the commandments of the better law. Nor will it place him in the position where he would have been had he not committed wrong. He has lost something which can never be regained, notwithstanding the perfection, the loving mercy, the kindness and forgiveness of the Lord God.   —*Joseph F. Smith,* IE 7:226-227, January, 1904

Repentance is a thing that cannot be trifled with every day. Daily transgression and daily repentance is not that which is pleasing in the sight of God.
—*Joseph Smith, Jr.,* DHC 3:379, June 27, 1839

CHAPTER X

The First Ordinances of the Gospel

A. BAPTISM

UPON LOOKING over the sacred pages of the Bible, searching into the prophets and sayings of the apostles, we find no subject so nearly connected with salvation as that of *baptism*. In the first place, however, let us understand that the word baptize is derived from the Greek verb *"baptiso,"* and means to immerse or overwhelm, and that sprinkle is from the Greek verb *"rantiso,"* and means to scatter on by particles; then we can treat the subject as one inseparably connected with our eternal welfare; and always bear in mind that it is one of the only methods by which we can obtain a remission of sins in this world and be prepared to enter into the joys of our Lord in the world to come. —*Joseph Smith, Jr.*, TS 3:903, September 1, 1842

In the former ages of the world, before the Savior came in the flesh, "the Saints" were baptized in the name of Jesus Christ to come, because there never was any other name whereby men could be saved; and after He came in the flesh and was crucified, then the Saints were baptized in the name of Jesus Christ, crucified, risen from the dead and ascended into heaven, that they might be buried in baptism like Him, and be raised in glory like Him, that as there was but *one* Lord, *one* faith, *one* baptism, and *one* God and Father of us all, even so there was but *one* door to the mansions of bliss.
—*Joseph Smith, Jr.*, TS 3:905, September 1, 1842

Baptism is a holy ordinance preparatory to the reception of the Holy Ghost; it is the channel and key by which the Holy Ghost will be administered.
—*Joseph Smith, Jr.*, DHC 3:379, June 27, 1839

Is there any difference between the baptized and the unbaptized man? All the difference in the world, I tell you, but it is only discernible through the Spirit. It is a vast difference too great for one not in possession of the Spirit to comprehend.

Take two men, they may be equals in point of goodness, they may be equally moral, charitable, honest and just, but one is baptized and the other is not. There is a mighty difference between them, for one is the son of God redeemed by compliance with His laws, and the other remains in darkness.

—*Joseph F. Smith*, GD, p. 97, February 2, 1909

We hold the opinion that in every stake of Zion there should be opportunity for baptism every day of every month and every month in every year.

—*Joseph F. Smith*, JI 40:337, June 1, 1905

FAITH AND REPENTANCE SHOULD PRECEDE BAPTISM

No person can be properly baptized unless he has faith in the Lord Jesus Christ and has repented of his sins, with a repentance that need not be repented of. But faith comes by hearing the word of God. This implies that the candidate must be taught. Efficient teaching and preparation must precede the ordinance, so that the candidate may have a proper appreciation and conception of its purposes. The call to baptism, in the mission of our Savior, was always preceded by instruction in the doctrines which He taught.

—*Joseph F. Smith*, IE 14:266, January, 1911

Baptism itself without faith in God avails nothing.

—*Joseph F. Smith*, JI 37:177, March, 1902

Some suppose they must *obtain religion* before they are baptized; but the Savior and apostles teach us to be baptized in order to get religion. Be baptized, says Peter, for the remission of sins, and ye shall receive the Holy Ghost. To obtain the gift of the Holy Ghost is to obtain religion. Faith and repentance were to go before baptism; but remission of sins, and gift of the Holy Ghost, were to follow this ordinance.

—*Lorenzo Snow*, OWTBS, p. 3, a. 1851

Has water, in itself, any virtue to wash away sin? Certainly not; but the Lord says, "If the sinner will repent of his sins, and go down into the waters of baptism, and there be buried in the likeness of being put into the earth and buried, and again be delivered from the water, in the likeness of being born—if in the sincerity of his heart he will do this, his sins shall be washed away." Will the water of itself wash them away? No; but keeping the commandments of God will cleanse away the stain of sin.   —*Brigham Young,* JD 2:4, October 23, 1853

AUTHORITY OF PRIESTHOOD NECESSARY TO BAPTIZE

Baptism means immersion in water, and it is to be administered by one having authority, in the name of the Father, and of the Son, and of the Holy Ghost. Baptism without divine authority is not valid. It is a symbol of the burial and resurrection of Jesus Christ and must be done in the likeness thereof, by one commissioned of God, in the manner prescribed, otherwise it is illegal and will not be accepted by Him, nor will it effect a remission of sins, the object for which it is designed, but whosoever hath faith, truly repents and is "buried with Christ in baptism," by one having divine authority, shall receive a remission of sins and is entitled to the gift of the Holy Ghost by the laying on of hands.
                    —*Joseph F. Smith,* JD 19:190, September 30, 1877

We claim . . . authority and declare to all the world that John the Baptist, who held the keys of authority to baptize, restored the Aaronic Priesthood and bestowed it upon Joseph Smith and Oliver Cowdery.
                    —*Heber J. Grant,* CR, p. 8, April, 1935

You have not the power to baptize yourselves, neither have you power to resurrect yourselves; and you could not legally baptize a second person for the remission of sins until some person first baptized you and ordained you to this authority.
                    —*Brigham Young,* JD 6:275, August 28, 1852

I want to say to the elders who go forth to preach the gospel —no matter who may apply to you for baptism, even if you have good reason to believe they are unworthy, if they require it forbid them not, but perform that duty and administer the ordinances for them; it clears the skirts of your garments, and the responsibility is upon them.
                    —*Brigham Young,* JD 14:78, April 9, 1871

BAPTISM NECESSARY TO ENTER THE KINGDOM
OF GOD

No man can enter into the kingdom of God except he is born of the water and of the Spirit. Men may be judged and their bodies lie in the grave until the last resurrection, to come forth and receive of a telestial glory, but no man will receive of the celestial glory except it be through the ordinances of the House of God.   —*Wilford Woodruff*, JD 19:361, June 30, 1878

The baptism of water, without the baptism of fire and the Holy Ghost attending it, is of no use; they are necessarily and inseparably connected. An individual must be born of water and the Spirit in order to get into the kingdom of God.
    —*Joseph Smith, Jr.*, TS August 15, 1844, Delivered April, 1844

God has made certain decrees which are fixed and immovable; for instance,—God set the sun, the moon, and the stars in the heavens, and gave them their laws, conditions and bounds, which they cannot pass, except by His commandments; they all move in perfect harmony in their sphere and order and are as lights, wonders and signs unto us. The sea also has its bounds which it cannot pass. God has set many signs on the earth, as well as in the heavens; for instance, the oak of the forest, the fruit of the tree, the herb of the field—all bear a sign that seed hath been planted there; for it is a decree of the Lord that every tree, plant, and herb bearing seed should bring forth of its kind, and cannot come forth after any other law or principle. Upon the same principle do I contend that baptism is a sign ordained of God, for the believer in Christ to take upon himself in order to enter into the kingdom of God, "for except ye are born of water and of the Spirit ye cannot enter into the kingdom of God," said the Savior. It is a sign and a commandment which God has set for man to enter into His kingdom. Those who seek to enter in any other way will seek in vain; for God will not receive them, neither will the angels acknowledge their works as accepted, for they have not obeyed the ordinances, nor attended to the signs which God ordained for the salvation of man, to prepare him for, and give him a title to a celestial glory; and God had decreed that all who will not obey His voice shall not escape the damnation of hell. What is the damnation of hell? To go with that society who have not obeyed His commands.

Baptism is a sign to God, to angels, and to heaven that we do the will of God, and there is no other way beneath the heavens whereby God hath ordained for man to come to Him to be saved and enter into the kingdom of God, except faith in Jesus Christ, repentance, and baptism for the remission of sins, and any other course is in vain; then you have the promise of the gift of the Holy Ghost.

—Joseph Smith, Jr., DHC 4:554-555, March 20, 1842

There is but one way in which men can receive salvation, exaltation and glory, and that is through the order of baptism and the ordinances connected therewith. No mortal man or woman will ever receive celestial glory unless he or she has been baptized, receiving this ordinance personally or by proxy. That is the order that God has established.

—Lorenzo Snow, DWN 54:482, March 13, 1897

It may be asked whether any person can be saved, except those who are baptized. Yes, all the inhabitants of the earth will be saved, except those that sin against the Holy Ghost. Will they come into the presence of the Father and the Son? Not unless they are baptized for the remission of sins and live faithfully in the observance of the words of life all the rest of their days.

—Brigham Young, JD 9:315, July 13, 1862

"WE BELIEVE IN . . . BAPTISM BY IMMERSION"

The gospel requires baptism by immersion for the remission of sins, which is the meaning of the word in the original language—namely, to bury or immerse.

—Joseph Smith, Jr., DHC 4:554, March 20, 1842

It says of John, that he baptized at AEnon, because there was much water; then, if sprinkling had been the mode, we can hardly suppose he would have gone to AEnon, because there was much water at that place: for a very little water indeed would have sprinkled all Judea, which he could have obtained without having performed a journey to AEnon. We are told, also, that he baptized in Jordan, and that, after the ordinance was administered to our Savior, he came up out of the water, expressly signifying that he had been down into the water, in order that the ordinance might be administered in a proper manner. Again, as it speaks of the Eunuch, that he went down into the water with Phillip, and then came up out of the water. Now, it must be acknowledged, by every one who makes any pretensions to reason and consistency, that had sprinkling a little water on the forehead answered the purpose, then those persons never would have gone into the water to receive the ordinance. Paul, in writing to the Saints, gives us a plain testimony in favor of immersion—(Colossians 2:12; also, Romans 6:4). That apostle states there, that the Saints had been buried with Christ by baptism.

It is plainly evident they could not have been buried by baptism, without having been entirely overwhelmed or covered in water. An object cannot be said to be buried when any portion of it remains uncovered; so, also, a man is not buried in water by baptism, unless his whole person is put into the watery element. This explanation of the apostle, upon the mode baptism, very beautifully corresponds with that given by our Savior, "Except ye be born of water," etc. To be born of a thing signifies being placed in that thing, and emerging or coming forth from it; to be born of water must also signify being placed in the womb of waters, and being brought forth again. I trust sufficient has already been said to convince every reasonable and unprejudiced mind, that immersion was the mode in which the ordinance of baptism was administered in the early days of Christianity, when the gospel was proclaimed in its purity and fullness. —*Lorenzo Snow, OWTBS, p. 5, a. 1851*

BAPTISM IS FOR THE REMISSION OF SINS

We, the Latter-day Saints, believe in being baptized by immersion for the remission of sins, according to the testimony of the disciples of Jesus and the revelations of the Lord given in these last days. Infants are pure, they have neither sorrow of heart, nor sins to repent of and forsake, and consequently are incapable of being baptized for the remission of sin. If we have sinned, we must know good from evil; an infant does not know this, it cannot know it; it has not grown into the idea of contemplation of good and evil; it has not the capacity to listen to the parent or teacher or to the priest when they tell what is right or wrong or what is injurious; and until these things

are understood a person cannot be held accountable and consequently cannot be baptized for the remission of sin.
                              —*Brigham Young*, JD 13:237, February 20, 1870

The Lord has instituted laws and ordinances, and all have
their peculiar design and meaning. And though we may not
know the origin of the necessity of being baptized for the remission of sins, it answers that portion of the law we are now under
to teach the people in their ignorance that water is designed
for purification and to instruct them to be baptized therein for
the remission of their sins. If the people could fully understand
this matter, they would perceive that it is perfectly reasonable
and has been the law to all worlds.
                              —*Brigham Young*, JD 7:162–163, June 5, 1859

Some deem it wrong to number baptism among the essential
principles ordained of God, to be attended to in obtaining remission of sins. In reply, we say that the Savior and apostles
have done so before us; therefore, we feel obligated to follow
their example.   —*Lorenzo Snow*, OWTBS, p. 3, a. 1851

Baptism for the remission of sin, by one having authority,
is an eternal principle, for God devised it and commanded it,
and Christ Himself was not above obeying it; He had to obey
it in order to fulfill the law of righteousness.
                              —*Joseph F. Smith*, CR, p. 11, October, 1912

BAPTISM OF CHILDREN NOT SCRIPTURAL

The doctrine of baptizing children, or sprinkling them, or
they must welter in hell is a doctrine not true, not supported
in Holy Writ, and is not consistent with the character of God.
                              —*Joseph Smith, Jr.*, DHC 4:554, March 20, 1842

Faith and repentance go before baptism; and baptism before
the remission of sins, and the reception of the Holy Ghost.
Hence, we see the useless and unscriptural practice of baptizing
infants. They cannot exercise faith and repentance, qualifications necessary previous to baptism; then, why require the outward work?   —*Lorenzo Snow*, OWTBS, p. 2, a. 1851

The sprinkling of infants or the doctrine that infants go to hell under any circumstances is a doctrine ordained of man and not of God, and is therefore of no avail and entirely wrong and displeasing in the sight of God. . . . they are redeemed by the blood of Jesus Christ, and when they die, whether of Christian, Pagan or Jewish parentage, their spirits are taken home to God who gave them, and never go to suffer torments of any kind. —*Wilford Woodruff*, JD 23:126, May 14, 1882

BAPTISM FOR THE DEAD

The Latter-day Saints believe in baptism for the dead, in salvation for those who have died without a knowledge of the gospel—that all human beings should have the privilege of receiving or rejecting the gospel.
—*Heber J. Grant*, DWN 44:593, April 17, 1892

Let me say to you, if it is true that no man can enter the kingdom of God unless he is born of the water and of the Spirit, God must provide a plan by which those who have died ignorant of the gospel may have the privilege of doing so, or He would appear to be a partial Being. Has He provided that way? He has.
—*Brigham Young*, JD 13:329, April 24, 1870

If there is one word of the Lord that supports the doctrine of baptism for the dead, it is enough to establish it as a true doctrine. Again; if we can, by the authority of the priesthood of the Son of God, baptize a man in the name of the Father, of the Son, and of the Holy Ghost, for the remission of sins, it is just as much our privilege to act as an agent and be baptized for the remission of sins for and in behalf of our dead kindred, who have not heard the gospel, or the fullness of it.
—*Joseph Smith, Jr.*, DHC 4:569, March 27, 1842

They will not baptize anybody in the spirit world; there is no baptism there; there is no marrying or giving in marriage there; all these ordinances have to be performed on the earth. Paul says, in referring to this subject—"Why are ye baptized for the dead? If the dead rise not why then are ye baptized for the dead?" The Lord holds us responsible for going to and building temples, that we may attend therein to the ordinances necessary for the salvation of the dead.
—*Wilford Woodruff*, JD 18:114, September 12, 1875

We have a great work before us in the redemption of our dead. . . . Those persons may receive their testimony, but they cannot be baptized in the spirit world, for somebody on the earth must perform this ordinance for them in the flesh before they can receive part in the first resurrection and be worthy of eternal life. It takes as much to save a dead man as a living one . . . Have we any time to spend in trying to get rich and in neglecting our dead? I tell you no.
—*Wilford Woodruff*, JD 22:234, June 26, 1881

We know something about our progenitors, and God has taught us how to be saviors for them by being baptized for them in the flesh, that they may live according to God in the spirit.
—*John Taylor*, JD 14:187, March 20, 1870

The doctrine of baptism for the dead is clearly shown in the New Testament; and if the doctrine is not good, then throw the New Testament away; but if it is the word of God, then let the doctrine be acknowledged; and it was the reason why Jesus said unto the Jews, "How oft would I have gathered thy children together, even as a hen gathereth her chickens under her wings, and ye would not!"—that they might attend to the ordinances of baptism for the dead as well as other ordinances of the priesthood, and receive revelations from heaven, and be perfected in the things of the kingdom of God—but they would not.
—*Joseph Smith, Jr.*, DHC 5:425, June 11, 1843

GENERAL CHARACTERISTICS OF BAPTISM FOR THE DEAD

All persons baptized for the dead must have a recorder present, that he may be an eyewitness to record and testify of the truth and validity of his record. It will be necessary, in the Grand Council, that these things be testified to by competent witnesses. Therefore let the recording and witnessing of baptisms for the dead be carefully attended to from this time forth. If there is any lack, it may be at the expense of our friends; they may not come forth.
—*Joseph Smith, Jr.*, DHC 5:141, August 31, 1842

It was revealed that if a woman was baptized for a man, she could not be ordained for him, neither could she be made an apostle or a patriarch for the man, consequently the sisters are to be baptized for their own sex only.
— *Brigham Young,* JD 16:166, August 31, 1873

One of the ordinances of the House of the Lord is baptism for the dead. God decreed before the foundation of the world that that ordinance should be administered in a font prepared for that purpose in the House of the Lord.
— *Joseph Smith, Jr.,* DHC 5:424, June 11, 1843

Every man that has been baptized and belongs to the kingdom has a right to be baptized for those who have gone before; and as soon as the law of the gospel is obeyed here by their friends who act as proxy for them, the Lord has administrators there to set them free.
— *Joseph Smith, Jr.,* DHC 6:365, May 12, 1844

This doctrine presents in a clear light the wisdom and mercy of God in preparing an ordinance for the salvation of the dead, being baptized by proxy, their names recorded in heaven and they judged according to the deeds done in the body . . . Those Saints who neglect it in behalf of their deceased relatives, do it at the peril of their own salvation.
— *Joseph Smith, Jr.,* DHC 4:426, October 3, 1841

B.   LAYING ON OF HANDS FOR THE GIFT OF THE HOLY GHOST

Now, if you have the Holy Ghost with you, . . . I can say unto you that there is no greater gift, there is no greater blessing, there is no greater testimony given to any man on earth. You may have the administration of angels; you may see many miracles; you may see many wonders in the earth; but I claim that the gift of the Holy Ghost is the greatest gift that can be bestowed upon man.
— *Wilford Woodruff,* DWN 38:451, March 5, 1889

I often think that our elders themselves hardly realize the significance of the situation they occupy when they say to him that believes, repents and is baptized, "Receive thou the Holy

Ghost." Is there a thing of more importance that we can think of anywhere than this which so many of us treat so lightly. The idea of a man, human and fallible, pronouncing the reception of the Holy Ghost upon his fellow man, and his fellow receiving that heavenly treasure, is one of the greatest manifestations of the faithfulness of God, in sanctioning the acts of His elders that it is possible for us to conceive of. He has said that through these ordinances He would confer the Holy Ghost; He has also fulfilled it, as the thousands who hear me today can bear record.   —*John Taylor*, JD 21:346, January 2, 1881

The gift of the Holy Ghost by the laying on of hands cannot be received through the medium of any other principle than the principle of righteousness, for if the proposals are not complied with, it is of no use, but withdraws.
                         —*Joseph Smith, Jr.*, DHC 3:379, June 27, 1839

In order that men may indeed become the children of God, He has introduced in the first principles of the gospel the means of their becoming possessed of His Spirit through baptism and laying on of hands by those having authority, being sent and ordained and authorized by Him that they may receive the Holy Ghost. What can be a stronger evidence to any man than an evidence of this kind? It is not something that affects the outward ear alone; it is not something that affects simply his judgment, but it affects his inner man; it affects the spirit that dwells within him; it is a part of God imparted unto man, if you please, giving him an assurance that God lives.
                         —*John Taylor*, JD 11:22, December 11, 1864

To obtain religion that will save us in the presence of God, we must obtain the Holy Ghost, and, in order to obtain the Holy Ghost, we must believe on the Lord Jesus Christ, then repent of our sins (that is, forsake them) then go forward and be immersed in water for the remission of sins, then receive the laying on of hands.   —*Lorenzo Snow*, OWTBS, p. 7, a. 1851

We believe that the Holy Ghost comes to all those who are faithful, who repent of their sins, who are baptized, and that it is received by all the members of the Church through the laying on of hands. —*Heber J. Grant*, LEJ 19:306, November 20, 1921

The sun shines upon the evil and the good; but the Holy Ghost descends only upon the righteous and upon those who are forgiven of their sins.

—Joseph F. Smith, JD 24:176, April 8, 1883

The disciples of Christ were without the gift of the Holy Ghost until after His resurrection. . . . it was not until the evening of the day on which Jesus came out of the grave that He bestowed upon them this inestimable gift.

—Joseph F. Smith, JD 23:174, June 18, 1882

THE PURPOSE OF LAYING ON OF HANDS

Let me here speak of a simple principle; there are three that bear record on earth; the water, the Spirit and the blood, and these three are one; and there are three that bear record in heaven; the Father, the Son, and the Holy Spirit, and these three are one. Thus, there are three in heaven and three on the earth. The Spirit of the Lord is one of the witnesses both in heaven and on earth. When a man is confirmed, he receives the witness of the Divine Spirit, and thus, if lived up to, a connecting link is established between man and God.

—John Taylor, MS 19:194, November 2, 1856

When men obey the gospel with pure hearts—when they are baptized in the name of Jesus Christ for the remission of sins and have hands laid upon them for the gift of the Holy Ghost, and they receive that Spirit and live in obedience to the dictates of that Spirit, it will bring things past and present to their remembrance, lead them into all truth, and show them things to come. This is part and parcel of our belief.

—John Taylor, JD 6:106, December 6, 1857

This gift of the Holy Ghost is a different principle from anything that we see manifested in the sectarian world. It is a principle of intelligence and revelation. It is a principle that reveals things past, present and to come, and these gifts of the Holy Ghost were to be received through obedience to the requirements of the gospel as proclaimed by the elders of the Church of Jesus Christ of Latter-day Saints in these days.

—Lorenzo Snow, JD 20:330, October 6, 1879

THE GIFT OF THE HOLY GHOST CONFERRED ONLY
BY LAYING ON OF HANDS

We believe that the Holy Ghost is imparted by the laying on of hands of those in authority, and that the gift of tongues, and also the gift of prophecy are gifts of the Spirit, and are obtained through that medium.

—Joseph Smith, Jr., DHC 5:27-28, June 15, 1842

This holy gift (the Holy Ghost) is bestowed today as it was anciently, by the laying on of hands by men possessing the authority to administer in the ordinances of the gospel.

—Wilford Woodruff, JD 23:127, May 14, 1882

God has not and will not suffer the gift of the Holy Ghost to be bestowed upon any man or woman, except through compliance with the laws of God. Therefore, no man can obtain a remission of sins; no man can obtain the gift of the Holy Ghost . . . except through compliance with the requirements of heaven.

—Joseph F. Smith, JD 24:175, April 8, 1883

The gift of the Holy Ghost . . . is not given unto all men until they repent of their sins and come into a state of worthiness before the Lord. Then they receive it by the laying on of hands of those who are authorized of God to bestow His blessings upon the heads of the children of men.

—Joseph F. Smith, IE 11:380, March 16, 1902

Every elder of the Church who has received the Holy Ghost by the laying on of hands, by one having authority, has power to confer that gift upon another; it does not follow that a man who has received the presentation or gift of the Holy Ghost shall always receive the recognition and witness and presence of the Holy Ghost himself, or he may receive all these, and yet the Holy Ghost not tarry with him, but visit him from time to time (Doc. and Cov., Sec. 130:23); and neither does it follow that a man must have the Holy Ghost present with him when he confers the Holy Ghost upon another, but he possesses the gift of the Holy Ghost, and it will depend upon the worthiness of him unto whom the gift is bestowed whether he receive the Holy Ghost or not . . .

Therefore, the presentation or "gift" of the Holy Ghost simply confers upon a man the right to receive at any time, when he is worthy of it and desires it, the power and light of truth of the Holy Ghost, although he may often be left to his own spirit and judgment.

—Joseph F. Smith, IE 12:390, March, 1909

People should be made to understand that just to bow before the Lord in prayer does not give them divine authority. To live up to the requirements that are made of honesty, virtue, truth, etc., does not give them divine authority. Our Heavenly Father has made it plain to the children of men that only under the hands of those who possess divine authority may we obtain the power to become members of the celestial kingdom.

—George Albert Smith, CR, p. 28, April, 1934

DISTINCTION BETWEEN HOLY GHOST AND GIFT OF THE HOLY GHOST

It is a very common saying with us, as elders, in our remarks concerning the gifts of the gospel to speak of confirming the gifts of the Holy Ghost by the laying on of hands. There is no difference with regard to our faith, opinions or views, as a Church, pertaining to this principle; it is only in the manner in which we use our language. There is a difference between the gifts of the Holy Ghost and the Holy Ghost itself. . . . we receive the laying on of hands for the reception of the Holy Ghost; but the elders, when speaking on this principle, instead of saying so, not infrequently say "for the reception of the gifts of the Holy Ghost." Now we have no right, power nor authority to seal the gifts of the Holy Ghost upon anybody, they are the property of the Holy Ghost itself . . .

We lay hands upon the heads of those who embrace the gospel and we say unto them, "In the name of the Lord Jesus Christ receive ye the Holy Ghost." We seal this blessing upon the heads of the children of men, just as Jesus and His apostles and the servants of God have done in every age when preaching the gospel of Christ. But the gifts of the Holy Ghost are his property to bestow as he sees fit. To one is given the spirit of prophecy, to another a tongue, to another the interpretation of tongues and to another the gift of healing. All these gifts are by the same Spirit, but all are the gifts of the Holy Ghost, to bestow as he sees fit, as the messenger of the Father and the Son to the children of men.

—*Wilford Woodruff*, JD 13:156-157, December 12, 1869

The sign of Peter was to repent and be baptized for the remission of sins, with the promise of the gift of the Holy Ghost; and in no other way is the gift of the Holy Ghost obtained.

There is a difference between the Holy Ghost and the gift of the Holy Ghost. Cornelius received the Holy Ghost before he was baptized, which was the convincing power of God unto him of the truth of the gospel, but he could not receive the gift of the Holy Ghost until after he was baptized. Had he not taken this sign or ordinance upon him, the Holy Ghost which convinced him of the truth of God, would have left him. Until he obeyed these ordinances and received the gift of the Holy Ghost, by the laying on of hands, according to the order of God, he could not have healed the sick or commanded an evil spirit to come out of a man, and it obey him; for the spirits might say unto him, as they did to the sons of Sceva: "Paul we know and Jesus we know, but who are ye?"

—*Joseph Smith, Jr.*, DHC 4:555, March 20, 1842

CHAPTER XI

Temple Ordinances for the Living and the Dead

THE REDEMPTION OF MANKIND

THE GREAT Jehovah contemplated the whole of the events connected with the earth, pertaining to the plan of salvation, before it rolled into existence . . . He comprehended the fall of man and his redemption; He knew the plan of salvation and pointed it out . . . He knows the situation of both the living and the dead, and has made ample provision for their redemption, according to their several circumstances, and the laws of the kingdom of God, whether in this world, or in the world to come. *—Joseph Smith, Jr.*, DHC 4:597, April 15, 1842

To my mind, there isn't anything so great and so glorious in this world as to labor for the salvation of the living and for the redemption of the dead.
—Joseph F. Smith, YWJ 23:130, January, 1912

If we preserve ourselves in the truth and live so that we shall be worthy of the celestial kingdom, by and by we can officiate for those who have died without law [the gospel]—the honest, honorable, good, truthful, virtuous and pure. By and by it will be said unto us, "Go ye forth and be baptized for them, and receive the ordinances for them;" and the hearts of the children will be turned to the fathers who have slept in their graves, and they will secure to them eternal life. This must be, lest the Lord come and smite the earth with a curse.
—Brigham Young, JD 14:151, June 25, 1871

We have blessings which have never been given to any other generation since the days of Jesus Christ and the Apostles . . . You hold the keys of the destiny of your fathers, your mothers, your progenitors, from generation to generation; you hold the keys of their salvation. God has put that power into your hands. But if we do not do what is required of us in this thing, we are under condemnation.
—Wilford Woodruff, CR, p. 38, October, 1897

THE NEED FOR TEMPLE WORK

God is no respecter of persons; He will not give privileges to one generation and withhold them from another; and the whole human family, from father Adam down to our day, have got to have the privilege, somewhere, of hearing the gospel of Christ; and the generations that have passed and gone without hearing that gospel in its fullness, power and glory will never be held responsible by God for not obeying it, neither will He bring them under condemnation for rejecting a law they never saw or understood; and if they live up to the light they had they are justified so far, and they have to be preached to in the spirit world. But nobody will baptize them there, and somebody has got to administer for them by proxy here in the flesh, that they may be judged according to men in the flesh and have part in the first resurrection.

—Wilford Woodruff, JD 18:190-191, April 6, 1876

The greatest responsibility in this world that God has laid upon us is to seek after our dead.

—Joseph Smith, Jr., TS August 15, 1844, Delivered April 7, 1844

We have got to enter into those temples and redeem our dead—not only the dead of our own family, but the dead of the whole spirit world . . . This is the great work of the last dispensation—the redemption of the living and the dead.

—Wilford Woodruff, JD 21:192;194, July 3, 1880

One of the great works in this gospel of salvation, devolving upon us as Saints, is to labor in the temples of God for the salvation of our dead.   *—Heber J .Grant*, CR, p. 87, October, 1913

We are building temples to the name of the Lord. What are we building them for? That we may enter in and redeem our dead.   *—Wilford Woodruff*, JD 22:209, January 9, 1881

It depends upon the living here to erect temples, that the ordinances for the dead may be attended to, for by and by you will meet your progenitors in the spirit world who never heard the sound of the gospel. You who are here in Zion have power to be baptized for and to redeem your dead.

—Wilford Woodruff, JD 17:250, October 9, 1874

THE PURPOSE OF TEMPLE ORDINANCES

These ordinances have been revealed unto us for this very purpose, that we might be born into the light from the midst of this darkness—from death into life.

—Joseph F. Smith, JD 19:265, April 11, 1878

It is absolutely necessary that the Saints should receive the further ordinances of the House of God before this short existence shall come to a close, that they may be prepared and fully able to pass all the sentinels leading into the celestial kingdom and into the presence of God.

—Brigham Young, JD 12:163-164, February 16, 1868

The work for our dead . . . should not be neglected. We should avail ourselves of those sacred and potent ordinances of the gospel which have been revealed as essential to the happiness, salvation and redemption of those who have lived in this world when they could not learn the gospel and have died without the knowledge of it and are now waiting for us, their children, who are living in an age when these ordinances can be performed, to do the work necessary for their release from the prison-house. Through our efforts in their behalf their chains of bondage will fall from them, and the darkness surrounding them will clear away, that light may shine upon them and they shall hear in the spirit world of the work that has been done for them by their children here and will rejoice with you in your performance of these duties.

—Joseph F. Smith, CR, p. 6, October, 1916

While the priesthood behind the veil are operating and preaching to the spirits that are in prison that have been there from the different ages, He [God] calls upon us to build temples that we may administer for the bodies of these people that have died without the gospel, that they may be judged according to men in the flesh and live after God in the spirit.

—John Taylor, JD 21:96, April 13, 1879

We hope to see the day when we shall have temples built in the various parts of the land where they are needed for the convenience of the people; for we realize that one of the greatest responsibilities that rests upon the people of God today is that their hearts shall be turned unto their fathers, and that they shall do the work that is necessary to be done for them in order that they may be joined together fitly in the bond of the new and everlasting covenant from generation to generation. For the Lord has said, through the Prophet Joseph, that this is one of the greatest responsibilities devolving upon us in this latter day.   *—Joseph F. Smith*, CR, p. 3, October, 1902

This great work for the redemption of our dead, the uniting together of the living and the dead, the sealing power that takes the living children and unites them in the bond of the new and everlasting covenant with their fathers and mothers who have gone before them; the great principle that binds on earth and it is bound in heaven, that takes the woman, chosen by the man, and seals her to the husband of her choice with an everlasting, unbreakable covenant, or a covenant that can only be broken by sin or by the transgression of the laws of God; a covenant that can never be broken by death, by time, or distance, because God has confirmed it, it is sealed by His power for time and for all eternity; the work of baptism and other saving ordinances for the dead; the endowments, and all the ordinances that have been revealed to be performed in the sacred edifices called temples, which we are under commandment from God always to build unto His holy name,—(Doc. and Cov., Sec. 124:39) these things have been revealed to us in this dispensation in greater fullness and in greater plainness than ever before in the history of the world so far as we know.
                              —Joseph F. Smith, CR, p. 9-10, October, 1913

GOSPEL ORDINANCES THE SAME FOR LIVING AND DEAD

The same principles that apply to the living apply also to the dead. "For for this cause," said the apostle, "was the gospel preached also to them that are dead, that they might be judged according to men in the flesh, but live according to God in the spirit." And so we are baptized for those that are dead. The living cannot be made perfect without the dead, nor the dead be made perfect without the living, There has got to be a welding together and a joining together of parents and children and

children and parents until the whole chain of God's family shall be welded together into one chain, and they shall all become the family of God and His Christ.
—*Joseph F. Smith*, MS 68:628-629, August 26, 1906

Ordinances instituted in the heavens before the foundation of the world, in the priesthood, for the salvation of men, are not to be altered or changed. All must be saved on the same principles.   —*Joseph Smith, Jr.*, DHC 5:423, June 11, 1843

There is but one way by which exaltation and glory can be secured. We have to be baptized for the remission of sins and have hands laid upon us for the reception of the Holy Ghost. These and other ordinances are absolutely necessary for exaltation and glory; and where individuals have lived when the Gospel has not been accessible, these things can be attended to by their friends. We have come into the world now in order to do these things . . . we cannot lay too great stress upon the importance of this work. —*Lorenzo Snow*, MS 57:405, April 6, 1895

It takes just as much to save a dead man as a living man.
—*Wilford Woodruff*, JD 19:228, September 16, 1877

It is not only necessary that you should be baptized for your dead, but you will have to go through all the ordinances for them, the same as you have gone through to save yourselves.
—*Joseph Smith, Jr.*, DHC 6:365, May 12, 1844

Every man who wishes to save his father, mother, brothers, sisters and friends, must go through all the ordinances for each one of them separately, the same as for himself, from baptism to ordination, washings and anointings, and receive all the keys and powers of the priesthood, the same as for himself.
—*Joseph Smith, Jr.*, DHC 6:319, April 8, 1844

The same gospel, the same ordinances, the same authority and blessings that were administered by the Prophet Joseph Smith and taught by him to his associates are now being enjoyed by and taught to the Latter-day Saints.
—*Joseph F. Smith*, CR, p. 46, October, 1900

The question is frequently asked, "Can we not be saved without going through with all those ordinances, etc?" I would answer, No, not the fullness of salvation. Jesus said, "There are many mansions in my Father's house, and I will go and prepare a place for you." *House* here named should have been translated kingdom; and any person who is exalted to the highest mansion has to abide a celestial law, and the whole law too.
                         —Joseph Smith, Jr., DHC 6:184, January 21, 1844

THE HOLY ENDOWMENT

Let me give you the definition in brief. Your *endowment* is to receive all those ordinances in the House of the Lord, which are necessary for you, after you have departed this life, to enable you to walk back to the presence of the Father, passing the angels who stand as sentinels, being enabled to give them the key words, the signs and tokens, pertaining to the Holy Priesthood, and gain your eternal exaltation in spite of earth and hell.   *—Brigham Young*, JD 2:31, April 6, 1853

Joseph Smith himself organized every endowment in our Church and revealed the same to the Church, and he lived to receive every key of the Aaronic and Melchizedek Priesthoods from the hands of the men who held them while in the flesh, and who hold them in eternity.
                         —Wilford Woodruff, JD 23:131, May 14, 1882

The endowment you are so anxious about, you cannot comprehend now, nor could Gabriel explain it to the understanding of your dark minds; but strive to be prepared in your hearts, be faithful in all things, that when we meet in the solemn assembly, that is, when such as God shall name out of all the official members shall meet, we must be clean every whit . . .

You need an endowment, brethren, in order that you may be prepared and able to overcome all things; and those that reject your testimony will be damned.
                         —Joseph Smith, Jr., DHC 2:309, November 12, 1835

THE SEALING ORDINANCE

With the introduction of the priesthood upon the earth was also introduced the sealing ordinance, that the chain of the priesthood from Adam to the last generation might be united in one unbroken continuance. It is the same power and the same keys that Elijah held and was to exercise in the last days. . . . By this power men will be sealed to men back to Adam, completing and making perfect the chain of the priesthood from his day to the winding up scene.

—*Brigham Young*, JD 9:269, April 6, 1862

Four destroying angels [are] holding power over the four quarters of the earth until the servants of God are sealed in their foreheads, which signifies sealing the blessing upon their heads, meaning the everlasting covenant, thereby making their calling and election sure. When a seal is put upon the father and mother, it secures their posterity so that they cannot be lost, but will be saved by virtue of the covenant of their father and mother.

—*Joseph Smith, Jr.*, DHC 5:530, August 13, 1843

The ordinances of sealing must be performed here man to man, and woman to man, and children to parents, etc., until the chain of generation is made perfect in the sealing ordinances back to father Adam; hence, we have been commanded to gather ourselves together, to come out from Babylon and sanctify ourselves and build up the Zion of our God, by building cities and temples, redeeming countries from the solitude of nature, until the earth is sanctified and prepared for the residence of God and angels.

—*Brigham Young*, JD 12:165, February 16, 1868

When the ordinances are carried out in the temples that will be erected, men will be sealed to their fathers and those who have slept clear up to Father Adam. This will have to be done, because of the chain of the priesthood being broken upon the earth . . . This priesthood has been restored again, and by its authority we shall be connected with our fathers, by the ordinance of sealing, until we shall form a perfect chain from Father Adam down to the closing up scene.

—*Brigham Young*, JD 16:186, September 4, 1873

Unto the Latter-day Saints the sealing ordinances have been revealed, and they will have effect after death and . . . will reunite men and women eternally in the family organization . . . We could not obtain a fullness of celestial glory without this sealing ordinance . . . which is one of the most glorious principles of our religion.

—*Wilford Woodruff*, JD 13:167, December 12, 1869

We want the Latter-day Saints from this time to trace their genealogies as far as they can and to be sealed to their fathers and mothers. Have children sealed to their parents and run this chain through as far as you can get it. When you get to the end, let the last man be adopted to Joseph Smith, who stands at the head of the dispensation. This is the will of the Lord to this people, and I think when you come to reflect upon it you will find it to be true.

—*Wilford Woodruff*, MS 56:338-339, April 8, 1894

COVENANTS WITH GOD

We entered into covenants with the Lord that we will keep ourselves pure and unspotted from the world. We have agreed before God, angels and witnesses, in sacred places, that we will not commit adultery, will not lie, that we will not steal or bear false witness against our neighbor, or take advantage of the weak, that we will help and sustain our fellow men in the right, and take such a course as will prove most effectual in helping the weak to overcome their weaknesses and bring themselves into subjection to the requirements of heaven. We cannot neglect, slight, or depart from the spirit, meaning, intent and purpose of these covenants and agreements that we have entered into with our Father in heaven, without shearing ourselves of our glory, strength, right and title to His blessings and to the gifts and manifestations of His Spirit.

The Lord has given unto us garments of the Holy Priesthood, and you know what that means. And yet there are those of us who mutilate them, in order that we may follow the foolish, vain and (permit me to say) indecent practices of the world. In order that such people may imitate the fashions, they will not hesitate to mutilate that which should be held by them the most sacred of all things in the world, next to their own virtue, next to their own purity of life. They should hold these things that God has given unto them sacred, unchanged and unaltered from the very pattern in which God gave them. Let us have the moral courage to stand against the opinions of fashion, and especially where fashion compels us to break a covenant and so commit a grievous sin.

—*Joseph F. Smith,* IE 9:813, August, 1906

We enter into obligations here as young men or young women, or as old men or old women, as the case may be, no matter what or how we enter into covenants before God, holy angels and witnesses, and pledge ourselves in the most solemn manner to be true unto these covenants, and if we violate these covenants and trample under foot the ordinances of God, we ought to be dealt with by the Church and either repent of our sins or be cut off from the Church, so that by purging the Church from iniquity we may be acceptable before God.

—*John Taylor,* JD 25:165, June 15, 1884

A great many of you have had your endowments, and you know what a vote with uplifted hands mean.

It is a sign which you make in token of your covenant with God and with one another, and it is for you to perform your vows. When you raise your hands to heaven and let them fall and then pass on with your covenants unfulfilled, you will be cursed.

I feel sometimes like lecturing men and women severely, who enter into covenants without realizing the nature of the covenants they make, and who use little or no effort to fulfill them . . .

It is written in the Bible that every man should perform his own vows, even if to his own hurt; in this way you will show to all creation and to God that you are full of integrity.

—*Brigham Young,* JD 3:332, June 8, 1856

GOSPEL ORDINANCES STILL TO BE REVEALED

It is supposed by this people that we have all the ordinances in our possession for life and salvation, and exaltation, and that we are administering in these ordinances. This is not the case. We are in possession of all the ordinances that can be administered in the flesh; but there are other ordinances and administrations that must be administered beyond this world. I know you would ask what they are. I will mention one. We have not, neither can we receive here, the ordinance and the keys of the resurrection. They will be given to those who have passed off this stage of action and have received their bodies again, as many have already done and many more will. They will be ordained, by those who hold the keys of the resurrection, to go forth and resurrect the Saints, just as we receive the ordinance of baptism, then the keys of authority to baptize others for the remission of their sins. This is one of the ordinances we cannot receive here and there are many more. We hold the authority to dispose of, alter and change the elements; but we have not received authority to organize native elements, to even make a spear of grass grow . . .

Another item: We have not the power in the flesh to create and bring forth or produce a spirit; but we have the power to produce a temporal body. The germ of this, God has placed within us. And when our spirits receive their bodies and through our faithfulness we are worthy to be crowned, we will then receive authority to produce both spirit and body. But these keys we cannot receive in the flesh. Herein, brethren, you can perceive that we have not finished and cannot finish our work while we live here, no more than Jesus did while He was in the flesh.

We cannot receive, while in the flesh, the keys to form and fashion kingdoms and to organize matter, for they are beyond our capacity and calling, beyond this world. In the resurrection, men who have been faithful and diligent in all things in the flesh, have kept their first and second estate, and are worthy to be crowned Gods, even the Sons of God, will be ordained to organize matter. How much matter do you suppose there is between here and some of the fixed stars which we can see? Enough to frame many, very many millions of such earths as this, yet it is now so diffused, clear and pure that we look through it and behold the stars. Yet the matter is there. Can you form any conception of this? Can you form any idea of the minuteness of matter?

—*Brigham Young*, JD 15:136-137, August 24, 1872

THE LIVING NOT PERFECT WITHOUT THE DEAD

The dead are not perfect without us, neither are we without them. We have a mission to perform for and in their behalf; we have a certain work to do in order to liberate those who, because of their ignorance and the unfavorable circumstances in which they were placed while here, are unprepared for eternal life; we have to open the door for them, by performing ordinances which they cannot perform for themselves and which are essential to their release from the "prison-house," to come forth and live according to God in the spirit and be judged according to man in the flesh.

—*Joseph F. Smith,* JD 19:264, April 11, 1878

Others are operating with us, I mean all the men of God who ever lived, and they are as much interested as we are, and a good deal more, for they know more, and "they without us cannot be made perfect," neither can we be perfected without them. We are building temples for them and for their posterity, and we are going to operate in these temples, as we have done heretofore for their welfare and for the welfare of their posterity.

—*John Taylor,* JD 17:213, October 7, 1874

Every father and mother has a great responsibility resting upon them to redeem their dead. Do not neglect it. You will have sorrow if you do. Any man will who neglects the redemption of his dead that he has power to officiate for here. When you get to the other side of the veil, if you have entered into these temples and redeemed your progenitors by the ordinances of the House of God, you will hold the keys of their redemption from eternity to eternity. Do not neglect this!

—*Wilford Woodruff,* CR, p. 90, April 10, 1898

What do you suppose the fathers would say if they could speak from the dead? Would they not say: "We have lain here thousands of years in this prison-house, bound and fettered in the association of the filthy and the corrupt." If they had the power the very thunders of heaven would resound in our ears. All the angels in heaven are looking to this little handful of people. When I think upon this subject I want the tongue of seven thunders to awaken the people to action.

—*Brigham Young* "Wilford Woodruff" by Cowley, p. 494-495, January 1, 1877

LATTER-DAY SAINTS TO BECOME SAVIORS ON MOUNT ZION

But how are they to become saviors on Mount Zion? By building their temples, erecting their baptismal fonts, and going forth and receiving all the ordinances, baptisms, confirmations, washings, anointings, ordinations and sealing powers upon their heads, in behalf of all their progenitors who are dead, and redeem them that they may come forth in the first resurrection and be exalted to thrones of glory with them; and herein is the chain that binds the hearts of the fathers to the children, and the children to the fathers, which fulfills the mission of Elijah.
— *Joseph Smith, Jr.,* DHC 6:184, January 21, 1844

God is looking upon us and has called us to be saviors upon Mount Zion. And what does a savior mean? It means a person who saves somebody . . . Would we be saviors if we did not save somebody? I think not. Could we save anyone if we did not build temples? No, we could not; for God would not accept our offerings and sacrifices. — *John Taylor,* JD 22:308, August 28, 1881

We have a work to do just as important in its sphere as the Savior's work was in its sphere. Our fathers cannot be made perfect without us; we cannot be made perfect without them. They have done their work and now sleep. We are now called upon to do ours; which is to be the greatest work man ever performed on the earth. Millions of our fellow creatures who have lived upon the earth and died without a knowledge of the gospel must be officiated for in order that they may inherit eternal life (that is, all that would have received the gospel). And we are called upon to enter into this work.
— *Brigham Young,* JD 18:213, August 15, 1876

God has wrought out a salvation for all men, unless they have committed a certain sin; and every man who has a friend in the eternal world can save him, unless he has committed the unpardonable sin. And so you can see how far you can be a savior. — *Joseph Smith, Jr.,* TS August 15, 1844, Delivered April, 1844

You hold the keys of the destiny of your fathers, your mothers, your progenitors, from generation to generation; you hold the keys of their salvation. God has put that power into your hands. But if we do not do what is required of us in this thing, we are under condemnation. If we do attend to this, then when we come to meet our friends in the celestial kingdom, they will say, "You have been our saviors, because you had power to do it. You have attended to these ordinances that God has required." —*Wilford Woodruff*, CR, p. 38, October, 1897

We have the gospel of Jesus Christ restored to us; we have the plan of life and salvation; we have the ordinances of the gospel not only for the living but for the dead. We have all that is necessary, not only for our own salvation, but that we may be in very deed "Saviors upon Mount Zion," and enter into the temples of our God and save our ancestors who have died without a knowledge of the gospel.
—*Heber J. Grant*, CR, p. 28, April, 1899

RULES REGULATING TEMPLE WORK

In the first place people desirous to go and attend to ordinances in these houses must have a recommendation from their bishop . . . Then when they have obtained this recommendation from the bishop, it must be endorsed by the president of the stake and after that have the sanction of the President of the Church . . .

However, there is something far more difficult than that yet to come . . . The time will come when we shall not only have to pass by those officers whom I have referred to . . . but we are told in this book (the book of Doctrine and Covenants) that we shall have to pass by the angels and the Gods. We may have squeezed through the other; we may have gotten along tolerably well and been passed and acted upon, and sometimes a "tight squeeze" at that; but how will it be when we get on the other side, and we have the angels and the Gods to pass by before we can enter into our exaltation? If we cannot pass, what then? Well, we cannot, that is all. And if we cannot, shall we be able to enter into our exaltation? I think not. What do you think about it? —*John Taylor*, JD 25:161, June 15, 1884

The information needed to properly identify the dead, for whom temple ordinances are to be performed, includes the following: Names in full (maiden names of women). Date of

birth. Place of birth (Town, County and State or Country).
Date of death. Name of heir, or friend, at whose instance the
work is to be done, and his, or her, relationship to each one
named. When this information cannot be given as complete as
desired, that which is lacking may be approximately formulated,
by following instructions that will be published in periodicals
issued in various missions of the Church.
                    —*Joseph F. Smith*, MS 77:191, March, 1915

The gospel is now preached to the spirits in prison, and
when the time comes for the servants of God to officiate for
them, the names of those who have received the gospel in the
spirit will be revealed by the angels of God and the spirits of
just men made perfect; also the places of their birth, the age in
which they lived, and everything regarding them that is necessary to be recorded on earth, and they will then be saved so as
to find admittance into the presence of God, with their relatives
who have officiated for them.
                    —*Brigham Young*, JD 9:317, July 13, 1862

THE MISSION OF ELIJAH

The spirit, power, and calling of Elijah is, that ye have
power to hold the key of the revelation, ordinances, oracles,
powers and endowments of the fullness of the Melchizedek
Priesthood and of the kingdom of God on the earth; and to
receive, obtain, and perform all the ordinances belonging to the
kingdom of God, even unto the turning of the hearts of the
fathers unto the children, and the hearts of the children unto
the fathers, even those who are in heaven.
                    —*Joseph Smith, Jr.*, DHC 6:251, March 10, 1844

The spirit of Elias is first, Elijah second, and Messiah last.
Elias is a forerunner to prepare the way, and the spirit and power
of Elijah is to come after, holding the keys of power, building
the temple to the capstone, placing the seals of the Melchizedek
Priesthood upon the House of Israel, and making all things ready;
then Messiah comes to His Temple, which is last of all.
                    —*Joseph Smith, Jr.*, DHC 6:254, March 10, 1844

TEMPLE WORK IS THE GREAT WORK
OF THE MILLENNIUM

This work of administering the ordinances of the house of God to the dead . . . will require the whole of the Millennium, with Jesus at the head of the resurrected dead to attend to it. The ordinances of salvation will have to be attended to for the dead who have not heard the gospel, from the days of Adam down, before Christ can present this world to the Father, and say, "It is finished."

—Wilford Woodruff, JD 13:327, September 5, 1869

In relation to the deliverance of spirits from their prison-house, of course, we believe that can only be done after the gospel has been preached to them in the spirit, and they have accepted the same, and the work necessary to their redemption by the living be done for them. That this work may be hastened so that all who believe in the spirit world may receive the benefit of deliverance, it is revealed that the great work of the Millennium shall be the work in the temples for the redemption of the dead; and then we hope to enjoy the benefits of revelation through the Urim and Thummim, or by such means as the Lord may reveal concerning those for whom the work shall be done, so that we may not work by chance, or by faith alone, without knowledge, but with the actual knowledge revealed unto us. It stands to reason that, while the gospel may be preached unto all, the good and the bad, or rather those who would repent and those who would not repent in the spirit world, the same as it is here, redemption will only come to those who repent and obey.

—Joseph F. Smith, IE 5:146-147, December, 1901

We are trying to save the living and the dead. The living can have their choice, the dead have not. Millions of them died without the gospel, without the priesthood, without the opportunities that we enjoy. We shall go forth in the name of Israel's God and attend to the ordinances for them. And through the Millennium, the thousand years that the people will love and serve God, we will build temples and officiate therein for those who have slept for hundreds and thousands of years—those who would have received the truth if they had had the opportunity; and we will bring them up and form the chain entire, back to Adam.

—Brigham Young, JD 14:97, April 8, 1871

To accomplish this work there will have to be not only one temple but thousands of them, and thousands and tens of thousands of men and women will go into those temples and officiate for people who have lived as far back as the Lord shall reveal.
—*Brigham Young*, JD 3:372, June 22, 1856

Before this work is finished, a great many of the elders of Israel in Mount Zion will become pillars in the Temple of God, to go no more out: they will eat and drink and sleep there.
—*Brigham Young*, JD 6:295, August 15, 1852

THE NEED OF TEMPLES

The building of temples, places in which the ordinances of salvation are administered, is necessary to carry out the plan of redemption.   —*Brigham Young*, JD 13:262, October 6, 1870

Each of them (the temples) has been built to one great eternal purpose: to serve as a House of the Lord, to provide a place sacred and suitable for the performing of holy ordinances that bind on earth as in heaven—ordinances for the dead and for the living that assure those who receive them and who are faithful to their covenants, the possession and association of their families, worlds without end, and exaltation with them in the celestial kingdom of our Father.
—*George Albert Smith*, IE 48:561, October, 1945

We have now finished this temple, and some people inquire, what is it for? For many things: that our sealings and ordinances may be performed in a manner that will be acceptable before God and the holy angels; that whatsoever is bound on the earth according to the laws of the eternal priesthood shall be bound in the heavens; that there may be a connecting link between the living and the dead, . . . that there may be a royal priesthood, a holy people, a pure people, a virtuous people on the earth to officiate and operate in the interests of the living and the dead; . . . that they may be prepared to operate with the priesthood in the heavens in the redemption of the inhabitants of this world from the days of Adam unto the present time.

It is also intended to introduce the higher branches of education—literary, scientific, linguistic, philosophical and theological; for we are told to obtain a knowledge of laws, languages, governments, justice, equity, rule, authority, dominion, and all those great cosmopolitan principles exhibited in the laws of nature and among the peoples, by the wisdom, prescience, power and intelligence of "nature's God." That we may thus be acquainted with earthly and heavenly things, in accordance with everlasting laws that have existed in the heavens and on the earth from the beginning; and that all those great and eternal principles by which the worlds are governed may be comprehended by us.

—*John Taylor,* JD 25:185, May 18, 1884

He (Christ) has told us to . . . build temples. What for? To administer in them. Who for? For the dead who have died without a knowledge of the gospel, that they might participate with us in the blessings which they had not the privilege of enjoying on the earth . . . we are making preparations for saving the dead, according to the word of God.

—*John Taylor,* JD 20:118, January 6, 1879

This ordinance [sealing] will not be performed anywhere but in a temple; neither will children be sealed to their living parents in any other place than a temple. . . . Children born unto parents, before the latter enter into the fullness of the covenants, have to be sealed to them in a temple to become legal heirs of the priesthood.   —*Brigham Young,* JD 16:186, September 4, 1873

ON TEMPLE BUILDING

We that are here are enjoying a privilege that we have no knowledge of any other people enjoying since the days of Adam, that is, to have a temple completed, wherein all the ordinances of the House of God can be bestowed upon his people. . . . It is true that Solomon built a temple for the purpose of giving endowments, but from what we can learn of the history of that time they gave very few if any endowments. . . . I will not say but what Enoch had temples and officiated therein, but we have no account of it.   —*Brigham Young,* JD 18:303, January 1, 1877

These temples, erected by the Saints in the days of their poverty, bear witness to all the world of the inspiration of God to those men and to the truthfulness of the visions in the Kirtland Temple. No men and women would spend their money by the millions of dollars for the erection of temples, and spend their time, year after year, laboring for the salvation of their dead, if they did not have the witness of the Holy Spirit that in very deed the promise has been fulfilled that was made to the boy Joseph Smith ninety-six years ago, that Elijah should come and restore these keys.   —*Heber J. Grant*, CR, p. 23, October, 1919

I scarcely ever say much about revelations, or visions, but suffice it to say, five years ago last July I was here and saw in the Spirit the Temple not ten feet from where we have laid the chief corner stone. I have not inquired what kind of a temple we should build. Why? Because it was represented before me. I have never looked upon that ground, but the vision of it was there. I see it as plainly as if it was in reality before me. Wait until it is done. I will say, however, that it will have six towers, to begin with, instead of one. . . . The time will come when there will be one in the centre of temples we shall build, and, on the top, groves and fish ponds. But we shall not see them here, at present.   —*Brigham Young*, JD 1:133, April 6, 1853

I want to see the temple built in a manner that it will endure through the Millennium. This is not the only temple we shall build; there will be hundreds of them built and dedicated to the Lord. This temple will be known as the first temple built in the mountains by the Latter-day Saints. And when the Millennium is over, and all the sons and daughters of Adam and Eve, down to the last of their posterity, who come within the reach of the clemency of the gospel, have been redeemed in hundreds of temples through the administration of their children as proxies for them, I want that temple still to stand as a proud monument of the faith, perseverance and industry of the Saints of God in the mountains, in the nineteenth century.
—*Brigham Young*, JD 10:254, October 6, 1863

This entire continent is the land of Zion, and the time will come when there will be temples established over every portion of the land, and we will go into these temples and work for our kindred dead night and day, that the work of the Lord may be speedily accomplished, that Jesus may come and present the kingdom to His Father.   —*Lorenzo Snow*, MS 61:546, May 8, 1899

CHAPTER XII

Obtaining Salvation through the Gospel Plan

THE PLAN OF SALVATION

THERE is nothing under the heavens of so much importance to me or to the children of men as the great plan of life and salvation.
—*Joseph F. Smith,* CR, p. 2, October, 1913

God tells us in the Doctrine and Covenants there is no gift greater than the gift of salvation. We as Latter-day Saints have all started out for the gift of salvation, and we should so order our lives that when we have finished our work we shall be worthy to go back into the presence of our Father and be worthy not only to receive an exaltation ourselves, but also to receive our wives and our children that have been sealed unto us that we shall possess them. No amount of testimony, no amount of knowledge, even knowledge that this is God's work will ever save a man . . . but the keeping of the commandments of God will entitle him to that blessing.
—*Heber J. Grant,* CR, p. 59, October, 1900

Who but those who have duly considered the condescension of the Father of our spirits, in providing a sacrifice for His creatures, a plan of redemption, a power of atonement, a scheme of salvation, having as its great objects the bringing of men back into the presence of the King of heaven, crowning them in the celestial glory and making them heirs with the Son to that inheritance which is incorruptible, undefiled, and which fadeth not away—who but such can realize the importance of a perfect walk before all men and a diligence in calling upon all men to partake of these blessings? How indescribably glorious are these things to mankind!
—*Joseph Smith, Jr.,* DHC 2:5-6, January 22, 1834

WHAT IS SALVATION?

Salvation is nothing more nor less than to triumph over all our enemies and put them under our feet. And when we have power to put all enemies under our feet in this world and a knowledge to triumph over all evil spirits in the world to come, then we are saved, as in the case of Jesus, who was to reign until He had put all enemies under His feet, and the last enemy was death.

Perhaps there are principles here that few men have thought of. No person can have this salvation except through a tabernacle.
—*Joseph Smith, Jr.*, DHC 5:387-388, May 13, 1842

What is salvation? It is for man to be saved from the consequences of sin, whether by his own acts or those of another; for we know that sins of parents sometimes follow the children to the third and fourth generation. This is a true principle and we cannot change it. Now if the consequence of sin be entailed upon us by our parents, salvation is liberation and deliverance therefrom, making all men equally acceptable before God. As in the case of our father Adam, who by sin brought death into the world, salvation is redemption therefrom, that we might come forth in the resurrection and be again united with our bodies clothed upon by the power of God.
—*Joseph F. Smith*, MS 37:278-279, April 18, 1875

Salvation is for a man to be saved from all his enemies; for until a man can triumph over death, he is not saved. A knowledge of the priesthood alone will do this.
—*Joseph Smith, Jr.*, DHC 5:403, May 21, 1843

What is life and salvation? It is to take that course wherein we can abide forever and ever and be exalted to thrones, kingdoms, governments, dominions, and have full power to control the elements, according to our pleasure to all eternity.
—*Brigham Young*, JD 1:275, August 14, 1853

Salvation is the full existence of man, of the angels, and the Gods; it is eternal life—the life which was, which is, and which is to come. And we, as human beings, are heirs to all this life, if we apply ourselves strictly to obey the requirements of the law of God and continue in faithfulness.
—*Brigham Young*, JD 12:111, December 8, 1867

HOW TO GAIN SALVATION

If you want to know how to be saved, I can tell you: it is by keeping the commandments of God. No power on earth, no power beneath the earth, will ever prevent you or me or any Latter-day Saint from being saved, except ourselves. We are the architects of our own lives, not only of our lives here, but our lives to come in the eternity.

—Heber J. Grant, IE 48:123, March, 1945

"What shall we do to be saved" was the cry of the people who heard the preaching of Peter on the day of Pentecost, and the same may be said to be applicable to all men in every generation. The answer would be, obey the law of the gospel. This is the safe means given for the salvation of the human family.

—Wilford Woodruff, JD 23:126, May 14, 1882

To get salvation we must not only do some things, but everything which God has commanded.

—Joseph Smith, Jr., DHC 6:223, February 21, 1844

I realize that the salvation of this people does not depend upon the great amount of teaching, instruction, or revelation that is given unto them, but their salvation depends more upon their obeying the commandments of God which are given unto them, their becoming a doer of the word and following the counsel of those who are set to lead them.

—Wilford Woodruff, JD 4:190, January 25, 1857

Salvation will come only to those who repent and have their sins washed away by baptism, and who thereafter show by a godly life that their repentance is genuine.

—Heber J. Grant, IE 15:785, July, 1912

Every son and daughter of God is expected to obey with a willing heart every word which the Lord has spoken and which He will in the future speak to us. It is expected that we hearken to the revelations of His will, and adhere to them, cleave to them with all our might; for this is salvation, and anything short of this clips the salvation and the glory of the Saints.

—Brigham Young, JD 2:2, October 23, 1853

SALVATION IS AN INDIVIDUAL WORK

Salvation is an individual operation. I am the only person that can possibly save myself. When salvation is sent to me, I can reject or receive it. In receiving it, I yield implicit obedience and submission to its great Author throughout my life and to those whom He shall appoint to instruct me; in rejecting it, I follow the dictates of my own will in preference to the will of my Creator.   —*Brigham Young*, JD 1:312, February 20, 1853

Though our interest is one as a people, yet remember, salvation is an individual work; it is every person for himself. . . . There are those in this Church who calculate to be saved by the righteousness of others. They will miss their mark. They are those who will arrive just as the gate is shut, so in that case you may be shut out; then you will call upon some one, who, by their own faithfulness, through the mercy of Jesus Christ, have entered in through the celestial gate, to come and open it for you; but to do this is not their province. . . . I forewarn you therefore to cultivate righteousness and faithfulness in yourselves, which is the only passport into celestial happiness.
          —*Brigham Young*, JD 2:132, December 18, 1853

THE GOSPEL IS THE LAW OF SALVATION

The gospel of Jesus Christ is the law of salvation. No man can be saved without it. The gospel is the power of God unto salvation to everyone that believeth—to Jew or Greek, Catholic, Methodist, Baptist, or any other sect or party on the face of the earth.   —*Wilford Woodruff*, JD 25:8, January 6, 1884

The gospel of salvation is a portion of the law that pertains to the kingdom where God resides; and the ordinances pertaining to the Holy Priesthood are the means by which the children of men find access to the way of life, wherein they can extend their travels until they return to the presence of their Father and God.   —*Brigham Young*, JD 8:159, September 2, 1860

The gospel of salvation—the priesthood of the Son of God— is so ordered and organized, in the very nature of it, being a portion of that law of heaven by which worlds are organized, that it is calculated to enlighten the children of men and give

them power to save themselves. It is of the same nature as the
further principles of eternal existence by which the worlds are
and were and by which they will endure; and these principles
are pure in their nature, from the fact that they are of God, who
is pure; but, without the revelation of the Spirit of God, no man
can understand them. That is the peculiarity there is about this
mysterious work.   —*Brigham Young*, JD 7:54, June 27, 1858

The gospel which we preach is the gospel of life and salvation. The Church which we represent is the Church and kingdom
of God and possesses the only faith by which the children of
men can be brought back into the presence of our Father and
God. The Lord has set His hands to restore all things as in the
beginning and, by the administration of His Holy Priesthood,
save all who can be saved, cleanse from the world the consequences of the fall and give it to the hands of His Saints.
                        —*Brigham Young*, JD 12:205, May 10, 1868

No man ever did or ever will obtain salvation only through
the ordinances of the gospel and through the name of Jesus.
There can be no change in the gospel; all men that are saved
from Adam to infinitum are saved by the one system of salvation.
The Lord may give many laws and many commandments to suit
the varied circumstances and conditions of His children throughout the world, such as giving a law of carnal commandments to
Israel, but the laws and principles of the gospel do not change.
                        —*Wilford Woodruff*, JD 10:217, June 12, 1863

While the first principles of the gospel, faith in God, repentance, baptism for the remission of sins, and the laying on
of hands for the reception of the Holy Ghost, the healing of the
sick, the resurrection, and, for that matter, all the revealed principles of the gospel of Christ are necessary and essential in the
plan of salvation, it is neither good policy nor sound doctrine to
take any one of these, single it out from the whole plan of gospel
truth, make it a special hobby and depend upon it for our salvation and progress either in this world or in the world to come.
They are all necessary.   —*Joseph F. Smith*, IE 15:844, July, 1912

No man will be saved and come into the presence of the
Father only through the gospel of Jesus Christ—the same for one
as the other. The Lord has His cause, His ways, His work; He

will finish it up. Jesus is laboring with His might to sanctify and redeem the earth and to bring back His brethren and sisters into the presence of the Father. We are laboring with Him for the purification of the whole human family, that we and they may be prepared to dwell with God in His kingdom.

—Brigham Young, JD 13:150, July 11, 1869

WHO WILL BE SAVED?

All will be saved, as Jesus said, when speaking to the apostles, except the sons of perdition. They will be saved through the atonement and their own good works, according to the law that is given to them. Will the heathen be saved? Yes, so far as they have lived according to the best light and intelligence they had; but not in the celestial kingdom. Who will not be saved? Those who have received the truth, or had the privileges of receiving it, and then rejected it. They are the only ones who will become the sons of perdition, go into everlasting punishment, and become angels to the devil.

—Brigham Young, JD 8:35, April 6, 1860

God has wrought out a salvation for all men, unless they have committed a certain sin; and every man who has a friend in the eternal world can save him, unless he has committed the unpardonable sin. . . .

A man cannot commit the unpardonable sin after the dissolution of the body, and there is a way possible for escape. Knowledge saves a man; and in the world of spirits no man can be exalted but by knowledge. So long as a man will not give heed to the commandments, he must abide without salvation. If a man has knowledge, he can be saved; although, if he has been guilty of great sins, he will be punished for them. But when he consents to obey the gospel, whether here or in the world of spirits, he is saved.

—Joseph Smith, Jr., TS August 15, 1844, Delivered April, 1844

We [the Latter-day Saints] believe that even our enemies will be saved in the Lord's own due time. Read the revelations given upon the subject and you will find that all mankind, except those who have had the testimony of Christ and rejected it, denying the blood of Christ, will ultimately be saved.

—Heber J. Grant, Journal History:2, September 9, 1888

The names of every son and daughter of Adam are already written in the Lamb's Book of Life. . . . All the names of the human family are written there, and the Lord will hold them there until they come to the knowledge of the truth, that they can rebel against Him and can sin against the Holy Ghost; then they will be thrust down to hell, and their names be blotted out from the Lamb's Book of Life.

—*Brigham Young,* JD 6:297, August 15, 1852

CHAPTER XIII

The Atonement of Jesus Christ

LATTER-DAY SAINT CONCEPT OF THE ATONEMENT

THE Latter-day Saints believe . . . that Jesus is the Savior of the world; they believe that all who attain to any glory whatever, in any kingdom, will do so because Jesus has purchased it by His atonement.
—*Brigham Young*, JD 13:328, April 24, 1870

A man who says he does not believe in the atoning blood of Jesus Christ, who professes to be a member of the Church of Jesus Christ of Latter-day Saints, but who ignores and repudiates the doctrine of the atonement . . . —the man who denies that truth and who persists in his unbelief is not worthy of membership in the Church. —*Joseph F. Smith*, IE 21:7, September 13, 1917

If it were not for the atonement of Jesus Christ, the sacrifice He made, all the human family would have to lie in the grave throughout eternity without any hope. But God having provided, through the atonement of the Lord Jesus Christ, the medium whereby we can be restored to the bosom and presence of the Father, to participate with Him among the Gods in the eternal worlds—He, having provided for that, has also provided for the resurrection. —*John Taylor*, JD 22:356, January 29, 1882

The atonement made by Jesus Christ brought about the resurrection from the dead and restored life.
—*John Taylor*, MA, p. 178, Published in 1892

THE NEED OF THE ATONEMENT

Was it known that man would fall? Yes. We are clearly told that it was understood that man should fall, and it was understood that the penalty of departing from the law would be death, death temporal. And there was a provision made for that. Man was not able to make that provision himself, and hence we are told that it needed the atonement of a God to accomplish this purpose; and the Son of God presented Himself to carry out that object. And when He presented Himself for this position He was accepted by His Father, just the same as any man who owes a debt, if he is not able to pay that obligation, and somebody steps forward and says, I will go security for him. If the persons to whom he is indebted are willing to take him as security they will receive the security's note or obligation to meet the debt. So Jesus offered Himself. Now, man could not have done that. Man could do all that he is capable of doing. But there was an eternal law of God violated and it needed an eternal, infinite sacrifice to atone therefor; and Jesus offered Himself as that sacrifice to atone for the sins of the world; and hence it is written, He was the Lamb slain from before the foundation of the world. —*John Taylor*, JD 22:300, August 28, 1881

A divine debt has been contracted by the children, and the Father demands recompense. He says to His children on this earth, who are in sin and transgression, it is impossible for you to pay this debt; I have prepared a sacrifice; I will send my Only Begotten Son to pay this divine debt. Was it necessary then that Jesus should die? Do we understand why He should sacrifice His life? The idea that the Son of God, who never committed sin, should sacrifice His life is unquestionably preposterous to the minds of many in the Christian world. But the fact exists that the Father, the Divine Father, whom we serve, the God of the Universe, the God and Father of our Lord Jesus Christ, and the Father of our spirits, provided this sacrifice and sent His Son to die for us; and it is also a great fact that the Son came to do the will of the Father, and that He has paid the debt, in fulfillment of the Scripture which says, "He was the Lamb slain from the foundation of the world." . . .

Unless God provides a Savior to pay this debt it can never be paid. Can all the wisdom of the world devise means by which we can be redeemed and return to the presence of our Father and Elder Brother and dwell with holy angels and celestial beings? No; it is beyond the power and wisdom of the inhabitants of the earth that now live, or that ever did or ever will live, to prepare or create a sacrifice that will pay this divine debt. But

God provided it, and His Son has paid it, and we, each and every one, can now receive the truth and be saved in the kingdom of God.   —*Brigham Young*, JD 14:71-72, July 10, 1870

That man was not able himself to erect a system or plan with power sufficient to free him from a destruction which awaited him is evident from the fact that God . . . prepared a sacrifice in the gift of His own Son who should be sent in due time, to prepare a way, or open a door through which man might enter into the Lord's presence, whence he had been cast out for disobedience. From time to time these glad tidings were sounded in the ears of men in different ages of the world down to the time of Messiah's coming. By faith in this atonement or plan of redemption, Abel offered to God a sacrifice that was accepted, which was the firstlings of the flock. Cain offered of the fruit of the ground and was not accepted, because he could not do it in faith, he could have no faith or could not exercise faith contrary to the plan of heaven. It must be—shedding the blood of the Only Begotten to atone for man; for this was the plan of redemption; and without the shedding of blood was no remission.
                    —*Joseph Smith, Jr.*, DHC 2:15, January 22, 1834

THE PURPOSE OF THE ATONEMENT

How, and in what manner are men benefited by the atonement? . . . In this, that the atonement, having restored man to his former position before the Lord, has placed him in a position and made it possible for him to obtain that exaltation and glory which it would have been impossible for him to have received without it; even to become a son of God by adoption; and being a son, then an heir of God, and a joint heir with Jesus Christ; and that, as Christ overcame, He has made it possible and has placed it within the power of believers in Him also to overcome; and as He is authorized to inherit His Father's glory which He had with Him before the world was, with His resurrected body, so through the adoption may we overcome and sit down with Him upon His throne, as He has overcome and sat down upon His Father's throne.   —*John Taylor*, MA, p. 179, Published in 1892

Men cannot forgive their own sins; they cannot cleanse themselves from the consequences of their sins. Men can stop

sinning and can do right in the future and so far their acts are acceptable before the Lord and worthy of consideration. But who shall repair the wrongs they have done to themselves and to others, which it seems impossible for them to repair themselves? By the atonement of Jesus Christ, the sins of the repentant shall be washed away, though they be crimson they shall be made white as wool. This is the promise given to you.
—*Joseph F. Smith,* CR, p. 41, October, 1899

From the facts in the case and the testimony presented in the Scriptures it becomes evident that through the great atonement, the expiatory sacrifice of the Son of God, it is made possible that man can be redeemed, restored, resurrected and exalted to the elevated position designed for him in the creation as a Son of God: that eternal justice and law required the penalty to be paid by man himself, or by the atonement of the Son of God: that Jesus offered Himself as the great expiatory sacrifice; that this offering being in accordance with the demands or requirements of the law was accepted by the great Lawgiver; that it was prefigured by sacrifices and ultimately fulfilled by Himself according to the eternal covenant.
—*John Taylor,* MA, p. 170-171, Published in 1892

THE EFFECT OF THE ATONEMENT

In a manner to us incomprehensible and inexplicable, He [Christ] bore the weight of the sins of the whole world, not only of Adam, but of his posterity; and in doing that opened the kingdom of heaven, not only to all believers and all who obeyed the law of God, but to more than one-half of the human family who die before they come to years of maturity, as well as to the heathen, who, having died without law, will through His mediation be resurrected without law and be judged without law and thus participate, according to their capacity, works, and worth in the blessings of His Atonement.
—*John Taylor,* MA, p. 148-149, Published in 1892

We are told that "without shedding of blood is no remission" of sins. This is beyond our comprehension. Jesus had to take away sin by the sacrifice of Himself, the just for the unjust, but, previous to this grand sacrifice, these animals had to have their blood shed as types, until the great antitype should offer up

Himself once for all. And as He in His own person bore the sins of all and atoned for them by the sacrifice of Himself, so there came upon Him the weight and agony of ages and generations, the indescribable agony consequent upon this great sacrificial atonement wherein He bore the sins of the world and suffered in His own person the consequences of an eternal law of God broken by man. Hence His profound grief, His indescribable anguish, His overpowering torture, all experienced in the submission to the eternal fiat of Jehovah and the requirements of an inexorable law. *—John Taylor,* MA, p. 149-150, Published in 1892

The Savior thus becomes master of the situation—the debt is paid, the redemption made, the covenant fulfilled, justice satisfied, the will of God done, and all power is now given into the hands of the Son of God—the power of the resurrection, the power of the redemption, the power of salvation, the power to enact laws for the carrying out and accomplishment of this design. . . .

The plan, the arrangement, the agreement, the covenant was made, entered into and accepted before the foundation of the world; it was prefigured by sacrifices and was carried out and consummated on the cross. Hence, being the mediator between God and man, He becomes by right the dictator and director on earth and in heaven for the living and for the dead, for the past, the present and the future, pertaining to man as associated with this earth or the heavens, in time or eternity, the Captain of our salvation, the Apostle and High Priest of our profession, the Lord and Giver of life. *—John Taylor,* MA, p. 171, Published in 1892

TO WHOM DOES THE ATONEMENT EXTEND?

Jesus will bring forth, by His own redemption, every son and daughter of Adam, except the sons of perdition, who will be cast into hell. Others will suffer the wrath of God—will suffer all the Lord can demand at their hands or justice will require of them; and when they have suffered the wrath of God till the utmost farthing is paid, they will be brought out of prison.
—Brigham Young, JD 8:154, August 26, 1860

How far does this principle extend and to whom is it applicable? It extends to all the human family; to all men of every nation. . . .

Hence what was lost in Adam was restored in Jesus Christ, so far as all men are concerned in all ages, with some very slight exceptions arising from an abuse of privileges. Transgression of the law brought death upon all the posterity of Adam, the restoration through the atonement restored all the human family to life.   —*John Taylor*, MA, p. 178, Published in 1892

And this provision (the atonement) applies not only to the living, but also to the dead, so that all men who have existed in all ages, who do exist now, or who will exist while the earth shall stand, may be placed upon the same footing, and that all men may have the privilege, living or dead, of accepting the conditions of the great plan of redemption provided by the Father, through the Son, before the word was; and that the justice and mercy of God may be applied to every being, living or dead, that ever has existed, that does now exist, or that ever will exist.
                          —*John Taylor*, MA, p. 181, Published in 1892

Not only did Jesus come as a universal gift, He came as an individual offering with a personal message to each one of us. For each one of us He died on Calvary and His blood will conditionally save us. Not as nations, communities or groups, but as individuals.   —*Heber J. Grant*, JI 64:697, October 6, 1929

This gospel will save the whole human family; the blood of Jesus will atone for our sins, if we accept the terms He has laid down; but we must accept those terms or else it will avail nothing in our behalf.   —*Brigham Young*, JD 13:331, April 24, 1870

MEN WILL BE PUNISHED FOR THEIR OWN SINS

When men are called upon to repent of their sins, the call has reference to their own individual sins, not to Adam's transgressions. What is called the original sin was atoned for through the death of Christ, irrespective of any action on the part of man; also man's individual sin was atoned for by the same sacrifice, but on condition of his obedience to the gospel plan of salvation when proclaimed in his hearing.
                    —*Wilford Woodruff*, MS 51:659, September 1, 1889

We are informed that we will not be held responsible for the sin of Adam, but that we will be held responsible for our own sins. The atonement of Jesus Christ removed from us the responsibility of atoning for the sin of father Adam, and he has made it possible for us to live here upon the earth, and in due time, if we take advantage of our opportunities, we will be prepared to be resurrected from the dead when that time shall come.   —*George Albert Smith,* CR, p. 102, October, 1926

The original sin was atoned for by the death of Christ, although its effects we still see in the diseases, tempers and every species of wickedness with which the human family is afflicted.
                    —*Brigham Young,* JD 13:143, July 11, 1869

When we commit sin, it is necessary that we repent of it and make restitution as far as lies in our power. When we cannot make restitution for the wrong we have done then we must apply for the grace and mercy of God to cleanse us from that iniquity.
                    —*Joseph F. Smith,* CR, p. 41, October, 1899

CHAPTER XIV

Foreordination

THE PRINCIPLE OF FOREORDINATION

IN every dispensation the Lord has had those who were fore-ordained to do a certain work. We all dwelt in the presence of God before we came here, and such men as Abraham, Isaac, Jacob, the ancient prophets, Jesus and the Apostles received their appointments before the world was made. They were ordained before the foundation of the world to come and tabernacle here in the flesh and to work for the cause of God, and this because of their faith and faithfulness.

—Wilford Woodruff, JD 18:114, September 12, 1875

Here is the great trouble with men of the world and too much so with the elders of Israel; we forget that we are working for God; we forget that we are here in order to carry out certain purposes that we have promised the Lord that we would carry out. It is a glorious work that we are engaged in. It is the work of the Almighty; and He has selected the men and the women whom He knows from past experience will carry out His purposes, as a general thing.

—Lorenzo Snow, MS 56:452, April 7, 1894

FOREORDINATION IS NOT PREDESTINATION

It is a mistaken idea . . . that God has decreed all things whatsoever that come to pass, for the volition of the creature is as free as air. You may inquire whether we believe in fore-ordination; we do, as strongly as any people in the world. We believe that Jesus was foreordained before the foundations of the world were built, and His mission was appointed Him in eternity to be the Savior of the world, yet when He came in the flesh He was left free to choose or refuse to obey His Father. Had He refused to obey His Father, He would have become a son of perdition. We also are free to choose or refuse the principles of eternal life. God has decreed and foreordained many things that have come to pass, and He will continue to do so; but when He

decrees great blessings upon a nation or upon an individual they are decreed upon certain conditions. When He decrees great plagues and overwhelming destructions upon nations or people, those decrees come to pass because those nations and people will not forsake their wickedness and turn unto the Lord. It was decreed that Nineveh should be destroyed in forty days, but the decree was stayed on the repentance of the inhabitants of Nineveh. . . . God rules and reigns and has made all His children as free as Himself, to choose the right or the wrong, and we shall then be judged according to our works.
                              —*Brigham Young*, JD 10:324, July 31, 1864

We talk sometimes about free will; is that a correct principle? Yes; and it is a principle that has always existed and proceeded from God, our Heavenly Father. When God revealed Himself to Joseph Smith it was optional whether he obeyed His counsel or not; I suppose, however, looking at things as they exist, and as they are in truth, God understood that he would do it, he having been selected for that purpose a long, long time ago; and (I suppose) that the Lord knew that he would adhere to those principles and would carry out the designs of heaven as they should be communicated unto and required of him.
                                —*John Taylor*, JD 22:7, January 9, 1881

WHO WAS FOREORDAINED?

Every man who has a calling to minister to the inhabitants of the world was ordained to that very purpose in the Grand Council of heaven before this world was. I suppose that I was ordained to this very office in that Grand Council.
                          —*Joseph Smith, Jr.*, DHC 6:364, May 12, 1844

No doubt all the prominent men who have figured in any dispensation of the gospel since the days of our father, Adam, until the present, were inspired of the Almighty from their childhood and were chosen and selected even from or before their birth.   —*Joseph F. Smith*, JD 25:52, February 17, 1884

There are thousands of men upon the earth today, among the Saints of God, of whom it was decreed before they came that they should occupy the positions they have occupied and do occupy, and many of them have performed their part and gone home; others are left to still fulfill the duties and responsibilities devolving upon them.

—John Taylor, JD 23:177, July 24, 1882

My faith and feeling about this matter is that we were appointed before the world was, as much as the ancient apostles were, to come forth in the flesh and take hold of this kingdom, and we have it to do, or be damned.

—Wilford Woodruff, CR, p. 84-85, April, 1880

Here we are a handful of people chosen out of some twelve or fourteen hundred millions of people; and my faith in regard to this matter is that before we were born . . . we were chosen to come forth in this day and generation and do the work which God has designed should be done.

—Wilford Woodruff, JD 21:193, July 3, 1880

Joseph Smith was ordained before he came here, the same as Jeremiah was. Said the Lord unto him, "Before you were begotten I knew you," etc.

So do I believe with regard to this people, so do I believe with regard to the apostles, the high priests, seventies and the elders of Israel bearing the Holy Priesthood, I believe they were ordained before they came here; and I believe the God of Israel has raised them up and has watched over them from their youth, has carried them through all the scenes of life both seen and unseen, and has prepared them as instruments in His hands to take this kingdom and bear it off. If this be so, what manner of men ought we to be? If anything under the heavens should humble men before the Lord and before one another, it should be the fact that we have been called of God.

—Wilford Woodruff, JD 21:317, October 10, 1880

It was decreed in the councils of eternity, long before the foundations of the earth were laid, that he (Joseph Smith) should be the man, in the last dispensation of this world, to bring forth the word of God to the people and receive the fullness of the keys and power of the priesthood of the Son of God. The Lord had His eye upon him and upon his father, and upon his father's father, and upon their progenitors clear back to Abraham, and from Abraham to the flood, from the flood to Enoch, and from Enoch to Adam. He has watched that family and that blood as it has circulated from its fountain to the birth of that man. He was foreordained in eternity to preside over this last dispensation.   —*Brigham Young*, JD 7:289-290, October 9, 1859

I believe that God Almighty reserved a certain class of men to carry on His word. They have been born into the world in this generation. I believe this was the case with Joseph Smith. I believe he was ordained to this work before he tabernacled in the flesh.   —*Wilford Woodruff*, JD 22:206, January 9, 1881

I was ordained to dedicate this Salt Lake Temple fifty years before it was dedicated. I knew I should live to dedicate that Temple. I did live to do it.

—*Wilford Woodruff*, CR, p. 29, April, 1898

CHAPTER XV

Free Agency

THE PRINCIPLE OF FREE AGENCY

G OD HAS given to all men an agency and has granted to us the privilege to serve Him or serve Him not, to do that which is right or that which is wrong, and this privilege is given to all men irrespective of creed, color or condition . . . But He will hold us strictly to an account for the use that we make of this agency, and as it was said of Cain, so it will be said of us: "If thou doest well, shalt thou not be accepted? and if thou doest not well, sin lieth at the door." (Genesis 4:7) There are, however, certain blessings which God bestows upon the children of men only upon the condition of the rightful exercise of this agency. For instance, . . . no man can obtain a remission of sins; no man can obtain the gift of the Holy Ghost; no man can obtain the revelations of God; no man can obtain the priesthood and the rights, powers and privileges thereof; no man can become an heir of God and a joint heir with Jesus Christ, except through compliance with the requirements of heaven. These are universal blessings . . . which are open and free to all on certain conditions, but which no creature beneath the heavens can enjoy, but through walking in the channel that God has marked out by which they can obtain them.

—Joseph F. Smith, JD 24:175, April 8, 1883

Besides the preaching of the gospel, we have another mission, namely, the perpetuation of the free agency of man and the maintenance of liberty, freedom, and the rights of man. There are certain principles that belong to humanity outside of the Constitution, outside of the laws, outside of all the enactments and plans of man, among which is the right to live; God gave us the right and not man; no government gave it to us, and no government has a right to take it away from us.

We have a right to liberty—that was a right that God gave to all men; and if there has been oppression, fraud or tyranny in the earth, it has been the result of the wickedness and corruption of men and has always been opposed to God and . . . all principles that are calculated to elevate mankind.

—*John Taylor*, JD 23:63, April 9, 1882

Free agency and direct individual accountability to God are among the essentials of our Church doctrine.

—*Wilford Woodruff*, MS 52:34, December 12, 1889

FREE AGENCY IS AN ETERNAL PRINCIPLE

The volition of the creature is free; this is a law of their existence, and the Lord cannot violate His own law; were He to do that He would cease to be God. He has placed life and death before His children, and it is for them to choose. If they choose life, they receive the blessings of life; if they choose death, they must abide the penalty. This is a law which has always existed from all eternity and will continue to exist throughout all the eternities to come. Every intelligent being must have the power of choice, and God brings forth the results of the acts of His creatures to promote His kingdom and subserve His purposes in the salvation and exaltation of His children.

—*Brigham Young*, JD 11:272, August 19, 1866

With regard to the rights of the human family, I wish to say that God has given unto all of His children of this dispensation, as He gave unto all of His children of previous dispensations, individual agency. This agency has always been the heritage of man under the rule and government of God. He possessed it in the heaven of heavens before the world was, and the Lord maintained and defended it there against the aggression of Lucifer and those that took sides with Him to the overthrow of Lucifer and one-third part of the heavenly hosts. By virtue of this agency you and I and all mankind are made responsible beings, responsible for the course we pursue, the lives we live, the deeds we do in the body.

—*Wilford Woodruff*, MS 51:642, September 1, 1889

All intelligent beings are . . . endowed with certain inalienable rights, privileges, and powers inherent in them. When God organized intelligent beings, He organized them as independent beings to a certain extent, as He is Himself. And whether we see an evil act or a good one performed by an intelligent being, that being has performed the act by his will, by his own independent organization, which is capable of doing good or evil, of choosing light or darkness.

—*Brigham Young*, JD 6:146, December 27, 1857

FREEDOM OF MAN NECESSARY FOR FAIR JUDGMENT

The actions of men . . . are left free; they are agents to themselves and must act freely on that agency, or else how could they be judged for their actions? But God reserves the right to Himself to control the results of their acts, and this no man can hinder. —*Brigham Young*, JD 16:45-46, May 18, 1873

If man be not a moral agent, he cannot be responsible for the present position of the world; and it would be unjust in God to punish him for acts that were not his and for circumstances over which he had no control.

—*John Taylor*, GG, p. 47, Published August, 1852

After the flood we are told that the curse that had been pronounced upon Cain was continued through Ham's wife, as he had married a wife of that seed. And why did it pass through the flood? Because it was necessary that the devil should have a representation upon the earth as well as God; and that man should be a free agent to act for himself, and that all men might have the opportunity of receiving or rejecting the truth and be governed by it or not according to their wishes and abide the result. —*John Taylor*, JD 22:304, August 28, 1881

God has given us our agency. He will not take it from us, and if I do that which is wrong and get into the devil's territory, I do it because I have the will and power to do it. I cannot blame anybody else, and if I determine to keep the commandments of God and live as I ought to live and stay on the Lord's side of the line I do it because I ought to do it, and I will receive my blessing for it. It will not be the result of what somebody else may do. —*George Albert Smith*, CR, p. 27, October, 1932

The children of men are made as independent in their sphere as the Lord is in His, to prove themselves, pursue which path they please, and choose the evil or the good. For those who love the Lord and do His will, all is right, and they shall be crowned, but those who hate His ways shall be damned, for they choose to be damned. —*Brigham Young*, JD 1:49, April 9, 1852

FREE AGENCY NECESSARY FOR MAN'S EXALTATION

Men may believe what they will believe. They are free to believe as they choose. God has given to every soul the free agency to choose the good or the evil, and His children have been given a knowledge of good and evil. No man ever came to a state of perfection without the knowledge and love of God and the love of his neighbor.

—*Joseph F. Smith,* IE 21:358, November 11, 1917

I believe in the independence of men and women. I believe that men and women have the image of God given them—are formed after the image of God and possess Deity in their nature and character, and that their spiritual organization possesses the qualities and properties of God, and that there is the principle of God in every individual. It is designed that man should act as God and not be constrained and controlled in everything, but have an independency, an agency, and the power to spread abroad and act according to the principle of godliness that is in him, act according to the power and intelligence and enlightenment of God that he possesses, and not that he should be watched continually and be controlled and act as a slave in these matters.

—*Lorenzo Snow,* JD 20:367, October 19, 1879

The Lord Almighty never created a world like this and peopled it for six thousand years, as He has done, without having some motive in view. That motive was that we might come here and exercise our agency. The probation we are called upon to pass through is intended to elevate us so that we can dwell in the presence of God our Father. And that eternal variety of character which existed in the heavens among the spirits—from God upon His throne down to Lucifer the Son of the Morning—exists here upon the earth. That variety will remain upon the earth in the creations of God and for what I know, throughout the endless ages of eternity. Men will occupy different glories and positions according to their lives—according to the law they keep in the flesh.   —*Wilford Woodruff,* JD, 25:9, January 6, 1884

FREEDOM OF WORSHIP

We believe in freedom of conscience; we believe that all men should be guaranteed the right to worship God according to

the dictates of their conscience. Some may want to worship a God without body, parts or passions; a God that sits on the top of a topless throne; although to me the idea of worshiping such a God would be most ridiculous, if other people desire to do it, all right, and they should be protected in that right. But while we accord to all men the right to think and the right to worship as they please, we claim the same right for ourselves.
—*John Taylor,* JD 24:36-37, January 21, 1883

We deem it a just principle . . . that all men are created equal, and that all have the privilege of thinking for themselves upon all matters relative to conscience.
—*Joseph Smith, Jr.,* DHC 2:6, January 22, 1834

Would you allow everybody to worship as they please? Certainly. What? If you knew they were in error? Certainly. I would not wish to control the human mind. I would not control the actions of men, God does not do it, He leaves them to their own agency to combat with the trials, temptations, adversities and evils of every kind that are in the world, to which humanity is or can be incident. He puts within their reach, however, certain principles and would like to lead them to Himself if they would be led. If not, He then does the very best with them that He can.   —*John Taylor,* JD 21:16, February 8, 1880

I know that any ruler who claims to be the representative of Almighty God who would take away the liberties of his fellow men is not a representative from God. You can draw your own conclusions whom he does represent.
—*Heber J. Grant,* CR, p. 26, April, 1918

STRICT OBEDIENCE TO GOD IS NOT SLAVERY

In rendering strict obedience, are we made slaves? No, it is the only way on the face of the earth for you and me to become free, and we shall become the slaves of our own passions and of the wicked one and servants of the devil if we take any other course, and we shall be eventually cast into hell with the devils. Now to say that I do not enjoy the volition of my own will just as much when I pray as I would to swear is a false principle, it is false ground to take. You take the man who swears, and he has no more freedom and acts no more on his own will than

the man who prays; the man who yields strict obedience to the requirements of heaven acts upon the volition of his own will and exercises his freedom just as much as when he was a slave to passion; and I think it is much better and more honorable for us, whether children or adults, youthful, middle-aged or old, it is better to live by and better to die by, to have our hearts pure, and to yield strict obedience to the principles of life which the Lord has revealed, than be a slave to sin and wickedness.
—*Brigham Young*, JD 18:246, June 23, 1874

Obedience is a requirement of heaven and is therefore a principle of the gospel. Are all required to be obedient? Yes, all. What, against their will? Oh, no, not by any means. There is no power given to man, nor means lawful to be used to compel men to obey the will of God against their wish, except persuasion and good advice, but there is a penalty attached to disobedience, which all must suffer who will not obey the obvious truths or laws of heaven.   —*Joseph F. Smith*, JD 19:193, September 30, 1877

Obedience must be voluntary; it must not be forced; there must be no coercion. Men must not be constrained against their will to obey the will of God; they must obey it because they know it to be right, because they desire to do it and because it is their pleasure to do it. God delights in the willing heart.
—*Joseph F. Smith*, JD 25:59, February 17, 1884

PRESERVE YOUR BIRTHRIGHT!

A man can dispose of his agency or of his birthright, as did Esau of old, but when disposed of he cannot again obtain it; consequently, it behooves us to be careful, and not forfeit that agency that is given to us. The difference between the righteous and the sinner, eternal life or death, happiness or misery, is this, to those who are exalted there are no bounds or limits to their privileges, their blessings have a continuation, and to their kingdoms, thrones, and dominions, principalities, and powers there is no end, but they increase through all eternity; whereas, those who reject the offer, who despise the proffered mercies of the Lord and prepare themselves to be banished from His presence and to become companions of the devils, have their agency abridged immediately, and bounds and limits are put to their operations.   —*Brigham Young*, JD 3:267, July 14, 1855

There are two influences ever present in the world. One is constructive and elevating and comes from our Heavenly Father; the other is destructive and debasing and comes from Lucifer. We have our agency and make our own choice in life subject to these unseen powers. There is a division line well defined that separates the Lord's territory from Lucifer's. If we live on the Lord's side of the line Lucifer cannot come there to influence us, but if we cross the line into his territory we are in his power. By keeping the commandments of the Lord we are safe on His side of the line, but if we disobey His teachings we voluntarily cross into the zone of temptation and invite the destruction that is ever present there. Knowing this, how anxious we should always be to live on the Lord's side of the line.

—*George Albert Smith*, IE 38:278, May, 1935

Chapter XVI

The Dispensations of the Gospel

THE SERIES OF DISPENSATIONS

IT IS no light thing for any people of any age in the world to have a dispensation of the gospel of Jesus Christ committed into their hands, and when a dispensation has been given, those receiving it are held responsible before high heaven for the use they make of it.

—*Wilford Woodruff*, JD 22:205, January 9, 1881

We have had in the different ages various dispensations; for instance what may be called the Adamic dispensation, the dispensation of Noah, the dispensation of Abraham, the dispensation of Moses and of the prophets who were associated with that dispensation; the dispensation of Jesus Christ, when He came to take away the sins of the world by the sacrifice of Himself, and in and through those various dispensations, certain principles, powers, privileges and priesthoods have been developed. But in the dispensation of the fullness of times a combination or a fullness, a completeness of all those dispensations was to be introduced among the human family. If there was anything pertaining to the Adamic (or what we may term more particularly the patriarchal) dispensation, it would be made manifest in the last days. If there was anything associated with Enoch and his city and the gathering together of his people, or of the translation of his city, it would be manifested in the last days. If there was anything associated with the Melchizedek Priesthood in all its forms, powers, privileges and blessings at any time or in any part of the earth, it would be restored in the last days. If there was anything connected with the Aaronic Priesthood, that also would be developed in the last times. If there was anything associated with the Apostleship and Presidency that existed in the days of Jesus, or that existed on this continent, it would be developed in the last times; for this is the dispensation of the fullness of times, embracing all other times, all principles, all powers, all manifestations, all priesthoods, and the powers thereof that have existed in any age, in any part of the world. For, "Those things which never have been revealed from the foundation of the world, but have been kept hid from the wise and prudent, shall be revealed unto babes and sucklings in this the dispensation of the fullness of times." (Doc. and Cov., Sec. 128:18)

And who was to originate this? It originated with God the Father, and it was sustained by Jesus, the Mediator of the new covenant, and it was sanctioned by all the prophets . . . in former ages. And finally, when all the preparations were made and everything was ready, or the time had fully come, the Father and the Son appeared to the youth Joseph Smith to introduce the great work of the latter days.

—John Taylor, JD 22:298-299, August 28, 1881

THE GOSPEL BEFORE CHRIST

Perhaps our friends will say that the gospel and its ordinances were not known till the days of John, the son of Zacharias, in the days of Herod, the king of Judea. But we will here look at this point: For our own part we cannot believe that the ancients in all ages were so ignorant of the system of heaven as many suppose, since all that were ever saved were saved through the power of this great plan of redemption, as much before the coming of Christ as since; if not, God has had different plans in operation (if we may so express it), to bring men back to dwell with Himself; and this we cannot believe, since there has been no change in the constitution of man since he fell; and the ordinance or institution of offering blood in sacrifice was only designed to be performed till Christ was offered up and shed His blood—as said before—that man might look forward in faith to that time. It will be noticed that, according to Paul, (see Galatians 3:8) the gospel was preached to Abraham . . . We find also, that when the Israelites came out of Egypt they had the gospel preached to them, according to Paul in his letter to the Hebrews, which says: "For unto us was the gospel preached, as well as unto them: but the word preached did not profit them, not being mixed with faith in them that heard it" (see Hebrews 4:2). It is said again, in Galatians 3:19, that the law (of Moses, or the Levitical law) was "added" because of transgression. What, we ask, was this law added to, if it was not added to the gospel? It must be plain that it was added to the gospel, since we learn that they had the gospel preached to them . . .

We may conclude, that though there were different dispensations, yet all things which God communicated to His people were calculated to draw their minds to the great object and to teach them to rely upon God alone as the Author of their salvation, as contained in His law.
                —*Joseph Smith, Jr.*, DHC 2:16-17, January 22, 1834

In the days of Noah the gospel which we have espoused was proclaimed to the people of his generation, and the same prospects as are presented to us were presented to them, temporal advantages, temporal salvation, and spiritual exaltation and glory.
                —*Lorenzo Snow*, CR, p. 1-2, October, 1900

PREPARATION FOR THE LAST DISPENSATION

The preparation for the ushering in of the gospel of Jesus Christ in this latter dispensation was indicated in the reign of Nebuchadnezzar and repeated again in the days of the Apostles, and then the foundation was laid for the organization of the government of the United States by men and women who believed in the divine mission of Jesus Christ. The stage was not set hastily; it was preparing through hundreds of years . . . Our Heavenly Father prepared the way for the coming of the gospel of Jesus Christ, which was to precede the second coming of our Lord.   —*George Albert Smith*, CR, p. 65, April, 1930

The opening of a new gospel dispensation was not a thing of chance. Jesus Christ, through His messenger, had declared to John while he was upon the isle of Patmos, that an angel would come flying through the midst of the heavens, having the everlasting gospel to preach to them that dwell upon the earth, calling them back to the worship of God . . . The Redeemer Himself had declared that before the time of His glorious appearance, to assume His rightful place among His people, the gospel of His kingdom should be preached in all the world, for a witness unto all nations, before the coming of the end.
                —*Heber J. Grant*, CR, p. 7, April, 1930

THE DISPENSATION OF THE FULLNESS OF TIMES

We are living in an age pregnant with greater events than any other age the world has ever seen . . . It is not merely the word of the Lord to one man or to a few men, or a peculiar dispensation to the Israelites or the Nephites; but it is the dispensation of the fullness of times when God will gather together all things in one and when He will settle up the affairs of the nations of the earth and the people of the earth, whether they be living or dead, whether they have slept thousands of years or have yet to come into existence. It is the time in which He has organized His Church according to the pattern that exists in the heavens, in which all the various organizations and priesthood that ever existed are concentrated. This is the age when the Saints are no longer to be trodden down or wickedness and iniquity triumph, but when the righteous shall bear rule and the dominion of God be established.

—Joseph F. Smith, JD 12:348, January 10, 1869

We are living in a marvelous age, in the dispensation of the fullness of times. All the other dispensations that have gone before are culminating in this one. The Lord tells us in the Book of Mormon, . . . that at the time of the coming forth of that book, He would commence His work among all the nations, and it is remarkable that since the publication of the Book of Mormon more important discoveries and inventions have been presented to mankind than in all the ages that have gone before . . . We have the accumulated information of the ages, and surely we ought to be inclined to take advantage of that information in order that we might enjoy our lives here and be prepared to enjoy them eternally. *—George Albert Smith, CR, p. 143, April, 1926*

We are living in the dispensation of the fullness of times, when all things are to be restored, and every gift and blessing of the gospel of our Master should be enjoyed by the Saints.

—Heber J. Grant, YWJ 16:128, January 13, 1905

The dispensation in which we live . . . differs from all other dispensations in that it is the dispensation of the fullness of times, embracing all other dispensations, all other powers, all other keys and all other privileges and immunities that ever existed upon the face of the earth. *—John Taylor, JD 20:175, April 8, 1879*

We are living in the last dispensation. Joseph Smith, I expect, will sound the sixth trumpet. He will be at the head of this dispensation. *—Wilford Woodruff, JD 21:196, July 3, 1880*

Our dispensation differs from others which have preceded it. It is kind of a time for settling up accounts. You know when a man goes to work on Monday, Tuesday, Wednesday, Thursday and Friday he keeps account of what he does, and when Saturday comes it is a kind of settling-up day. It is so with us, it is so with the world, our day is a kind of settling-up day.

—John Taylor, JD 17:212, October 7, 1874

THE WORK OF THE LAST DISPENSATION

We are living in a very important day and age of the world, in a time which is pregnant with greater events than any other period that we know of, or in any other dispensation that has existed upon the earth. It is called "the dispensation of the fullness of times," when God "will gather together in one all things in Christ, both which are in heaven, and which are on earth;" for the heavens, the Gods in the eternal worlds, the holy priesthood that has existed upon the earth, the living that live upon the face of the earth, and the dead that have departed this life are all interested in the work in which we are engaged. Consequently, it is of the greatest importance that everything we do, that every ordinance we administer, that every principle we believe in should be strictly in accordance with the mind and word, the will and law of God.

—John Taylor, JD 25:177, May 18, 1884

The day has already dawned when the light of heaven is to fill the earth; the day in which the Lord has said that nothing should be kept hidden, whether it be things pertaining to one God or many Gods, to thrones, principalities or powers; the day in which everything that has been kept from the knowledge of man ever since the foundation of the earth must be revealed; and it is a day in which the ancient prophets looked forward to with a great deal of interest and anxiety.

It is a day in which the gospel is to be preached to every nation, tongue and people for a witness of what shall follow; a day in which the Israel of God who receive it in their dispersed and scattered condition are to gather together to the place appointed of God, the place where they will perform the "marvelous work and wonder" spoken of by the ancients who, in vision, saw our day; and where they will begin to inherit the promises made to the fathers respecting their children.

The work that is to be so marvelous in the eyes of men has already commenced and is assuming shape and proportions; but they cannot see it. It will consist in preaching the gospel to all the world, gathering the Saints from the midst of all those nations who reject it; building up the Zion of God; establishing permanently in the earth His kingdom; preparing for the work of the gathering of the Jews and the events that will follow their settlement in their own lands, and in preparing for ourselves holy places in which to stand when the judgments of God shall overtake the nations. This is truly a good work; and it is a marvel (when we look at it with our natural eyes) how this people are sustained in their faith and hope of accomplishing it, besides having to provide for the wants of themselves and families, which is of itself as much as most men can accomplish.

—*Wilford Woodruff*, JD 24:51, January 27, 1883

The Lord has a work to perform upon the earth; and the ancient priesthood who have lived upon the earth and who now live in heaven have also a work to perform. And this gospel and this kingdom has been introduced that there might be a priesthood upon the earth to operate with God and with the priesthood in the heavens, for the accomplishment of His purposes, for the redemption of the living, even all who desire to love the truth and work righteousness, and for the salvation and redemption of the dead; that the purposes of God from before the foundation of the world may be carried out, and that the laws, principles, rules and government as they exist in heaven may be taught to man upon the earth; and that through the operation and co-operation of the heavenly priesthood and the earthly priesthood, and God the Father, and Jesus the Mediator of the new covenant an organization may take place, a union be formed, truth developed, and a kingdom established that the will of God may be done upon the earth as it is done in heaven.

—*John Taylor*, JD 20:19-20, July 7, 1878

There never was a dispensation on the earth when prophets and apostles, the inspiration, revelation and power of God, the Holy Priesthood and the keys of the kingdom were needed more than they are in this generation. There never has been a dispensation when the friends of God and righteousness among the children of men needed more faith in the promises and pro-

phecies than they do today; and there certainly never has been a generation of people on the earth that has had a greater work to perform than the inhabitants of the earth in the latter days.
                              —*Wilford Woodruff*, JD 15:8, April 6, 1872

This is the great dispensation in which the Zion of God must be built up, and we as Latter-day Saints have it to build . . . We are obliged to build cities, towns and villages, and we are obliged to gather the people from every nation under heaven to the Zion of God, that they may be taught in the ways of the Lord. We have only just begun to prepare for the celestial law when we are baptized into the Church of Jesus Christ of Latter-day Saints.   —*Wilford Woodruff*, JD 16:268-269, October 8, 1873

THIS CHURCH AND KINGDOM WILL NOT BE DESTROYED

Any Latter-day Saint who thinks for one minute that this Church is going to fail is not a really converted Latter-day Saint. There will be no failure in this Church. It has been established for the last time, never to be given to another people and never to be thrown down.   —*Heber J. Grant*, DNCS, September 8, 1934
                                        Delivered July 13, 1934

This is the only dispensation which God has ever established that was foreordained, before the world was made, not to be overcome by wicked men and devils.
                              —*Wilford Woodruff*, JD 17:245, October 9, 1874

The powers of earth and hell have striven to destroy this kingdom from the earth. The wicked have succeeded in doing so in former ages; but this kingdom they cannot destroy, because it is the last dispensation—because it is the fullness of times. It is the dispensation of all dispensations and will excel in magnificence and glory every dispensation that has ever been committed to the children of men upon this earth. The Lord will bring again Zion, redeem His Israel, plant His standard upon the earth and establish the laws of His kingdom, and those laws will prevail.   —*Brigham Young*, JD 8:36, April 6, 1860

A VISION CONCERNING THIS WORK

Joseph Smith visited me a great deal after his death and taught me many important principles . . . The last time I saw him was in heaven. In the night vision I saw him at the door of the temple in heaven. He came to me and spoke to me. He said he could not stop to talk with me because he was in a hurry. The next man I met was Father Smith; he could not talk with me because he was in a hurry. I met half a dozen brethren who had held high positions on earth, and none of them could stop to talk with me because they were in a hurry. I was much astonished. By and by I saw the Prophet again and I got the privilege of asking him a question.

"Now," said I, "I want to know why you are in a hurry. I have been in a hurry all my life; but I expected my hurry would be over when I got into the kingdom of heaven, if I ever did."

Joseph said: "I will tell you, Brother Woodruff. Every dispensation that has had the priesthood on the earth and has gone into the celestial kingdom has had a certain amount of work to do to prepare to go to the earth with the Savior when He goes to reign on the earth. Each dispensation has had ample time to do this work. We have not. We are the last dispensation; so much work has to be done that we need to be in a hurry to accomplish it."

Of course, that was satisfactory, but it was a new doctrine to me.   —*Wilford Woodruff*, MS 67:637-638, October 19, 1896

CHAPTER XVII

Spiritual Gifts that Accompany the Gospel

THE GIFTS OF THE HOLY SPIRIT

THE Latter-day Saints are the only people on the face of the earth who claim to possess divine authority as restored to the earth in the nineteenth century and who testify that they enjoy the same gifts and blessings that the Saints in ancient days rejoiced in.   *—Heber J. Grant, DWN 47:568, October, 1893*

We believe in the gift of the Holy Ghost being enjoyed now, as much as it was in the apostles' days; we believe that it (the gift of the Holy Ghost) is necessary to make and to organize the priesthood, that no man can be called to fill any office in the ministry without it; we also believe in prophecy, in tongues, in visions, and in revelations, in gifts, and in healings; and that these things cannot be enjoyed without the gift of the Holy Ghost.   *—Joseph Smith, Jr., DHC 5:27, June 15, 1842*

We are asked if signs follow the believer in our day as in days of old. We answer, they do. The blind see, the lame leap, the deaf hear, the gift of prophecy is manifest, also the gift of healing, the gift of revelation, the gift of tongues and the interpretation of tongues. Jesus said that these signs should follow them that believe. His Church and kingdom always have these signs which follow the believer in all ages when the true Church is in existence.   *—Brigham Young, JD 12:208, May 10, 1868*

The fact is that every principle of healing, every principle of the power of the Holy Ghost, and of God, which have been manifested to the Saints in all ages, have been bestowed upon the Latter-day Saints. There is no principle, there is no blessing, there is no advantage, there is no truth in any other religious society or organization which are not included in the gospel of Jesus Christ as taught by Joseph Smith, the Prophet, and after him by the leaders and elders of this Church.   *—Joseph F. Smith, IE 12:562, May, 1909*

Christ set in His Church apostles and prophets; He also set in His Church evangelists, pastors and teachers; also the gifts of the Spirit, such as diverse tongues, healing the sick, discernment of spirits, and various other gifts. Now, I would ask the whole world, who has received revelation that the Lord has discontinued these offices and gifts in His Church? I have not. I have had revelation that they should be in the Church, and that there is no Church without them.

—Brigham Young, JD 13:144, July 11, 1869

I rejoice . . . that every Latter-day Saint, every humble son and daughter of God that has embraced the gospel and become a member of the Church of Jesus Christ of Latter-day Saints has received the witness of the Holy Spirit, that the gift of tongues, the gift of prophecy, of healing, and other gifts and blessings, are found in the Church, and are not confined to men that hold responsible positions in the Church.

—Heber J. Grant, CR, p. 64, April, 1901

HOW THESE GIFTS ARE MADE MANIFEST

We believe that the Holy Ghost is imparted by the laying on of hands of those in authority, and that the gift of tongues and also the gift of prophecy are gifts of the Spirit and are obtained through that medium.   *—Joseph Smith, Jr.,* DHC 5:27, June 15, 1842

There is a variety of blessings; a different blessing being probably given to one, two, three or four of this congregation. Thus, one will have faith to lay hands upon the sick and rebuke disease and drive it from the person afflicted. Many may receive this blessing of faith, the gift of healing. Some may receive faith to the discerning of spirits; they can discern the spirit of a person, whether it is good or evil. They have such power, that when a person enters this congregation they can tell the spirit of such a person . . . Some may receive the gift of tongues, that they will get up and speak in tongues and speak in many other languages beside their mother tongue . . . These are the blessings; but others might receive the gift of prophecy, get up and prophesy what is to befall this nation, . . . what will befall the different nations of the earth, etc.

—Brigham Young, JD 16:164, August 31, 1873

There are several gifts mentioned here (I Corinthians 12), yet which of them all could be known by an observer at the imposition of hands? The word of wisdom, and the word of knowledge, are as much gifts as any other, yet if a person possessed both of these gifts, or received them by the imposition of hands, who would know it? Another might receive the gift of faith, and they would be as ignorant of it. Or suppose a man had the gift of healing or power to work miracles, that would not then be known; it would require time and circumstances to call these gifts into operation. Suppose a man had the discerning of spirits, who would be the wiser for it? Or if he had the interpretation of tongues, unless someone spoke in an unknown tongue, he of course would have to be silent; there are only two gifts that could be made visible—the gift of tongues and the gift of prophecy.   —*Joseph Smith, Jr.,* DHC 5:29-30, June 15, 1842

The gift of seeing with the natural eyes is just as much a gift as the gift of tongues. The Lord gave that gift and we can do as we please with regard to seeing; we can use the sight of the eye to the glory of God or to our own destruction . . .

The gift of communicating one with another is the gift of God, just as much so as the gift of prophecy, of discerning spirits, of tongues, of healing, or any other gift, though sight, taste, and speech are so generally bestowed that they are not considered in the same miraculous light as are those gifts mentioned in the gospel.   —*Brigham Young,* JD 3:364, June 22, 1856

THESE GIFTS ONLY FOR THE FAITHFUL

Miracles, or these extraordinary manifestations of the power of God, are not for the unbeliever; they are to console the Saints and to strengthen and confirm the faith of those who love, fear, and serve God and not for outsiders.
          —*Brigham Young,* JD 12:97, June 30, 1867

The gospel plan is so devised that a miracle to make people believe would only be a condemnation to them . . . No person, unless he is an adulterer, a fornicator, covetous, or an idolater, will ever require a miracle; in other words, no good, honest person ever will.   —*Brigham Young,* JD 8:42, April 8, 1860

Men may receive the visitation of angels; they may speak in tongues; they may interpret; they may prophesy; they may heal the sick by the laying on of hands; they may have visions and dreams; but except they are faithful and pure in heart, they become an easy prey to the adversary of their souls, and he will lead them into darkness and unbelief more easily than others.
                                        —*Joseph F. Smith,* CR, p. 41, April, 1900

There is but one witness—one testimony, pertaining to the evidence of the gospel of the Son of God, and that is the Spirit that He diffused among His disciples. Do His will, and we shall know whether He speaks by the authority of the Father or of Himself. Do as He commands us to do, and we shall know of the doctrine, whether it is of God or not. It is only by the revelations of the Spirit that we can know the things of God.
                                        —*Brigham Young,* JD 9:2, April 6, 1861

THE GIFT OF HEALING

I can bear testimony that the sick have been healed, the blind have been made to see, the deaf to hear, and the lame to walk, and devils have been cast out, by the power of God. These gifts and graces have been with this people from the organization of the Church until the present hour.
                                        —*Wilford Woodruff,* DWN 38:451, March 5, 1889

The Latter-day Saints believe in the power of God to heal the sick through the administration of the priesthood. They believe that the signs promised in the Scriptures do follow the believer, that through faith in Christ and in the ordinances which He has instituted men and women may be healed and may do many wonderful works. They believe that through the priesthood the servants of Jesus Christ may cast out evil spirits, speak in tongues, lay hands on the sick, in His name, to their recovery; and that by the power of faith in Christ people may be preserved from poisonous reptiles and other dangers.
                                        —*Joseph F. Smith,* IE 14:1033, September, 1911

The diseases that are and ever have been prevalent among the human family are from beneath and are entailed upon them through the fall—through the disobedience of our first parents;

but Jesus, having the issues of life at His command, could counter-
act those diseases at His pleasure. The case of the Centurion's
servant is a striking instance of this. The Centurion sent and
besought Jesus to heal his servant. "Say in a word," said he,
"and my servant shall be healed." Jesus, seeing the man's earnest-
ness and solicitude, said, "I have not found so great faith, no,
not in Israel." And it is said that they who were sent, returned
to the Centurion's house and found the servant healed. Jesus
counteracted the disease preying upon the system of this man,
but to Himself, knowing the principle by which the disease was
rebuked, it was no miracle.
                          —*Brigham Young,* JD 13:141, July 11, 1869

Do you suppose that Jesus Christ healed every person that
was sick or that all the devils were cast out in the country where
He sojourned? I do not. Working miracles, healing the sick,
raising the dead, and the like were almost as rare in His day as
in this our day. Once in a while the people would have faith in
His power, and what is called a miracle would be performed, but
the sick, the blind, the deaf and dumb, the crazy, and those
possessed with different kinds of devils were around Him and
only now and then could His faith have power to take effect,
on account of the want of faith in the individuals.
                          —*Brigham Young,* JD 3:45-46, October 6, 1855

I bear my witness to you that if a record had been made of
all those who have been afflicted, those who have been given up
to die, and who have been healed by the power of God since
the establishment of the Church of Christ in our day, it would
make a book much larger than the New Testament. More
miracles have been performed in the Church of Jesus Christ of
Latter-day Saints than we have any account of in the days of
the Savior and His Apostles. Today, sickness is cured by spiritual
power . . . The dead have been raised. My own brother was
announced to be dead, but by the prayer of faith he lives and
presides over one of the stakes of Zion. I know, as I know I live,
that the healing power of Almighty God . . . is in the Church
of Christ of which you and I are members.
                          —*Heber J. Grant,* CR, p. 119, October 6, 1910

THE CORRECT ORDER OF ADMINISTERING
TO THE SICK

What is the sign of the healing of the sick? The laying on of hands is the sign or way marked out by James and the custom of the ancient Saints as ordered by the Lord, and we cannot obtain the blessing by pursuing any other course except the way marked out by the Lord.

—Joseph Smith, Jr., DHC 4:555, March 20, 1842

We have several instances where Christ laid His hands upon the sick and healed them; and, in His commission to the Apostles, last chapter of Mark, He says—These signs shall follow them that believe; they shall lay hands on the sick, and they shall recover, etc. Ananias laid his hands on Saul, who immediately received his sight, after this ordinance was administered. Paul, when shipwrecked upon the island of Melita, laid his hands upon the father of Publius, the governor of the island, and healed him of a fever. These few remarks show clearly that laying on of hands has been appointed of God, to be a medium through which heavenly blessings may be obtained.

—Lorenzo Snow, OWTBS, p. 6, a. 1851

When I lay hands on the sick, I expect the healing power and influence of God to pass through me to the patient and the disease to give way . . . Do you see the reason and propriety of laying hands on each other? When we are prepared, when we are holy vessels before the Lord, a stream of power from the Almighty can pass through the tabernacle of the administrator to the system of the patient, and the sick are made whole; the headache, fever or other disease has to give way. My brethren and sisters, there is virtue in us if we will do right; if we live our religion we are the temples of God wherein He will dwell; if we defile ourselves, these temples God will destroy.

—Brigham Young, JD 14:72, July 10, 1870

In the matter of administering to the sick, according to the order and practice established in the Church, care should be taken to avoid unwarranted repetitions. When an administration is made, and when the blessing pronounced upon the afflicted one has been received, the ordinance should not be repeated, rather let the time be given to prayer and thanksgiving for the manifestation of divine power already granted and realized. No limit should be or can be set to the offering of prayer and the rendering of praise to the Giver of good, for we are specially told to pray without ceasing, and no special authority of the priesthood or standing in the Church is essential to the offering of prayer; but the actual administration by anointing with oil and by the imposition of hands by those who hold the proper office in the priesthood is an authoritative ordinance, too sacred in its nature to be performed lightly or to be repeated loosely when the blessing has been gained.

—*Joseph F. Smith, JI 38:19, January, 1902*

I believe, according to my understanding of the principles of eternal truth, that I should have implicit faith in our God; and when we are where we have no help for ourselves in the case of diseases, that we have the right to ask the Father, in the name of Jesus, to administer by His power and heal the sick, and I am sure it will be done to those who have implicit confidence in Him.   —*Brigham Young, JD 4:25, August 17, 1856*

I am sent for continually, though I only go occasionally, because it is the privilege of every father, who is an elder in Israel, to have faith to heal his family; and if he does not do it he is not living up to his privilege.

—*Brigham Young, JD 3:46, October 6, 1855*

THE GIFT OF TONGUES

I know that there are no gifts, no graces, no authority which were possessed in the days of the Savior by His Apostles which are not possessed today by the people of God. I know that the gift of tongues and the interpretation thereof exist in this Church of Christ.   —*Heber J. Grant, CR, p. 14, October, 1917*

Be not so curious about tongues, do not speak in tongues except there be an interpreter present; the ultimate design of tongues is to speak to foreigners, and if persons are very anxious to display their intelligence, let them speak to such in their own tongues. The gifts of God are all useful in their place, but when they are applied to that which God does not intend, they prove an injury, a snare and a curse instead of a blessing.

—*Joseph Smith, Jr., DHC 5:31-32, June 15, 1842*

If you have a matter to reveal, let it be in your own tongue; do not indulge too much in the exercise of the gift of tongues, or the devil will take advantage of the innocent and unwary. You may speak in tongues for your own comfort, but I lay this down for a rule, that if anything is taught by the gift of tongues, it is not to be received for doctrine.

—*Joseph Smith, Jr.*, DHC 4:607, April 28, 1842

I want to say to you who are in the habit of desiring to hear the gift of tongues and the interpretation thereof, to seek better things. The gift of inspiration and the gift of prophecy and the gift of faith. These are the gifts you should seek for more than the gift of tongues. After you get the Spirit of inspiration that comes from the Lord it will lead you into all truth and show you all evil that you may shun and avoid it. You are then entitled to the title prophet, because you are then a prophet; you possess the spirit of prophecy . . . Paul said that he would rather that the people should seek to prophecy than speak in tongues; because when you speak in tongues it is the Spirit that is speaking and not the understanding.

—*Joseph F. Smith*, MS 68:723, September 2, 1906

Tongues were given for the purpose of preaching among those whose language is not understood; as on the day of Pentecost, etc., and it is not necessary for tongues to be taught to the Church particularly, for any man that has the Holy Ghost can speak of the things of God in his own tongue as well as to speak in another; for faith comes not by signs, but by hearing the word of God.   —*Joseph Smith, Jr.*, DHC 3:379, June 27, 1839

There is perhaps no gift of the Spirit of God more easily imitated by the devil than the gift of tongues. Where two men or women exercise the gift of tongues by the inspiration of the Spirit of God, there are a dozen perhaps who do it by the inspiration of the devil . . .

I believe in the gifts of the Holy Spirit unto men, but I do not want the gift of tongues, except when I need it . . .

So far as I am concerned, if the Lord will give me ability to teach the people in my native tongue, or in their own language to the understanding of those who hear me, that will be sufficient gift of tongues to me. Yet if the Lord gives you the gift of tongues, do not despise it, do not reject it. For if it comes from the Spirit of God, it will come to those who are worthy to receive it, and it is all right. —*Joseph F. Smith*, CR, p. 41, April, 1900

DREAMS AND VISIONS

Holy men and holy women have had heavenly visions, by the hundreds and by the thousands, yea by the tens of thousands since this gospel was restored to the earth in our day.
                              —*Heber J. Grant*, CR, p. 92, October, 1913

There are a great many things taught us in dreams that are true, and if a man has the Spirit of God he can tell the difference between what is from the Lord and what is not. And I want to say to my brethren and sisters, that whenever you have a dream that you feel is from the Lord, pay attention to it.
                              —*Wilford Woodruff*, JD 22:333, October 8, 1881

But what I want to say in regard to these matters is, that the Lord does communicate some things of importance to the children of men by means of visions and dreams as well as by the records of divine truth. And what is it all for? It is to teach us a principle. We may never see anything take place exactly as we see it in a dream or a vision, yet it is intended to teach us a principle.   —*Wilford Woodruff*, JD 22:333, October 8, 1881

The Lord will not condemn any man for following counsel and keeping the commandments; and a faithful man will have dreams about the work he is engaged in. If he is engaged in building the temple, he will dream about it; and if in preaching, he will dream about that; and not, when he is laboring on the temple, dream that it is his duty to run off preaching and leave his family to starve. Such dreams are not of God.
                              —*Brigham Young*, DHC 5:350, April 10, 1843

We may look for angels and receive their ministration, but we are to try the spirits and prove them, for it is often the case that men make a mistake in regard to these things. God has so ordained that, when He has communicated, no vision is to be taken but what you see by the seeing of the eye, or what you hear by the hearing of the ear. When you see a vision, pray for the interpretation. If you get not this, shut it up. There must be certainty in this matter.
                              —*Joseph Smith, Jr.*, JD 6:240, June 2, 1839

God never bestows upon His people, or upon an individual, superior blessings without a severe trial to prove them, to prove that individual, or that people, to see whether they will keep their covenants with Him and keep in remembrance what He has shown them. Then the greater the vision, the greater the display of the power of the enemy . . .

So when individuals are blessed with visions, revelations, and great manifestations, look out, then the devil is nigh you, and you will be tempted in proportion to the vision, revelation, or manifestation you have received.

—*Brigham Young*, JD 3:205-206, February 17, 1856

ON TESTIMONY BEARING

The individual testimony is a personal possession. One cannot give his testimony to another, yet he is able to aid his earnest brother in gaining a true testimony for himself. The over-zealous missionary may be influenced by the misleading thought that the bearing of his testimony to those who have not before heard the gospel message is to convince or condemn, as the hearers accept or reject. The elder is sent into the field to preach the gospel—the good news of its restoration to earth, showing by scriptural evidence the harmony of the new message with the predictions of earlier times; expounding the truths embodied in the first principles of the gospel; then if he bears his testimony under divine inspiration, such a testimony is as a seal attesting the genuineness of the truths he has declared and so appealing to the receptive soul whose ears have been saluted by the heaven-sent message . . .

But the voicing of one's testimony, however eloquently phrased or beautifully expressed, is no fit or acceptable substitute for the needed discourse of instruction and counsel expected in a general gathering of the people.

—*Joseph F. Smith*, JI 41:465, August, 1906

Testimony bearing should have a strong educational influence upon the feelings and lives of the children, and it is intended to cultivate within them feelings of thankfulness and appreciation for the blessings they enjoy. The Spirit of God may work within the life of a child and make the child realize and know that this is the work of God. The child knows it rather because of the Spirit than because of some physical manifestation which he may have witnessed . . .

Testimony bearing is chiefly for the benefit of those who bear the testimony, in that their gratitude and appreciation are deepened. Testimony bearing is not the accumulation of arguments or evidences solely for the satisfaction and testimony of others. Let the testimonies then of the young people include the training of their feelings by way of making them more appreciative and more thankful for the blessings they enjoy, and the children should be made to understand what these blessings are and how they come to them. It is an excellent way to make people helpful and thankful to others, by first making them thankful to God.   —*Joseph F. Smith*, JI 38:245-246, April, 1903

CONCERNING FALSE GIFTS

If a man is called to be a prophet, and the gift of prophecy is poured upon him, though he afterwards actually defies the power of God and turns away from the holy commandments, that man will continue in his gift and will prophesy lies.

He will make false prophecies, yet he will do it by the spirit of prophecy; he will feel that he is a prophet and can prophesy, but he does it by another spirit and power than that which was given him of the Lord. He uses the gift as much as you and I use ours.   —*Brigham Young*, JD 3:364, June 22, 1856

When you hear elders . . . say that God does not now reveal through the President of the Church that which they know and tell wonderful things, you may generally set it down as a God's truth that the revelation they have had is from the devil and not from God. If they had received from the proper source, the same power that revealed to them would have shown them that they must keep the things revealed in their own bosoms, and they seldom would have a desire to disclose them to the second person.   —*Brigham Young*, JD 3:318, April 20, 1856

Spiritualism started in the United States about the time that Joseph Smith received his visions from the heavens. What more natural than that Lucifer should begin revealing himself to men in his cunning way, in order to deceive them and to distract their minds from the truth that God was revealing?
           —*Joseph F. Smith*, CR, p. 73, April, 1901

BOOK THREE

The Priesthood

The study of the subject of the Holy or Melchizedek Priesthood, including the Aaronic, is one of vast importance to the human family. The student of the true science of theology will readily comprehend the necessity of its existence among men, for the reason that true theology, or the Church of Jesus Christ, cannot exist without it. It lies at the foundation of the Church, it is the authority by which the Church is established or organized . . . Therefore, where the Melchizedek or Holy Priesthood does not exist, there can be no true Church of Christ in its fullness.

—JOSEPH F. SMITH
"The Contributor"
10:307
June, 1889

CHAPTER XVIII

Definition and Nature of the Priesthood

WHAT IS PRIESTHOOD?

IT IS THE rule and government of God, whether on earth or in the heaven; and it is the only legitimate power, the only authority that is acknowledged by Him to rule and regulate the affairs of His kingdom. When every wrong thing shall be put right and all usurpers shall be put down, when He whose right it is to reign shall take the dominion, then nothing but the priesthood will bear rule; it alone will sway the sceptre of authority in heaven and on earth, for this is the legitimacy of God.
—*John Taylor*, JD 1:224, April 8, 1853

The priesthood of the Son of God is the law by which the worlds are, were, and will continue for ever and ever. It is that system which brings worlds into existence and peoples them, gives them their revolutions—their days, weeks, months, years, their seasons and times and by which they . . . go into a higher state of existence. —*Brigham Young*, JD 15:127, August 11, 1872

The Holy Priesthood is the channel through which God communicates and deals with man upon the earth; and the heavenly messengers that have visited the earth to communicate with man are men who held and honored the priesthood while in the flesh; and everything that God has caused to be done for the salvation of man, from the coming of man upon the earth to the redemption of the world, has been and will be by virtue of the everlasting priesthood.
—*Wilford Woodruff*, MS 51:657, September 1, 1889

The priesthood or authority in which we stand is the medium or channel through which our Heavenly Father has purposed to communicate light, intelligence, gifts, powers, and spiritual and temporal salvation unto the present generation.
—*Lorenzo Snow*, MS 2:39, May, 1841

It is nothing more nor less than the power of God delegated to man by which man can act in the earth for the salvation of the human family, in the name of the Father and the Son and the Holy Ghost, and act legitimately; not assuming that authority, not borrowing it from generations that are dead and gone, but authority that has been given in this day in which we live by ministering angels and spirits from above, direct from the presence of Almighty God . . . It is the same power and priesthood that was committed to the disciples of Christ while He was upon the earth; that whatsoever they should bind on earth should be bound in heaven and whatsoever they should loose on earth should be loosed in heaven.

—Joseph F. Smith, CR, p. 5, October, 1904

The priesthood after the order of the Son of God is the ruling, presiding authority in the Church . . . In other words, there is no government in the Church of Jesus Christ separate and apart, above, or outside of the Holy Priesthood or its authority.   *—Joseph F. Smith, IE 6:705, July, 1903*

The priesthood . . . is the authority of God in heaven to the sons of men to administer in any of the ordinances of His house. There never was a man and never will be a man, in this or any other age of the world, who has power and authority to administer in one of the ordinances of the House of God, unless he is called of God, . . . unless he has the Holy Priesthood and is administered to by those holding that authority.

—Wilford Woodruff, JD 16:266, October, 8, 1873

THE PURPOSE OF THE PRIESTHOOD

To restore creation to its pristine excellency and to fulfill the object of creation—to redeem, save, exalt, and glorify man— to save and redeem the dead and the living, and all that shall live according to its laws is the design and object of the establishment of the priesthood on the earth in the last days; it is for the purpose of fulfilling what has not heretofore been done—that God's works may be perfected—that the time of the restitution of all things may be brought about, and that, in conjunction with the eternal priesthood in the heavens (who without us, nor we without them, could not be made perfect), we may bring to pass all things which have been in the mind of God or spoken of by the Spirit of God.   *—John Taylor, MS 9:321-322, May 7, 1847*

What is the priesthood for? It is to administer the ordinances of the gospel, even the gospel of our Father in heaven, the eternal God, the Elohim of the Jews and the God of the Gentiles, and all He has ever done from the beginning has been performed by and through the power of that priesthood, which is "without father, without mother, without descent, having neither beginning of days, nor end of life," and the administration of His servants holding this priesthood is binding, being the savior of life unto life or death unto death.
—*Wilford Woodruff*, JD 19:360, June 30, 1878

God has organized a priesthood, and that priesthood bears rule in all things pertaining to the earth and the heavens; one part of it exists in the heavens, another part on the earth; they both cooperate together for the building up of Zion, the redemption of the dead and the living, and the bringing to pass the "times of the restitution of all things;" and as they are thus closely united, it is necessary that there should be a communication between the one and the other, and that those on the earth should receive instructions from those in the heavens, who are acquainted with earthly as well as heavenly things, having had the experience of both, as they once officiated in the same priesthood on the earth.
—*John Taylor*, MS 9:322, May 7, 1847

Our Heavenly Father performs all His works—the creation of worlds, the redemption of worlds—by the power of the eternal priesthood. And no man on the earth, from the days of Father Adam to the present time, has ever had power to administer in any of the ordinances of life and salvation only by the power of the Holy Priesthood. You will find this to be the case in the whole history of the prophets of God.
—*Wilford Woodruff*, JD 24:242, July 20, 1883

THE RESTORATION OF THE PRIESTHOOD

According to Joseph the Prophet, who claimed to have received these priesthoods through angelic ministrations, the time of their restoration was several months before the organization of the Church. The Aaronic Priesthood came first, being conferred by John the Baptist upon Joseph Smith and Oliver Cowdery, May 14th, 1829. The Melchizedek Priesthood came soon

after, when they were ordained under the hands of Apostles
Peter, James and John.

-*Joseph F. Smith,* MS 67:628, September, 1905

The Lord Almighty will not suffer His priesthood to be again
driven from the earth, even should He permit the wicked to kill
and destroy His people. The government of the United States
and all the world may go to war with us, but God will preserve
a portion of the meek and humble of this people to bear off the
kingdom to the inhabitants of the earth and will defend His
priesthood, for it is the last time, the last gathering time, and
He will not suffer the priesthood to be again driven from the
earth.

-*Brigham Young,* "Brigham Young" by Nibley, p. 229, February, 1855

ETERNAL NATURE OF THE PRIESTHOOD

The priesthood of the Son of God is from everlasting to
everlasting; it is without beginning of days or end of years,
or time. It is without father, without mother, without descent;
it is the power by which the worlds are and were created and
the power by which they are now held in existence and by which
all that are yet to come will be organized, governed, controlled
and sustained.

-*Brigham Young,* "Brigham Young" by Nibley, p. 453, October, 1869

The priesthood of God that was given to the ancients and
is given to men in the latter-days is co-equal in duration with
eternity—is without beginning of days or end of life. It is unchangeable in its system of government and its gospel of salvation.   -*Brigham Young,* JD 10:5, September 28, 1862

The priesthood was first given to Adam; he obtained the First
Presidency and held the keys of it from generation to generation. He obtained it in the Creation, before the world was
formed . . .

The priesthood is an everlasting principle and existed with
God from eternity and will to eternity, without beginning of
days or end of years. The keys have to be brought from heaven
whenever the gospel is sent. When they are revealed from heaven
it is by Adam's authority.

-*Joseph Smith, Jr.,* DHC 3:385-386, July 2, 1839

There is no change in the eternal and everlasting priesthood. It is without beginning of days or end of years. It is from eternity unto eternity. By the power of that priesthood God, our Eternal Father, has organized all worlds and redeemed all worlds that have ever been redeemed.

—Wilford Woodruff, DWN 38:450, March 5, 1889

THE PRIESTHOOD IN THE HEREAFTER

The same priesthood exists on the other side of the veil. Every man who is faithful in his quorum here will join his quorum there. When a man dies and his body is laid in the tomb he does not lose his position. The Prophet Joseph Smith held the keys of this dispensation on this side of the veil, and he will hold them throughout the countless ages of eternity.

—Wilford Woodruff, JD 22:333, October 8, 1881

And are the priesthood operating behind the veil? Yes, and we are operating here. And we have a priesthood here, and they have one there. Have we a Presidency? They have one there. Have we a Twelve? So they have there. Have we seventies here? They have there. Have we high priests here? They have there. Have we various quorums? Yes, and we operate in them; and when we get through we join our quorums above.

—John Taylor, JD 22:308, August 28, 1881

When the faithful elders, holding this priesthood, go into the spirit world they carry with them the same power and priesthood that they had while in the mortal tabernacle.

—Brigham Young, JD 3:371, June 22, 1856

We expect in the resurrection to exercise the powers of our priesthood—we can exercise them only in proportion as we secure its righteousness and perfections; these qualifications can be had only as they are sought and obtained, so that in the morning of the resurrection we will possess those acquisitions only which we secured in this world! Godliness cannot be *conferred* but must be *acquired.* *—Lorenzo Snow*, MS 13:362, December 1, 1851

We have received the Holy Priesthood. There is no change in that priesthood. It belongs to the celestial kingdom of our God. It does not belong to the terrestrial nor to the telestial kingdom. *—Wilford Woodruff*, MS 51:596, July 29, 1889

THE PRIESTHOOD AS A SYSTEM OF GOVERNMENT

The Holy Priesthood is a system of laws and government that is pure and holy; and if it is adhered to by intelligent man, whom God has created a little lower than angels, it is calculated to preserve our tabernacles in eternal being; otherwise they will be resolved into native element.
                                        —*Brigham Young*, JD 7:202, July 31, 1859

When we talk of the celestial law which is revealed from heaven, that is, the priesthood, we are talking about the principle of salvation, a perfect system of government, of laws and ordinances, by which we can be prepared to pass from one gate to another and from one sentinel to another, until we go into the presence of our Father and God. This law has not always been upon the earth; and in its absence, other laws have been given to the children of men for their improvement, for their education, for their government, and to prove what they would do when left to control themselves; and what we now call tradition has grown out of these circumstances.
                                        —*Brigham Young*, JD 2:139, December 3, 1854

MAIN SECTIONS WITHIN THE PRIESTHOOD

There are two priesthoods spoken of in the Scriptures, viz., the Melchizedek and the Aaronic or Levitical. Although there are two priesthoods, yet the Melchizedek Priesthood comprehends the Aaronic or Levitical Priesthood and is the grand head and holds the highest authority which pertains to the priesthood and the keys of the kingdom of God in all ages of the world to the latest posterity on the earth; it is the channel through which all knowledge, doctrine, the plan of salvation and every important matter is revealed from heaven.

Its institution was prior to "the foundation of this earth, or the morning stars sang together, or the Sons of God shouted for joy," and is the highest and holiest priesthood; it is after the order of the Son of God, and all other priesthoods are only parts, ramifications, powers and blessings belonging to the same and are held, controlled, and directed by it.
                                        —*Joseph Smith, Jr.*, DHC 4:207, October 5, 1840

The Church has two characteristics—the temporal and the spiritual, and one is not without the other. We maintain that both are essential and that one without the other is incomplete and ineffectual. Hence, the Lord instituted in the government of the Church two priesthoods—the lesser or Aaronic, having special charge of the temporal, and the higher or Melchizedek, looking to the spiritual welfare of the people.

—*Joseph F. Smith,* IE 8:620, June, 1905

The Aaronic Priesthood, as the Melchizedek, is an everlasting priesthood, . . . and continueth forever as an appendage to the Melchizedek Priesthood; and hence in the old apostolic days, when under an organization of the Melchizedek, the latter is the most prominent, and very little is said about the Levitical or Aaronic.   —*John Taylor,* "Items on Priesthood," p. 17, 1881

The Melchizedek Priesthood holds the right from the eternal God and not by descent from father and mother; and that priesthood is as eternal as God Himself, having neither beginning of days nor end of life.

The Second Priesthood is Patriarchal authority. Go to and finish the temple, and God will fill it with power, and you will then receive more knowledge concerning this priesthood.

The third is what is called the Levitical Priesthood, consisting of priests to administer in outward ordinance, made without an oath; but the Priesthood of Melchizedek is by an oath and covenant.   —*Joseph Smith, Jr.,* DHC 5:555, August 27, 1843

CHAPTER XIX

Keys, Powers and Authority of the Priesthood

DEFINITION OF THE KEYS OF THE PRIESTHOOD

THE PRIESTHOOD in general is the authority given to man to act for God. Every man that has been ordained to any degree of the priesthood has this authority dedicated to him.

But it is necessary that every act performed under this authority shall be done at the proper time and place, in the proper way, and after the proper order. The power of directing these labors constitutes the *keys* of the priesthood. In their fullness, these keys are held by only one person at a time, the Prophet and President of the Church. He may delegate any portion of this power to another, in which case that person holds the keys of that particular labor. Thus, the president of a temple, the president of a stake, the bishop of a ward, the president of a mission, the president of a quorum, each holds the keys of the labors performed in that particular body or locality. His priesthood is not increased by this special appointment, for a seventy who presides over a mission has no more priesthood than a seventy who labors under his direction; and the president of an elders' quorum, for example, has no more priesthood than any member of that quorum. But he holds the power of directing the official labors performed in the mission or the quorum, or in other words, *the keys* of that division of that work. So it is throughout all the ramifications of the priesthood—a distinction must be carefully made between the general authority and the directing of the labors performed by that authority.

—*Joseph F. Smith*, IE 4:230, January, 1901

I say that the priesthood who are the agents of our Heavenly Father hold the keys of the ministering of angels. What is a key? It is the right or privilege which belongs to and comes with the priesthood, to have communication with God. Is not that a key? Most decidedly. We may not enjoy the blessings,

or key, very much, but the key is in the priesthood. It is the right to enjoy the blessing of communication with the heavens and the privilege and authority to administer in the ordinances of the gospel of Jesus Christ, to preach the gospel of repentance and of baptism by immersion for the remission of sins.
—Joseph F. Smith, IE 14:176, December, 1910

THE RESTORATION OF THE KEYS TO JOSEPH SMITH

He (Joseph Smith) lived until he received every key, ordinance and law ever given to any man on the earth, from Father Adam down, touching this dispensation. He received powers and keys from under the hands of Moses for gathering the House of Israel in the last days; he received under the hands of Elijah the keys of sealing the hearts of the fathers to the children and the hearts of the children to the fathers; he received under the hands of Peter, James and John, the apostleship, and everything belonging thereto; he received under the hands of Moroni all the keys and powers required of the stick of Joseph in the hands of Ephraim; he received under the hands of John the Baptist the Aaronic Priesthood, with all its keys and powers, and every other key and power belonging to this dispensation, and I am not ashamed to say that he was a Prophet of God, and he laid the foundation of the greatest work and dispensation that has ever been established on the earth.
—Wilford Woodruff, JD 16:267, October 8, 1873

I say to the Latter-day Saints the keys of the kingdom of God are here, and they are going to stay here, too, until the coming of the Son of Man. Let all Israel understand that. They may not rest upon my head but a short time, but they will then rest on the head of another apostle, and another after him, and so continue until the coming of the Lord Jesus Christ in the clouds of heaven to "reward every man according to the deeds done in the body." . . .
I say to all Israel at this day, I say to the whole world, that the God of Israel, who organized this Church and kingdom, never ordained any President or Presidency to lead it astray. Hear it, ye Israel, no man who has ever breathed the breath of life can hold these keys of the kingdom of God and lead the people astray.
—Wilford Woodruff, MS 51:547, June 2, 1889

We claim . . . that John the Baptist, who held the keys of authority to baptize, restored the Aaronic Priesthood and bestowed it upon Joseph Smith and Oliver Cowdery, also that Peter, James and John, Apostles of the Lord Jesus Christ, restored the higher or Melchizedek Priesthood, by ordaining these same men to the apostleship.   —*Heber J. Grant,* MS 97:355, May 12, 1935

Joseph Smith did not call upon any man to ordain or to baptize him, but he waited until the Lord sent forth His servants to administer unto him. He was commanded of the Lord to go forth and be baptized, but not until he had received the priesthood. Where did he get it? . . . Why, the Lord sent unto him John the Baptist, who, when upon the earth, held the Aaronic Priesthood . . . He laid his hands upon the head of Joseph Smith and ordained him to the Aaronic Priesthood . . . Joseph was then qualified to baptize for the remission of sins, but he had not the authority to lay on hands for the reception of the Holy Ghost, and he never attempted to administer in this ordinance until Peter, James and John . . . laid their hands upon the head of Joseph Smith and sealed upon him every power, principle, ordinance and key belonging to the apostleship.
—*Wilford Woodruff,* JD 16:266, October 8, 1873

THE POWERS OF THE PRIESTHOOD

First—We find . . . that there are two distinctive general priesthoods, namely, the Melchizedek and Aaronic, including the Levitical Priesthood.

Second—That they are both conferred by the Lord; that both are everlasting and administer in time and eternity.

Third—That the Melchizedek Priesthood holds the right of Presidency and has power and authority *over all the offices in the Church,* in all ages of the world, *to administer in spiritual things.*

Fourth—That the second priesthood is called the priesthood of Aaron; because it was conferred upon Aaron and his seed throughout all their generations.

Fifth—That the lesser priesthood is a part of, or an appendage to the greater, or the Melchizedek Priesthood, and has power in administering outward ordinances. The lesser or Aaronic Priesthood can make appointments for the greater, in preaching, can baptize, administer the sacrament, attend to the tithing, buy lands, settle people on possessions, divide inheritances, look after the poor, take care of the properties of the Church, attend generally to temporal affairs; act as common judges in Israel, and assist in ordinances of the temple, under the direction of the greater or Melchizedek Priesthood. They hold the keys of the ministering of angels and administer in outward ordinances, *the letter of the gospel,* and the baptism of repentance for the remission of sins.

Sixth—That there is a Presidency over each of these priesthoods, both over the Melchizedek and the Aaronic.

Seventh—That while the power of the higher, or Melchizedek, is to hold the keys *of all the* spiritual *blessings of the Church* . . . and to preside over all the spiritual officers of the Church, yet the *Presidency* of the High Priesthood, after the order of Melchizedek, have a right to officiate in *all the offices of the Church,* both spiritual and temporal. . . .

Eighth—. . . That the position which a bishop holds depends upon his calling and appointment, and that, although a man holding the bishopric is eligible to any office in the bishopric, yet he cannot officiate legally in any, except by selection, calling and appointment.

Ninth—That the power and right of selecting and calling of the presiding bishop and general bishops is vested in the First Presidency, who also must try those appointed by them in case of transgression, except in the case of a literal descendant of Aaron; who, if the firstborn, possesses a legal right to the keys of this priesthood; but even he must be sanctioned and appointed by the First Presidency. This arises from the fact that the Aaronic is an appendage to the Melchizedek Priesthood.

That the presiding bishop, who presides over all bishops and all of the lesser priesthood, should consult the First Presidency in all important matters pertaining to the Bishopric.

Tenth—That in regard to the appointment and trial of ward bishops, it appears that they stand in the same relationship to the presidents of stakes as the early bishops did to the First Presidency, who presided over the Stake at Kirtland; but that those presidents should consult with the First Presidency on these and other important matters and officiate under their direction in their several stakes.

—John Taylor, "Items on Priesthood," p. 36-39, 1881

AUTHORITY NECESSARY TO ORGANIZE THE KINGDOM OF GOD ON EARTH

Suppose . . . there had been only Joseph Smith left of the First Presidency, would he alone have had authority to set in order the Kingdom of God on earth? Yes. Again: suppose that eleven of the Twelve had been taken away by the power of the adversary, that one apostle has the same power that Joseph had and could preach, baptize, and set in order the whole kingdom of God upon the earth as much so as the Twelve, were they all together. Again: If in the province of God He should permit the enemy to destroy these two first quorums and then destroy the quorum of the seventy, all but one man, what is his power? It would be to go and preach, baptize, confirm, lay on hands, ordain, set in order, build up, and establish the whole kingdom of God as it is now. . . . Suppose the enemy had power to destroy all but one of the high priests from the face of the earth, what would that one possess in the power of his priesthood? He would have power and authority to go and preach, baptize, confirm, ordain, and set in order the kingdom of God in all its perfection on the earth. Could he do this without revelation? No. Could the seventies? No. Could the Twelve? No. And we ask, could Joseph Smith or the First Presidency do this without revelation? No; not one of them could do such work without revelation direct from God. I can go still further. Whoever is ordained to the office of an elder to a certain degree possesses the keys of the Melchizedek Priesthood; and suppose only one elder should be left on the earth, could he go and set in order the kingdom of God? Yes, by revelation. —*Brigham Young*, JD 9:88, May 7, 1861

If it were necessary—though I do not expect the necessity will ever arise—and there was no man left on earth holding the Melchizedek Priesthood, except an elder, that elder, by the inspiration of the Spirit of God and by the direction of the Almighty could proceed, and should proceed, to organize the Church of Jesus Christ in all its perfection, because he holds the Melchizedek Priesthood. —*Joseph F. Smith*, CR, p. 87, October, 1903

PRIESTHOOD NECESSARY IN THE TRUE
CHURCH OF CHRIST

As to the question of authority, nearly everything depends upon it. No ordinance can be performed to the acceptance of God without divine authority. . . . Some suppose this authority may be derived from the Bible, but nothing could be more absurd. . . . If by reading and believing the Bible this authority could be obtained, all who read the Bible and believed it would have it—one equally with another. . . . God Almighty is the only source from whence this knowledge, power and authority can be obtained and that through the operations of the Holy Ghost. The Scriptures may serve as a guide to lead us to God and hence to the possession of all things necessary to life and salvation, but they can do no more.

—*Joseph F. Smith,* JD 19:191, September 30, 1877

The Church of Jesus Christ of Latter-day Saints is no partisan Church. It is not a sect. It is *The Church of Jesus Christ of Latter-day Saints.* It is the only one today existing in the world that can and does legitimately bear the name of Jesus Christ and His divine authority. . . .

Many of our great writers have recently been querying and wondering where the divine authority exists today to command in the name of the Father and of the Son and of the Holy Ghost, so that it will be in effect and acceptable at the throne of the Eternal Father. I will announce here and now, presumptuous as it may seem to be to those who know not the truth, that the divine authority of Almighty God, to speak in the name of the Father and of the Son, is here in the midst of these everlasting hills, in the midst of this inter-mountain region, and it will abide and will continue, for God is its source.

—*Joseph F. Smith,* IE 21:639, April 6, 1918

It is well understood in our Church that those holding the Aaronic Priesthood have authority to officiate only in outward ordinances. By virtue of this priesthood, faith and repentance may be preached and baptism by immersion (in the temporal element of water) administered. But it requires the imposition of hands by those holding the higher or Melchizedek Priesthood to bestow the Holy Ghost and induct the convert into the spiritual concern of the kingdom.

—*Joseph F. Smith,* MS 67:628, September, 1905

THE POWERS OF THE APOSTLESHIP

Could he (Joseph Smith) have built up the kingdom of God without first being an apostle? No, he never could. The keys of the eternal priesthood, which is after the order of the Son of God, is comprehended by being an apostle. All the priesthood, all the keys, all the gifts, all the endowments, and everything preparatory to entering back into the presence of the Father and of the Son is in, composed of, circumscribed by, or I might say incorporated within the circumference of the apostleship.

—*Brigham Young,* MS 15:489, April 6, 1853

THE CALLING OF A PATRIARCH

Every father, after he has received his patriarchal blessing, is a patriarch to his own family and has the right to confer patriarchal blessings upon his family; which blessings will be just as legal as those conferred by any patriarch of the Church: in fact it is his right; and a patriarch in blessing his children can only bless as his mouthpiece.

A patriarch to the Church is appointed to bless those who are orphans or have no father in the Church to bless them . . . Where the Church is so extensive . . . other patriarchs have been ordained . . . to assist the patriarch to the Church and hence the provision made in the book of Doctrine and Covenants: "It is the duty of the Twelve, in *all* large branches of the Church, to ordain *evangelical ministers,* (patriarchs) as they shall be designated unto them by revelation." (Doc. and Cov. 107:39) And should any of those patriarchs remove here they have just as much right to administer in their patriarchal office under the direction of the patriarch to the Church as an elder or priest would, who should remove from one of the branches to this place, under the direction of the Presidency.

—*John Taylor,* TS 6:921, June 1, 1845

PRIESTHOOD THE SAME BUT THE CALLINGS ARE DIFFERENT

There are different callings, and offices, and stations, and authorities in the Holy Priesthood, but it is all the same priesthood; and there are different keys, and powers, and responsibilities, but it is the same government; and all the priesthood are

agents in that government, and all are requisite for the organization of the body, the upbuilding of Zion, and the government
of His kingdom.   —*John Taylor,* MS 9:322, May 7, 1847

A person who is ordained to the office of an elder in this
kingdom has the same priesthood that the high priests, that the
Twelve Apostles, that the seventies, and that the First Presidency
hold; but all are not called to be one of the Twelve Apostles,
nor are all called to be one of the First Presidency, nor to be
one of the first presidents of all the seventies, nor to be one of
the presidents of a quorum of seventies, nor to preside over the
high priests' quorum; but every man in his order and place,
possessing a portion of the same priesthood, according to the gifts
and callings to each.   —*Brigham Young,* JD 9:89, May 7, 1861

Which is the greater—the high priest or the seventy, the
seventy or the high priest? I tell you that neither of them is the
greater, and neither of them is the lesser. Their callings lie
in different directions, but they are from the same priesthood. If
it were necessary, the seventy, holding the Melchizedek Priesthood, as he does, I say *if it were necessary*—he could ordain a
high priest; and if it were necessary for a high priest to ordain a
seventy, he could do that. Why? Because both of them hold
the Melchizedek Priesthood.
          —*Joseph F. Smith,* CR, p. 87, October, 1903

When the Twelve were called and ordained they possessed
the same power and authority as the three First Presidents . . .
The seventies possess the same power and authority; they hold
the keys of establishing, building up, regulating, ordaining, and
setting in order the kingdom of God in all its perfections upon
the earth. We have a quorum of high priests, and there are a
great many of them. They are a local body—they tarry at home;
but the seventies travel and preach; so also do the high priests,
when they are called upon. They possess precisely the same
priesthood that the seventies and the Twelve and the First
Presidency possess; but are they ordained to officiate in all the
authority, powers, and keys of this priesthood? No, they are
not. Still they are high priests of God; and if they magnify their
priesthood they will receive at some time all the authority and
power that it is possible for man to receive.
          —*Brigham Young,* JD 9:87-88, May 7, 1861

THE POWER OF THE PRIESTHOOD EXTENDS
BEYOND THE GRAVE

When . . . any man holding the priesthood officiates, he administers by the authority of the Lord Jesus Christ; then that priesthood has effect, and all the blessings that a servant of God bestows upon the children of men will take effect both in this life and in that which is to come. If I have a blessing given to me by the Holy Priesthood, or if I receive a blessing from a patriarch, those gifts and blessings will reach into the other world; and if I am true to my covenants through this life, I can claim every blessing that has been conferred upon me, because that authority by which they were conferred is ordained of God; and it is that authority by which the sons of the Most High administer unto the children of men the ordinances of life and salvation; and those official acts will have their effect upon those persons beyond the grave as well as in this life.

—*Wilford Woodruff*, JD 9:162-163, December 1, 1861

CHAPTER XX

The Priesthood Bearer

THE SACRED CALLING OF THE PRIESTHOOD BEARER

THE HIGHEST calling the Lord ever called any human being to, in any age of the world, has been to receive the Holy Priesthood, with its keys and powers.
—*Wilford Woodruff, MS 58:305, April 5, 1896*

Some of the brightest spirits who dwell in the bosom of the Father are making their appearance among this people, of whom the Lord will make a Royal Priesthood, a peculiar nation that He can own and bless, talk with, and associate with.
—*Brigham Young, JD 11:132, Augusut, 1865*

The truths and revelations which have been made known unto this people, for their salvation and exaltation, and glory, and for the salvation of all men, both the living and the dead, are of great value and worth unto us,—and unto all men, if they would receive them. We are the only people to whom this holy gospel, priesthood, and covenants have been committed in our day; and we shall be held responsible for the use we make of them. —*Wilford Woodruff, JD 5:86, April 9, 1857*

The priesthood that you hold is not the priesthood of Joseph Smith, or Brigham Young, or any other men who have been called to leadership of the Church at home or abroad. The priesthood that you hold is the power of God, conferred upon you from on high. Holy beings had to be sent to earth a little over a hundred years ago in order to restore that glorious blessing that had been lost to the earth for hundreds of years. Surely we ought to be grateful for our blessings.
—*George Albert Smith, CR, p. 118, October, 1945*

RESPONSIBILITIES DEVOLVING UPON PRIESTHOOD BEARERS

O, ye elders of Israel, who have received the Holy Priesthood, we have this work laid upon our shoulders, we have to

take hold and build up this kingdom or be damned. This is our condition; we cannot get away from it; the ancient apostles could not; we cannot. It is the greatest dispensation God ever gave to the human family in any age of the world, and we are commanded to carry it forward. We cannot afford to treat lightly this work. We cannot undertake to serve God and mammon. We cannot undertake to serve the world and fulfill our missions as apostles and elders of the Lord Jesus Christ. We have got to take one side or the other.
                                    —*Wilford Woodruff*, JD 22:206, January 9, 1881

We have the same priesthood that Jesus had, and we have got to do as He did, to make sacrifice of our own desires and feelings as He did, perhaps not to die martyrs as He did, but we have got to make sacrifices in order to carry out the purposes of God, or we shall not be worthy of this Holy Priesthood and be saviors of the world.
                                    —*Lorenzo Snow*, JD 23:341-342, November 4, 1882

I say to you that it is not an insignificant thing to hold the priesthood of God—to have the right to influence the powers of the heavens for good; and it is not a slight thing for us to neglect to honor . . . the priesthood of God in those who preside over us.
                                    —*Heber J. Grant*, IE 48:123, March, 1945

The priesthood is received by man, but the use of it determines whether it remains with him. The right to use it vanishes under the cloud of unrighteous living, for nothing so grieves our Heavenly Father as to have those who have received great knowledge deny it and return to untruth. This view of the priesthood is not always remembered by those who are tempted, after having been ordained, to depart from the paths of righteousness. . . .

This makes a very serious matter of receiving this covenant and this priesthood; for those who receive it must, like God Himself, abide in it and must not fail and must not be moved out of the way; for those who receive this oath and covenant and turn away from it and cease to do righteously and to honor this covenant, who will to abide in sin and repent not, there is no forgiveness for them, either in this life or in the world to come.   —*Joseph F. Smith*, CR, p. 65, April, 1898

If we have the Holy Priesthood upon our heads and do not live our religion, of all men we are under the greatest condemnation.   —*Wilford Woodruff*, JD 21:125, June 6, 1880

I believe the Lord has held every man responsible, from the day of our great progenitor, father Adam, into whose hands the Holy Priesthood and the keys of the kingdom of God have been committed; and I believe that every man, every set of men, and every people will be held responsible, in time and eternity, for the use they have made of the gifts, blessings, and promises which have been given unto them.
                                    —*Wilford Woodruff*, JD 18:187, April 6, 1876

We have been ordaining men in the various quorums for the last forty years; and what for? Merely to give them a place and position and the priesthood? No, I tell you nay; but that holding the Holy Priesthood you may magnify it and become the saviors of men . . .
It is time we were waking up to a sense of the position we occupy before God; for the day is not far distant when we will hear of wars and rumors of war; not only rumors of wars, but wars themselves . . . and general carnage will spread through the lands, and if you do not magnify your callings, God will hold you responsible for those whom you might have saved had you done your duty.   —*John Taylor*, JD 20:22-23, July 7, 1878

Let all Israel remember that the eternal and everlasting priesthood is bestowed upon us for the purpose alone of administering in the ordinances of life and salvation, both for the living and the dead, and no man on earth can use that priesthood for any other purpose than for the work of the ministry, the perfecting of the Saints, edifying the body of Christ, establishing the kingdom of heaven, and redeeming Zion. If we attempt to use it for unrighteous purposes, like lightning from heaven, our power, sooner or later, falls, and we fail to accomplish the designs of God.
                                    —*Wilford Woodruff*, MS 49:546, August, 1887

PRIESTHOOD BEARERS SHOULD SET THE EXAMPLE FOR THE CHURCH

Think what it means to hold keys of authority which—if exercised in wisdom and in righteousness—are bound to be respected by the Father, the Son, and the Holy Ghost! Do you honor this priesthood? Do you respect the office and honor the key of authority that you possess in the Melchizedek Priesthood, which is after the order of the Son of God? Will you, who hold this priesthood, profane the name of Deity? Would you be riotous and eat and drink with the drunken, with the unbelieving and with the profane? Would you, holding that priesthood, forget your prayers and fail to remember the Giver of all good? Would you, . . . possessing the right and authority from God to administer in the name of the Father, and of the Son, and of the Holy Ghost, violate the confidence and the love of God, the hope and desire of the Father of all of us? . . . Would you, as an elder in the Church of Jesus Christ, dishonor your wife or your children? . . . Will you honor the Sabbath day and keep it holy? Will you observe the law of tithing and all the other requirements of the gospel? Will you carry with you at all times the spirit of prayer and the desire to do good? Will you teach your children the principles of life and salvation, so that when they are eight years old they will *desire* baptism, of their own accord?   —*Joseph F. Smith,* IE 21:105-106, December, 1917

There is no authority associated with the Holy Priesthood except on the principle of persuasion, and no man has a right to plume himself upon any position he occupies in this Church, for he is simply a servant of God and a servant of the people, and if any man attempts to use any kind of arbitrary authority and act with any degree of unrighteousness, God will hold that man to an account for it, and we all of us have to be judged according to the deeds done in the body. We are here as saviors of men and not as tyrants and oppressors.
                              —*John Taylor,* JD 24:268, June 24, 1883

If I find a man, as I do once in a while, who thinks that he ought to be sustained in a higher position than he occupies, that proves to me that he does not understand his true position and is not capable of magnifying it. Has he not already the privilege of exhibiting all the talents he has—of doing all the good he is capable of in this kingdom? Is he curtailed in the least, in anywise or place, in bringing forth his wisdom and powers and exhibiting them before the community and leading out? No, not in the least.

—Brigham Young, JD 7:161-162, June 5, 1859

Every man should be willing to be presided over; and he is not fit to preside over others until he can submit sufficiently to the presidency of his brethren.

—Joseph F. Smith, IE 21:105, December, 1917

It is extremely hurtful for any man holding the priesthood and enjoying the gift of the Holy Ghost to harbor a spirit of envy, or malice, of retaliation, or intolerance toward or against his fellow man. We ought to say in our hearts, let God judge between me and thee, but as for me I will forgive. I want to say to you that Latter-day Saints who harbor a feeling of unforgiveness in their souls are more guilty and more censurable than the one who has sinned against them.

—Joseph F. Smith, CR, p. 86-87, October, 1902

BENEFITS DERIVED BY WORTHY PRIESTHOOD BEARERS

It is the priesthood that will give you character, renown, wisdom, power, and authority, and build you up here below among the children of men; and above, exalt you to peace and happiness, to thrones and dominions, even through countless eternities. *—Lorenzo Snow,* BFRLS, p. 192, 1851

And now, where is the man among you having once burst the veil and gazed upon this purity, the glory, the might, majesty, and dominion of a perfected man, in celestial glory, in eternity, will not cheerfully resign life, suffer the most excruciating tortures, let limb be torn from limb sooner than dishonor or resign his priesthood. *—Lorenzo Snow,* MS 13:363, December 1, 1851

It is the privilege of every person who is faithful to the priesthood . . . to live upon the earth until his appointed time; and he may know, see, and understand, by revelation, the things of God just as naturally as we understand natural things that are around us. *—Brigham Young,* JD 3:192-193, January 27, 1856

To be ordained to the priesthood may not prove a blessing. We should not at any time feel that it will be a blessing to us, unless we honor it, unless we magnify it, and have in our hearts the desire that the Lord intended we should have, when He bestowed that gift upon us, and we should always desire to do good.   —*George Albert Smith,* CR, p. 27, April, 1941

If we perform our duties, each one of us in our proper position, God gives us power to accomplish the object we have in view, no matter what it is, or what priesthood we hold.
                    —*John Taylor,* JD 21:211, March 1, 1880

An individual who holds a share in the priesthood and continues faithful to his calling . . . will secure to himself not only the privilege of receiving, but the knowledge how to receive the things of God, that he may know the mind of God continually; and he will be enabled to discern between right and wrong, between the things of God and the things that are not of God. And the priesthood—the Spirit that is within him, will continue to increase until it becomes like a fountain of living water; until it is like the tree of life; until it is one continued source of intelligence and instruction to that individual.
                    —*Brigham Young,* JD 3:192, January 27, 1856

PRIESTHOOD TO EVENTUALLY EXTEND TO ALL

When all the other children of Adam have had the privilege of receiving the priesthood, and of coming into the kingdom of God, and of being redeemed from the four quarters of the earth, and have received their resurrection from the dead, then it will be time enough to remove the curse from Cain and his posterity. He deprived his brother of the privilege of pursuing his journey through life and of extending his kingdom by multiplying upon the earth and because he did this, he is the last to share the joys of the kingdom of God.
                    —*Brigham Young,* JD 2:143, December 3, 1854

Any man having one drop of the seed of Cain in him cannot receive the priesthood; but the day will come when all that race will be redeemed and possess all the blessings which we now have.
                    —*Brigham. Young,* "Wilford Woodruff" by Cowley, p. 351, a. 1852

The Lamanites or Indians are just as much the children of our Father and God as we are. So also are the Africans. But we are also the children of adoption through obedience to the gospel of His son. Why are so many of the inhabitants of the earth cursed with a skin of blackness? It comes in consequence of their fathers rejecting the power of the Holy Priesthood and the law of God. They will go down to death. And when all the rest of the children have received their blessings in the Holy Priesthood, then that curse will be removed from the seed of Cain, and they will then come up and possess the priesthood and receive all the blessings which we now are entitled to.

—*Brigham Young,* JD 11:272, August 19, 1866

TITLES OF THE PRIESTHOOD ARE SACRED

The titles "Prophet, Seer and Revelator," "Apostles," etc. . . . are too sacred to be used indiscriminately in our common talk. There are occasions when they are quite proper and in place; but in our everyday conversations it is sufficient honor to address any brother holding the Melchizedek Priesthood as elder. The term elder is a general one, applying to all those who hold the higher priesthood, whether they be apostles, patriarchs, high priests or seventies; and to address a brother as Apostle So-and-So, or Patriarch Such-a-One in the common talk of business and the like is using titles too sacred to be in place on such occasion. . . . The use of all these titles continuously and indiscriminately savors somewhat of blasphemy and is not pleasing to our Heavenly Father.

—*Joseph F. Smith,* JI 38:20, January 1, 1903

HOW THE PRIESTHOOD MAY BE LOST

An officer in the Church in one of the stakes of Zion asks whether a man's priesthood may be taken from him in any other way than by excommunication. In other words, can a man's ordination to the priesthood be made null and void and he still be permitted to retain his membership in the Church; or must he be excommunicated before the priesthood can be taken from him? The reply must be that only by excommunication in the appointed way can the priesthood be taken from a person. We know of no other means provided by which a man who has had the priesthood conferred upon him can be deprived of it. The constituted authorities of the Church may, however, after proper authorized hearing, decide that a man has forfeited his right to act in the priesthood, and for this cause he may be silenced and his certificate of ordination be taken from him, and thus have his right suspended to officiate in the ordinances of the gospel or to exercise the priesthood which has been conferred upon him. Then, if he persists in exercising his priesthood and former calling, he may be taken to account for the insubordination and excommunicated.

Several examples have occurred in the history of the Church where men through transgression, duly proved and decided upon by the constituted authorities, have been stopped from acting in the priesthood, which is just as effectual as taking away their priesthood would be, if it were possible; but this has taken no ordination from them, and if in such cases the transgressors should repent and make complete and satisfactory restitution, they would still hold the same priesthood which they held before they were silenced or stopped from acting. A person once ordained a bishop, an elder, or high priest, continues to hold those offices. A bishop is still a bishop though he may remove to another ward or for other reasons temporarily lose his calling. But in case he is wanted to act in a new office, or place, and the proper authorities call him to act, it is not necessary to reordain him a bishop; he would only need to be set apart for his new calling. So with other officers in the priesthood, once having received the priesthood, it cannot be taken from them, except by transgression so serious that they must forfeit their standing in the Church. But, as stated, their right to officiate may be suspended or stopped. The Lord can take away the power and efficacy of their ordinations and will do so if they transgress. No endowments or blessings in the House of the Lord, no patriarchal blessings, no ordination to the priesthood can be taken away, once given. To prevent a person for cause from exercising the rights and privileges of acting in the offices of the priesthood may be and has been done, and the person so silenced still remains a member of the Church, but this does not take away from him any priesthood that he held.

—*Joseph F. Smith*, IE 11:465-466, April, 1908

CHAPTER XXI

Church Organization and Government

OFFICE HOLDING IN THE LATTER-DAY SAINT CHURCH

GOD HAS ordained His Holy Priesthood upon the earth with presidents, apostles, bishops, high councils, seventies, high priests, and the order and organization of the Church and kingdom of God in its fullness and completeness, more complete perhaps than it ever was since the world was framed. Why? Because it is the dispensation of the fullness of times, embracing all other times that have ever existed since the world was, and He has gathered us together for that purpose.
—*John Taylor*, JD 21:117, November 28, 1879

As regards our religious principles, we are not indebted to any men who live upon the earth for them. These principles emanated from God. They were given by revelation, and if we have a First Presidency, if we have high priests, if we have seventies, if we have bishops, elders, priests, and teachers, if we have stake and other organizations, we have received them all from God. If we have temples, if we administer in them, it is because we have received instruction in relation thereto from the Lord. If we know anything pertaining to the future, it comes from Him, and in fact we live in God, we move in God, and from Him we derive our being.
—*John Taylor*, JD 26:30, December 14, 1884

There is no office growing out of this priesthood that is or can be greater than the priesthood itself. It is from the priesthood that the office derives its authority and power. No office gives authority to the priesthood. No office adds to the power of the priesthood. But all offices in the Church derive their power, their virtue, their authority from the priesthood.
—*Joseph F. Smith*, CR, p. 87, October, 1903

The Church is patriarchal in its character and nature, and it is highly proper and right that the head of the family, the father,

should be consulted by officers in all things that pertain to the calling of his children to any of the duties in the Church.
                              —Joseph F. Smith, IE 5:307-308, February, 1902

A SYNOPSIS OF CHURCH OFFICES

THE OFFICE OF PRESIDENCY

Does a man's being a *Prophet* in this Church prove that he shall be the *President* of it? I answer, no! A man may be a Prophet, Seer, and Revelator, and it may have nothing to do with his being the President of the Church. Suffice it to say, that Joseph was the President of the Church, as long as he lived: the people chose to have it so. . . . The *keys* of the *priesthood* were committed to Joseph, to build up the *kingdom of God* on the *earth,* and were not to be taken from him in time or in eternity; but when he was called to preside over the Church, it was by the voice of the people; though he held the keys of the *priesthood, independent* of their voice.
                              —Brigham Young, JD 1:133, April 6, 1853

There never can be and never will be, under God's direction, two equal heads at the same time. That would not be consistent; it would be irrational and unreasonable, contrary to God's will. There is one head, and He is God, the head of all. Next to Him stands the man He puts in nomination to stand at the head on the earth, with his associates; and all the other organizations and heads, from him to the last, are subordinate to the first, otherwise there would be discord, disunion, and disorganization.   *—Joseph F. Smith,* IE 6:707, July, 1903

I testify in the name of Israel's God that He will not suffer the head of the Church, him whom He has chosen to stand at the head, to transgress His laws and apostatize; the moment he should take a course that would in time lead to it, God would take him away. Why? Because to suffer a wicked man to occupy that position would be to allow, as it were, the fountain to become corrupted, which is something He will never permit.
                              —Joseph F. Smith, JD 24:192, June 21, 1883

When the Lord wishes to give a revelation to His people, when He wishes to reveal new items of doctrine to them or ad-

minister chastisement, He will do it through the man whom He has appointed to that office and calling. The rest of the offices and callings of the Church are helps . . . to strengthen the hands of the Presidency of the whole Church.
—Brigham Young, JD 11:135-136,August, 1865

The Apostleship

The highest office that any man has ever held on the face of the earth in this or any other generation is that of an apostle.
—Wilford Woodruff, JD 13:319, September 5, 1869

This Church has been established by raising up prophets, unto whom have been given the keys of the kingdom of God—the keys of the Holy Priesthood and apostleship of the Son of God, with power to organize the Church and kingdom of God on the earth, with all its gifts, graces, ordinances, and orders, as proclaimed by all the apostles and prophets who have lived since the world began. *—Wilford Woodruff, JD 14:2-3, January 1, 1871*

The Twelve are set apart as special witnesses to the nations of the earth and are empowered and authorized to open up the gospel, to introduce it, and to turn the keys thereof to all people. . . . This is just as it was in former ages.
—John Taylor, JD 24:288, October 7, 1883

What position can any man occupy on the face of the earth that is more noble, Godlike, high and glorious than to be a messenger of salvation unto the human family? What more responsible position can a man occupy than to be an apostle of the Lord Jesus Christ? I do not know of any in this or any other generation. *—Wilford Woodruff, JD 13:319, September 5, 1869*

The Position of Patriarch

An evangelist is a patriarch, even the oldest man of the blood of Joseph or of the seed of Abraham. Wherever the Church of Christ is established in the earth there should be a patriarch for the benefit of the posterity of the Saints, as it was with Jacob in giving his patriarchal blessing unto his sons.
—Joseph Smith, Jr., DHC 3:381, June 27, 1839

Why do we believe in evangelists? Because they have the inspiration of God, the inspiration of their office and they are able to foretell the lives of the men and women upon whom they place their hands. —*Heber J. Grant*, CR, p. 31, October, 1919

QUORUM OF HIGH PRIESTS

In addition to these organizations we have in each stake of Zion an organization called the high priests' quorum, to which all high priests of the Church belong, including the presidency and the high councilors of the stake, and also the bishops and their counselors, all the patriarchs and all others who have been ordained to the office of high priest in the Church, which office is the office of presidency in the Melchizedek Priesthood, not that every man who holds the office of high priest is a president. Only he who is called, appointed and set apart to preside among the high priests holds the presiding authority and office.
—*Joseph F. Smith*, CR, p. 3, October, 1904

COUNCIL OF SEVENTIES

The seventies are . . . a sort of traveling council or priesthood and may preside over a church or churches, until a high priest can be had. The seventies are to be taken from the quorum of elders and are not to be high priests. They are subject to the direction and dictation of the Twelve, who have the keys of the ministry. All are to preach the gospel, by the power and influence of the Holy Ghost; and no man can preach the gospel without the Holy Ghost.
—*Joseph Smith, Jr.*, DHC 2:477, April 6, 1837

To assist the Twelve in the labors in which they are engaged are the seventies, who are called as special witnesses to the nations of the earth.   —*John Taylor*, JD 24:288, October 7, 1883

THE BISHOPRIC

The office of a bishop belongs to the lesser priesthood. He is the highest officer in the Aaronic Priesthood and has the privilege of using the Urim and Thummim—has the administration of angels, if he has faith, and lives so that he can receive and enjoy all the blessings Aaron enjoyed.
—*Brigham Young*, JD 9:87, May 7, 1861

The bishop is a high priest and necessarily so, because he is to preside over that particular branch of Church affairs that is denominated the lesser priesthood and because we have no direct lineal descendant of Aaron, to whom it would of right belong.
                    —*Joseph Smith, Jr.*, DHC 2:477, April 6, 1837

A bishop in his calling and duty is with the Church all the time; he is not called to travel abroad to preach, but is at home; he is not abroad in the world, but is with the Saints.
                    —*Brigham Young*, JD 2:89, October 6, 1854

Instead of my believing for a moment that Paul wished to signify to Timothy that he must select a man to fill the office of a bishop that would have but *one* wife, I believe directly the reverse; but his advice to Timothy amounts simply to this—it would not be wise for you to ordain a man to the office of a bishop unless he has a *wife*; you must not ordain a *single* or *unmarried* man to that calling.
                    —*Brigham Young*, JD 2:88, October 6, 1854

THE ORDER OF CHURCH GOVERNMENT

The First Presidency has authority over all matters pertaining to the Church.

The next in order are the Twelve Apostles, whose calling is to preach the gospel, or see it preached, to all the world. They hold the same authority in all parts of the world that the First Presidency does at home, and act under their direction. They are called by revelation and sanctioned by the people. The Twelve have a president. . . . This presidency is obtained by seniority of age and ordination.

There are then the seventies. . . . It is their office also to preach the gospel to all the world. There is a presidency over each quorum. And again there are seven presidents with their president, who preside over the presidents of the quorums of seventy.

There are then the elders, of whom there are many. It is their business to preach the gospel in different parts of the earth, where they are located, according to circumstances; but they are not bound, as the seventies are, to go to different parts of the earth, only as their circumstances will admit. But they have power to preach, to baptize, to lay on hands for the gift of the Holy Ghost, and to attend to other ordinances of the Church.

There are then the priests, whose duty it is to preach and baptize, but not to lay on hands for the gift of the Holy Ghost.

There are also teachers, whose business it is to visit the members in the different branches of the Church where they live, and to see that they attend to their family duties, prayers, etc.; to watch over the spiritual interests of those under their care; and to see that there is no hard feeling, contention, evil speaking, or wickedness.

There are then deacons, whose business it is to assist the teachers and attend to the temporal affairs of the branches where they may happen to be situated.

There is then a quorum of high priests, of whom there are many. It is their business generally to preside over churches, and assist on councils as they may be directed, whether at home or abroad. But a seventy, or an elder, can do this in their absence or when others have not been appointed.

There are also evangelists, or patriarchs.

The above is an outline of the organization for the purpose of preaching the gospel to all the world and carrying out the order of God as revealed unto His Church.

—John Taylor, MS 13:337-338, November 15, 1851

Ascending the scale of authority, the titles and callings of deacon, teacher, priest and bishop come within the purview of the Aaronic Priesthood; while those of elder, seventy, high priest, patriarch, apostle and president are offices and callings in the Melchizedek Priesthood, to which the Aaronic Priesthood is an appendage. A full equipment is thus shown for the government and conduct of the Church both spiritually and temporally.

—Joseph F. Smith, MS 67:628, September, 1905

It [the kingdom of God] has its First Presidency, its Prophets and Apostles, its seventies and high priests, its bishops, teachers, and deacons, and every appendage that is necessary to completeness and to promote the happiness and welfare of the human family and for all purposes of government on this earth and in the heavens. Or, in other words, this organization is a pattern of things in the heavens and is the medium or channel through which the blessings of God flow to His people on the earth and through which intelligence is communicated concerning all subjects with which the Saints are concerned, whether they relate to this world or to the world which is to come. *—John Taylor,* JD 7:323, October 7, 1859

How came these apostles, these seventies, these high priests, and all this organization we now enjoy? It came by revelation. . . . In the year 1831 the Prophet went to Ohio. . . They held a General Conference, which was the first General Conference ever called or held in Ohio. Joseph then received a revelation and ordained high priests. . . . These were the first that were ordained to this office in the Church. I relate this to show you how Joseph proceeded step by step in organizing the Church. At that time there were no seventies nor Twelve Apostles. *—Brigham Young,* JD 9:88-89, May, 1861

THE CORRECT LINE OF AUTHORITY

If the Presidency were to be killed off, then the Council of the Twelve Apostles would stand in their place and preside until the Presidency should be restored; and if they and the First Presidency were all killed off, then the seventies would come forward and they would establish the order of Zion and renew the order of the priesthood upon the earth; and if all the seventies were killed off, and yet there was one elder possessing the Melchizedek Priesthood, he would have authority to organize the Church, under the command of God and the guidance of His Holy Spirit, as Joseph did in the beginning; that it should be re-established in its perfect form. So you can see that this organization is well-nigh undestructible. *—Joseph F. Smith,* LEJ 4:45-46, September 7, 1895

I want here to correct an impression that has grown up to some extent among the people and that is, that the Twelve Apostles possess equal authority with the First Presidency in the Church. This is correct when there is no other Presidency but the Twelve Apostles; but so long as there are three presiding elders who possess the presiding authority in the Church, the authority of the Twelve Apostles is not equal to theirs. If it were so, there would be two equal authorities and two equal quorums in the priesthood, running parallel, and that could not be, because there must be a head. Therefore, so long as there is a First Presidency in the Church they hold supreme authority in the Church, and the Twelve Apostles are subject unto them and do not possess the same authority as they do as a presiding quorum. When the Presidency are not here, or when the Lord takes away the man who is called to be the President of the Church and the quorum of the three Presidents is thereby dissolved, then the authority of the Twelve rises to the dignity of Presidents of the Church and *not* till then. Some people have thought also that the quorum of seventies possess equal authority with the First Presidency and with the Twelve. So they would if there was no Presidency and no Twelve and only seven elders called seventies in the Church, but their authority is not equal to that of the First Presidency while the First Presidency lives, nor to that of the Twelve Apostles.

—Joseph F. Smith, LEJ 4:43, September 7, 1895

THE QUESTION OF SUCCESSION
TO THE PRESIDENCY

In answer to the question "Do you know of any reason in case of the death of the President of the Church why the Twelve Apostles should not choose some other person than the President of the Twelve to be the President of the Church?" Wilford Woodruff wrote:

I know several reasons why they should not. First, at the death of the President of the Church the Twelve Apostles become the presiding authority of the Church, and the president of the Twelve is really the President of the Church by virtue of his office as much while presiding over the Twelve Apostles as while presiding over his two counselors. . . . Second, in case of the death of the President of the Church it takes a majority of the Twelve Apostles to appoint the President of the Church, and it is very unreasonable to suppose that the majority of that quorum could be converted to depart from the course marked out by inspiration and followed by the Apostles at the death of Christ and by the Twelve Apostles at the death of Joseph Smith.   *— Wilford Woodruff,* "Wilford Woodruff" by Cowley, p. 561,
March 28, 1887

The Twelve are not subject to any other than the First Presidency, viz. myself, . . . Sidney Rigdon, and Frederick G. Williams, who are now my Counselors; and where I am not, there is no First Presidency over the Twelve.
　　　　　　—Joseph Smith, Jr., DHC 2:374, January 16, 1836

THE POWER OF THE ORGANIZATION
OF THE PRIESTHOOD

Take away the organization of the Church, and its power would cease. Every part of its organization is necessary and essential to its perfect existence. Disregard, ignore, or omit any part and you start imperfection in the Church; and if we should continue in that way we would find ourselves like those of old, being led by error, superstition, ignorance, and by the cunning and craftiness of men. We would soon leave out here a little and there a little, here a line and there a precept, until we would become like the rest of the world, divided, disorganized, confused, and without knowledge, without revelation or inspiration, and without Divine authority or power.
　　　　　　—Joseph F. Smith, CR, p. 5, April, 1915

I am for the kingdom of God. I like a good government and then I like to have it wisely and justly administered. The government of heaven, if wickedly administered, would become one of the worst governments upon the face of the earth. No matter how good a government is, unless it is administered by righteous men, an evil government will be made of it.
　　　　　　—Brigham Young, JD 10:177, May 24, 1863

We can accept nothing as authoritative but that which comes directly through the appointed channel, the constituted organizations of the priesthood, which is the channel that God has appointed through which to make known His mind and will to the world. . . .

Whenever you see a man rise up claiming to have received direct revelation from the Lord to the Church, independent of the order and channel of the priesthood, you may set him down as an impostor.　　　*—Joseph F. Smith,* JD 24:188-189, June 21, 1883

I have in mind our auxiliary organizations; what are they? Helps to the standard organizations of the Church. They are not independent. I want to say to the Young Men's and Young Ladies' Mutual Improvement Associations, and to the Relief Society, and to the Primaries, and to the Sunday Schools, and Religion Classes, and all the rest of the organizations in the Church that not one of them is independent of the priesthood of the Son of God, not one of them can exist a moment in the acceptance of the Lord when they withdraw from the voice and from the counsel of those who hold the priesthood and preside over them. They are subject to the powers and authority of the Church, and they are not independent of them; nor can they exercise any rights in their organizations independently of the priesthood and of the Church.

                              —*Joseph F. Smith*, CR, p. 7, April, 1913

We expect to see the day . . . when every council of the priesthood in the Church of Jesus Christ of Latter-day Saints will understand its duty, will assume its own responsibility, will magnify its calling, and fill its place in the Church, to the uttermost, according to the intelligence and ability possessed by it. When that day shall come, there will not be so much necessity for work that is now being done by the auxiliary organizations, because it will be done by the regular quorums of the priesthood. The Lord designed and comprehended it from the beginning, and He has made provision in the Church whereby every need may be met and satisfied through the regular organizations of the priesthood.   —*Joseph F. Smith*, CR, p. 3, April, 1906

CONCERNING THE SUSTAINING OF
CHURCH OFFICERS

The First Presidency and the Twelve are presented before all the Church in all parts of the world, for acceptance or rejection, twice every year in the several conferences; and any member of the Church has a perfect right to arise and testify, if he knows anything objectionable against these persons. The above rule applies to all other officers, whether at home or abroad.   —*John Taylor*, MS, 13:339, November 15, 1851

There is no officer in the Church of Jesus Christ of Latter-day Saints chosen by the body. The Lord has given us His way to do these things. He has revealed to us that it is the duty of the presiding authorities to appoint and call; and then those whom they choose for any official position in the Church shall be presented to the body. If the body reject them, they are responsible for that rejection. They have the right to reject, if they will, or to receive them and sustain them by their faith and prayers. —*Joseph F. Smith*, CR, p. 4, April, 1907

Who have we for our ruling power? Where and how did he obtain his authority? . . . It is by the voice of God and the voice of the people that our present President obtained his authority. . . . He obtains his authority first from God and secondly from the people. . . . Is there a monarch, potentate, or power under the heavens that undergoes a scrutiny as fine as this? No, there is not; and yet this is done twice a year, before all the Saints in. the world. Here are legitimacy and rule. You place the power in their hands to govern, dictate, regulate, and put in order the affairs of the kingdom of God. This is, Vox Dei, vox populi. God appoints, the people sustain.
—*John Taylor* JD, 1:229-230, April 8, 1853

We hold up our right hand when voting in token before God that we will sustain those for whom we vote; and if we cannot feel to sustain them, we ought not to hold up our hands, because to do this would be to act the part of hypocrites. And the question naturally arises, how far shall we sustain them? Or in other words, how far are we at liberty to depart from this covenant which we make before each other and before our God? For when we lift up our hands in this way, it is in token to God that we are sincere in what we do, and that we will sustain the parties we vote for. . . . If we agree to do a thing and do not do it, we become covenant breakers and violators of our obligations, which are, perhaps, as solemn and binding as anything we can enter into. . . .

What is meant by sustaining a person? . . . It is a very simple thing to me. . . . For instance, if a man be a teacher, and I vote that I will sustain him in his position, when he visits me in an official capacity I will welcome him and treat him with consideration, kindness and respect and if I need counsel I will ask it at his hand, and I will do everything I can to sustain him. That would be proper and a principle of righteousness, and I would not say anything derogatory to his character. . . .

But suppose he should do something wrong, supposing he
should be found lying or cheating, or defrauding somebody; or
stealing or anything else, or even become impure in his habits,
would you still sustain him? It would be my duty then to talk
with him as I would with anybody else and tell him that I had
understood that things were thus and so and that under these
circumstances I could not sustain him; and if I found that I had
been misinformed I would withdraw the charge; but if not it
would then be my duty to see that justice was administered to
him, that he was brought before the proper tribunal to answer
for the things he had done; and in the absence of that I would
have no business to talk about him.

—*John Taylor*, JD 21:207-208, March 1, 1880

THE SETTLEMENT OF DISPUTES AMONG
CHURCH MEMBERS

The youth of Zion should remember that the foundation
principle in settling difficulties lies in the persons themselves
who are in difficulty making the adjustments and settlements.
If those who vary cannot adjust their differences, it is infinitely
more difficult, if not impossible, for a third or fourth party to
create harmony between them. In any event, such outside
parties can only aid the contending persons to come to an
understanding.

But, in case it is necessary to call in the priesthood as a
third party, there is a proper order in which this should be done.
If no conclusion can be arrived at, in a difficulty or difference
between two members of the Church, the ward teachers should
be called to assist; failing then, appeal may be made to the
bishop, then to the high council of the stake, and only after
the difficulty has been tried before that body should the matter
ever come before the general presiding quorum of the Church.
It is wrong to disregard any of these authorized steps, or
authorities.   —*Joseph F. Smith*, IE 5:230, January, 1902

The bishoprics and the presidents of stakes have exclusive
jurisdiction over the membership or the standing of men and
women in their wards and in their stakes. I want to state that
pretty plain—that is to say, it is not my duty, it is not the duty
of the seven presidents of seventies, nor of the council of the

Twelve Apostles to go into a stake of Zion and try for membership or for standing in the Church any member of a stake or ward. We have no business to do it; it belongs to the local authorities, and they have ample authority to deal with the membership in their wards and in their stakes. The bishops may try an elder for misconduct, for un-Christianlike conduct, for apostasy, or for wickedness of any kind that would disqualify him for membership in the Church, and they may pass upon him their judgment that he is unworthy of fellowship in the Church, and they may withdraw from him their fellowship. Then they may refer his case to the presidency and high council, and it will be the duty of the presidency and high council of the stake to deal with him, even to the extent of excommunication from the Church; and there is no remedy for this, only the right of appeal to the Presidency of the Church. If there may be perchance any injustice and partiality, lack of information or understanding on the part of the bishopric, which may not be corrected and therefore might be perpetuated by the decision of the high council and the party aggrieved does not feel that he has had justice dealt out to him, he then has a right, under the laws of the Church, to appeal to the Presidency of the Church, but not otherwise. —*Joseph F. Smith*, CR, p. 5, April, 1913

BOOK FOUR

The Last Days

The daily press brings to us accounts of disasters that are everywhere—the sea being tempestuous and loss of life upon it, earthquakes, great tornadoes, such as we have been told would occur in the last days—and it does seem to me . . . if men are thinking seriously, if they are reading the Scriptures, they must know the happenings that the Lord said would occur in the last days are occurring. The fig tree is surely putting forth its leaves, and . . . those things that the Lord has predicted as preceding His second coming are now coming to pass.

—GEORGE ALBERT SMITH
CR, p. 44
April, 1932

CHAPTER XXII

Conditions Existing in the Last Days

CALAMITIES TO COME

Do you think there is calamity abroad now among the people? Not much.

All we have yet heard and we have experienced is scarcely a preface to the sermon that is going to be preached. When the testimony of the elders ceases to be given, and the Lord says to them, "Come home; I will now preach my own sermons to the nations of the earth," all you now know can scarcely be called a preface to the sermon that will be preached with fire and sword, tempests, earthquakes, hail, rain, thunders and lightnings, and fearful destruction. What matters the destruction of a few railway cars? You will hear of magnificent cities, now idolized by the people, sinking in the earth, entombing the inhabitants. The sea will heave itself beyond its bounds, engulfing mighty cities. Famine will spread over the nations, and nation will rise up against nation, kingdom against kingdom, and states against states, in our own country and in foreign lands; and they will destroy each other, caring not for the blood and lives of their neighbors, of their families, or for their own lives.

—Brigham Young, JD 8:123, July 15, 1860

My testimony is this unto all men and nations, that you live in the day and hour of the judgments of God Almighty. You live in the day and generation when the God of Israel has set His hand to perform His work, His strange work in the latter days. You live in the age in which God will bring to pass the fulfillment of that word of prophecy and prediction which has been spoken by all the prophets since the world began. . . .

Thrones will be cast down, nations will be overturned, anarchy will reign, all legal barriers will be broken down, and the laws will be trampled in the dust. You are about to be visited with war, the sword, famine, pestilence, plague, earthquake, whirlwinds, tempests, and with the flame of devouring fire. By fire and with the sword will God plead with all flesh, and the slain of the Lord will be many. The anger of the Lord is kindled and His sword is bathed in heaven and is about to fall upon Idumea, or the world. . . . The fig trees are leafing, and the signs of all heaven and earth indicate the coming of the Son of Man. The seals are about to be opened; the plagues to be poured forth. Your rivers and seas will be turned to blood and to gall. And the inhabitants of the earth will die of plagues. . . . The question may be asked why these judgments are coming upon the world in the last days? I answer because of the wickedness of the inhabitants thereof. . . . The Lord has raised up prophets and apostles who have cried aloud to this generation, with the proclamation of the gospel for half a century, and warned them of the judgments which were to come, and the inhabitants of the earth have rejected this testimony and shed the blood of the Lord's anointed, persecuted the Saints of God, and the consequence is this, "Darkness covers the earth, and gross darkness the people," and the Lord is withholding His Spirit from the inhabitants of the earth, and the devil is ruling over his own kingdom, and wickedness and abominations of every kind have increased a hundred fold within the last few years, until the whole earth is filled with murders, whoredoms, blasphemies, and every crime in the black catalogue that was manifest in the antedeluvain world, or Sodom and Gomorrah, until the whole earth groans under its abominations, and the heavens weep, and all eternity is pained, and the angels are waiting the great command to go forth and reap down the earth. This testimony I bear to all nations under heaven, and I know it is true by the inspiration of Almighty God.

—*Wilford Woodruff*, MS 41:241; 245-246, April 21, 1879

I prophesy, in the name of the Lord God of Israel, anguish and wrath and tribulation and the withdrawing of the Spirit of God from the earth await this generation, until they are visited with utter desolation. This generation is as corrupt as the generation of the Jews that crucified Christ; and if He were here today and should preach the same doctrine He did then, they would put Him to death.   —*Joseph Smith, Jr.*, DHC 6:58, October 15, 1843

We see nations rising against nations; we hear of the pestilence destroying its thousands in one place and its tens of thousands in another; the plague consuming all before it, and we witness this terror that reigns in the hearts of the wicked, and we are ready to exclaim, "The Lord is certainly about bringing the world to an account of its iniquity." Let us reflect, then, in the last days, that there was to be great tribulations; for the Savior says, nation shall rise against nation, kingdom against kingdom, and there shall be famine, pestilence, and earthquakes in divers places, and the prophets have declared that the valleys should rise; that the mountains should be laid low; that a great earthquake should be, in which the sun should become black as sackcloth of hair, and the moon turn into blood; yea, the Eternal God hath declared that the great deep shall roll back into the north countries and that the land of Zion and the land of Jerusalem shall be joined together, as they were before they were divided in the days of Peleg. No wonder the mind starts at the sound of the last days.

—*Joseph Smith, Jr.,* "Inspired Prophetic Warnings" by Lundwall, p. 41-42, a. 1844

We read in the Scriptures of a time that is coming when there will be a howling among the merchants in Babylon, for men will not be found to buy their merchandise. This is in accordance with the prediction of John the Revelator. And the gold and the silver and the fine linen, etc., in Babylon will be of no avail. But before that time comes, we as a people must prepare for those events, that we may be able to live and sustain ourselves when in the midst of convulsions that by and by will overtake the nations of the earth and among others, this nation. The time that is spoken of is not very far distant.

—*John Taylor,* JD 21:33, April 9, 1879

JUDGMENTS TO BEGIN AT ZION

The judgments will begin at the house of God. We have to pass through some of these things, but it will only be a very little compared with the terrible destruction, the misery and suffering that will overtake the world who are doomed to suffer the wrath of God. It behooves us, as the Saints of God, to stand firm and faithful in the observance of His laws, that we may be worthy of His preserving care and blessing.

—*John Taylor,* JD 21:100, April 13, 1879

It is a false idea that the Saints will escape all the judgments, whilst the wicked suffer; for all flesh is subject to suffer, and "the righteous shall hardly escape;" still many of the Saints will escape, for the just shall live by faith; yet many of the righteous shall fall a prey to disease, to pestilence, etc., by reason of the weakness of the flesh, and yet be saved in the kingdom of God.   *—Joseph Smith, Jr.*, DHC 4:11, September 29, 1839

WARS AND RUMORS OF WAR

The time is soon coming when no man will have any peace but in Zion and her stakes.

I saw men hunting the lives of their own sons, and brother murdering brother, women killing their own daughters, and daughters seeking the lives of their mothers. I saw armies arrayed against armies. I saw blood, desolation, fires. The Son of Man has said that the mother shall be against the daughter, and the daughter against the mother. These things are at our doors. They will follow the Saints of God from city to city. Satan will rage, and the spirit of the devil is now enraged. I know not how soon these things will take place; but with a view of them, shall I cry peace? No! I will lift up my voice and testify of them.   *—Joseph Smith, Jr.*, DHC 3:391, July 2, 1839

War! Yes; war is one of the troubles that belong to the generation in which we live. . . . They are as sure to come to pass as that God lives. There is no power on earth, nor beneath the earth, nor anywhere else, that can stay the fulfillment of these things. And they are at our doors.
            —Wilford Woodruff, CR, p. 32, April, 1898

I fear that the time is coming . . . unless we can call the people of this world to repent of their sins and turn from the error of their ways, that the great war that has just passed will be an insignificant thing, as far as calamity is concerned, compared to that which is before us.
            —George Albert Smith, CR, p. 149, October, 1946

The world will soon be devastated with war and carnage, with plague and all the distresses that the Lord has promised unless they repent; but He has indicated that they will not repent, and distress must come.
            —George Albert Smith, CR, p. 36, April, 1937

By and by the nations will be broken up on account of their wickedness, the Latter-day Saints are not going to move upon them with their little army, they will destroy themselves with their wickedness and immorality. They will contend and quarrel one with another, state after state and nation after nation, until they are broken up, and thousands, tens of thousands and hundreds of thousands will undoubtedly come and seek protection at the hands of the servants of God.

—*Lorenzo Snow*, JD 14:309, January 14, 1872

KINGDOMS TO BE DESTROYED, THRONES CAST DOWN

This nation and other nations will be overthrown, not because of their virtue, but because of their corruption and iniquity. The time will come, for the prophecies will be fulfilled, when kingdoms will be destroyed, thrones cast down, and the powers of the earth shaken, and God's wrath will be kindled against the nations of the earth.

—*John Taylor*, JD 17:4, February 1, 1874

A terrible day of reckoning is approaching the nations of the earth; the Lord is coming out of His hiding place to vex the inhabitants thereof; and the destroyer of the Gentiles, as prophesied of, is already on his way. Already the monarchs of the earth are trembling from conspiracies among their own people. . . . Already have two of the Presidents of this Republic been laid low by the hands of the assassin; and the spirit of insubordination, misrule, lynching, and mobocracy of every kind is beginning to ride rampant through the land; already combinations are being entered into which are very ominous for the future prosperity, welfare and happiness of this great Republic. The volcanic fires of disordered and anarchical elements are beginning to manifest themselves and exhibit the internal forces that are at work among the turbulent and unthinking masses of the people. —*John Taylor*, JD 23:62, April 9, 1882

Why is it that thrones will be cast down, empires dissolved, nations destroyed, and confusion and distress cover all people, as the prophets have spoken? Because the Spirit of the Lord will be withdrawn from the nations in consequence of their wickedness, and they will be left to their own folly.

—*John Taylor*, JD 6:24, November 1, 1857

CRIMES AND WICKEDNESS TO INCREASE

The Lord is withdrawing His Spirit from the nations of the earth, and the power of the devil is gaining dominion over the children of men. See how crime is increasing. Fifty years ago . . . there was not one murder where there are a thousand today; there was not one whoredom where there are a thousand today; and so you may go through the whole black catalogue of crime. . . . What will the end be? Death, destruction, whirlwinds, pestilence, famine and the judgments of God will be poured out upon the wicked; for the Lord has withheld these judgments until the world is fully warned.

—Wilford Woodruff, JD 22:175, June 12, 1881

The wickedness committed today in the Christian world in twenty-four hours is greater than would have been committed in a hundred years at the ratio of fifty years ago. And the spirit of wickedness is increasing, so that I no longer wonder that God Almighty will turn rivers into blood; I do not wonder that He will open the seals and pour out the plagues and sink great Babylon, as the angel saw, like a millstone cast into the sea, to rise no more for ever. I can see that it requires just such plagues and judgments to cleanse the earth, that it may cease to groan under the wickedness and abomination in which the Christian world welters today.   *—Wilford Woodruff*, JD 14:3, January 1, 1871

Consider for a moment, brethren, the fulfillment of the words of the prophet; for we behold that darkness covers the earth, and gross darkness the minds of the inhabitants thereof—that crimes of every description are increasing among men—vices of great enormity are practiced—the rising generation growing up in the fullness of pride and arrogance—the aged losing every sense of conviction and seemingly banishing every thought of a day of retribution—intemperance, immorality, extravagance, pride, blindness of heart, idolatry, the loss of natural affection; the love of this world, and indifference toward the things of eternity increasing among those who profess a belief in the religion of heaven, and infidelity spreading itself in consequence of the same—men giving themselves up to commit acts of the foulest kind and deeds of the blackest dye, blaspheming, defrauding, blasting the reputation of neighbors, stealing, robbing, murdering; advocating error and opposing the truth, forsaking the covenant of heaven, and denying the faith of Jesus—and in the midst of all this, the day of the Lord fast approaching when none except those who have won the wedding garment will be permitted to eat and drink in the presence of the Bridegroom, the Prince of Peace! *—Joseph Smith, Jr.*, DHC 2:5, January 22, 1834

WILL THE UNITED STATES ESCAPE THESE JUDGMENTS?

When I contemplate the condition of our nation and see that wickedness and abominations are increasing, so much so that the whole heavens groan and weep over the abominations of this nation and the nations of the earth, I ask myself the question, can the American nation escape? The answer comes, No; its destruction, as well as the destruction of the world, is sure; just as sure as the Lord cut off and destroyed the two great and prosperous nations that once inhabited this continent of North and South America, because of their wickedness, so will He them destroy, and sooner or later they will reap the fruits of their own wicked acts and be numbered among the past.

I cannot help it; I would to God they would repent, that their eyes might be opened to see their condition; but the devil has power over them; he rules the children of men, he holds Babylon in his own hand and leads the people whithersoever he will. There are changes awaiting us, they are even nigh at our very doors, and I know it by the revelations of Jesus Christ.
—Wilford Woodruff, JD 21:301, August 1, 1880

I prophesy, in the name of the Lord God of Israel, unless the United States redress the wrongs committed upon the Saints in the State of Missouri and punish the crimes committed by officers, that in a few years the government will be utterly overthrown and wasted, and there will not be so much as a potsherd left for their wickedness in permitting the murder of men, women and children, and the wholesale plunder and extermination of thousands of her citizens to go unpunished, thereby perpetrating a foul and corroding blot upon the fair fame of this great republic, the very thought of which would have caused the high-minded and patriotic framers of the Constitution of the United States to hide their faces with shame.
—Joseph Smith, Jr., "Historical Record," p. 514, May 18, 1843

You will see worse things than that [the Civil War] for God will lay His hand upon this nation, and they will feel it more terribly than ever they have done before; there will be more bloodshed, more ruin, more devastation than ever they have seen before. . . . There is yet to come a sound of war, trouble and distress, in which brother will be arrayed against brother, father against son, son against father, a scene of desolation and destruction that will permeate our land until it will be a vexation to hear the report thereof. —*John Taylor*, JD 20:318, October 6, 1879

And now I am prepared to say by the authority of Jesus Christ, that not many years shall pass away before the United States shall present such a scene of *bloodshed* as has not a parallel in the history of our nation; pestilence, hail, famine, and earthquake will sweep the wicked of this generation from off the face of the land, to open and prepare the way for the return of the lost tribes of Israel from the north country.
—*Joseph Smith, Jr.*, DHC 1:315, January 4, 1833

Do I not know that a nation like that in which we live, a nation which is blessed with the freest, the most enlightened and magnificent government in the world today, with privileges which would exalt people to heaven if lived up to—do I not know that if they do not live up to them, but violate them and trample them under their feet, and discard the sacred principles of liberty by which we ought to be governed—do I not know that their punishment will be commensurate with the enlightment which they possess? I do. And I know—I cannot help but know—that there are a great many more afflictions yet awaiting this nation.
—*John Taylor*, JD 22:141, July 3, 1881

THE CONSTITUTION TO HANG BY A THREAD

How long will it be before the words of the Prophet Joseph will be fulfilled? He said if the Constitution of the United States were saved at all it must be done by this people. It will not be many years before these words come to pass.
—*Brigham Young*, JD 12:204, April 8, 1868

When the Constitution of the United States hangs, as it were, upon a single thread, they will have to call for the "Mormon" elders to save it from utter destruction; and they will step forth and do it.   —*Brigham Young*, JD 2:182, February 18, 1855

When the people shall have torn to shreds the Constitution of the United States, the elders of Israel will be found holding it up to the nations of the earth and proclaiming liberty and equal rights to all men and extending the hand of fellowship to the oppressed of all nations. This is part of the program and as long as we do what is right and fear God He will help us and stand by us under all circumstances.

—John Taylor, JD 21:8, August 31, 1879

THE VERY ELECT MAY BE DECEIVED

We are living in perilous times. The Scriptures are being fulfilled, and as it appears to me this is the particular time when, if it were possible, the very elect would be deceived. It is remarkable how easy it is for those who desire to advance their financial interests in the world to find a reason for setting aside the plain teachings of the Lord with reference to our lives. And it is strange to me how many people fall into the habit of listening to those who say things that are contrary to the revealed will of our Heavenly Father. . . .

I fear that the Latter-day Saints, in many cases, are blinded by their own vanity, by their desire to be what the world is; and we have been told in such plain language by our Heavenly Father that we cannot live as the world lives and enjoy His Spirit.

—George Albert Smith, CR, p. 30, April, 1929

We are living in a period of time when upheavals in the world are daily, almost momentary. Marvelous things are occurring. The map of the world is changing. The order of government is being modified. In our own nation we are almost helpless before the problems that confront us, notwithstanding we are probably the wealthiest and most powerful nation in all the world. What is our difficulty, brethren and sisters? It is that men refuse to hear what the Lord has said. They refuse to pay attention to His wise counsel. They absolutely neglect to give credence to the things that He teaches us, and *He will not be mocked.* He gives us the advice and the counsel that we need, but He will not compel us. But if we refuse we lose our opportunity and it passes away from us, in many cases to return again no more forever.

—George Albert Smith, CR, p. 71, April, 1933

THE ESTABLISHMENT OF THE KINGDOM OF GOD

In making a brief summary of . . . the means to be employed for the establishment of the kingdom of God, we find the following:—

First.—That it will be not only a spiritual kingdom, but a temporal and literal one also.

Second.—That if it is the kingdom of heaven, it must be revealed from the heavens.

Third.—That a standard is to be lifted up, by the Lord, to the nations.

Fourth.—That an angel is to come with the everlasting gospel, which is to be proclaimed to every nation, kindred, people, and tongue; that it is to be the same as the ancient one, and that the same powers and blessings will attend it.

Fifth.—That not only will the ancient gospel be preached, but there will accompany it a declaration of judgment to the nations.

Sixth.—That there will be a literal Zion, or gathering of the Saints to Zion, as well as a gathering of the Jews to Jerusalem.

Seventh.—That when this has taken place, the Spirit of God will be withdrawn from the nations, and they will war with and destroy each other.

Eighth.—That judgments will also overtake them, from the Lord, plague, pestilence, famine, etc.

Ninth.—That the nations, having lost the Spirit of God, will assemble to fight against the Lord's people, being full of the spirit of unrighteousness and opposed to the rule and government of God.

Tenth.—That when they do, the Lord will come and fight against them Himself, overthrow their armies, assert His own right, rule the nations with a rod of iron, root the wicked out of the earth, and take possession of His own kingdom. . . . He will issue His commands, and they must be obeyed; and if the nations of the earth observe not His laws, "they will have no rain." And they will be taught by more forcible means than moral suasion that they are dependent upon God; for the Lord will demand obedience, and the Scriptures say, time and again, that the wicked shall be rooted out of the land, and the righteous and the meek shall inherit the earth.

—*John Taylor,* GG, p. 103-104, August, 1852

THE ANGELS OF DESTRUCTION

What is the matter with the world today? What has created this change that we see coming over the world? Why these terrible earthquakes, tornadoes, and judgments? What is the meaning of all these mighty events that are taking place? The meaning is, these angels that have been held for many years in the temple of our God have got their liberty to go out and commence their mission and their work in the earth, and they are here today in the earth.

—Wilford Woodruff, MS 56:643, July 15, 1894

I want to bear testimony to this congregation and to the heavens and the earth that the day is come when those angels are privileged to go forth and commence their work. They are laboring in the United States of America; they are laboring among the nations of the earth; and they will continue. These things are at our doors, and neither you nor I can hinder them. We need not marvel or wonder at anything that is transpiring in the earth. *—Wilford Woodruff*, MS 58:738-739, October 4, 1896

God has held the angels of destruction for many years, lest they should reap down the wheat with the tares. But I want to tell you now that those angels have left the portals of heaven, and they stand over this people and this nation now and are hovering over the earth waiting to pour out the judgments. And from this very day they shall be poured out.

—Wilford Woodruff, YW 5:512, June, 1894

The destroying angels have got their sharp sickles in their hands, and they are going to reap the earth. Everything that has been spoken by the prophets under the inspiration of the Holy Ghost will come to pass in the generation in which we live. Do not forget it. *—Wilford Woodruff*, CR, p. 90, April, 1898

THE SIGNS IN THE HEAVENS

A personage appeared to me and showed me the great scenes that should take place in the last days. One scene after another passed before me. I saw the sun darkened; I saw the moon become as blood; I saw the stars fall from heaven; I saw seven golden lamps set in the heavens, representing the various dispensations of God to man—a sign that would appear before the coming of Christ. —*Wilford Woodruff*, JD 22:332-333, October 8, 1881

We see that perilous times have come, as was testified of. We may look, then, with most perfect assurance, for the fulfillment of all those things that have been written and with more confidence than ever before, lift up our eyes to the luminary of day and say in our hearts, Soon thou wilt veil thy blushing face. He that said "Let there be light," and there was light, hath spoken this word. And again, Thou moon, thou dimmer light, thou luminary of night, shalt turn to blood.

> —*Joseph Smith, Jr.*, DHC 3:291, March 25, 1839

All these judgments will come. The seals will be opened; plague will follow plague; the sun and the moon will be darkened; and the unbelief of the world will make no difference to all these things coming to pass.

> —*Wilford Woodruff*, JD 22:175-176, June 12, 1881

GOD RULES OVER ALL

If your eyes were opened, you would see His hand in the midst of the nations of the earth in the setting up of governments and in the downfall of kingdoms—in the revolutions, wars, famine, distress, and wretchedness among the inhabitants of the earth. In these manifestations you would discern the foosteps of the Almighty just as plainly as you may see the footsteps of your children upon the soft earth.

> —*Brigham Young*, JD 7:144, May 22, 1859

The earth is groaning under corruption, oppression, tyranny and bloodshed; and God is coming out of His hiding place, as He said He would do, to vex the nations of the earth.

> —*Joseph Smith, Jr.*, DHC 5:65, July 15, 1842

The Latter-day Saints . . . believe that great judgments are coming upon the world because of iniquity; they firmly believe in the statements of the Holy Scriptures, that calamities will befall the nations, as signs of the coming of Christ to judgment. They believe that God rules in the fire, the earthquake, the tidal wave, the volcanic eruption, and the storm. Him they recognize as the Master and Ruler of nature and her laws and freely acknowledge His hand in all things. We believe that His judgments are poured out to bring mankind to a sense of His power and His purposes, that they may repent of their sins and prepare themselves for the second coming of Christ to reign in righteousness upon the earth. —*Joseph F. Smith,* IE 9:653, June, 1906

In relation to events that will yet take place and the kind of trials, troubles, and sufferings which we shall have to cope with, it is to me a matter of very little moment; these things are in the hands of God, He dictates the affairs of the human family and directs and controls our affairs; and the great thing that we, as a people, have to do is to seek after and cleave unto our God, to be in close affinity with Him and to seek for His guidance and His blessing and Holy Spirit to lead and guide us in the right path. Then it matters not what it is nor who it is that we have to contend with, God will give us strength according to our day. —*John Taylor,* JD 18:281, November 5, 1876

HOW TO ESCAPE THESE JUDGMENTS

I will proceed to tell you what the Lord requires of all people, high and low, rich and poor, male and female, ministers and people, professors of religion and non-professors, in order that they may enjoy the Holy Spirit of God to a fullness and escape the judgments of God, which are almost ready to burst upon the nations of the earth. Repent of all your sins and be baptized in water for the remission of them, in the name of the Father, and of the Son, and of the Holy Ghost, and receive the ordinance of the laying on of hands of him who is ordained and sealed unto this power, that ye may receive the Holy Spirit of God; and this is according to the Holy Scriptures and the Book of Mormon and the only way that man can enter into the celestial kingdom. —*Joseph Smith, Jr.,* DHC 1:314, January 4, 1833

Can you tell me where the people are who will be shielded and protected from these great calamities and judgments which are even now at our door? I'll tell you. The priesthood of God who honor their priesthood and who are worthy of their blessings are the only ones who shall have this safety and protection. They are the only mortal beings. No other people have a right to be shielded from these judgments. They are at our very doors; not even this people will escape them entirely.

> —*Wilford Woodruff*, YWJ 5:512, June, 1894

The Lord has provided, when the days of trouble come upon the nations, a place for you and me, and we will be preserved as Noah was preserved, not in an ark, but we will be preserved by going into these principles of union by which we can accomplish the work of the Lord and surround ourselves with those things that will preserve us from the difficulties that are now coming upon the world, the judgments of the Lord.

> —*Lorenzo Snow*, CR, p. 4, October, 1900

We firmly believe that Zion—which is the pure in heart— shall escape, if she observes to do all things whatsoever God has commanded; but, in the opposite event, even Zion will be visited "with sore affliction, with pestilence, with plague, with sword, with vengeance, and with devouring fire." (Doc. and Cov. 97:26) All this that her people may be taught to walk in the light of truth and in the way of the God of their salvation.

> —*Joseph F. Smith*, IE 9:653, June, 1906

CHAPTER XXIII

The Gathering of Israel

ISRAEL TO GATHER HOME

ONE OF the most important points in the faith of the Church of the Latter-day Saints, through the fullness of the everlasting gospel is the gathering of Israel (of whom the Lamanites constitute a part)—that happy time when Jacob shall go up to the House of the Lord, to worship Him in spirit and in truth, to live in holiness; when the Lord will restore His judges as at first and His counselors as at the beginning; when every man may sit under his own vine and fig tree, and there will be none to molest or make afraid; when He will turn to them a pure language, and the earth will be filled with sacred knowledge, as the waters cover the great deep; when it shall no longer be said, the Lord lives that brought up the children of Israel out of the land of Egypt, but the Lord lives that brought up the children of Israel from the land of the north and from all the lands whither He has driven them. That day is one, all important to all men.   —*Joseph Smith, Jr.,* DHC 2:357, January 6, 1836

The Jews will be moved upon by and by, and they will return to the land of their fathers, and they will rebuild Jerusalem. These Lamanites here will receive the gospel of Christ in fulfillment of the revelations of God. The prophets which have been shut up in the north country with the nine and a half tribes led away by Shalmanezer, King of Assyria, thousands of years ago, will come in remembrance before God; they will smite the rocks and mountains of ice will flow down before them, and those long lost tribes will come forth in your day and mine, if we live a few years longer, and they will be crowned under the hands of the children of Ephraim—the elders of Israel who dwell in the land of Zion.   —*Wilford Woodruff,* JD 18:38, June 27, 1875

By and by the Jews will be gathered to the land of their fathers, and the ten tribes, who wandered into the north, will be gathered home, and the blood of Ephraim, the second son of

Joseph, who was sold into Egypt, will be gathered from among the Gentiles, and the Gentiles who will receive and adhere to the principles of the gospel will be adopted and initiated into the family of Father Abraham, and Jesus will reign over His own and Satan will reign over his own.

—*Brigham Young*, JD 12:38, April 14, 1867

THE PURPOSE OF THE GATHERING

It was the design of the councils of heaven before the world was that the principles and laws of the priesthood should be predicated upon the gathering of the people in every age of the world. Jesus did everything to gather the people, and they would not be gathered, and He therefore poured out curses upon them. Ordinances instituted in the heavens before the foundation of the world, in the priesthood, for the salvation of men, are not to be altered or changed. All must be saved on the same principles.

It is for the same purpose that God gathers together His people in the last days, to build unto the Lord a House to prepare them for the ordinances and endowments, washings and anointings, etc.   —*Joseph Smith, Jr.*, DHC 5:423-424, June 11, 1843

We have been gathered to the valleys of these mountains for the express purpose of purifying ourselves, that we may become polished stones in the temple of God. . . . We are here for the purpose of establishing the kingdom of God on the earth. To be prepared for this work it has been necessary to gather us out from the nations and countries of the world, for if we had remained in those lands we could not have received the ordinances of the Holy Priesthood of the Son of God, which are necessary for the perfection of the Saints preparatory to His coming.   —*Brigham Young*, JD 12:161, February 16, 1868

We have been gathered together from among the nations the earth in order that God might have a people who would obey His law; who had been baptized into one baptism; who had all been partakers of the same spirit, and who had . . . learned to approach the Lord in the proper way; for there is a medium opened out whereby man can approach God and learn His mind and will.   —*John Taylor*, JD 24:200, June 18, 1883

What was the object of gathering the Jews or the people of God in any age of the world? . . . The main object was to build unto the Lord a house whereby He could reveal unto His people the ordinances of His house and the glories of His kingdom and teach the people the way of salvation; for there are certain ordinances and principles that, when they are taught and practiced, must be done in a place or house built for that purpose.

—Joseph Smith, Jr., DHC 5:423, June 11, 1843

The gathering of this people is as necessary to be observed by believers as faith, repentance, baptism, or any other ordinance. It is an essential part of the gospel of this dispensation, as much so as the necessity of building an ark by Noah, for his deliverance, was a part of the gospel of his dispensation.

—Joseph F. Smith, JD 19:192, September 30, 1877

THE RETURN OF THE JEWS TO JERUSALEM

The Lord has decreed that the Jews should be gathered from all the Gentile nations where they have been driven, into their own land, in fulfillment of the words of Moses their law-giver. . . . O house of Judah, . . . it is true that after you return and gather your nation home and rebuild your city and temple, that the Gentiles may gather together their armies to go against you to battle, to take you a prey and to take you as a spoil, which they will do, for the words of your prophets must be fulfilled; but when this affliction comes, the living God that led Moses through the wilderness will deliver you, and your Shiloh will come and stand in your midst and will fight your battles; and you will know Him, and the afflictions of the Jews will be at an end, while the destruction of the Gentiles will be so great that it will take the whole House of Israel who are gathered about Jerusalem seven months to bury the dead of their enemies, and the weapons of war will last them seven years for fuel, so that they need not go to any forest for wood. These are tremendous sayings—who can bear them? Nevertheless they are true and will be fulfilled, according to the sayings of Ezekiel, Zechariah, and other prophets. Though the heavens and the earth pass away, not one jot or tittle will fall unfulfilled.

—Wilford Woodruff, "Wilford Woodruff" by Cowley, p. 509-510, February 22, 1879

The Jews have got to gather to their own land in unbelief. They will go and rebuild Jerusalem and their temple. They will take their gold and silver from the nations and will gather to the Holy Land, and when they have done this and rebuilt their city the Gentiles . . . will go up against Jerusalem to battle and to take a spoil and a prey; and then, when they have taken one-half of Jerusalem captive and distressed the Jews for the last time on the earth, their Great Deliverer, Shiloh, will come. They do not believe in Jesus of Nazareth now, nor ever will until He comes and sets His foot on Mount Olivet and it cleaves in twain, one part going towards the east and the other towards the west. Then, when they behold the wounds in His hands and in His feet, they will say, "Where did you get them?" And he will reply, "I am Jesus of Nazareth, King of the Jews, your Shiloh, Him whom you crucified." Then, for the first time will the eyes of Judah be opened. They will remain in unbelief until that day. This is one of the events that will transpire in the latter day.
                    —*Wilford Woodruff*, JD 15:277-278, January 12, 1873

The time is not far distant when the rich men among the Jews may be called upon to use their abundant wealth to gather the dispersed of Judah and purchase the ancient dwelling places of their fathers in and about Jerusalem and rebuild the holy city and temple. For the fullness of the Gentiles has come in, and the Lord has decreed that the Jews should be gathered from all the Gentile nations where they have been driven, into their own land, in fulfillment of the words of Moses their law-giver.
                    —*Wilford Woodruff*, MS 41:244, April 21, 1879

When the Gentiles reject the gospel it will be taken from them and go to the House of Israel, to that long suffering people that are now scattered abroad through all the nations upon the earth, and they will be gathered home by thousands, and by hundreds of thousands, and they will rebuild Jerusalem their ancient city and make it more glorious than at the beginning, and they will have a leader in Israel with them, a man that is full of the power of God and the gift of the Holy Ghost; but they are held now from this work, only because the fullness of the Gentiles has not yet come in.
                    Wilford Woodruff, JD 2:200, February 25, 1855

The gospel has been offered to the Gentiles for almost a hundred years. The time is rapidly approaching when it will be preached to the Jews, who are to gather in from their long dispersion, upon the land of their inheritance. Palestine is to be inhabited as a city without walls and the glory of the Lord will rest upon His chosen people, when they repent of their sins and turn unto Him.   —*George Albert Smith*, MS 83:2, January, 1921

You cannot convert a Jew. They will never believe in Jesus Christ until He comes to them in Jerusalem, until these fleeing Jews take back their gold and silver to Jerusalem and rebuild their city and temple, and they will do this as the Lord lives. Then the Gentiles will say, "Come let us go to Jerusalem; let us go up and spoil her. The Jews have taken our gold and silver from the nations of the earth—come let us go up and fight against Jerusalem." Then will the prophecies that are before you be fulfilled.   —*Wilford Woodruff*, JD 22:173, June 12, 1881

By the authority of the Holy Priesthood of God that has again been restored to the earth, and by the ministration under the direction of the Prophet of God, apostles of the Lord Jesus Christ have been to the Holy Land and have dedicated that country for the return of the Jews; and we believe that in due time of the Lord they shall be in the favor of God again.
        —*Heber J. Grant*, CR, p. 124, April, 1921

The time has at last arrived when the God of Abraham, of Isaac, and of Jacob has set His hand again the second time to recover the remnants of His people . . . and with them to bring in the fullness of the Gentiles and establish that covenant with them, which was promised when their sins should be taken away.
        —*Joseph Smith, Jr.*, DHC 1:313, January 4, 1833

THE GATHERING TO THE AMERICAN ZION

There will be a literal Zion, or gathering of the Saints to Zion, as well as a gathering of the Jews to Jerusalem.
        —*John Taylor*, GG, p. 104, Published August, 1852

When God commanded Noah to build an ark, he saved himself with his family by gathering into it. When the angels commanded Lot to flee to Zoar, he saved himself by fleeing thence.

. . . And as the Lord has said by the ancient prophets, in the last days there should be deliverance in Jerusalem and in Mount Zion; and by the mouth of the modern prophet, seer, and revelator, [He] pointed out the location of Zion and commanded the Saints among the Gentiles to gather thereunto and build it up, while the Jews gather to Jerusalem. The safety of the Saints depends as much upon their fulfilling His commandments as the safety of Noah and Lot depended upon their obedience to the commands of God in their day and generation.
                        —Wilford Woodruff, MS 6:3, June 15, 1845

The principle of gathering has been preached for the past thirty-seven years. . . . We have gathered here for the purpose of establishing Zion, which, according to the Scriptures, must be before the gospel can be sent to the Jews.
                        —Wilford Woodruff, JD 18:221, August 13, 1876

From whence has come this congregation; from whence have come the Saints gathered together throughout these mountains of Israel? They have been gathered from every nation as far as the gospel has been preached. We have been gathered together by the power of the gospel. Yet, . . . if we had preached until we were as old as Methuselah, we could never have gotten men and women to leave their homes if they had not been moved upon by the Holy Ghost.
                        —Wilford Woodruff, JD 22:344, October 23, 1881

Why is it that you are here today? And what brought you here? Because the keys of the gathering of Israel from the four quarters of the earth have been committed to Joseph Smith, and he has conferred those keys upon others that the gathering of Israel may be accomplished, and in due time the same thing will be performed to the tribes in the land of the north. It is on this account, and through the unlocking of this principle and through these means, that you are brought together as you are today.   —John Taylor, JD 25:179, May 18, 1884

Our mission is to preach the gospel and then to gather the people who embrace it. And why? That there might be a nucleus formed, a people gathered who would be under the inspiration of the Almighty and who would be willing to listen to the voice of God, a people who would receive and obey His word when it was made known to them. And this people in their gathered condition are called Zion, or the pure in heart.

—*John Taylor*, JD 23:262, October 8, 1882

The Spirit of the Lord Jesus Christ is a gathering spirit. Its tendency is to gather the virtuous and good, the honest and meek of the earth, and, in fine, the Saints of God. The time has come when the Lord is determined to fulfill His purposes. . . .

The Lord does not require every soul to leave his home as soon as he believes. Some may be wanted to go to the isles of the sea, and some to go north, and some south. But He does require them to hearken to counsel and follow that course which He points out, whether to gather or stay to do some other work. . . .

Perhaps some of you are ready to ask, "Cannot the Lord save us as well where we are as to gather together?" Yes, if the Lord says so. But if He commands us to come out and gather together, He will not save us by staying at home.

—*Brigham Young*, DHC 6:12 September 9, 1843

THE RESTORATION OF THE TEN TRIBES

All that God has said with regard to the ten tribes of Israel, strange as it may appear, will come to pass. They will, as has been said concerning them, smite the rock, and the mountains of ice will flow before them, and a great highway will be cast up, and their enemies will become a prey to them; and their records and other choice treasures they will bring with them to Zion. These things are as true as God lives.

—*Wilford Woodruff*, JD 21:301, August 1, 1880

Again, here are the ten tribes of Israel; we know nothing about them only what the Lord has said by His prophets. There are prophets among them, and by and by they will come along, and they will smite the rocks, and the mountains of ice will flow down at their presence, and a highway will be cast up before them, and they will come to Zion, receive their endowments and be crowned under the hands of the children of Ephraim, and there are persons before me in this assembly today who will assist to give them their endowments.

—*Wilford Woodruff*, JD 4:231-232, February 22, 1857

CHAPTER XXIV

The Building Up of Zion

LATTER-DAY ZION TO BE BUILT

THE BUILDING up of Zion is a cause that has interested the people of God in every age; it is a theme upon which prophets, priests and kings have dwelt with peculiar delight; they have looked forward with joyful anticipation to the day in which we live; and fired with heavenly and joyful anticipations they have sung and written and prophesied of this our day; but they died without the sight; we are the favored people that God has made choice of to bring about the Latter-day glory.
—*Joseph Smith, Jr.*, DHC 4:609-610, May 2, 1842

We will build up our Zion after the pattern that God will show us, and we will be governed by His law and submit to His authority and be governed by the Holy Priesthood and by the word and will of God. And then when the time comes that these calamities we read of shall overtake the earth, those that are prepared will have the power of translation, as they had in former times, and the city will be translated. And Zion that is on the earth will rise, and the Zion above will descend, as we are told, and we will meet and fall on each other's necks and embrace and kiss each other. And thus the purposes of God to a certain extent will then be fulfilled.
—*John Taylor*, JD 21:253, March 21, 1880

In regard to the building up of Zion, it has to be done by the counsel of Jehovah, by the revelations of heaven; and we should feel to say, "If the Lord go not with us, carry us not up hence."
—*Joseph Smith, Jr.*, DHC 5:65, July 15, 1842

And now, I ask, how righteousness and truth are going to sweep the earth as with a flood? I will answer. Men and angels are going to be co-workers in bringing to pass this great work, and Zion is to be prepared, even a new Jerusalem, for the elect that are to be gathered from the four quarters of the earth and

to be established an holy city, for the tabernacle of the Lord
shall be with them. . . .

There is a New Jerusalem to be established on this continent,
and also Jerusalem shall be rebuilt on the eastern continent.

—Joseph Smith, Jr., DHC 2:260; 262, November, 1835

WHAT IS ZION?

The Zion of God. What does it mean? The pure in heart
in the first place. In the second place those who are governed
by the law of God—the pure in heart who are governed by the
law of God.   *—John Taylor*, JD 26:109, October 20, 1881

And what is Zion? In one sense Zion is the pure in heart.
But is there a land that ever will be called Zion? Yes, brethren.
What land is it? It is the land that the Lord gave to Jacob, who
bequeathed it to his son Joseph and his posterity, and they inhabit it, and that land is North and South America. That is Zion
as to land, as to territory, and location. The children of Zion
have not yet much in their possession, but their territory is North
and South America to begin with. As to the spirit of Zion, it
is in the hearts of the Saints, of those who love and serve the
Lord with all their might, mind, and strength.

—Brigham Young, JD 2:253, April 6, 1855

WHERE IS ZION?

This American continent will be Zion; for it is so spoken of
by the prophets. Jerusalem will be rebuilt and will be the place
of gathering, and the tribe of Judah will gather there; but this
continent of America is the land of Zion.

—Brigham Young, JD 5:4, July 5, 1857

*The whole of America is Zion itself from north to south and
is described by the prophets, who declare that it is the Zion
where the mountain of the Lord should be and that it should
be in the center of the land.* When elders shall take up and examine the old prophecies in the Bible, they will see it.

—Joseph Smith, Jr., DHC 6:318-319, April 8, 1844

The land of Joseph is the land of Zion; and it takes North
and South America to make the land of Joseph.

—Brigham Young, JD 6:296, August 15, 1852

Where is Zion? Where the organization of the Church of God is. And may it dwell spiritually in every heart; and may we so live as to always enjoy the Spirit of Zion!
—*Brigham Young*, JD 8:205, October 8, 1860

This land, North and South America, is the land of Zion; it is a choice land—the land that was given by promise from old father Jacob to his grandson and his descendants, the land on which the Zion of God should be established in the latter days.
—*Wilford Woodruff*, JD 15:279, January 12, 1873

Zion will extend, eventually, all over this earth. There will be no nook or corner upon the earth but what will be in Zion. It will all be Zion.
—*Brigham Young*, JD 9:138, July 28, 1861

BUILDING UP THE CENTER STAKE OF ZION

This is the land of Zion; but we are not yet prepared to go and establish the Center Stake of Zion. The Lord tried this in the first place. He called the people together to the place where the New Jerusalem and the great temple will be built and where He will prepare for the City of Enoch. And He gave revelation after revelation; but the people could not abide them, and the Church was scattered and peeled, and the people hunted from place to place till, finally, they were driven into the mountains, and here we are. Now, it is for you and me to prepare to return back again . . . to build up the Center Stake of Zion.
—*Brigham Young*, JD 11:324, February 10, 1867

When will Zion be redeemed? . . . Just as soon as the Latter-day Saints are ready and prepared to return to Independence, Jackson County, in the State of Missouri, North America, just so soon will the voice of the Lord be heard, "Arise now, Israel, and make your way to the Center Stake of Zion."
—*Brigham Young*, JD 9:137, July 28, 1861

If we don't go back there [to Jackson County] our sons and daughters will; and a great temple will be built upon the consecrated spot and a great many more besides that.
—*Brigham Young*, JD 6:296, August 15, 1852

Now the time is fast approaching when a large portion of the people that I am now addressing will go back to Jackson County. . . . A large portion of the Latter-day Saints that now dwell in these valleys will go back to Jackson County to build a holy city to the Lord, as was decreed by Jehovah and revealed through Joseph Smith. . . .

We will not take possession of the land of Zion by force. If we should do, it would turn out to us as it did with the people who were upon the land of Zion when this revelation was given. As the Lord here tells us, there are only two ways in which we can come in possession of that land. One way is by purchase, "and if by purchase, behold you are blessed." The other way is by blood, "and if by blood, as you are forbidden to shed blood, lo, your enemies are upon you, and ye shall be scouraged from city to city and from synagogue to synagogue, and but few shall stand to receive an inheritance." These are the words of God.

—*Lorenzo Snow,* CR, p. 61-62, October, 1900

You will see the day; if you live properly, observe the Word of Wisdom and do that which is required you will go back to Jackson County, many of you whom I am addressing this afternoon. I am sure of this. . . .

We are not going tomorrow, nor next day, this week or next week; but we are going, and there are many—hundreds and hundreds within the sound of my voice—that will live to go back to Jackson County and build a holy temple to the Lord our God.

—*Lorenzo Snow,* CR, p. 14;64, April, 1898

THE WONDERS OF THE LATTER-DAY ZION

When Zion is established in her beauty and honor and glory, the kings and princes of the earth will come, in order that they may get information and teach the same to their people. They will come as they came to learn the wisdom of Solomon.

—*John Taylor,* JD 6:169, January 17, 1858

The day will come when it will be said of our children as the old prophets have prophesied, that such and such a one was born in Zion. It will be considered a great blessing and one of the greatest honors that could have been inherited by our children to have been born in Zion among the people of God.

—*John Taylor,* JD 22:317, October 19, 1881

We are here to build up the Church of God, the Zion of
God, and the kingdom of God and to be on hand to do whatever
God requires—first to purge ourselves from all iniquity, from
covetousness and evil of every kind: to forsake sin of every sort,
cultivate the Spirit of God, and help to build up His kingdom;
to beautify Zion and have pleasant habitations, and pleasant
gardens and orchards, until Zion shall be the most beautiful
place there is on the earth. Already Zion is attracting the attention of the people of the world. I have all kinds of people calling
on me—lords, admirals, senators, members of the House of Representatives, members of the Parliament of England, of the Reich-
stag of Germany, and the Chamber of Deputies of France—all
classes come and they say, "You have a most beautiful place
here!" Why, yes. And by and by the kings of the earth will come
to gaze upon the glory of Zion, and we are here to build it up
under the instruction of God our Heavenly Father. Zion shall
yet become the praise and the glory of the whole earth.
                              —John Taylor, JD 24:201, June 18, 1883

Jesus will never receive the Zion of God unless its people
are united according to celestial law, for all who go into the
presence of God have to go there by this law. Enoch had to
practice this law, and we shall have to do the same if we are
ever accepted of God as he was. It has been promised that the
New Jerusalem will be built up in our day and generation, and
it will have to be done by the United Order of Zion and according to celestial law. —Wilford Woodruff, JD 17:250, October 9, 1874

We will have to go to work and get the gold out of the mountains to lay down, if we ever walk in streets paved with gold.
The angels that now walk in their golden streets, and they have
the tree of life within their paradise, had to obtain that gold
and put it there. When we have streets paved with gold, we
will have placed it there ourselves. When we enjoy a Zion in
its beauty and glory, it will be when we have built it. If we
enjoy the Zion that we now anticipate, it will be after we redeem
and prepare it.   —Brigham Young, JD 8:354, March 3, 1861

When we have faith to understand that He must dictate and
that we must be perfectly submissive to Him, then we shall begin
to rapidly collect the intelligence that is bestowed upon the na-

tions, for all this intelligence belongs to Zion. All the knowledge, wisdom, power, and glory that have been bestowed upon the nations of the earth, from the days of Adam till now, must be gathered home to Zion. —*Brigham Young*, JD 8:279, June 3, 1860

I will say to the Latter-day Saints that we have been more blessed in this land than has any other dispensation or generation of men. The Lord has been at work for the last three hundred years preparing this land, with a government and constitution which would guarantee equal rights and privileges to the inhabitants thereof, in the midst of which He could establish His kingdom. The kingdom is established, the work of God is manifest in the earth, the Saints have come up here into the valleys of the mountains, and they are erecting the house of God in the tops thereof, for the nations to flow unto. A standard of truth has been lifted up to the people, and from the commencement of this work the Latter-day Saints have been fulfilling that flood of revelation and prophecy which was given formerly concerning this great work in the last days. I rejoice in this and also because we have every reason to expect a continuation of these blessings unto Zion. —*Wilford Woodruff*, JD 15:10, April 6, 1872

ZION A PLACE OF SAFETY

Let me go to the Zion, which God hath prepared
As the hope of the Saints—as rest and reward,
Where the fountains and rivers in purity flow,
And the earth teems with plenty—oh! there let me go.
—*John Taylor*, MS 12:208, July 1, 1850

He [the Lord] has told us in great plainness that the world will be in distress, that there will be warfare from one end of the world to the other, that the wicked shall slay the wicked and that peace shall be taken from the earth. And He has said, too, that the only place where there will be safety will be in Zion. Will we make this Zion? Will we keep it to be Zion, because Zion means the pure in heart?
—*George Albert Smith*, CR, p. 99, October, 1941

The time will yet come when he that will not take up his sword to fight against his neighbor must needs flee to Zion for safety. All those who are not fond of blood and carnage and desolation, if they want to be preserved will flee to Zion. Have we not got to have a Zion for them to flee to? Yes. And what is Zion? The pure in heart. We want to organize in such a way and advocate and maintain such correct principles, that they will become the admiration of all honest men, who will feel that they can be protected and find safety and an asylum in Zion.

—John Taylor, JD 20:266, March 2, 1879

LATTER-DAY ZION TO ASCEND

In regard to the work in which we are engaged. Will it go on? I tell you it will. Will Zion be built up? I tell you it will. Will the Zion that Enoch built up, descend? It most assuredly will, and this that we are building up will ascend, and the two will meet and the peoples thereof will fall on each other's necks and embrace each other. So says the word of God to us.

—John Taylor, JD 26:37, December 14, 1884

We have no business here other than to build up and establish the Zion of God. It must be done according to the will and law of God, after that pattern and order by which Enoch built up and perfected the former-day Zion, which was taken away to heaven, hence the saying went abroad that Zion had fled. By and by it will come back again, and as Enoch prepared his people to be worthy of translation, so we, through our faithfulness, must prepare ourselves to meet Zion from above when it shall return to earth and to abide the brightness and glory of its coming.   *—Brigham Young,* JD 18:356, April 6, 1877

When Zion descends from above, Zion will also ascend from beneath, and be prepared to associate with those from above. The people will be so perfected and purified, ennobled, exalted, and dignified in their feelings and so truly humble and most worthy, virtuous and intelligent that they will be fit, when caught up, to associate with that Zion that shall come down from God out of heaven.   *—John Taylor,* JD 10:147, April 6, 1863

WOE TO THOSE WHO FIGHT AGAINST ZION!

God is with us and will be with us and will sustain us, and no power on earth or in hell can stop the progress of this work;

for it is onward according to the decree of Almighty God and will be from this time henceforth and forever. And as the prophets have said, so say I, woe to those men and woe to that nation or to those nations that lift up their hands against Zion, for God will destroy them. I prophesy that in the name of the Lord God of hosts. And He will be with His Israel and will sustain His people and bring them off victorious; and if faithful to the end we shall obtain thrones, principalities, powers, dominions, exaltations, and eternal lives in the kingdom of our God.

—John Taylor, JD 23:180, July 24, 1882

There is a change coming over the world with regard to Zion. The day is coming when the world will say, "Let us not go up to battle against Zion, for the inhabitants of Zion are terrible; wherefore we cannot stand." They will find that the power of God is with this people.

—Wilford Woodruff, MS 56:644, July 15, 1894

CHAPTER XXV

The Second Coming of Christ

CHRIST TO REIGN ON EARTH

THE LORD JESUS CHRIST is coming to reign on earth. The world may say that He delays His coming until the end of the earth. But they know neither the thoughts nor the ways of the Lord. The Lord will not delay His coming because of their unbelief, and the signs both in heaven and earth indicate that it is near. The fig trees are leafing in sight of all the nations of the earth, and if they had the Spirit of God they could see and understand them.   —*Wilford Woodruff*, JD 16:35, April 7, 1873

Do you know that it is the eleventh hour of the reign of Satan on the earth? Jesus is coming to reign, and all you who fear and tremble because of your enemies, cease to fear them and learn to fear to offend God, fear to transgress His laws, fear to do any evil to your brother, or to any being upon the earth, and do not fear Satan and his power, nor those who have only power to slay the body, for God will preserve His people.
—*Brigham Young*, JD 10:250, October 6, 1863

We believe that Jesus Christ will descend from heaven to earth again even as He ascended into heaven. "Behold, He cometh with clouds, and every eye shall see Him, and they also which pierced Him: and all kindreds of the earth shall wail because of Him." He will come to receive His own and rule and reign King of Nations as He does King of Saints; "For He must reign, till He hath put all enemies under His feet. The last enemy that shall be destroyed is death." He will banish sin from the earth and its dreadful consequences, tears shall be wiped from every eye and there shall be nothing to hurt or destroy in all God's holy mountain.
—*Brigham Young*, JD 11:123-124, June 18, 1865

You and I live in a day in which the Lord our God has set His hand for the last time, to gather out the righteous and to prepare a people to reign on this earth,—a people who will be purified by good works, who will abide the faith of the living God and be ready to meet the Bridegroom when He comes to reign over the earth, even Jesus Christ . . . and be prepared for that glorious event—the coming of the Son of Man—which I believe will not be at any great distant day.

—Joseph F. Smith, MS 36:220, March 29, 1874

WHEN WILL THE SECOND COMING TAKE PLACE?

No man knows the day or the hour when Christ will come, yet the generation has been pointed out by Jesus Himself . . . The Savior, when speaking to His disciples of His second coming and the establishment of His kingdom on the earth, said the Jews should be scattered and trodden under foot until the times of the Gentiles were fulfilled. But, said He, when you see light breaking forth among the Gentiles, referring to the preaching of His gospel amongst them; when you see salvation offered to the Gentiles, and the Jews—the seed of Israel—passed by, the last first and the first last; when you see this you may know that the time of my second coming is at hand as surely as you know that summer is nigh when the fig tree puts forth its leaves; and when these things commence that generation shall not pass away until all are fulfilled.

We are living in the dispensation and generation to which Jesus referred. *—Wilford Woodruff, JD 14:5, January 1, 1871*

I will take the responsibility upon myself to prophesy in the name of the Lord, that Christ will not come this year . . . and I also prophesy, in the name of the Lord, that Christ will not come in forty years; and if God ever spoke by my mouth, He will not come in that length of time. Brethren, when you go home, write this down, that it may be remembered.

Jesus Christ never did reveal to any man the precise time that He would come. Go and read the Scriptures, and you cannot find anything that specifies the exact hour He would come; and all that say so are false teachers.

—Joseph Smith, Jr., DHC 6:254, March 10, 1844

There are those of the rising generation who shall not taste death till Christ comes.

I was once praying earnestly upon this subject, and a voice said unto me, "My son, if thou livest until thou art eighty-five years of age, thou shalt see the face of the Son of Man," I was left to draw my own conclusions concerning this; and I took the liberty to conclude that if I did live to that time, He would make His appearance. But I do not say whether He will make His appearance or I shall go where He is. I prophesy in the name of the Lord God, and let it be written—the Son of God will not come in the clouds of heaven till I am eighty-five years old.

—Joseph Smith, Jr., DHC 5:336, April 6, 1843

I believe there are many children now living in the mountains of Israel who will never taste death, that is, they will dwell on the earth at the coming of the Lord Jesus Christ. I will acknowledge that there is a great deal to be done, and the Lord has not revealed to man the day or the hour, but He has revealed the generation; and the fig trees are now putting forth their leaves in the eyes of all the nations, indicating the near approach of the second coming of the Son of Man. It is my faith that hundreds and thousands of the children that have been given to us will be alive in the flesh when Christ comes in the clouds of heaven in power and great glory.

—Wilford Woodruff, JD 18:37, June 27, 1875

Many of these young men and maidens that are here today will, in my opinion, if they are faithful, stand in the flesh when Christ comes in the clouds of heaven. . . . Therefore, I say, our young men cannot begin too quickly to qualify themselves by treasuring up wisdom and calling upon God and getting the Holy Priesthood; for they have got to stand in holy places while these judgments are poured out upon the earth.

—Wilford Woodruff, MS 51:595-596, July 29, 1889

Many of you will be living in Jackson County and there you will be assisting in building the temple; and if you will not have seen the Lord Jesus at that time you may expect Him very soon, to see Him, to eat and drink with Him, to shake hands with Him and to invite Him to your houses as He was invited when He was here before. I am saying things to you now of which I know something of the truth of them.

—Lorenzo Snow, DN, June 15, 1901

I will say here that I shall not live to see it, you may not live to see it; but these thousands of Latter-day Saint children that belong to the Sabbath schools, I believe many of them will stand in the flesh when the Lord Jesus Christ visits the Zion of God here in the mountains of Israel.

—*Wilford Woodruff*, CR, p. 57, April, 1898

When they got through the Prophet said: "Brethren I have been very much edified and instructed in your testimonies here tonight, but I want to say to you before the Lord, that you know no more concerning the destinies of the Church and kingdom than a babe upon its mother's lap. You don't comprehend it." I was rather surprised. He said: "It is only a little handful of priesthood you see here tonight, but this Church will fill North and South America—it will fill the world." Among other things he said; "It will fill the Rocky Mountains. There will be tens of thousands of Latter-day Saints who will be gathered in the Rocky Mountains, and there they will open the door for the establishing of the gospel among the Lamanites, who will receive the gospel and their endowments and the blessings of God. This people will go into the Rocky Mountains; they will there build temples to the Most High. They will raise up a posterity there, and the Latter-day Saints who dwell in these mountains will stand in the flesh until the coming of the Son of Man. The Son of Man will come to them while in the Rocky Mountains."

—*Wilford Woodruff*, CR, p. 57, April 8, 1898

EVENTS TO PRECEDE THE SECOND COMING

I will prophesy that the signs of the coming of the Son of man are already commenced. One pestilence will desolate after another. We shall soon have war and bloodshed. The moon will be turned into blood. I testify of these things and that the coming of the Son of Man is nigh, even at your doors.

—*Joseph Smith, Jr.*, DHC 3:390, July 2, 1839

We are approaching some of the most tremendous judgments God ever poured out upon the world. You watch the signs of the times, the sign of the coming of the Son of Man. They are beginning to be manifest both in heaven and on earth. As has been told by the apostles, Christ will not come until these things come to pass. Jerusalem has got to be rebuilt. The temple has got to be built. Judah has got to be gathered and the House of Israel. And the Gentiles will go forth to battle against Judah and Jerusalem before the coming of the Son of Man. These things have been revealed by the prophets; they will have their fulfillment.   —*Wilford Woodruff*, MS 52:740, October 6, 1890

Judah must return, Jerusalem must be rebuilt, and the temple, and water come out from under the temple, and the waters of the Dead Sea be healed. It will take some time to rebuild the walls of the city and the temple, etc.; and all this must be done before the Son of Man will make His appearance. There will be wars and rumors of wars, signs in the heavens above and on the earth beneath, the sun turned into darkness and the moon to blood, earthquakes in divers places, the seas heaving beyond their bounds; then will appear one grand sign of the Son of Man in heaven. But what will the world do? They will say it is a planet, a comet, etc. But the Son of Man will come as the sign of the coming of the Son of Man, which will be as the light of morning cometh out of the east.
                              —*Joseph Smith, Jr.*, DHC 5:336-337, April 6, 1843

I have asked of the Lord concerning His coming; and while asking the Lord, He gave a sign and said, "In the days of Noah I set a bow in the heavens as a sign and token that in any year that the bow should be seen the Lord would not come; but there should be seed time and harvest during that year; but whenever you see the bow withdrawn, it shall be a token that there shall be famine, pestilence, and great distress among the nations, and that the coming of the Messiah is not far distant."
                              —*Joseph Smith, Jr.*, DHC 6:254, March 10, 1844

He will never come until the Jews are gathered home and have rebuilt their temple and city and the Gentiles have gone up there to battle against them. He will never come until His Saints have built up Zion and have fulfilled the revelations which have been spoken concerning it. He will never come until the Gentiles throughout the whole Christian world have been warned by the inspired elders of Israel.
                              —*Wilford Woodruff*, JD 18:111, September 12, 1875

The gospel of Jesus Christ must be preached to all nations for a witness and a testimony; for a sign that the day has come, the set time for the Lord to redeem Zion and gather Israel, preparatory to the coming of the Son of Man.

—Brigham Young, JD 3:91, August 8, 1852

The hour and day of the Lord's future advent is withheld from the knowledge of both men and angels; yet the signs, so definitely specified as harbingers of His coming, are multiplying apace. The prevailing unrest among men and nations, the fury of the elements, widespread destruction by land and sea, the frequency and intensity of volcanic and earthquake disturbances —all tell to the well-tuned and listening ear that the gladsome yet terrible day of the Lord is nigh—aye, even at the doors!

A sure indication of the great event, as specified by the Lord Himself, was and is that the gospel of the kingdom shall be preached in all the world. The missionary service of the Church of Jesus Christ of Latter-day Saints attests the progressive fulfillment of this prediction.

—Heber J. Grant, MS 91:34, January, 1929

THE FUTURE MISSION OF JESUS CHRIST

There is something also to be looked to in the future. The Son of God has again to figure in the grand drama of the world. He has been here once and "In His humiliation His judgment was taken away.". . . Jesus accomplished what He was sent to do, and feeling satisfied of this, when He was about to leave the earth He said He had finished the work His Father gave Him to do. But there was another work, another event that was to transpire in the latter days, when He should not be led as a lamb to the slaughter or be like a sheep before the shearers; when He would not act in that state of humiliation and quiescence, but when He will go forth as a man of war and tread down the people in His anger and trample them in His fury, when blood should be on His garments and the day of vengeance in His heart, when He would rule the nations with an iron rod and break them to pieces like a potter's vessel. . . .

When He comes again He comes to take vengeance on the ungodly and to bring deliverance unto His Saints; "For the day of vengeance," it is said, "is in mine heart, and the year of my redeemed is come." (Isaiah 63:4) It behooves us to be made well aware which class we belong to, that if we are not already among the redeemed we may immediately join that society, that when the Son of God shall come the second time with all the holy angels with Him, arrayed in power and great glory to take vengeance on them that know not God and obey not the gospel, or when He shall come in flaming fire, we shall be among that number who shall be ready to meet Him with gladness in our hearts and hail Him as our great Deliverer and friend.

—*John Taylor*, JD 10:115-116, February 22, 1863

Jesus has been upon the earth a great many more times than you are aware of. When Jesus makes His next appearance upon the earth, but few of this Church and kingdom will be prepared to receive Him and see Him face to face and converse with Him; but He will come to His temple. Will He remain and dwell upon the earth a thousand years, without returning? He will come here and return to His mansion where He dwells with His Father, and come again to the earth, and again return to His Father, according to my understanding. Then angels will come and begin to resurrect the dead, and the Savior will also raise the dead, and they will receive the keys of the resurrection and will begin to assist in that work. Will the wicked know of it? They will know just as much about that as they now know about "Mormonism" and no more.

—*Brigham Young*, JD 7:142, May 22, 1859

CHAPTER XXVI

The Millennium

THE MILLENNIUM IS DAWNING

W E ARE living at the commencement of the Millennium and
near the close of the 6,000th year of the world's history.
Tremendous events await this generation.
—*Wilford Woodruff*, JD 25:10, January 6, 1884

The Millennium is dawning upon the world, we are at the
end of the sixth thousand years; and the great day of rest, the
Millennium of which the Lord has spoken, will soon dawn and
the Savior will come in the clouds of heaven to reign over His
people on the earth one thousand years.
—*Wilford Woodruff*, JD 18:113, September 12, 1875

The Millennium consists in this—every heart in the Church
and kingdom of God being united in one; the kingdom increasing
to the overcoming of everything opposed to the economy of
heaven and Satan being bound and having a seal set upon him.
All things else will be as they are now, we shall eat, drink, and
wear clothing.   —*Brigham Young*, JD 1:203, April 6, 1852

THE WORK OF THE MILLENNIUM

The great work of the Millennium shall be the work in the
temples for the redemption of the dead; and then we hope to
enjoy the benefits of revelation through the Urim and Thummim,
or by such means as the Lord may reveal concerning those for
whom the work shall be done, so that we may not work by
chance, or by faith alone, without knowledge, but with the
actual knowledge revealed unto us.
—*Joseph F. Smith*, IE 5:146-147, December, 1901

Do you know what the Millennium is for and what work
will have to be done during that period? Suppose the Christian
world were now one in heart, faith, sentiment and works, so
that the Lord could commence the Millennium in power and
glory, do you know what would be done? Would you sit and

sing yourselves away to everlasting bliss? No, I reckon not. I think there is a work to be done then which the whole world seems determined we shall not do. What is it? To build temples. . . . What are we going to do in these temples? . . . In these temples we will officiate in the ordinances of the gospel of Jesus Christ for our friends, for no man can enter the kingdom of God without being born of the water and of the Spirit. We will officiate for those who are in the spirit world, where Jesus went to preach to the spirits, as Peter has written in the third chapter, verses 18, 19, 20, of his first epistle.

We will also have hands laid on us for the reception of the Holy Ghost; and then we will receive the washing and anointings for and in their behalf, preparatory to their becoming heirs of God and joint-heirs with Christ.

—*Brigham Young*, JD 13:329, April 24, 1870

In the Millennium, when the kingdom of God is established on the earth in power, glory and perfection, and the reign of wickedness that has so long prevailed is subdued, the Saints of God will have the privilege of building their temples and of entering into them, becoming, as it were, pillars in the temples of God, and they will officiate for their dead. Then we will see our friends come up and perhaps some that we have been acquainted with here. If we ask who will stand at the head of the resurrection in this last dispensation, the answer is—Joseph Smith, Junior, the Prophet of God. He is the man who will be resurrected and receive the keys of the resurrection, and he will seal this authority upon others, and they will hunt up their friends and resurrect them when they shall have been officiated for and bring them up. And we will have revelations to know our forefathers clear back to Father Adam and Mother Eve, and we will enter into the temples of God and officiate for them. Then man will be sealed to man until the chain is made perfect back to Adam, so that there will be a perfect chain of priesthood from Adam to the winding-up scene.

This will be the work of the Latter-day Saints in the Millennium.   —*Brigham Young*, JD 15:138-139, August 24, 1872

Satan will be bound for a thousand years, and during that time we will have a chance to build temples and to be baptized for the dead and to do a work pertaining to the world that has been, as well as to the world that now is, and to operate under the direction of the Almighty in bringing to pass those designs which He contemplated from the foundation of the world.

—John Taylor, JD 24:235, a. June 1883

When the Savior comes, a thousand years will be devoted to this work of redemption; and temples will appear all over this land of Joseph,—North and South America—and also in Europe and elsewhere; and all the descendants of Shem, Ham, and Japheth, who received not the gospel in the flesh, must be officiated for in the temples of God, before the Savior can present the kingdom to the Father, saying, "It is finished."

—Wilford Woodruff, JD 19:230 September 16, 1877

We have at least one thousand years, counting three hundred and sixty-five days, five hours, forty-eight minutes, and fifty-seven seconds to the year, if I recollect right, wherein the elders of Israel will enter holy temples of the Lord and officiate for just such persons as you and me, that have done the work we were called to do in our day, whether it was much or little. There will be hundreds of thousands of the sons of Jacob to administer in these temples for you and me.

—Brigham Young, JD 6:308, April 8, 1853

RELIGIOUS FREEDOM DURING THE MILLENNIUM

If the Latter-day Saints think, when the kingdom of God is established on the earth, that all the inhabitants of the earth will join the Church called Latter-day Saints, they are egregiously mistaken. I presume there will be as many sects and parties then as now. Still, when the kingdom of God triumphs, every knee shall bow and every tongue confess that Jesus is the Christ, to the glory of the Father. Even the Jews will do it then; but will the Jews and Gentiles be obliged to belong to the Church of Jesus Christ of Latter-day Saints? No; not by any means. . . . They will cease their persecutions against the Church of Jesus Christ, and they will be willing to acknowledge that the Lord is God and that Jesus is the Savior of the world.

—Brigham Young, JD 11:275, December 23, 1866

In the Millennium men will have the privilege of being Presbyterians, Methodists, or Infidels, but they will not have the

privilege of treating the name and character of Deity as they
have done heretofore. No, but every knee shall bow and every
tongue confess to the glory of God the Father that Jesus is the
Christic.   *—Brigham Young, JD 12:274, August 16, 1868*

The order of society will be as it is when Christ comes to
reign a thousand years; there will be every sort of sect and party
and every individual following what he supposes to be the best
in religion and in everything else, similar to what it is now.
                           —Brigham Young, JD 2:316, July 8, 1855

When Jesus comes to rule and reign King of Nations as He
now does King of Saints, the veil of the covering will be taken
from all nations, that all flesh may see His glory together, but
that will not make them all Saints. Seeing the Lord does not
make a man a Saint, seeing an angel does not make a man a
Saint by any means. A man may see the finger of the Lord and
not thereby become a Saint; the veil of the covering may be
taken from before the nations and all flesh see His glory together,
and at the same time declare they will not serve Him.
                           —Brigham Young, JD 2:316, July 8, 1855

When all nations are so subdued to Jesus that every knee
shall bow and every tongue shall confess, there will still be
millions on the earth who will not believe in Him; but they will
be obliged to acknowledge His kingly government.
                           —Brigham Young, JD 7:142, May 22, 1859

When the kingdom of God is fully set up and established on
the face of the earth and takes the pre-eminence over all other
nations and kingdoms, it will protect the people in the enjoyment of all their rights, no matter what they believe, what they
profess, or what they worship. If they wish to worship a god
of their own workmanship, instead of the true and living God,
all right, if they will mind their own business and let other
people alone. . . .
As observed by one of the speakers this morning, that kingdom grows out of the Church of Jesus Christ of Latter-day Saints,
but it is not the Church, for a man may be a legislator in that
body which will issue laws to sustain the inhabitants of the earth
in their individual rights and still not belong to the Church of
Jesus Christ at all.   *—Brigham Young, JD 2:310, July 8, 1855*

CHRIST TO RULE OVER THE EARTH

It startles men when they hear the elders of Israel tell about the kingdoms of this world becoming the kingdom of our God and His Christ. They say it is treason for men to teach that the kingdom Daniel saw is going to be set up and bear rule over the whole earth. Is it treason for God Almighty to govern the earth? Who made it? God, did He not? Who made you? God, if you have any Eternal Father. Well, whose right is it to rule and reign over you and the earth? It does not belong to the devil, nor to men. It has never been given to men yet: it has never been given to the nations. It belongs solely to God and He is coming to rule and reign over it.

—*Wilford Woodruff*, JD 13:164, December 12, 1869

The world has had a fair trial for six thousand years; the Lord will try the seventh thousand Himself. . . . Satan will be bound, and the works of darkness destroyed; righteousness will be put to the line and judgment to the plummet, and "he that fears the Lord will alone be exalted in that day."

—*Joseph Smith, Jr.*, DHC 5:64-65, July 15, 1842

In relation to the kingdom of God, what is it? Is it a spiritual kingdom? Yes. Is it a temporal kingdom? Yes. Does it relate to the spiritual affairs of men? Yes. Does it relate to the temporal of men? Yes. And when it is fully established upon the earth, the will of God will be done upon the earth precisely as it is done in heaven.

—*John Taylor*, JD 6:23, November 1, 1857

When the will of God is done on earth as it is in heaven, the priesthood will be the only legitimate ruling power under the whole heavens; for every other power and influence will be subject to it. When the Millennium . . . is introduced all potentates, powers, and authorities—every man, woman, and child will be in subjection to the kingdom of God; they will be under the power and dominion of the priesthood of God; then the will of God will be done on the earth as it is done in heaven.

—*John Taylor*, JD 6:25, November 1, 1857

The government of the Almighty has always been very dissimilar to the governments of men, whether we refer to His religious government or to the government of nations. The government of God has always tended to promote peace, unity, harmony, strength and happiness; while that of man has been productive of confusion, disorder, weakness, and misery.

—Joseph Smith, Jr., DHC 5:61, July 15, 1842

Christ and the resurrected Saints will reign over the earth during the thousand years. They will probably not dwell upon the earth, but will visit it when they please or when it is necessary to govern it. There will be wicked men on the earth during the thousand years. The heathen nations who will not come up to worship will be visited with the judgments of God and must eventually be destroyed from the earth.

—Joseph Smith, Jr., DHC 5:212, December 30, 1842

We believe this Church will prepare the way for the coming of Christ to reign as King and that this Church will then develop into the kingdom of God, which all Christians pray will come; that the will of God may be done on earth as it is in heaven. We believe in the full and free agency of man and that when that kingdom is established there will be perfect liberty on earth, civil, political and religious.

—Wilford Woodruff, MS 52:162, February 11, 1890

It has been the design of Jehovah, from the commencement of the world, and is His purpose now to regulate the affairs of the world in His own time, to stand as a head of the universe and take the reins of government in His own hand. When that is done judgment will be administered in righteousness; anarchy and confusion will be destroyed, and "nations will learn war no more." It is for want of this great governing principle that all this confusion has existed; "for it is not in man that walketh, to direct his steps;" this we have fully shown.

—Joseph Smith, Jr., DHC 5:63, July, 1842

CHAPTER XXVII

The Story of the Earth

THE EARTH'S POSITION IN THE GREAT PLAN

THIS EARTH is our home, it was framed expressly for the habitation of those who are faithful to God and who prove themselves worthy to inherit the earth when the Lord shall have sanctified, purified and glorified it and brought it back into His presence, from which it fell far into space. . . . When the earth was framed and brought into existence and man was placed upon it, it was near the throne of our Father in heaven. And when man fell . . . the earth fell into space and took up its abode in this planetary system, and the sun became our light. When the Lord said—"Let there be light," there was light, for the earth was brought near the sun that it might reflect upon it so as to give us light by day and the moon to give us light by night. This is the glory the earth came from, and when it is glorified it will return again into the presence of the Father, and it will dwell there, and these intelligent beings that I am looking at, if they live worthy of it, will dwell upon this earth.
—*Brigham Young*, JD 17:143, July 19, 1874

We begin to find out that we are earthly, we came from the earth, our feelings cling to it, when we die we return to the earth, and when we come forth in the resurrection it will be as immortal beings to dwell on a celestial earth; it will be renovated and so will the people that dwell on it. It is a natural desire for us to possess the earth, and for this thousands of persons have been laid low, in order to gain possession of it, but the Savior has promised that the meek shall inherit it.
—*John Taylor*, MS 16:49, October 8, 1853

When sin and iniquity are driven from the earth, and the spirits that now float in this atmosphere are driven into the place prepared for them; and when the earth is sanctified from the effects of the fall, and baptized, cleansed, and purified by fire, and returns to its paradisiacal state, and has become like a sea of glass, a Urim and Thummim; when all this is done, and the

Savior has presented the earth to His Father, and it is placed in the cluster of the celestial kingdoms, and the Son and all His faithful brethren and sisters have received the welcome plaudit— "Enter ye into the joy of your Lord," and the Savior is crowned, then and not till then will the Saints receive their everlasting inheritances. I want you to understand this.

—Brigham Young, JD 17:117, June 28, 1874

The earth is very good in and of itself and has abided a celestial law, consequently we should not despise it nor desire to leave it, but rather desire and strive to obey the same law that the earth abides and abide it as honorably as does the earth.

—Brigham Young, JD 2:302-303, June 3, 1855

CONCERNING THE CREATION OF THE EARTH

All this vast creation was produced from element in its unorganized state; the mountains, rivers, seas, valleys, plains, and the animal, vegetable, and mineral kingdoms beneath and around us, all speaking forth the wonderful works of the Great God. Shall I say that the seeds of vegetables were planted here by the Characters that formed and built this world—that the seeds of every plant composing the vegetable kingdom were brought from another world? This would be news to many of you. Who brought them here? . . . It was some Being who had power to frame this earth with its seas, valleys, mountains, and rivers and cause it to teem with vegetable and animal life.

—Brigham Young, JD 7:285, October 9, 1859

It is true that the earth was organized by three distinct characters, namely, Elohim, Jehovah, and Michael, these three forming a quorum, as in all heavenly bodies and in organizing element, perfectly represented in the Deity as Father, Son, and Holy Ghost.   *—Brigham Young, JD 1:51, April 9, 1852*

Though we have it in history that our Father Adam was made of the dust of this earth and that he knew nothing about his God previous to being made here, yet it is not so; and when we learn the truth we shall see and understand that he helped to make this world and was the chief manager in that operation.

He was the person who brought the animals and the seeds from other planets to this world and brought a wife with him and stayed here. You may read and believe what you please as to what is found written in the Bible. Adam was made from the dust of an earth, but not from the dust of this earth. He was made as you and I are made, and no person was ever made upon any other principle.

Do you not suppose that he was acquainted with his associates, who came and helped to make this earth? Yes, they were just as familiar with each other as we are with our children and parents. —*Brigham Young*, JD 3:319, April 20, 1856

Things upon the earth, so far as they have not been perverted by wickedness, are typical of things in heaven. Heaven was the prototype of this beautiful creation when it came from the hand of the Creator and was pronounced "good."
—*Joseph F. Smith*, JD 23:175, June 18, 1882

THE EARTH TO RECEIVE ITS PARADISIACAL GLORY

The Lord never created this world at random; He has never done any of His work at random. The earth was created for certain purposes; and one of these purposes was its final redemption and the establishment of His government and kingdom upon it in the latter days, to prepare it for the reign of the Lord Jesus Christ, whose right it is to reign. That set time has come, that dispensation is before us, we are living in the midst of it.
—*Wilford Woodruff*, JD 15:8, April 6, 1872

The Prophet asked the Lord whether there would ever be a time when the earth should rest; and the Lord answered that in the dispensation of the fullness of times the earth would fill the measure of its days and then it would rest from wickedness and abominations, for in that day He would establish His kingdom upon it, to be thrown down no more forever.
—*Wilford Woodruff*, JD 17:245, October 9, 1874

Who placed the dark stain of sin upon this fair creation? Man. Who but man shall remove the foul blot and restore all things to their primeval purity and innocence? But can he do this independently of heavenly aid? He can not. To aid him in this work heavenly grace is here; heavenly wisdom, power, and help are here, and God's laws and ordinances are here; the angels and spirits of just men made perfect are here; Jesus Christ, our Great High Priest, with prophets, apostles, and Saints, ancient and modern, are here to help man in the great work of sanctifying himself and the earth for final glorification in its paradisiacal state. All this will be accomplished through the law of the Holy Priesthood.   —*Brigham Young*, JD 10:301, June 4, 1864

THE EARTH TO BE CELESTIALIZED

This earth, after wading through all the corruptions of men, being cursed for his sake and not permitted to shed forth its full lustre and glory, must yet take its proper place in God's creations; be purified from that corruption under which it has groaned for ages and become a fit place for redeemed men, angels, and God to dwell upon.
                            —*John Taylor*, GG, p. 82, Published August, 1852

This earth is the property of our Heavenly Father. Some day it will be cleansed and purified by fire. All disease and sorrow will be banished from it and it will become the celestial kingdom.   —*George Albert Smith*, DNCS, June 17, 1944

This earth in its present condition and situation, is not a fit habitation for the sanctified; but it abides the law of its creation, has been baptized with water, will be baptized by fire and the Holy Ghost, and by-and-by will be prepared for the faithful to dwell upon.   —Brigham Young, JD 8:83, June 12, 1860

The earth, also, abideth the law and filleth the measure of its creation and though it shall die, it shall be resurrected in glory, a sanctified creation suitable for the residence of celestial beings. The elements will be burned and purified and be renewed; but not one atom of earth's organism will be lost; for that which is governed by law shall be preserved by law.
                                    —*Brigham Young*, LEJ 1:155, 1875

The earth will abide its creation and will be counted worthy of receiving the blessings designed for it, and it will ultimately roll back into the presence of God who formed it and established its mineral, vegetable, and animal kingdoms. These will all be retained upon the earth, come forth in the resurrection, and abide for ever and ever.   —*Brigham Young*, JD 8:8, March 4, 1860

When that time comes [the resurrection] this earth will have been cleansed by fire and purified, all sickness, sorrow and disease will have been banished, all those who dwell here will be glorified immortal beings, men, women and children, who will dwell in the presence of our Heavenly Father throughout the ages of eternity. —*George Albert Smith*, DNCS, March 17, 1945

God has said if we will honor Him and keep His commandments—if we will observe His laws He will fight our battles and destroy the wicked, and when the time comes He will come down in heaven—not from heaven—but He will bring heaven with Him —and this earth upon which we dwell will be the celestial kingdom. —*George Albert Smith*, CR, p. 49, October, 1942

The whole earth is the Lord's. The time will come when it will be translated and be filled with the spirit and power of God. The atmosphere around it will be the spirit of the Almighty. We will breathe that Spirit instead of the atmosphere that we now breathe. —*Lorenzo Snow*, MS 61:546, May 8, 1899

I suppose this is one of the lowest kingdoms that ever the Lord Almighty created and on that account is capable of becoming exalted to be one of the highest kingdoms that has ever had an exaltation in all the eternities. In proportion as it has been reduced so it will be exalted, with that portion of its inhabitants who in their humiliation have cleaved to righteousness and acknowledged God in all things.
—*Brigham Young*, JD 10:175, May 24, 1863

THE EARTH AS A BODY OF LIGHT

When we are in eternity we shall be on this earth, which will be brought into the immediate presence of the Father and the Son. We shall inhabit different mansions, and worlds will continue to be made, formed, and organized, and messengers from this earth will be sent to others. This earth will become a celestial body—be like a sea of glass, or like a Urim and Thummim; and when you wish to know anything you can look in this earth and see all the eternities of God. We shall make our home here and go on our missions as we do now, but at greater than railroad speed. —*Brigham Young*, JD 8:200, October 6, 1860

I remarked to my family and friends present that when the earth was sanctified and became like a sea of glass, it would be one great Urim and Thummim, and the Saints could look in it and see as they are seen.

—Joseph Smith, Jr. DHC 5:279, February 18, 1843

By and by the Lord will purify the earth, and it will become pure and holy, like a sea of glass; then it will take its place in the rank of the celestial ones and be recognized as celestial, but at the present time it is a dark, little speck in space.

—Brigham Young, JD 14:136, May 21, 1871

And this world . . . when it becomes celestialized, it will be like the sun. . . . It will not then be an opaque body as it now is, but it will be like the stars of the firmament, full of light and glory; it will be a body of light.

—Brigham Young, JD 7:163, June 5, 1859

BOOK FIVE

General Church Doctrines and Practices

> After all our endeavors to obtain wisdom from the best books, etc., there still remains an open fountain for all; "If any man lack wisdom let him ask of God." Let every Latter-day Saint constantly practice himself in the performance of every good word and work, to acknowledge God to be God, to be strict in keeping His laws and learning to love mercy, eschew evil and delight in constantly doing that which is pleasing to God. This is the only sure way to obtain influence with God and all good men.
>
> —BRIGHAM YOUNG
> JD 9:370
> August 31, 1862

CHAPTER XXVIII

The Godhead

THE NATURE OF THE GODHEAD

I HAVE ALWAYS declared God to be a distinct personage, Jesus Christ a separate and distinct personage from God the Father, and that the Holy Ghost was a distinct personage and a Spirit: and these three constitute three distinct personages and three Gods.
—*Joseph Smith, Jr.*, DHC 6:474, June 16, 1844

The personality of the Godhead is an absolute doctrine of the Church regarding which there can be no doubt or controversy. The Father, the Son and the Holy Ghost are three separate and distinct personages; the first two with glorified tabernacles of flesh and bone, the third a personage of spirit. If this fact is never lost sight of, there will be no difficulty in explaining any passage of Scripture bearing on this subject.

But there is a *oneness* in the Godhead as well as a distinctness of personality. This oneness is emphasized in the sayings and writings of prophets and apostles in order to guard against the erroneous idea that these three may be distinct and independent deities and rivals for our worship. The stress laid upon this unity by the Bible has led to the error, so prevalent in the sectarian denominations, that this is a unity of personality—that there is only one personage, manifesting Himself in three different ways. This error must be carefully guarded against.
—*Joseph F. Smith*, IE 4:228, January, 1901

The teachers of the day say that the Father is God, the Son is God, and the Holy Ghost is God, and they are all in one body and one God. . . . If I were to testify that the Christian world were wrong on this point, my testimony would be true.

Peter and Stephen testify that they saw the Son of Man standing on the right hand of God. Any person that had seen the heavens opened knows that there are three personages in the heavens who hold the keys of power, and one presides over all.
—*Joseph Smith, Jr.*, DHC 5:426, June 11, 1843

"And that I am in the Father, and the Father in me, and the Father and I are one."

I do not apprehend that any intelligent person will construe these words to mean that Jesus and His Father are one person, but merely that they are one in knowledge, in truth, in wisdom, in understanding, and in purpose; just as the Lord Jesus Himself admonished His disciples to be one with Him, and to be in Him, that He might be in them. It is in this sense that I understand this language and not as it is construed by some people, that Christ and His Father are one person. I declare to you that they are not one person, but they are two persons, two bodies, separate and apart, and as distinct as are my father and son within the sound of my voice.   —*Joseph F. Smith*, IE 11:382, March, 1908

I now see before me beings who are in the image of these heavenly personages who are enthroned in glory and crowned with eternal lives, in the very image of those beings who organized the earth and its fullness and who constitute the Godhead.   —*Brigham Young*, JD 9:246, March 23, 1862

The God of heaven, whom we worship, is represented as the Father, the Son, and the Holy Ghost. The Father and Son have tabernacles, and they created man after their own image. But the Holy Ghost is a spirit and a witness and a testimony of the Father and the Son. This Holy Ghost and witness are promised unto all men who will obey the law of the gospel, which God has revealed to the human family.
                              —*Wilford Woodruff*, MS 48:802, October 26, 1886

We believe God to be a person. We believe absolutely that we are made in the image of God. We believe that Jesus Christ was actually the Son of His Father, as I am the son of my father, and as you are of your father, and we believe they are personages.
                              —*Heber J. Grant*, DNCS, September 3, 1938

The thing I want to impress upon you is that God is real, a person of flesh and bones, the same as you are and I am. Christ is the same, but the Holy Ghost is a person of spirit.
                              —*Joseph F. Smith*, Logan Journal, March 14, 1911

We believe in one God, one Mediator and one Holy Ghost. We cannot believe for a moment that God is destitute of body, parts, passions or attributes. Attributes can be made manifest only through an organized personage. All attributes are couched in and are the results of organized existence.

—Brigham Young, JD 10:192, May 31, 1863

A. ELOHIM, GOD THE FATHER

GOD IS THE FATHER OF OUR SPIRITS

I want to tell you, each and every one of you, that you are well acquainted with God our Heavenly Father, or the great Elohim. You are all well acquainted with Him, for there is not a soul of you but what has lived in His house and dwelt with Him year after year; and yet you are seeking to become acquainted with Him, when the fact is, you have merely forgotten what you did know. . . .

There is not a person here today but what is a son or a daughter of that Being. In the spirit world their spirits were first begotten and brought forth, and they lived there with their parents for ages before they came here. This, perhaps, is hard for many to believe, but it is the greatest nonsense in the world not to believe it. If you do not believe it, cease to call Him Father; and when you pray, pray to some other character.

—Brigham Young, JD 4:216, February 8, 1857

We consider that God is Father of the spirits of all flesh, not only of those that fear Him, but of those who do not fear Him, and who disobey His laws. He is the Father of the spirits of all.

—John Taylor, JD 21:14, February 8, 1880

Man is the offspring of God. . . . We are as much the children of this great Being as we are the children of our mortal progenitors. We are flesh of His flesh, bone of His bone, and the same fluid that circulates in our bodies, called blood, once circulated in His veins as it does in ours. As the seeds of grains, vegetables and fruits produce their kind, so man is in the image of God.   *—Brigham Young, JD 9:283, February 23, 1862*

We are the children of God. He is the Father of our spirits. We have not come from some lower form of life, but God is the Father of our spirits, and we belong to the royal family, because He is our Father.   *—George Albert Smith, CR, p. 125, April, 1946*

We are the children of God our Heavenly Father. And is God our Father? The Scriptures say so. But what of the rest of the world—say of this nation and all other nations—what of them? Whose children are they? They are also the children of our Heavenly Father, and He is interested in their welfare as He is in ours; and as a kind and beneficent father towards His children, He has been seeking from generation to generation to promote the welfare, the happiness, and the exaltation of the human family.   —*John Taylor*, JD 24:125, April 8, 1883

What is our relationship to God? . . . The position that we stand in to Him is that of a son. Adam is the father of our bodies, and God is the father of our spirits.
                    —*John Taylor*, GG, p. 30, Published August, 1852

We are the offspring of our Father in heaven, and we possess in our spiritual organizations the same capabilities, powers and faculties that our Father possesses, although in an infantile state.   —*Lorenzo Snow*, DWN 20:597, January 14, 1872

If any of us could now see the God we are striving to serve— if we could see our Father who dwells in the heavens, we should learn that we are as well acquainted with Him as we are with our earthly father; and He would be as familiar to us in the expression of His countenance and we should be ready to embrace Him and fall upon His neck and kiss Him, if we had the privilege. And still we, unless the vision of the Spirit is opened to us, know nothing about God. You know much about Him, if you did but realize it. And there is no other one item that will so astound you, when your eyes are opened in eternity, as to think that you were so stupid in the body.
                    —*Brigham Young*, JD 8:30, March 25, 1860

MAN IS FORMED IN THE IMAGE OF ELOHIM

In the first place, I wish to go back to the beginning—to the morn of creation. There is the starting point for us to look to, in order to understand and be fully acquainted with the mind, purposes and decrees of the Great Elohim, who sits in yonder heavens as He did at the creation of this world. . . .
What sort of a being was God in the beginning? . . .

God Himself was once as we are now and is an exalted man and sits enthroned in yonder heavens! That is the great secret. If the veil were rent today and the great God who holds this world in its orbit and who upholds all worlds and all things by His power was to make Himself visible,—I say, if you were to see Him today, you would see Him like a man in form—like yourselves in all the person, image, and very form as a man; for Adam was created in the very fashion, image and likeness of God and received instruction from, and walked, talked and conversed with Him, as one man talks and communes with another. . . .

It is the first principle of the gospel to know for a certainty the character of God and to know that we may converse with Him as one man converses with another and that He was once a man like us; yea, that God Himself, the Father of us all, dwelt on an earth, the same as Jesus Christ Himself did; and I will show it from the Bible.

—*Joseph Smith, Jr.*, TS August 15, 1844, Delivered April, 1844

We believe absolutely that God is a personal being. We believe in the Scripture which states that we were made in the image of God—"in the image of God created He him, male, and female created He them." Therefore, the God that all Latter-day Saints believe in and worship is a God of individuality. Nothing can be made in your image that does not have all the parts that we have. We do not believe that God is a mere congeries of laws floating in the universe—but we believe that we are the children of God, made in His image.

—*Heber J. Grant*, MS 84:1, November 20, 1921

We know that we are created in the image of God, both male and female; and whoever goes back into the presence of God our Eternal Father will find that He is a noble man, a noble God, tabernacled in a form similar to ours, for we are created after His own image; they will also learn that He has placed us here that we may pass through a state of probation and experience, the same as He Himself did in His day of mortality.

—*Wilford Woodruff*, JD 18:32, June 27, 1875

The Lord has blessed us with a knowledge that He lives and has a body and that we are created in His image. We do not

believe that He is some kind of essence or that He is incomprehensible . . . I know that our Heavenly Father has revealed Himself to the children of men, that He is a personal God, that we are created in His image, that our spirits were begotten by Him, that He has given us an opportunity to dwell upon the earth to receive a physical tabernacle, in order that we may be prepared to return unto His presence and live eternally with Him.
—*George Albert Smith*, CR, p. 39, October, 1921

Man is made in the image of his maker, . . . he is His exact image, having eye for eye, forehead for forehead, eyebrows for eyebrows, nose for nose, cheekbones for cheekbones, mouth for mouth, chin for chin, ears for ears, precisely like our Father in heaven.   —*Brigham Young*, JD 13:146, July 11, 1869

God Has a Body of Flesh and Bone

Our Father in heaven is a personage of tabernacle, just as much as I am . . . and He has all the parts and passions of a perfect man, and His body is composed of flesh and bones, but not of blood.   —*Brigham Young*, JD 19:64, July 24, 1877

Jesus is the express image and likeness of His Father; therefore, as Jesus is a personage of flesh and bones, having a body as tangible as that of man, bearing in it the wounds of the nails and of the spear, so is the body of the Father just as tangible; it is just as real as that of the Son.
—*Joseph F. Smith*, MS 68:690, September 2, 1906

The Lord is our God and it is He whom we serve; and we say to the whole world that He is a tangible Being. We have a God with ears, eyes, nose, mouth; He can and does speak. He has arms, hands, body, legs and feet; He talks and walks; and we are formed after His likeness. The good book—the Bible, tells us what kind of a character our Heavenly Father is. In the first chapter of Genesis and the 17th verse, speaking of the Lord creating men, it reads as plain as it can read, "and He created man in His own image and likeness;" and if He created Adam and Eve in His own image, the whole human family are like Him.   —*Brigham Young*, JD 13:308-309, November 13, 1870

God possesses a body of flesh and bone, as tangible as man. Joseph Smith proclaimed that. Christ Himself proclaimed it, in His teachings, and in the example of His own existence. "He that hath seen me hath seen the Father," He said. Why? Because He was in the express image of His Father's person.

—Joseph F. Smith, IE 20:828, July, 1917

What Does God Do?

He governs this and other worlds, regulates all the systems and gives them their motions and revolutions. He preserves them in their various orbits and governs them by unerring, unchangeable laws, as they traverse the immensity of space. In our world He gives day and night, summer and winter, seedtime and harvest; He adapts man, the beasts of the field, the fowls of the air and the fishes of the sea to their various climates and elements. He takes care of and provides for not only the hundreds of millions of the human family, but the myriads of beasts, fowls and fishes; He feeds and provides for them day by day, giving them their breakfast, dinner and supper; He takes care of the reptiles and other creeping things, and feeds the myriads of animalculae, which crowd earth, air and water. His hand is over all and His providence sustains all.

—John Taylor, JD 10:260, October 10, 1863

He is our Heavenly Father; He is also our God and the Maker and upholder of all things in heaven and on earth. He sends forth His counsels and extends His providences to all living. He is the Supreme Controller of the universe. At His rebuke the sea is dried up, and the rivers become a wilderness. He measures the waters in the hollow of His hand, and meteth out heaven with a span, and comprehendeth the dust of the earth in a measure, and weigheth the mountains in scales, and the hills in a balance; the nations to Him are as a drop in a bucket, and He taketh up the isles as a very little thing; the hairs of our heads are numbered by Him, and not a sparrow falleth to the ground without our Father; and He knoweth every thought and intent of the hearts of all living, for He is everywhere present by the power of His Spirit—His minister, the Holy Ghost. He is the Father of all, is above all, through all, and in you all; He

knoweth all things pertaining to this earth, and He knows all things pertaining to millions of earths like this.
                    —*Brigham Young*, JD 11:41, January 8, 1865

If we could see our Heavenly Father, we should see a being similar to our earthly parent, with this difference, our Father in heaven is exalted and glorified. He has received His thrones, His principalities and powers, and He sits as a governor, as a monarch, and overrules kingdoms, thrones, and dominions that have been bequeathed to Him.
                    —*Brigham Young*, JD 4:54, September 21, 1856

B. JEHOVAH, JESUS CHRIST THE SON

THE DIVINE CONCEPTION

There cannot be any doubt in the heart of a Latter-day Saint regarding Jesus Christ's being the Son of the living God, because God Himself introduced Him to Joseph Smith. . . . Any individual who does not acknowledge Jesus Christ as the Son of God, the Redeemer of the world, has no business to be associated with the Church of Jesus Christ of Latter-day Saints.
                    —*Heber J. Grant*, CR, p. 7, October, 1924

Jesus Christ is the Son of Elohim both as spiritual and bodily offspring; that is to say, Elohim is literally the Father of the spirit of Jesus Christ and also of the body in which Jesus Christ performed His mission in the flesh, and which body died on the cross and was afterward taken up by the process of resurrection and is now the immortalized tabernacle of the eternal spirit of our Lord and Savior.   —*Joseph F. Smith*, IE 19:935, June 30, 1916

We believe absolutely that Jesus Christ is the Son of God, begotten of God, the first-born in the spirit and the only begotten in the flesh; that He is the Son of God just as much as you and I are the sons of our fathers.
                    —*Heber J. Grant*, MS 84:2, November 20, 1921

When the time came that His first-born, the Savior, should come into the world and take a tabernacle, the Father came Himself and favored that spirit with a tabernacle instead of letting any other man do it. The Savior was begotten by the Father and His spirit by the same Being who is the Father of our spirits, and that is all the organic difference between Jesus Christ and you and me.

—Brigham Young, JD 4:218, February 8, 1857

Christ announced Himself the Son of God, stating that those who had seen Him had seen the Father; that He was in the express image of the Father. If He were not the Son of God, then He could not be a great moral teacher, because the foundation of His teachings would be a falsehood.

—Heber J. Grant, MS 92:679, August 24, 1930

Jesus Christ Is Our Elder Brother

We believe that Jesus Christ is our elder brother—that He is actually the Son of our Father and that He is the Savior of the world and was appointed to this before the foundations of this earth were laid.

—Brigham Young, JD 13:235-236, February 20, 1870

He [Jehovah] was the Son of our Heavenly Father, as we are the sons of our earthly fathers. God is the Father of our spirits, which are clothed upon by fleshly bodies, begotten for us by our earthly fathers. Jesus is our elder brother spirit clothed upon with an earthly body begotten by the Father of our spirits.

—Brigham Young, JD 10:2, September 28, 1862

Among the spirit children of Elohim the firstborn was and is Jehovah or Jesus Christ to whom all others are juniors. . . . There is no impropriety, therefore, in speaking of Jesus Christ as the elder brother of the rest of human kind. . . . Let it not be forgotten, however, that He is essentially greater than any and all others by reason (1) of His seniority as the oldest or firstborn; (2) of His unique status in the flesh as the offspring of a mortal mother and of an immortal, or resurrected and glorified, Father; (3) of His selection and foreordination as the one and only Redeemer and Savior of the race; and (4) of His transcendent sinlessness.

Jesus Christ is not the Father of the spirits who have taken or yet shall take bodies upon this earth, for He is one of them. He is the Son, as they are sons or daughters of Elohim.

—Joseph F. Smith, IE 19:941-942, June 30, 1916

Our Lord Jesus Christ—the Savior, who has redeemed the world and all things pertaining to it, is the only begotten of the Father pertaining to the flesh. He is our elder brother and the heir of the family and as such we worship Him.
—*Brigham Young*, JD 12:69, June 23, 1867

The Divine Mission of Jesus Christ

We believe Jesus Christ to be not only one of the great moral teachers, the greatest the world has ever known, but the Son of God, the Redeemer of mankind, that He came to earth with a divinely appointed mission, to die on the cross, in order that you and I and all eventually may have part in the resurrection.   —*Heber J. Grant*, CR, p. 10, April, 1935

Jesus is the Redeemer of the world, the Savior of mankind, who came to the earth with a divinely appointed mission to die for the redemption of mankind. Jesus Christ is literally the Son of God, the only begotten in the flesh.
—*Heber J. Grant*, CR, p. 203, April, 1921

Jesus Christ . . . came in the meridian of time to redeem the earth and the children of men from the original sin that was committed by our first parents and bring to pass the restoration of all things through His death and sufferings, open wide to all believers the gates of life and salvation and exaltation to the presence of the Father and the Son to dwell with them for evermore.   —*Brigham Young*, JD 11:122, June 18, 1865

Jesus Christ is the Son of the living God, the Redeemer of the world, and . . . He came to this earth with a divine mission to die upon the cross as the Redeemer of mankind, atoning for the sins of the world.   —*Heber J. Grant*, IE 44:315, May, 1941

It has been justly remarked this afternoon that "Jesus paid the debt; He atoned for the original sin; He came and suffered and died on the cross." He is now King of kings and Lord of lords, and the time will come when every knee will bow and every tongue confess, to the glory of God the Father, that Jesus is the Christ. That very character that was looked upon, not as the Savior, but as an outcast, who was crucified between two thieves and treated with scorn and derision, will be greeted by all men as the only Being through whom they can obtain salvation.　　　　　　　　*—Brigham Young,* JD 13:59, July 18, 1869

He had power, when all mankind had lost their life, to restore life to them again; and hence He is the Resurrection and the Life, which power no other man possesses.
—John Taylor, MA, p. 135, Published in 1892

When Jesus came, He came as a sacrifice not simply in the interest of Israel . . . but in the interest of the whole human family, that in Him all men might be blessed, that in Him all men might be saved; and His mission was to make provision by which the whole human family might receive the benefits of the everlasting gospel, . . . not alone those dwelling upon the earth, but those also in the spirit world.
—Lorenzo Snow, DWN 32:18, November 4, 1882

The Sufferings of Jesus Necessary For His Exaltation

I have always looked upon the life of our Savior—who descended beneath all things that He might rise above all things —as an example for His followers. And yet it has always, in one sense of the word, seemed strange to me that the Son of God, the first begotten in the eternal worlds of the Father and the only begotten in the flesh, should have to descend to the earth and pass through what He did—born in a stable, cradled in a manger, persecuted, afflicted, scorned, a hiss and byword to almost all the world and especially to the inhabitants of Jerusalem and Judea. There was apparently nothing that the Savior could do that was acceptable in the eyes of the world; anything and almost everything He did was imputed to an unholy influence. When He cast out devils the people said He did it through the power of Beelzebub, the prince of devils; when He opened the eyes of the blind, the Pharisees and priests of the day told the man to "give God the glory; we know this man is a sinner." And so all His life through, to the day of His death upon the cross. There is something about all this that appears sorrowful; but it seemed necessary for the Savior to descend below all things that He might ascend above all things. So it has been with other men.
—Wilford Woodruff, JD 23:327, December 10, 1882

We all know that no one ever lived upon the earth that exerted the same influence upon the destinies of the world as did our Lord and Savior Jesus Christ; and yet He was born in obscurity, cradled in a manger. He chose for His apostles poor, unlettered fishermen. More than nineteen hundred years have passed and gone since His crucifixion, and yet all over the world, in spite of all strife and chaos, there is still burning in the hearts of millions of people a testimony of the divinity of the work that He accomplished.   —*Heber J. Grant*, IE 43:713, December, 1940

As to whether the Savior has got a body or not is no question with those who possess the gift and power of the Holy Ghost and are endowed with the Holy Priesthood; they know that He was a man in the flesh and is now a man in the heavens; He was a man subject to sin, to temptation, and to weaknesses; but He is now a man that is above all this— a man in perfection.
—*Brigham Young*, JD 11:42, January 8, 1865

C. THE HOLY GHOST

The Holy Ghost Is a Distinct Personage

The Holy Ghost is a personage and is in the form of a personage. It does not confine itself to the *form* of the dove, but in *sign* of the dove. The Holy Ghost cannot be transformed into a dove; but the sign of a dove was given to John to signify the truth of the deed, as the dove is an emblem or token of truth and innocence.   —*Joseph Smith, Jr.*, DHC 5:261, January 29, 1843

The Holy Ghost, who is a member of the Trinity in the Godhead, has not a body of flesh and bones, like the Father and the Son, but is a personage of Spirit. . . .
The Holy Ghost as a personage of Spirit can no more be omnipresent in person than can the Father or the Son, but by his intelligence, his knowledge, his power and influence, over and through the laws of nature, he is and can be omnipresent throughout all the works of God. . . .
The Holy Ghost in person may visit men and will visit those who are worthy and bear witness to their spirit of God and Christ but may not tarry with them.
—*Joseph F. Smith*, IE 12:389-390, March, 1909

The Holy Ghost, we believe, is one of the characters that form the Trinity, or the Godhead. Not one person in three, nor three persons in one; but the Father, Son, and Holy Ghost are one in essence, as the hearts of three men who are united in all things. . . . Lest you mistake me, I will say that I do not wish you to understand that the Holy Ghost is a personage having a tabernacle, like the Father and the Son; but he is God's messenger that diffuses his influence through all the works of the Almighty. —*Brigham Young, JD 6:95, November 29, 1857*

THE MISSION OF THE HOLY GHOST

The Holy Ghost is the Spirit of the Lord and issues forth from himself and may properly be called God's minister to execute His will in immensity; being called to govern by His influence and power; but he is not a person of tabernacle as we are and as our Father in heaven and Jesus Christ are.
—*Brigham Young, JD 1:50, April 9, 1852*

We are all dependent upon the Holy Ghost. And what is the Holy Ghost? The testimony of the Father and the Son. It is one of the Godhead—God the Father, God the Son, and God the Holy Ghost. Will the Holy Ghost deceive any man? It will not. When a man speaks as he is moved upon by the Holy Ghost, it is the spirit of inspiration; it is the word of God; it is the will of God. It cannot lie; it cannot deceive. It leads into all truth and reveals to man the will of his Maker.
—*Wilford Woodruff, MS 51:786, October 6, 1889*

Without the aid of the Holy Ghost no man can know the will of God or that Jesus is the Christ.
—*Joseph F. Smith, JD 19:187, September 30, 1877*

I have proven to my satisfaction, according to the best knowledge I can gather, that man can be deceived by the sight of the natural eye, he can be deceived by the hearing of the ear and by the touch of the hand; that he can be deceived in all of what are called the natural senses. But there is one thing in which he cannot be deceived. What is that? It is the operations of the Holy Ghost, the Spirit and power of God upon the creature. It teaches him of heavenly things; it directs him in

the way of life; it affords him the key by which he can test the devices of man and which recommends the things of God.
—*Brigham Young*, JD 18:230, September 17, 1876

We do not believe that the Holy Ghost ever dictated, suggested, moved, or pretended to offer a plan, except that which the Eternal Father dictated. . . .

Have we not learned enough with regard to the character of the Father, Son, and Holy Ghost to at once believe, admit, and affirm that the Holy Ghost always has and always will operate precisely according to the suggestion of the Father? Not a desire, act, wish, or thought does the Holy Ghost indulge in contrary to that which is dictated by the Father.
—*Brigham Young*, JD 6:95, November 29, 1857

The Lord said, speaking through Joseph Smith: "And whatsoever they shall speak when moved upon by the Holy Ghost, shall be Scripture, shall be the will of the Lord, shall be the mind of the Lord, shall be the voice of the Lord, and the power of God unto salvation."

Why is this? Because *the Holy Ghost is one of the Godhead and consequently when a man speaks by the Holy Ghost, it is the word of the Lord.* —*Wilford Woodruff*, MS 51:596, July 29, 1889

The Holy Ghost has no other effect than pure intelligence. It is more powerful in expanding the mind, enlightening the understanding, and storing the intellect with present knowledge of a man who is the literal seed of Abraham, than one that is a Gentile, though it may not have half as much visible effect upon the body; for as the Holy Ghost falls upon one of the literal seed of Abraham, it is calm and serene; and his whole soul and body are only exercised by the pure spirit of intelligence; while the effect of the Holy Ghost upon a Gentile is to purge out the old blood and make him actually of the seed of Abraham. That man that has none of the blood of Abraham (naturally) must have a new creation by the Holy Ghost. In such a case there may be more of a powerful effect upon the body, and visible to the eye, than upon an Israelite, while the Israelite at first might be far before the Gentile in pure intelligence.
—*Joseph Smith Jr.*, DHC 3:380, June 27, 1839

How then can we *know* "the only true and living God and
Jesus Christ whom He has sent?"—for to obtain this knowledge
would be to obtain the secret or key to eternal life. It must be
through the Holy Ghost, whose office is to reveal the things of
the Father to man and to bear witness in our hearts of Christ,
and Him crucified and risen from the dead. . . . How shall we
obtain the Holy Ghost? . . . We are told to have faith in God,
to repent of our sins, . . . then to be baptized for the remission
of our sins, by one having authority; and when this ordinance
of the gospel is complied with, we may receive the gift of the
Holy Ghost by the laying on of the hands of those clothed with
the authority of the priesthood.

—Joseph F. Smith, JD 19:22, April 2, 1877

The Holy Ghost reveals unto you things past, present, and to
come; it makes your minds quick and vivid to understand the
handy work of the Lord. —*Brigham Young, JD 4:22, August 17, 1856*

DISTINCTION BETWEEN THE SPIRIT OF GOD
AND THE HOLY GHOST

The question is often asked, is there any difference between
the Spirit of the Lord and the Holy Ghost? . . . The Holy Ghost
is a personage in the Godhead and is not that which lighteth
every man that comes into the world. It is the Spirit of God
which proceeds through Christ to the world, that enlightens
every man that comes into the world and that strives with the
children of men and will continue to strive with them, until it
brings them to a knowledge of the truth and the possession of
the greater light and testimony of the Holy Ghost.

—Joseph F. Smith, IE 11:381-382, March 16, 1902

The Holy Ghost . . . is different from the common Spirit of
God, which we are told lighteth every man that cometh into the
world. The Holy Ghost is only given to men through their
obedience to the gospel of Christ; and every man who receives
that Spirit has a comforter within—a leader to dictate and guide
him. This Spirit reveals, day by day, to every man who has faith,
those things which are for his benefit. As Job said, "There is a
spirit in man and the inspiration of the Almighty giveth it understanding." It is this inspiration of God to His children in every
age of the world that is one of the necessary gifts to sustain man

and enable him to walk by faith and to go forth and obey all the dictations and commandments and revelations which God gives to His children to guide and direct them in life.

—*Wilford Woodruff*, JD 13:157, December 12, 1869

There is a great difference between the possession of the Holy Ghost and the mere possession of the Spirit of God. Everybody has the Spirit of God, that is, the honest hearted, those who are living according to the best light they have. . . .

When the gospel reached us in the different nations whence we came, the Spirit of the Lord gave us convictions of its truth, and, in the honesty of our hearts, we received it and its blessings, otherwise we would have stayed at our several homes. It was promised to us by the several elders who proclaimed the gospel unto us, that if we would do the will of God, if we would obey the gospel, we should receive the gift of the Holy Ghost. . . .

I say that any man who will humble himself before God and will be immersed in water, after repentance, for the remission of his sins shall receive, through the laying on of hands, the gift of the Holy Ghost. Can I give this to him? No, . . . I simply lay my hands upon him for the reception of the Holy Ghost, then God, from His presence, acknowledges my authority, acknowledges that I am His messenger, and confers the Holy Ghost upon the individual.

—*Lorenzo Snow*, JD 14:304; 305; 307, January 14, 1872

The Scripture . . . says, He [God] has given unto them a portion of His Spirit to profit withal. But there is quite a distinction between the position that these people occupy and the one which we occupy. We have something more than that portion of the Spirit of God which is given to every man, and it is called the gift of the Holy Ghost, which is received through obedience to the first principles of the gospel of Christ, by the laying on of hands of the servants of God. . . . It is this Spirit that brings us into relationship with God, and it differs very materially from the portion of spirit that is given to all men to profit withal. The special gift of the Holy Ghost is obtained, as I have said, through obedience to the first principles of the gospel. Its province is to lead us into all truth and to bring to our remembrance things past, present and to come. It contemplates the future and unfolds things we had not thought of heretofore.

—*John Taylor*, JD 23:321, November 23, 1882

CHAPTER XXIX

Prophecy and Revelation

THE GIFT OF PROPHECY AND REVELATION

A S WE ARE all made in the image of God, and as God is the God and Father of the spirits of all flesh, it is His right, it is His prerogative to communicate with the human family. We are told that there is a spirit in man and the inspiration of the Almighty giveth it understanding. God having made the earth, made the people to inhabit it and made all things that exist therein, has a right to dictate, has a right to make known His will, has a right to communicate with whom He will and control matters as He sees proper: it belongs to Him by right.
—*John Taylor*, JD 23:260, October 8, 1882

We believe that it is necessary for man to be placed in communication with God; that he should have revelation from Him, and that unless he is placed under the influences of the inspiration of the Holy Spirit he can know nothing about the things of God. I do not care how learned a man may be or how extensively he may have traveled; I do not care what his talent, intellect or genius may be, at what college he may have studied, how comprehensive his views or what his judgment may be on other matters, he cannot understand certain things without the Spirit of God, and that necessarily introduces the principle I before referred to—the necessity of revelation. Not revelation in former times, but present and immediate revelation, which shall lead and guide those who possess it in all the paths of life here and to eternal life hereafter. A good many people, and those professing Christians, will sneer a good deal at the idea of present revelation. Whoever heard of true religion without communication with God? To me the thing is the most absurd that the human mind could conceive of. I do not wonder, when the people generally reject the principle of present revelation, that skepticism and infidelity prevail to such an alarming extent. I do not wonder that so many men treat religion with contempt and regard it as something not worth the attention of intelligent beings, for without revelation religion is a mockery and a farce. If I can not have a religion that will lead me to God and place me *en rapport* with Him and unfold to my mind the principles of immortality and eternal life, I want nothing to do with it.

The principle of present revelation, then, is the very foundation of our religion.   —*John Taylor*, JD 16:371, February 1, 1874

We believe in the principle of direct revelation from God to man. . . . It is not a hereditary principle, it cannot be handed down from father to son, nor from generation to generation, but is a living, vital principle to be enjoyed on certain conditions only, namely—through absolute faith in God and obedience to His laws and commandments.

                    —*Joseph F. Smith*, JD 19:192, September 30, 1877

I would to God that the inhabitants of the earth would get rid of the idea that revelation ceased when Christ was put to death. It is a false doctrine. Revelation belongs to the salvation of the children of men.

                    —*Wilford Woodruff*, MS 57:739, October 6, 1895

THE TESTIMONY OF JESUS IS THE SPIRIT OF PROPHECY

If any person should ask me if I were a prophet, I should not deny it, as that would give me the lie; for, according to John, the testimony of Jesus is the spirit of prophecy; therefore, if I profess to be a witness or teacher and have not the spirit of prophecy, which is the testimony of Jesus, I must be a false witness; but if I be a true teacher and witness, I must possess the spirit of prophecy, and that constitutes a prophet; and any man who says he is a teacher or preacher of righteousness and denies the spirit of prophecy is a liar, and the truth is not in him; and by this key false teachers and impostors may be detected.   —*Joseph Smith, Jr.*, DHC 5:215-216, January 1, 1843

He [Brigham Young] is a prophet, I am a prophet, you are, and anybody is a prophet who has the testimony of Jesus Christ, for that is the spirit of prophecy. The elders of Israel are prophets. A prophet is not so great as an apostle. Christ has set in His Church, first, apostles; they hold the keys of the kingdom of God.   —*Wilford Woodruff*, JD 13:165, December 12, 1869

We must have the testimony of the Lord Jesus to enable us to discern between truth and error, light and darkness, him who is of God, and him who is not of God, and to know how to place everything where it belongs. That is the only way to be a scientific Christian; there is no other method or process which will actually school a person so that he can become a Saint of God and prepare him for a celestial glory; he must have within him the testimony of the spirit of the gospel.

—*Brigham Young*, JD 3:155, May 6, 1855

You need have no fear . . . that when one of the apostles of the Lord Jesus Christ delivers a prophecy in the name of Jesus Christ, because he is inspired to do that, that it will fall by the wayside. I know of more than one prophecy, which, looking at it naturally, seemed as though it would fall to the ground as year after year passed, but lo and behold, in the providences of the Lord, that prophecy was fulfilled.

—*Heber J. Grant*, IE 40:735, December, 1937

There is no prophecy of Scripture of any private interpretation, but holy men of old spoke as they were moved upon by the Holy Ghost, and their words will be fulfilled to the very letter, and it certainly is time that we prepare ourselves for that which is to come.

—*Wilford Woodruff*, JD 18:128, October 8, 1875

CHARACTERISTICS OF THE PRINCIPLE
OF REVELATION

The action of the angels, or messengers of God, upon our minds so that the heart can conceive things past, present, and to come, and revelations from the eternal world is, among a majority of mankind, a greater mystery than all the secrets of philosophy, literature, superstition, and bigotry put together: though some men try to deny it, and some try to explain away the meaning; still there is so much testimony in the Bible and among a respectable portion of the world, that one might as well undertake to throw the water out of this world into the moon with a teaspoon, as to do away with the supervision of angels upon the human mind.

—*John Taylor*, TS 6:824, March 1, 1845

A person may profit by noticing the first intimation of the spirit of revelation; for instance, when you feel pure intelligence flowing into you, it may give you sudden strokes of ideas, so that by noticing it you may find it fulfilled the same day or soon; (i.e.) those things that were presented unto your minds by the Spirit of God will come to pass; and thus by learning the Spirit of God and understanding it you may grow into the principle of revelation, until you become perfect in Christ Jesus.
—*Joseph Smith, Jr.,* DHC 3:381, June 27, 1839

When the Spirit of revelation from God inspires a man, his mind is opened to behold the beauty, order, and glory of the creation of this earth and its inhabitants, the object of its creation, and the purpose of its Creator in peopling it with His children. He can then clearly understand that our existence here is for the sole purpose of exaltation and restoration to the presence of our Father and God, where we may progress endlessly in the power of godliness. After the mind has thus been illuminated, the ignorance and blindness of the great mass of mankind are more apparent.   —*Brigham Young,* JD 9:256, March 16, 1862

There is a principle existing by which God is able to communicate His will unto man and make known the truths of heaven. It is revelation. When God has a Church upon the earth, this important principle of communication must of necessity be possessed by its members; it is by this they are distinguished from the world at large or from those who are not adopted into the fold, in distinction to the sheep who *know* His voice and will follow it, and not the voice of a stranger. The devil also possesses power to imitate very closely this principle by which God conveys knowledge unto man, but his is the voice of the stranger, and the sheep will not follow it, for they have learned and do know the voice of the true Shepherd.
—*Joseph F. Smith,* MS 37:88, February 9, 1875

By the revelations of the Lord Jesus we understand things as they were, that have been made known unto us; things that are in the life which we now enjoy and things as they will be, not to the fullest extent, but all that the Lord designs that we should understand, to make it profitable to us, in order to give us the experience necessary in this life to prepare us to enjoy eternal life hereafter. —*Brigham Young,* JD 12:112, December 8, 1867

What is revelation? It is the inspiration of the Holy Ghost to man. This is the key, the foundation stone of all revelation.
—*Wilford Woodruff*, MS 53:642, August 10, 1891

What is revelation? The testimony of the Father and Son. How many of you have had revelation? How many of you have had the Spirit of God whisper unto you—the still small voice? . . . I have been blessed at times with certain gifts and graces, certain revelations and ministrations; but with them all I have never found anything that I could place more dependency upon than the still small voice of the Holy Ghost.
—*Wilford Woodruff*, JD 21:195-196, July 3, 1880

THE LATTER-DAY SAINT CHURCH IS FOUNDED ON REVELATION

This Church is built upon the rock of revelation, through which means the constituted authorities thereof receive authority from God direct, to act in their callings and to enjoy the gifts and powers of the gospel.   —*Heber J. Grant*, IE 23:473, April, 1920

God established the Church of Jesus Christ of Latter-day Saints, by direct revelation; this is a FACT, clearly and distinctly revealed to thousands. The so-called "Mormon" people, in these valleys, are the acknowledged people of God, and are here, not by their own choice, but by immediate command of God. The work and management is the Lord's—not the people's—they do His bidding, and He, alone, is responsible for the result.
—*Lorenzo Snow*, JD 26:367, January 10, 1886

We, as a people, profess emphatically to be governed by revelation. . . . We believe that God has spoken, that angels have appeared, that the everlasting gospel in its purity has been restored; we believe that God has organized His Church and kingdom on the earth, and that, through channels which He has appointed and ordained, He manifests His will first to the Saints and then to the world.   —*John Taylor*, JD 12:49, May 19, 1867

The distinction between this great Church and that of all other churches from the beginning has been that we believe in divine revelation; we believe that our Father speaks to man today

as He has done from the time of Adam. We believe and we know —which is more than mere belief—that our Father has set His hand in this world for the salvation of the children of men.
—*George Albert Smith, CR, p. 37, April, 1917*

The Lord never had—and never will have to the end of time —a Church on the earth without prophets, apostles, and inspired men. Whenever the Lord had a people on the earth that He acknowledged as such, that people were led by revelation.
—*Wilford Woodruff, JD 24:240, July 20, 1883*

Permit me . . . to quote what Jesus promised, viz: "Blessed art thou, Simon Barjona: for flesh and blood hath not revealed it unto thee, but my Father which is in heaven. And upon this *rock* I will build my Church; and the gates of hell shall not prevail against it." Peter had obtained a *revelation* which Jesus called a *Rock,* which every man might receive individually for himself to build upon, with perfect assurance and safety—on which he could anchor his hopes and prospects of salvation. Peter, on the day of Pentecost, promised the Holy Ghost to those who would repent and receive baptism. That principle imparts the knowledge or the *rock* of *revelation* upon which the Savior declared His people should be established; and we constitute the only religious community which dares to assume this Scriptural position.   —*Lorenzo Snow, JD 26:376, March, 1886*

LIVING ORACLES IN THE CHURCH

Now, we may take the Bible, the Book of Mormon and Doctrine and Covenants, and we may read them through and every other revelation that has been given to us, and they would scarcely be sufficient to guide us twenty-four hours. We have only an outline of our duties written; we are to be guided by the living oracles.   —*Wilford Woodruff, JD 9:324, April 8, 1862*

Without revelation direct from heaven it is impossible for any person to fully understand the plan of salvation. We often hear it said that the living oracles must be in the Church, in order that the kingdom of God may be established and prosper on the earth. I will give another version of this sentiment. I say that the living oracles of God, or the Spirit of revelation,

must be in each and every individual to know the plan of salvation and keep in the path that leads them to the presence of God.
—*Brigham Young*, JD 9:279, April 7, 1862

Yes, we have revelation. The Church of God could not live twenty-four hours without revelation.
—*Wilford Woodruff*, DWN 45:545, October 9, 1892

There is an appointed way, however, by which revelation from the Lord for the government of His Church is received. There is but one man on the earth, at a time, who holds this power. But every individual member has the privilege of receiving revelation from the Lord for his guidance in his own affairs and to testify to him concerning the correctness of public teachings and movements.
—*Wilford Woodruff*, MS 50:307-308, April 7, 1888

It is impossible for a prophet of Christ to live in an adulterous generation without speaking of the wickedness of the people, without revealing their faults and their failings, and there is nothing short of death that will stay him from it, for a prophet of God will do as he pleases.
—*Brigham Young*, JD 3:48, October 6, 1855

This Church has been led by revelation, and unless we forsake the Lord entirely, so that the priesthood is taken from us, it will be led by revelation all the time. The question arises with some, who has the right to revelation? . . . Every member has the right of receiving revelation for himself. It is the very life of the Church of the living God, in all ages of the world.
—*Brigham Young*, MS 5:117, October 6, 1844

Salvation cannot come without revelation; it is in vain for anyone to minister without it. No man is a minister of Jesus Christ without being a prophet. No man can be a minister of Jesus Christ except he has the testimony of Jesus; and this is the spirit of prophecy. —*Joseph Smith, Jr.*, DHC 3:389, July 2, 1839

Now I would ask this congregation; I would ask all the Jews, the Catholics, the Protestants, I would ask the clergy of all nations: Can this mighty dispensation of which every prophet has spoken be fulfilled and can these great events transpire in the

earth, without revelation from God? No, most assuredly not. God never gave . . . a greater dispensation than the one in which Joseph Smith was called and ordained of God to organize the Church of Jesus Christ of Latter-day Saints. It required revelation. It will require it to the winding-up scene. Zion cannot be built up . . . nor can the nations of the earth be warned of the great judgments that are at the door without it.
—*Wilford Woodruff*, MS 57:739, October 6, 1895

ALL CHURCH MEMBERS ARE ENTITLED TO REVELATION

Every man or woman that has ever entered into the Church of God and been baptized for the remission of sins, has a right to revelation, a right to the Spirit of God, to assist them in their labors, in their administrations to their children, in counseling their children and those over whom they are called upon to preside. The Holy Ghost is not restricted to men, nor to apostles or prophets; it belongs to every faithful man and woman and to every child who is old enough to receive the gospel of Christ.
—*Wilford Woodruff*, MS 51:548, June 2, 1889

The gift of revelation does not belong to one man solely; it is not a gift that pertains to the Presidency of the Church and the Twelve Apostles alone. It is not confined to the presiding authorities of the Church, it belongs to every individual member of the Church; and it is the right and privilege of every man, every woman, and every child who has reached the years of accountability to enjoy the spirit of revelation and to be possessed of the spirit of inspiration in the discharge of their duties as members of the Church.   —*Joseph F. Smith*, CR, p. 5, April, 1912

The Lord gives to many of us the still, small voice of revelation. It comes as vividly and strongly as though it were with a great sound. It comes to each man, according to his needs and faithfulness, for guidance in matters that pertain to his own life. For the Church as a whole it comes to those who have been ordained to speak for the Church as a whole. This certain knowledge which we have that the guiding influence of the Lord may be felt in all the ways of life, according to our needs and faithfulness, is among the greatest blessings God grants unto

men. With this blessing comes the responsibility to render strict obedience to the "still small voice."
—Heber J. Grant, IE 41:712, December, 1938

What business have we with this priesthood, if we have not power to receive revelation? What is the priesthood given for? If we do not have revelation, it is because we do not live as we should live, because we do not magnify our priesthood as we ought to; if we did we would not be without revelation, none would be barren or unfruitful. We have one man who holds the keys of the kingdom of God upon the earth, and it is his business to give the word of the Lord for the guidance of the Church. But here we have apostles and men of God, holding the Holy Priesthood, acting in behalf of the Church in different parts of this Territory and also in different parts of the earth: . . . is it the right of such men to have revelation from the Lord to guide them in their operations? Yes, it is; and no man should undertake to act in positions affecting the interests of Zion, unless he lives so as to be guided and directed by revelations of God. . . . This idea that no man has any right to call upon God and receive revelation is wrong, and it has been wrong whenever it has existed in any age of the world. As was said of old, when a complaint was made concerning certain of the elders prophesying in the camp of Israel, so say I: "I would to God that all were prophets;" because the spirit of prophecy is the testimony of Jesus.
—Wilford Woodruff, JD 21:298, August 1, 1880

REVELATION IS THE SOURCE OF ALL TRUTH

No person receives knowledge only upon the principle of revelation, that is, by having something revealed to them. . . . Who reveals? Everybody around us; we learn of each other. I have something which you have not, and you have something which I have not; I reveal what I have to you, and you reveal what you have to me. I believe that we are revelators to each other. Are the heavens opened? Yes, to some at times, yet upon natural principles, upon the principle of natural philosophy.
—Brigham Young, JD 3:209, February 17, 1856

"Have you had revelations?" Yes, I have them all the time, I live constantly by the principle of revelation. I never received

one iota of intelligence, from the letter A to what I now know,
I mean that, from the very start of my life to this time, I have
never received one particle of intelligence only by revelation, no
matter whether father or mother revealed it, or my sister, or
neighbor.   —*Brigham Young, JD 3:209, February 17, 1856*

Every new truth which grows into living action in the lives
of men is a revelation in itself from God, and without the revelation of additional truth men would not progress in this
world, but, left to themselves, would retrograde, being cut off
from the light and life of the great fountain of all intelligence,
the Father of all.

What is revelation but the uncovering of new truths, by Him
who is the Fountain of all Truth? To say that there is no need
of new revelation is equivalent to saying that we have no need
of new truths—a ridiculous assertion.
                        —*Joseph F. Smith, IE 5:805-806, August, 1902*

NO REVELATION IS PERFECT IN ITS FULLNESS

The laws that the Lord has given are not fully perfect, because the people could not receive them in their perfect fullness;
but they can receive a little here and a little there, . . . and a
little more in advance of that next year, if they make a wise improvement upon every little they receive; if they do not, they are
left in the shade, and the light which the Lord reveals will appear
darkness to them, and the kingdom of heaven will travel on and
leave them groping. Hence, if we wish to act upon the fullness
of the knowledge that the Lord designs to reveal, little by little,
to the inhabitants of the earth, we must improve upon every
little as it is revealed.   —*Brigham Young, JD 2:314, July 8, 1855*

I am so far from believing that any government upon this
earth has constitutions and laws that are perfect that I do not
even believe that there is a single revelation, among the many
God has given to the Church, that is perfect in its fullness. The
revelations of God contain correct doctrine and principle, so
far as they go; but it is impossible for the poor, weak, low,
grovelling, sinful inhabitants of the earth to receive a revelation
from the Almighty in all its perfections.
                         —*Brigham Young, JD 2:314, July 8, 1855*

CONCERNING FUTURE REVELATION

When we obey and are capable of observing the precepts of the gospel and the laws of God and the requirements of heaven, which have already been revealed, we will be far better off and nearer the goal of perfection in wisdom, knowledge and power than we are today. When that time comes, then there are other things still greater yet to be revealed to the people of God. Until we do our duty, however, . . . to add commandments, to add light and intelligence to us over that which we have already received, which we have not yet fully obeyed, would be to add condemnation upon our heads. It is enough for us to live in the light of present inspiration and present revelation and for each individual member of the Church to keep the commandments of the Lord and labor in the Church as the Spirit may give him and her guidance in the performance of duty.

—Joseph F. Smith, CR, p. 5, October, 1917

The channels of communication between God and man cannot be cut off nor closed by man nor ever will be while God has a purpose to accomplish by revealing Himself.

—Joseph F. Smith, YWJ 2:268, a. 1890

Chapter XXX

Temple Marriage

MARRIAGE IS ORDAINED OF GOD

"AND AGAIN, verily I say unto you, that whoso forbiddeth to marry is not ordained of God, for marriage is ordained of God unto man." (Doc. and Cov. 49:15)

I desire to emphasize this. I want the young men of Zion to realize that this institution of marriage is not a man-made institution. It is of God; it is honorable, and no man who is of marriageable age is living his religion who remains single. It is not simply devised for the convenience alone of man, to suit his own notions, and his own ideas; to marry and then divorce, to adopt and then to discard, just as he pleases. There are great consequences connected with it, consequences which reach beyond this present time, into all eternity, for thereby souls are begotten into the world, and men and women obtain their being in the world. Marriage is the preserver of the human race. Without it, the purposes of God would be frustrated; virtue would be destroyed to give place to vice and corruption, and the earth would be void and empty.

—Joseph F. Smith, IE 5:713-714, July, 1902

Marriage constitutes the most sacred relationship existing between man and woman. It is of heavenly origin and is founded upon eternal principles. As a part and portion of the great plan of salvation devised for Adam's race before this world was made, it is destined to continue not only while time shall last but throughout all eternity. Indeed it is an exigency upon which man's happiness, the perpetuity of his earthly existence, and his future dominion, glory and exaltation depend and which, in the wisdom of God, must of necessity continue as the seal of the natural, legitimate and inevitable domestic union of the sexes forever.

—Joseph F. Smith, MS 36:312, May 19, 1874

And I would say, as no man can be perfect without the woman, so no woman can be perfect without a man to lead her, I tell you the truth as it is in the bosom of eternity; and I say so to every man upon the face of the earth: if he wishes to be saved he cannot be saved without a woman by his side.

—Brigham Young, TS 6:955, April 6, 1845

The first marriage on record appertaining to this earth was solemnized by the Almighty. The first couple married were immortal beings—Adam and Eve, our first parents—before they had partaken of the forbidden fruit and became subject to the penalty of death. Marriage, as then understood, could not have been what it is now popularly supposed to be by the so-called Christian world. Then the marriage vow was made and the ceremony was performed by immortal or celestial beings, with no reference to death or to a time when that sacred and holy union should cease. *—Joseph F. Smith, MS 36:312, May 19, 1874*

THE NATURE OF A CELESTIAL MARRIAGE

Celestial marriage—that is, marriage for time and eternity—and polygamous or plural marriage are not synonymous terms. Monogamous marriages for time and eternity, solemnized in our temples in accordance with the word of the Lord and the laws of the Church, are celestial marriages.

—Heber J. Grant, MS 95:588, September, 1933

The Lord has revealed unto us the ancient law, which was revealed to Adam through the gospel and which is called the law of celestial marriage. This . . . applies only to certain conditions of men and can only be enjoyed by parties who have obeyed the everlasting gospel. It is one of the eternal principles associated therewith, uniting mortal and immortal beings by eternal covenants, that will live and endure forever. . . . But with regard to the law of celestial marriage, there are certain safeguards thrown around it, as there always were, and those safeguards are, and always were, in the hands of the proper authorities and priesthood, delegated by God to man for the protection and preservation and right use of this most important, sacred, exalting and eternal ceremony or covenant. These things are clearly defined in the revelation on celestial marriage and can rightly only be enjoyed and participated in by such as are considered worthy, according to the laws, rites, privileges and immunities connected therewith. . . . Are the barriers placed around this sacred institution to be broken down and trampled underfoot? And are unworthy characters who do not fulfill the requirements of the gospel to have conferred upon them the blessings of eternal lives, of thrones, and powers, and principalities in the celestial kingdom of God? We emphatically answer, No!

—*John Taylor,* Article "On Marriage," p. 5-6, Published 1882

It (celestial marriage) is one of the greatest blessings that ever was conferred upon the human family. It is an eternal law which has always existed in other worlds as well as in this world.

—*John Taylor,* JD 24:229, a. June, 1883

BENEFITS OF MARRIAGE IN A TEMPLE

The Eternal Nature of the Marriage Covenant

Grateful should we be for a knowledge of the eternity of the marriage covenant. If in this life only had we hope, we would indeed be of all men most miserable. The assurance that our relationship here as parents and children, as husbands and wives will continue in heaven and that this is but the beginning of a great and glorious kingdom that our Father has destined we shall inherit on the other side fills us with hope and joy. One of the greatest evidences to me of the divinity of this work is that it teaches there is eternal life on the other side and that there will be a reunion there of the loved ones who have known each other here. Consequently, as parents, we may well be patient and loving toward our children, for they will eternally abide with us on the other side, if we and they are faithful. The few years that we live here may be regarded as a time in which we become acquainted, but, when we mingle in the other life, we will know each other better than we have here.

—*George Albert Smith,* CR, p. 29, October, 1905

We are living for eternity and not merely for the moment. Death does not part us from one another, if we have entered into sacred relationships with each other by virtue of the authority that God has revealed to the children of men. Our relationships are formed for eternity. We are immortal beings, and we are looking forward to the growth that is to be attained in an exalted life after we have proved ourselves faithful and true to the covenants that we have entered into here and then we will receive a fullness of joy. *—Joseph F. Smith,* RSM, 4:316, June, 1917

There is no doubt in the mind of any true Latter-day Saint, man or woman, as to the fact of individual existence beyond the grave, as to the fact that we shall know each other, and as to the endless duration of the covenant of marriage that has been performed in the House of the Lord for time and eternity.
—Heber J. Grant, IE 44:329, June, 1941

THE BLESSING OF ETERNAL LIVES

Except a man and his wife enter into an everlasting covenant and be married for eternity, while in this probation, by the power and authority of the Holy Priesthood, they will cease to increase when they die; that is, they will not have any children after the resurrection. But those who are married by the power and authority of the priesthood in this life and continue without committing the sin against the Holy Ghost will continue to increase and have children in the celestial glory. The unpardonable sin is to shed innocent blood or be accessory thereto. All other sins will be visited with judgment in the flesh and the spirit being delivered to the buffetings of Satan until the day of the Lord Jesus. . . .

"In the celestial glory there are three heavens or degrees; and in order to obtain the highest, a man must enter into this order of the priesthood (meaning the new and everlasting covenant of marriage); and if he does not, he cannot obtain it. He may enter into the other, but that is the end of his kingdom; he cannot have an increase." (Doc. and Cov. 131:1-4)
—Joseph Smith, Jr., DHC 5:391-392, May 16, 1843

Those who are faithful will continue to increase and this is the great blessing the Lord has given to, or placed within the reach of, the children of man, even to be capable of receiving eternal lives.

To have such a promise so sealed upon our heads, which no power on earth, in heaven, or beneath the earth can take from us, to be sealed up to the day of redemption and have the promise of eternal lives is the greatest gift of all.
—Brigham Young, JD 2:301, June 3, 1855

When two Latter-day Saints are united together in marriage, promises are made to them concerning their offspring that reach from eternity to eternity. They are promised that they shall have the power and the right to govern and control and administer salvation and exaltation and glory to their offspring worlds without end. And what offspring they do not have here, undoubtedly there will be opportunities to have them hereafter. What else could man wish? A man and a woman in the other life, having celestial bodies, free from sickness and disease, glorified and beautified beyond description, standing in the midst of their posterity, governing and controlling them, administering life, exaltation and glory, worlds without end.
    —*Lorenzo Snow,* DWN 54:481, March 13, 1897

FAMILY RELATIONSHIPS ENDURE THROUGHOUT ETERNITY

These women that are sealed to us for time and eternity will, with our children, be ours in the other life, going on in honor and glory.   —*Lorenzo Snow,* CR, p. 56, October, 1898

When a man and woman have received their endowments and sealings and then had children born to them afterwards, those children are legal heirs to the kingdom and to all its blessings and promises, and they are the only ones that are on this earth. There is not a young man in our community who would not be willing to travel from here to England to be married right, if he understood things as they are; there is not a young woman in our community, who loves the gospel and wishes its blessings, that would be married in any other way; they would live unmarried until they were as old as Sarah before she had Isaac born to her.   —*Brigham Young,* JD 11:118, a. June, 1865

Bless your souls, if you lived here in the flesh a thousand years, as long as Father Adam, and lived and labored all your life in poverty and when you got through, if, by your acts, you could secure your wives and children in the morning of the first resurrection, to dwell with you in the presence of God, that one thing would amply pay you for the labors of a thousand years.   —*Wilford Woodruff,* JD 21:284, July 4, 1880

PRIESTHOOD AUTHORITY NECESSARY TO
PERFORM TEMPLE MARRIAGES

Any man that marries a wife by any other authority than the authority of the Holy Priesthood is simply married for time, "or until death do you part." When you go into the spirit world you have no claim on your wife and children. The ordinance of having them sealed to you by one having the authority of the Holy Priesthood must be attended to in this world.
—*Wilford Woodruff*, JD 24:243-244, July 20, 1883

God has shown us, in regard to our marital relations, that our wives are to be sealed to us for time and eternity. By what authority? By the authority of that Holy Priesthood that administers on the earth and in heaven and of which Jesus said that whatever they should bind on earth should be bound in heaven. —*Wilford Woodruff*, JD 18:141, October 10, 1875

To this I add that we believe in the eternal union of the sexes in the married state. That marriage is an ordinance of the gospel and not merely a civil contract. That, according to God's law, it is inevitably as binding in eternity as it possibly can be in "time." That all marriage contracts should be solemnized and confirmed by that authority and power which was conferred by the Savior of the world upon Peter and the apostles. "That whatsoever they should bind on earth should be bound in heaven," and *vice versa.* That all marriages not solemnized and confirmed by this authority pertain only to time and are of no force or effect in the resurrection, where "there is neither marrying nor giving in marriage."
—*Joseph F. Smith*, MS 37:242, March 23, 1875

Why is a woman sealed to man for time and all eternity? Because there is legitimate power on earth to do it. This power will bind on earth and in heaven; it can loose on earth, and it is loosed in heaven; it can seal on earth, and it is sealed in heaven. There is a legitimate, authorized agent of God upon earth; this sealing power is regulated by him; hence what is done by that is done right and is recorded. When the books are opened, every one will find his proper mate and have those that belong to him, and every one will be deprived of that which is surreptitiously obtained. —*John Taylor*, JD 1:232, April 8, 1853

Unless man and wife are married by the power of God and by His authority they become single again, they have no claim upon each other after death; their contract is filled by that time and is therefore of no force in and after the resurrection from the dead, nor after they are dead. . . . Therefore, when they are out of the world they neither marry nor are given in marriage, but become as angels in heaven.

—Joseph F. Smith, IE 5:716-717, July, 1902

ADVICE TO YOUNG LATTER-DAY SAINT MEMBERS

I believe that no worthy young Latter-day Saint man or woman should spare any reasonable effort to come to a house of the Lord to begin life together. The marriage vows taken in these hallowed places and the sacred covenants entered into for time and all eternity are proof against many of the temptations of life that tend to break homes and destroy happiness. . . .

The blessings and promises that come from beginning life together, for time and eternity, in a temple of the Lord, cannot be obtained in any other way and worthy young Latter-day Saint men and women who so begin life together find that their eternal partnership under the everlasting covenant becomes the foundation upon which are built peace, happiness, virtue, love, and all of the other eternal verities of life, here and hereafter.

—Heber J. Grant, IE 39:198-199, April, 1936

How is it with you, sisters? Do you distinguish between a man of God and a man of the world? It is one of the strangest things that happens in my existence, to think that any man or woman can love a being that will not receive the truth of heaven. The love this gospel produces is far above the love of women; it is the love of God—the love of eternity—of eternal lives.

—Brigham Young, JD 8:199-200, October 7, 1860

When the daughters of Zion are asked by the young men to join them in marriage, instead of asking—"Has this man a fine brick house, a span of fine horses and a fine carriage?" they should ask—"Is he a man of God? Has he the Spirit of God with him? Is he a Latter-day Saint? Does he pray? Has he got the Spirit upon him to qualify him to build up the kingdom?" If he has that, never mind the carriage and brick house, take hold and unite yourselves together according to the law of God.

—Wilford Woodruff, JD 18:129-130, October 8, 1875

I believe that many of the troubles of those Latter-day Saints who have sorrow in their homes and difficulties with their families come from neglect in carrying out the commandments of God, one of the most important of which concerns temple marriage. Much sorrow is chargeable to indifference to this and other requirements.

One of the serious evils of our day is divorce, the breaking up of families, the infidelity of husband and wife. There are fewer divorces among the Latter-day Saints than among other people; and in our own communities the divorce rate is lower among members of our Church who have been properly married in the temple, as compared with those married by civil ceremony, showing that the teachings of the gospel of Jesus Christ, when observed, tend to make the marriage covenant sacred and thereby the evil of divorce is greatly lessened.

—Heber J. Grant, IE 44:329, June, 1941

FAMILY LIFE AND THE HOME

There is no substitute for the home. Its foundation is as ancient as the world, and its mission has been ordained of God from the earliest times. From Abraham sprang two ancient races represented in Isaac and Ishmael. The one built stable homes and prized its land as a divine inheritance. The other became children of the desert and as restless as its ever-shifting sands upon which their tents were pitched. From that day to the present, the home has been the chief characteristic of superior over inferior nations. The home then is more than a habitation, it is an institution which stands for stability and love in individuals as well as in nations. . . .

A Latter-day Saint who has no ambition to establish a home and give it permanency has not a full conception of a sacred duty the gospel imposes upon him. It may be necessary at times to change our abode; but a change should never be made for light or trivial reasons, nor to satisfy a restless spirit.

—Joseph F. Smith, JI 38:144; 145, March 1, 1903

To be a successful father or a successful mother is greater than to be a successful general or a successful statesman.

—Joseph F. Smith, JI 40:752, December 15, 1905

The parents in Zion will be held responsible for the acts of their children, not only until they become eight years old but, perhaps, throughout all the lives of their children, provided they have neglected their duty to their children while they were under their care and guidance, and the parents were responsible for them.   —*Joseph F. Smith,* CR, p. 6, April, 1910

There is no higher authority in matters relating to the family organization, especially when that organization is presided over by one holding the higher priesthood, than that of the father. This authority is time honored, and among the people of God in all dispensations it has been highly respected and often emphasized by the teachings of the prophets who were inspired of God. The patriarchal order is of divine origin and will continue throughout time and eternity. . . . This patriarchal order has its divine spirit and purpose, and those who disregard it under one pretext or another are out of harmony with the spirit of God's laws as they are ordained for recognition in the home. It is not merely a question of who is perhaps the best qualified. Neither is it wholly a question of who is living the most worthy life. It is a question largely of law and order, and its importance is seen often from the fact that the authority remains and is respected long after a man is really unworthy to exercise it.
                          —*Joseph F. Smith,* JI 37:146; 147, March 1, 1902

I regret, I think it is a crying evil, that there should exist a sentiment or a feeling among any members of the Church to curtail the birth of their children. I think that is a crime whereever it occurs, where husband and wife are in possession of health and vigor and are free from impurities that would be entailed upon their posterity. I believe that where people undertake to curtail or prevent the birth of their children that they are going to reap disappointment by and by. I have no hesitancy in saying that I believe this is one of the greatest crimes of the world today, this evil practice.   —*Joseph F. Smith,* RSM 4:318, June, 1917

LATTER-DAY SAINT MARRIAGES OUTSIDE THE TEMPLES

The question arises, What shall be done in regard to those persons who, being members of the Church, are not worthy to enter into those sacred and eternal relations of which we have been speaking? This is probably a question that concerns our civil polity rather than our religion, but we have deemed it worthy of our consideration and after due deliberation have determined that in cases where recommends cannot be justifiably given for the blessings of the House of the Lord the parties desiring marriage be united by the bishop, inasmuch as they are worthy of the recognition of their brethren and sisters and have not forfeited their right to be esteemed members of the Church, though not sufficiently valiant in the cause of righteousness to be deemed altogether worthy of these weightier blessings that belong to the new and everlasting covenant.

–*John Taylor*, Article "On Marriage," p. 7-8, Published, 1882

I would rather take one of my children to the grave than I would see him turn away from this gospel. I would rather follow their bodies to the cemetery and see them buried in innocence, than I would see them corrupted by the ways of the world. I would rather go myself to the grave than to be associated with a wife outside of the bonds of the new and everlasting covenant. Now, I hold it just so sacred; but some members of the Church do not so regard the matter. Some people feel that it does not make very much difference whether a girl marries a man in the Church, full of the faith of the gospel, or an unbeliever. Some of our young people have married outside the Church; but very few of those who have done it have failed to come to grief. . . . There is nothing that I can think of, in a religious way, that would grieve me more intensely than to see one of my boys marry an unbelieving girl, or one of my girls marry an unbelieving man.

–*Joseph F. Smith*, CR, p. 5-6, October, 1909

CHAPTER XXXI

The Word of Wisdom

PREPARE TO LIVE!

PREPARE to die is not the exhortation in this Church and kingdom; but prepare to live is the word with us and improve all we can in this life, that we may be the better prepared to enjoy a better life hereafter, wherein we may enjoy a more exalted condition of intelligence, wisdom, light, knowledge, power, glory, and exaltation. Then let us seek to extend the present life to the uttermost, by observing every law of health and by properly balancing labor, study, rest, and recreation and thus prepare for a better life. Let us teach these principles to our children that, in the morning of their days, they may be taught to lay the foundation of health and strength and constitution and power of life in their bodies.
—*Brigham Young,* JD 11:132, August, 1865

I am fully convinced that the Lord in His mercy, when He gave us the Word of Wisdom, gave it to us, not alone that we might have health while we live in the world, but that our faith might be strengthened, that our testimony of the divinity of the mission of our Lord and Master might be increased, that thereby we might be better prepared to return to His presence when our labor here is complete. —*George Albert Smith,* CR, p. 19, April, 1907

We are promised that if we obey the Word of Wisdom it will give us physical strength, whereby the destroying angel shall pass us by as he did the children of Israel. And we are promised that we shall have hidden treasures of knowledge if we live in accordance with the Word of Wisdom.
—*Heber J. Grant,* CR, p. 188, April, 1930

It is a piece of good counsel which the Lord desires His people to observe, that they may live on the earth until the measure of their creation is full. This is the object the Lord had in view in giving that Word of Wisdom. To those who observe it He will give great wisdom and understanding, increasing their

health, giving strength and endurance to the faculties of their bodies and minds until they shall be full of years upon the earth. This will be their blessing if they will observe His word with a good and willing heart and in faithfulness before the Lord.
—*Brigham Young*, JD 12:156, January 12, 1868

CONCERNING THE ORIGIN OF THE WORD OF WISDOM

I think I am as well acquainted with the circumstances which led to the giving of the Word of Wisdom as any man in the Church, although I was not present at the time to witness them. The first school of the prophets was held in a small room situated over the Prophet Joseph's kitchen, in a house which belonged to Bishop Whitney. . . . The brethren came to that place for hundreds of miles to attend school in a little room probably no larger than eleven by fourteen. When they assembled together in this room after breakfast, the first they did was to light their pipes and, while smoking, talk about the great things of the kingdom and spit all over the room, and as soon as the pipe was out of their mouths a large chew of tobacco would then be taken. Often when the Prophet entered the room to give the school instructions he would find himself in a cloud of tobacco smoke. This, and the complaints of his wife at having to clean so filthy a floor, made the Prophet think upon the matter, and he inquired of the Lord relating to the conduct of the elders in using tobacco, and the revelation known as the Word of Wisdom was the result of his inquiry. You know what it is and can read it at your leisure.
—*Brigham Young*, JD, 12:158, February 8, 1868

THE WORD OF WISDOM IS A COMMANDMENT OF GOD

The Word of Wisdom is today a commandment of the Lord to us, first given to us "not by constraint or commandment," but of later years given to us by the Prophet Brigham Young and by the Prophet Joseph F. Smith as a commandment to this people.
—*Heber J. Grant*, IE 19:833, June 9, 1916

Now, elders of Israel, if you have the right to chew tobacco, you have a privilege I have not; if you have a right to drink whisky, you have a right that I have not; if you have a right to transgress the Word of Wisdom, you have a right that I have not.
—*Brigham Young*, JD 12:30-31, April 7, 1867

Any Latter-day Saint who actually believes in the commandments contained in this book [Doctrine and Covenants] must have no regard for advancement in life when he fails to keep what is known as the Word of Wisdom. . . . There is absolutely no benefit to any human being derived from breaking the Word of Wisdom, but there is everything for his benefit, morally, intellectually, physically and spiritually in obeying it.
—Heber J. Grant, IE 31:514, February 12, 1928

"TOBACCO . . . IS NOT GOOD FOR MAN"

The Lord has pronounced tobacco not good for man, and this should be sufficient reason for the Latter-day Saints to abandon it. But instead, many of our people are becoming careless in the observance of this law and consider it a very slight matter to use tobacco in various ways. I cannot believe, nor have I ever believed, that it is a slight affair for any man, woman or child to do that which God, our Heavenly Father, has commanded us not to do.   *—Heber J. Grant, IE 24:260, January 1, 1921*

I have thought seriously that a boy or man who has become addicted to the use of tobacco in any form, to the extent that he is unable to resist his appetite for it, or who has practiced it until he is unable to resist or overcome it, is a man who is so mentally weakened, so morally degraded that he is not competent to perform and would not be worthy to be entrusted with any responsible duty. Why? because a man who has become so weak-minded and irresolute that he cannot overcome the temptation to do wrong or resist the power of an acquired, vicious appetite for poison, how can he be trusted? . . . You can't do it. You can't trust a man who has not the power of will to say "no" to temptation, to do evil or to that which entices to evil; he is only worthy of condemnation, and you cannot safely trust him, and you ought not to trust him.
—Joseph F. Smith, CR, p. 5, October, 1913

I want to say to you, in my judgment, that the use of tobacco, a little thing as it seems to some men, has been the means of destroying their spiritual life, has been the means of driving from them the companionship of the Spirit of our Father, has alienated them from the society of good men and women, and has brought upon them the disregard and reproach of the children

that have been born to them, and yet the devil will say to a man, Oh, it's only a little thing!
—*George Albert Smith,* CR, p. 40, April, 1918

There is something in the use of tobacco that blunts the finer susceptibilities, the gentlemanly instincts of men. I say nothing about destroying the finer, admirable, wonderful qualities of ladies, that every true man almost worships.
—*Heber J. Grant,* IE 24:876, August, 1921

One thing I deplore, and that is the fact that I can scarcely go onto the street or sidewalk but I see one to a dozen or more boys in their 'teens with pipes of tobacco in their mouths, puffing away in the open. . . . I deplore the sight of it wherever I see it; I want to tell those present, who are in the habit of using these things, that when you meet me in the street with a pipe, cigarette, or a cigar in your mouths, please do not recognize me— go right by, and I will do the same. I never did like to bow to a nasty, old, stinking pipe, nor to take my hat off to it. . . . I think it would be quite as manly if they would take directly to the use of opium and use it until they killed themselves quickly. It would be sooner over with to do that than to take the slower means of reaching death by sucking a pipe, cigarette, or something of that kind.   —*Joseph F. Smith,* CR, p. 6, April 3, 1910

I say to all the elders of Israel, if it makes you sick and so sleepy that you cannot keep out of bed unless you have tobacco, go to bed and there lie. How long? Until you can get up and go to your business like rational men, like men who have heads on their shoulders and who are not controlled by their foolish appetites.   —*Brigham Young,* JD 13:278, October 30, 1870

The cigarette creates an appetite for itself, and the habit of smoking cigarettes is one of the hardest and most difficult things in the world to overcome. It is absolutely no good morally, intellectually, physically, or in any other way.
—*Heber J. Grant,* RSM 25:14, September 30, 1937

Nothing is more detrimental to the physical and moral growth of a boy than the use of the cigarette.
—*Heber J. Grant,* IE 25:955, June 10, 1922

"STRONG DRINKS ARE NOT FOR THE BELLY"

"That inasmuch as any man drinketh wine or strong drink among you, behold it is not good, neither meet in the sight of your Father . . ." (Doc. and Cov. 89:5)

The Lord says it is not good. And all the legislatures and all the congresses and all the senators and all the officers in the kingdoms of the world can say otherwise, but that will not change the word of the Creator of heaven and earth.

—Heber J. Grant, CR, p. 7, April, 1933

There is no valid or convincing argument, economic, social, financial, moral or religious against wiping out the liquor traffic. On the contrary, every strong point favors the use of our franchise for the establishment of temperance, the abolishment of the saloon, and the absolute prohibition of the sale of liquor.

—Joseph F. Smith, IE 14:735, June, 1911

With the intelligence with which God has endowed me I believe, beyond a doubt, that more evil, suffering and crime has come into the world by the use of intoxicating liquors, and more misery has been brought into homes of the people, many, many times over, than was ever caused by slavery. I believe that the greatest financial, the greatest moral problem that is before the people of the United States today is this liquor problem.

—Heber J. Grant, CR, p. 26, April, 1914

We carry upon our shoulders the reputation, so to speak, of the Church, each and every one of us. The young men and young women of today who think they are being smart by getting a little wine and a little liquor in their homes, and doing that which the Lord tells them not to do, are laying a foundation that will lead to their destruction eventually. They cannot go on breaking the commandments of the Lord without getting into the rapids. And what are the rapids? The rapids of moderate drinking, nine times out of ten, lead to excessive drinking, and excessive drinking leads to the destruction of body and of mind and of faith.   *—Heber J. Grant, IE 31:514, February 12, 1928*

As with a person, as with a people, so it is with a nation. A drunken nation cannot expect that God will withhold His judgments, nor ward off the ravages of the destroyer. A drunken nation is a seedbed for disaster—political, moral, and spiritual. A drunken nation may not, even in its hours of direst distress, pray to God for help, with that simple assurance and unpolluted faith which brings aid and comfort to those who abide the law of sobriety and keep His commandments.

—Heber J. Grant, CR, p. 10, October, 1942

Over the earth, and it seems particularly in America, the demon drink is in control. Drunken with strong drink, men have lost their reason; their counsel has been destroyed; their judgment and vision are fled; they reel forward to destruction.

Drink brings cruelty into the home; it walks arm in arm with poverty; its companions are disease and plague; it puts chastity to flight; it knows neither honesty nor fair dealing; it is a total stranger to truth; it drowns conscience; it is the bodyguard of evil; it curses all who touch it.

Drink has brought more woe and misery, broken more hearts, wrecked more homes, committed more crimes, filled more coffins than all the wars the world has suffered.

—Heber J. Grant, CR, p. 8, October, 1942

Some mothers, when bearing children, long for tea and coffee, or for brandy and other strong drinks, and if they give way to that influence the next time they will want more and the next still more and thus lay the foundation for drunkenness in their offspring. An appetite is engendered, bred, and born in the child, and it is a miracle if it does not grow up a confirmed drunkard.   *—Brigham Young, JD 2:270, April 8, 1855*

Whisky-drinking makes fools of men. . . . Its effects are much worse than they used to be, for the liquor made now-a-days contains so much strychnine and arsenic that it is enough to kill anybody, and unless those who use it do lay it aside many will die.   *—Wilford Woodruff, JD 11:370, April 7, 1867*

And in regard to drunkenness, which has been of late a prevailing topic of conversation—what a nice creature is a drunken elder, a drunken Saint, a reeling, staggering, drunken Saint! What do you think of it? . . . We will not have such a person associated with us; we will not be contaminated nor disgraced with the name nor with the infamy of such conduct. And as regards the sellers of intoxicating drinks, they would many of them sell themselves. And any man who cannot let these things alone, any man that has not got manhood and respect enough to keep out of these pest-houses that disgrace our city, is not fit to associate with decent people, and respectable people ought to guard against him as they would against smallpox or any other pestiferous evil.   —*John Taylor*, JD 22:339, January 1, 1882

In the name of the Lord Jesus Christ, I command the elders of Israel—those who have been in the habit of getting drunk— to cease drinking strong drink from this time henceforth. . . . When you are tired and think you need a little spirituous liquor take some bread and butter, or bread and milk, and lie down and rest. Do not labor so hard as to deem it requisite to get half-drunk in order to keep up your spirits. If you will follow this counsel, you will be full of life and health, and you will increase your intelligence, your joy, and comfort.
          —*Brigham Young*, JD 7:337-338, October 8, 1859

Let me say to you Latter-day Saints that any man or woman professing to be a Latter-day Saint who keeps liquor in his or her home is not living the gospel of Jesus Christ. We know that there are girls—good, fine, true, virtuous girls—who have lost their virtue because of liquor in the homes of Latter-day Saints. They lose their senses, become drunk, stupid, and then they lose their virtue; and I know what I am talking about.
          —*Heber J. Grant*, CR, p. 12, April, 1937

How many saloons have we in Salt Lake City? (President Joseph F. Smith: Forty-five.) Forty-five rum shops in Salt Lake City! . . . Have we any people engaged in this degrading business that we know of? (President Joseph F. Smith: In Salt Lake City two, who profess to be Latter-day Saints.) They ought to be cut off from the Church. Any man who will deal in that liquid damnation ought to be cut off from the Church. They don't belong here. A saloon is not one of the institutions of Zion.
          —*John Taylor*, JD 24:354, December 9, 1883

Any man who will make whisky to use or sell would sell the kingdom of God for a picayune. I despise the whiskey-maker more than I do thieves, and I have no use for either. Harlots and publicans will enter the kingdom of God before the whisky dealer. "Cursed is he that putteth the cup to his brother's lips."
          —*Brigham Young*, "Life Story of Brigham Young" by Gates and Widtsoe, p. 164

"HOT DRINKS ARE NOT FOR THE BODY OR BELLY"

This Word of Wisdom prohibits the use of hot drinks and tobacco. I have heard it argued that tea and coffee are not mentioned therein; that is very true; but what were the people in the habit of taking as hot drinks when that revelation was given? Tea and coffee. We were not in the habit of drinking water very hot, but tea and coffee—the beverages in common use. And the Lord said hot drinks are not good for the body nor the belly.   —*Brigham Young,* JD 13:277, October 30, 1870

I understand that some of the people are excusing themselves in using tea and coffee, because the Lord only said "hot drinks" in the revelation of the Word of Wisdom. Tea and coffee are what the Lord meant when he said "hot drinks."
—*Joseph Smith, Jr.,* "The Word of Wisdom" by Widtsoe, p. 85, July, 1833

I have said to my family, and I now say to all the sisters in the Church, if you cannot get up and do your washing without a cup of tea in the morning go to bed and there lie. How long? Until the influence of tea is out of the system. Will it take a month? No matter if it does; if it takes three months, six months, or a year, it is better to lie there in bed until the influence of tea, coffee and liquor is out of the system, so that you may go about your business like rational persons, than to give way to these foolish habits. They are destructive to the human system; they filch money from our pockets, and they deprive the poor of the necessaries of life.   —*Brigham Young,* JD 13:278, October 30, 1870

It is a disgrace for a man blessed with the priesthood of God and with a testimony that God lives burning in his heart to be so weak that a little insignificant cup of coffee is his master. How he must swell up in vanity when he thinks what a wonderful man he is that a cup of coffee is his master! The example is pernicious.   —*Heber J. Grant,* CR, p. 35, October, 1900

FLESH OF BEASTS AND FOWLS TO BE USED SPARINGLY

A thorough reformation is needed in regard to our eating and drinking, and on this point I will freely express myself and shall be glad if the people will hear, believe and obey. If the people were willing to receive the true knowledge from heaven in regard to their diet they will cease eating swine's flesh. I know this as well as Moses knew it and without putting it in a code of commandments. . . . The beef fed upon our mountain grasses is as healthy food as we need at present. Beef, so fattened, is as good as wild meat, and is quite different in its nature from stall-fed meat. But we can eat fish; and I ask the people of this community, Who hinders you from raising fowls for their eggs? Who hinders you from cultivating fruit of every variety that will flourish in the different parts of this Territory? . . . Who hinders any person in this community from having these different kinds of food in their families? Fish is as healthy a food as we can eat, if we except vegetables and fruit, and with them will become a very wholesome diet.

—*Brigham Young*, JD 12:192-193, April 6, 1868

I think that another reason why I have very splendid strength for an old man is that during the years we have had a cafeteria in the Utah Hotel I have not, with the exception of not more than a dozen times, ordered meat of any kind. On these special occasions I have mentioned I have perhaps had a small, tender lamb chop. I have endeavored to live the Word of Wisdom, and that, in my opinion, is one reason for my good health.

—*Heber J. Grant*, CR, p. 15, April, 1937

CHURCH OFFICERS SHOULD OBEY THIS LAW OR RESIGN

No official member in this Church is worthy to hold an office after having the Word of Wisdom properly taught him; and he, the official member, neglecting to comply with and obey it.

—*Joseph Smith, Jr.*, TPJS, p. 117, a. 1834

The Word of Wisdom applies to Wilford Woodruff, the President of the Church, and it applies to all the leaders of Israel as well as to the members of the Church; and if there are any of these leading men who cannot refrain from using tobacco or liquor in violation of the Word of Wisdom let them resign and others take their places. As leaders of Israel, we have no business to indulge in these things.

—*Wilford Woodruff*, MS 56:737, October 7, 1894

We expect all the general officers of the Church, each and every one of them, from this very day, to be absolute, full-tithepayers, to really and truly observe the Word of Wisdom; and we ask all of the officers of the Church and all members of the general boards, and all stake and ward officers, if they are not living the gospel and honestly and conscientiously paying their tithing, to kindly step aside, unless from this day they live up to these provisions. . . .

No Latter-day Saint is entitled to anything that is contrary to the mind and will of the Lord, and the Word of Wisdom is the mind and the will of the Lord.

—*Heber J. Grant,* IE 40:665, October 3, 1937

If a man thinks more of a cup of tea or coffee, or a cigarette, or a chew of tobacco than he does of his priesthood, let him resign his priesthood.

—*Heber J. Grant,* DWN 50:1, October 6, 1894

Young men or middle-aged men who have had experience in the Church should not be ordained to the priesthood nor recommended to the privileges of the House of the Lord unless they will abstain from the use of tobacco and intoxicating drinks. This is the rule of the Church and should be observed by all its members. —*Joseph F. Smith,* IE 19:360, February, 1916

My own faith is that no one is fit to administer the sacrament, baptize the children of men, or administer in the House of God, unless he . . . keeps the Word of Wisdom. The Spirit of God will not dwell in unholy temples.

Wilford Woodruff, CR, p. 84, April, 1880

FINANCIAL REWARDS OF OBEYING THE WORD OF WISDOM

I want to say to the young people that, as a cold-blooded business proposition, as an investment, there is nothing that will give a young man more credit or better standing in the world, than to obey this simple law of God.

Many of the greatest corporations, employing thousands of men, will not employ a man who smokes; neither will they employ a man who drinks. They are beginning to find out that men who drink, who smoke, and break these commandments that the Lord has given to the Latter-day Saints lack the intellect, lack the physical strength, and the moral character which is so necessary to efficient service. They discover that those who break these laws of God are not so capable in the performance of any labor as are those who keep these laws. Now, let us fit and qualify ourselves morally, intellectually, and physically, that we may be able to fulfill every duty and obligation in all the walks of life. Let us have this capital as a part of our reserve; for it will prove to be one of the means by which we can make a success in the battle of life.   —*Heber J. Grant*, CR, p. 27, April, 1908

Do you want to know how to obtain temporal salvation? Not only the Latter-day Saints, but all the world would have the solution of that problem if there were no tea, coffee, liquor nor tobacco used in the world. Peace, prosperity, and happiness would come to the entire world.

—*Heber J. Grant*, CR, p. 9, October, 1933

I would like it known that if we as a people never used a particle of tea or coffee or of tobacco or of liquor, we would become one of the most wealthy people in the world. Why? Because we would have increased vigor of body, increased vigor of mind; we would grow spiritually; we would have a more direct line of communication with God, our Heavenly Father; we would be able to accomplish more—to say nothing about the fact that we do not produce these things that the Lord has told us to leave alone, and the money that is expended in breaking the Word of Wisdom goes away from our communities.

—*Heber J. Grant*, IE 44:73, February, 1941

I believe that if every dollar of money that is expended in Utah for liquor and for beer, tea, coffee and tobacco were saved, Utah would need no help from the United States government to take care of the poor, but peace, prosperity, happiness and abundance would be given to the people of our fair state and of every other state in the Union.   —*Heber J. Grant*, CR, p. 9, October, 1935

IN ALL THINGS BE TEMPERATE

How humiliating it must be to a thoughtful man to feel that he is a slave to his appetites, or to an over-weening and pernicious habit, desire or passion. We believe in strict temperance. We believe in abstinence from all injurious practices and from the use of all harmful things.   —*Joseph F. Smith*, CR, p. 4, April, 1908

Brethren, from henceforth, let truth and righteousness prevail and abound in you; and in all things be temperate; abstain from drunkenness, and from swearing, and from all profane language, and from everything which is unrighteous or unholy; also from enmity, and hatred, and covetousness, and from every unholy desire.   —*Joseph Smith, Jr.*, DHC, 3:233, December 16, 1838

Among these covenants are . . . that they will abstain from the use of intoxicants, from the use of strong drinks of every description, from the use of tobacco, from every vile thing, and from extremes in every phase of life.
                 —*Joseph F. Smith*, CR, p. 4, October, 1904

The best way to teach temperance is to keep the Word of Wisdom; and the next best is to assist others to keep it by removing artificial temptations from their lives. Such a temptation is the saloon, and it is time that the sentiment in the communities where the members of the Church reside should be declared against this soul-destroying evil.
                 —*Joseph F. Smith*, JI 46:333, June, 1911

There is a great destiny awaiting our young men. Therefore they ought to be temperate; not drink whisky, not chew or smoke tobacco, and not mingle with the drunken.
                 —*Wilford Woodruff*, MS 51:595, July 29, 1889

When I see men and women addicting themselves to the use of tea and coffee, or strong drinks, or tobacco in any form, I say to myself, here are men and women who do not appreciate the promise God has made unto them. . . They despise the word of God and go contrary to it in their actions. Then when afflicton overtakes them, they are almost ready to curse God, because He will not hear their prayers, and they are left to endure sickness and pain.
                 —*Joseph F. Smith*, JI 37:722, December, 1902

No member of the Church of Jesus Christ of Latter-day Saints can afford to do himself the dishonor or to bring upon himself the disgrace of crossing the threshold of a liquor saloon or a gambling hell, or of any house of ill-fame of whatever name or nature it may be. No Latter-day Saint, no member of the Church can afford it, for it is humiliating to him, it is disgraceful in him to do it, and God will judge him according to his works.
—*Joseph F. Smith*, CR, p. 7, October, 1908

The drunkard becomes a slave to his drink; others become slaves to the use of tea, coffee, and tobacco, and therefore they consider them necessary to their happiness; but they are not really necessary to their happiness nor to their health. Indeed, they are injurious to health. You cannot find an intelligent physician in the world that will tell you these things are not hurtful for common use.   —*Joseph F. Smith*, MS 56:819-820, October 5, 1894

CHAPTER XXXII

The Law of Tithing

WHAT IS TITHING?

WHAT IS tithing? The best and simplest answer, and from which all answers must in the end be taken, is that given by the Lord in reply to a similar question from the Prophet Joseph: "O Lord, show unto thy servants how much thou requirest of the properties of the people for a tithing?" The reply is plain: "Verily, thus saith the Lord, I require all their surplus property to be put into the hands of the bishop of my Church in Zion. . . . And this shall be the beginning of the tithing of my people. And after that, those who have thus been tithed shall pay one-tenth of all their interest annually; and this shall be a standing law unto them forever, for my Holy Priesthood, saith the Lord." (Doc. and Cov. 119:1;3-4)

Some persons are fond of caviling on the word interest, desiring to prove how little or how much should be paid in tithing. Such dickering and pinching, and such arguments, are not in line with the inspirations of the Spirit of God. Tithing is one-tenth.   —*Joseph F. Smith*, IE 2:782; 784, August, 1899

I do not suppose for a moment that there is a person in this Church who is unacquainted with the duty of paying tithing, neither is it necessary to have revelation every year upon the subject. There is the law—pay one-tenth.
—*Brigham Young*, JD 1:278, February 4, 1853

Here is a character—a man—that God has created, organized, fashioned and made,—every part and particle of my system from the top of my head to the soles of my feet has been produced by my Father in heaven; and He requires one-tenth part of my brain, heart, nerve, muscle, sinew, flesh, bone, and of my whole system for the building of temples, for the ministry, for sustaining missionaries and missionaries' families, for feeding the poor, the aged, the halt and blind, and for gathering them home from the nations and taking care of them after they are gathered.
—*Brigham Young*, JD 16:69, June 28, 1873

THE TITHING COVENANT

On the evening of the 29th of November, I united in prayer with Brother Oliver for the continuance of blessings. After giving thanks for the relief which the Lord had lately sent us by opening the hearts of the brethren from the east to loan us $430; after commencing and rejoicing before the Lord on this occasion, we agreed to enter into the following covenant with the Lord, viz.:

That if the Lord will prosper us in our business and open the way before us that we may obtain means to pay our debts; that we be not troubled nor brought into disrepute before the world, nor His people; after that, of all that He shall give unto us, we will give a tenth to be bestowed upon the poor in His Church, or as He shall command; and that we will be faithful over that which He has entrusted to our care, that we may obtain much; and that our children after us shall remember to observe this sacred and holy covenant; and that our children, and our children's children may know of the same, we have subscribed our names with our own hands.

—*Joseph Smith, Jr.*, DHC 2:174-175, November 29, 1834

TITHING IS OF THE LORD

The Lord instituted tithing; it was practiced in the days of Abraham, and Enoch and Adam.

—*Brigham Young*, JD 15:163, October 9, 1873

The law of tithing is an eternal law. The Lord Almighty never had His kingdom on the earth without the law of tithing being in the midst of His people, and He never will. It is an eternal law that God has instituted for the benefit of the human family, for their salvation and exaltation.

—*Brigham Young*, JD 14:89, April 9, 1871

The principle of tithing has been a principle of sacrifice in almost every age of the world; in fact, it was peculiarly so among the people in ancient days and among even the heathen nations of the earth. . . .

The law of tithing was carried out by all Israel, from the creation of the world down to the present time—that is, whenever God had a people upon the earth they observed the law of tithing.   —*Wilford Woodruff*, JD 22:207-208, January 9, 1881

THE PURPOSE OF TITHING

The purpose of the law of tithing is similar to that of the law of revenue which is enacted by every state, every country, and every municipality in the world. There is no such thing as an organization of men for any purpose of importance, without provisions for carrying out its designs. The law of tithing is the law of revenue for the Church of Jesus Christ of Latter-day Saints. Without it, it would be impossible to carry on the purposes of the Lord.   —*Joseph F. Smith*, CR, p. 28, October, 1897

The Lord revealed . . . the law of tithing, in order that there might be means in the storehouse of the Lord for the carrying out of the purposes He had in view; for the gathering of the poor, for the spreading of the gospel to the nations of the earth, for the maintenance of those who were required to give their constant attention, day in and day out, to the work of the Lord, and for whom it was necessary to make some provision. Without this law these things could not be done, neither could temples be built and maintained, nor the poor fed and clothed. Therefore the law of tithing is necessary for the Church, so much so that the Lord has laid great stress upon it.
—*Joseph F. Smith*, CR, p. 47, April, 1900

WHO SHOULD PAY TITHING?

All members who have an interest. That includes all who live.   —*Joseph F. Smith*, IE 2:782; 784, August, 1899

The bishop should encourage every man, woman and child that earns and receives in return for his labor to honor the Lord and to prove his obedience to the law of God by giving the one-tenth of that which he or she receives, as the Lord requires, so that they may have their names enrolled on the book of the law of the Lord, that their genealogies may be had in the archives of the Church, and that they may be entitled to the privileges and blessings of the House of God.
—*Joseph F. Smith*, CR, p. 48, April, 1900

WHEN TO PAY TITHING

The payment of our tithing in the season thereof—when we get our income—makes it come easy. I find that those who pay tithing every month have very much less difficulty in paying it than those who postpone payment to the end of the year. . . .

The Lord, you know, does not send collectors around once a month to collect bills; He does not send us our account once a month; we are trusted by the Lord; we are agents; we have our free will; and when the battle of life is over, we have had the ability and the power and the capacity to have done those things which the Lord required us to do and we cannot blame anybody else.   *—Heber J. Grant, IE 44:9; 56, January, 1941*

One of the best ways that I know of to pay my obligations to my brother, my neighbor, or business associate is for me first to pay my obligations to the Lord. I can pay more of my debts to my neighbors, if I have contracted them, after I have met my honest obligations with the Lord, than I can by neglecting the latter; and you can do the same. If you desire to prosper, and be free men and women and a free people, first meet your just obligations to God and then meet your obligations to your fellow-men.   *—Joseph F. Smith, CR, p. 2, April, 1903*

On the subject of tithing I heard a very splendid illustration given by a teacher in one of our children's classes: She brought with her ten beautiful red apples. She explained that everything we have in the world came to us from the Lord, and she said, "Now, if I give one of you these ten apples, will you give me one of them back again? Now, any one of you children that will do that, hold up your hand."

Of course, they all held up their hands. Then she said, "That is what the Lord does for us. He gives us the ten apples, but He requests that we return one to Him to show our appreciation of that gift."

The trouble with some people is that when they get the ten apples, they eat up nine of them, and then cut the other in two and give the Lord half of what is left. Some of them cut the apple in two and eat up one-half of it and then hold up the other half and ask the Lord to take a bite. That is about as near as they see fit to share properly and show their gratitude to the Lord.   *—Heber J. Grant, CR, p. 6, April, 1945*

TITHE PAYING IS NOT COMPULSORY

They say we cut people off the Church for not paying tithing; we never have yet, but they ought to be. God does not fellowship them. —*Brigham Young,* JD 14:89, April 9, 1871

The Lord has given us the privilege of contributing one-tenth of our interest for His Church, for the development of His work in the world. Those who pay their tithing receive their blessing. If we do not desire the blessing, we may withhold our contribution. The Lord promises His blessing if we honor His law and not otherwise. . . .

I suppose people think when they pay their tithing that they are making a sacrifice, but they are not; they are making a real investment that will return an eternal dividend. Our Heavenly Father gives us all that we have. He places all in our hands, authorizing us to retain for our own use nine-tenths of it, and then He asks that we put His tenth where He directs, where He knows it will accomplish the most good in developing His Church.
—*George Albert Smith,* CR, p. 25;28, April, 1941

HOW TITHING IS TO BE ADMINISTERED

The Lord has revealed how this means shall be cared for and managed; namely, by the Presidency of the Church and the High Council of the Church (that is, the Twelve Apostles), and the Presiding Bishopric of the Church. I think there is wisdom in this. It is not left for one man to dispose of it, or to handle it alone, not by any means. It devolves upon at least eighteen men . . . to dispose of the tithes of the people and to use them for whatever purposes in their judgment and wisdom will accomplish the most good for the Church.
—*Joseph F. Smith,* CR, p. 6, April, 1912

There is not one of the general authorities in the Church that draws one dollar from the tithes of the people for his own use. Well, you may say, how do they live? I will give you the key: The Church helped to support in its infancy the sugar industry in this country, and it has some means invested in that enterprise. The Church helped to establish the Z.C.M.I. and it has a little interest in that and in some other institutions which pay dividends. In other words, tithing funds were invested in these institutions, which give employment to many, for which the Trustee-in-Trust holds stock certificates, which are worth more today than what was given for them; and the dividends from these investments more than pay for the support of the general authorities of the Church. So we do not use one dollar of your tithing.   *—Joseph F. Smith,* CR, p. 7-8, April, 1907

THE TITHING BOOKS ARE OPEN TO TITHE PAYERS

The man that complains about not knowing what is done with the tithing, in ninety-nine cases out of a hundred, is the man who has no credit on the books of the Church for paying tithing. We do not care to exhibit the books of the Church to such carpers and to that class of people. But there is not a tithe-payer in the Church that cannot go to the Presiding Bishop's Office, or to the office of the Trustee-in-Trust, if he desires, and find his account and see to it that every dollar he has given to the Lord for tithing is credited to him. Then, if he wants to be more searching as a tithepayer and find out what is done with the tithing, we will set before him the whole thing, and if he has any good counsel to give us we will take it from him.
                                —Joseph F. Smith, CR, p. 6-7, April, 1906

I think our system of bookkeeping in relation to the tithes of the people is so perfect that every man who has ever paid tithing may go to the books and find there his credit. But the books here do not pretend to keep an account of that which you should pay; we simply keep an account of that which you do pay. But there is One above us who knows; and there may be a system of keeping accounts there wherein it will be known just what every man should pay to be honest with himself and the Lord.   *—Joseph F. Smith,* CR, p. 68, April, 1899

WHY OBSERVE THE LAW OF TITHING?

Tithing Is a Test of Faith

There is a great deal of importance connected with this principle [tithing] for by it it shall be known whether we are faithful or unfaithful. In this respect it is as essential as faith in God, as repentance of sin, as baptism for the remission of sin, or as the laying on of hands for the gift of the Holy Ghost.

The law of tithing is a test by which the people as individuals shall be proved. Any man who fails to observe this principle shall be known as a man who is indifferent to the welfare of Zion, who neglects his duty as a member of the Church, and who does nothing toward the accomplishment of the temporal advancement of the kingdom of God. He contributes nothing, either, toward spreading the gospel to the nations of the earth, and he neglects to do that which would entitle him to receive the blessings and ordinances of the gospel.
—Joseph F. Smith, CR, p. 47, April, 1900

Tithe Payment Is a Commandment With Promise of Blessing

It is not only a command, but it is given as the word of the Lord with promise; for by obedience to it are we to be delivered. When the earth shall be burned, and when the proud and they that do wickedly shall become as stubble under the feet of men, the Lord has declared that those who are tithed shall not be burned. *—Joseph F. Smith, CR, p. 69, April, 1901*

The promise is, that if we will obey the laws of God, if we will put our trust in Him, if we will draw near unto Him He will draw near unto us, and He will reward us with His favor, and His blessing. He will rebuke the devourer, and He will cause that the earth shall be fruitful, that it shall yield in its strength to the husbandman, the tiller of the soil, and to the herder of flocks, He will increase his kine, and will prosper him upon the right hand and upon the left, and he shall have an abundance, because he puts his trust in God; he draws near unto Him, and he is willing to prove Him, to see whether He will not open the windows of heaven and pour out blessings upon him that he shall not have room to contain them. Let every man who has received the gospel of Jesus Christ receive this saying and hearken to these words for all they are worth.
—Joseph F. Smith, CR, p. 28, October, 1897

Economic Advantages of Tithe Paying

I want to state here that which is in my heart. You may call it a prophecy if you will. Those who are and continue to be enrolled in the book of the law of the Lord—on the tithing records of the Church—will continue to prosper, their substance will increase, and they will have added unto them in greater abundance everything that they need; while those whose names are not recorded in the book of the law of the Lord will begin to diminish in that which they possess, until they will feel sorely the chastening hand of God.

—*Joseph F. Smith, CR, p. 70, April, 1901*

I want to repeat to the Latter-day Saints my firm belief that God our Heavenly Father prospers and blesses and gives wisdom to those men and to those women who are strictly honest with Him in the payment of their tithing. I believe that when a man is in financial difficulty, the best way to get out of that difficulty (and I speak from personal experience, because I believe that more than once in my life I have been in the financial mud as deep as almost anybody) is to be absolutely honest with the Lord and never to allow a dollar to come into our hands without the Lord receiving ten per cent of it.

—*Heber J. Grant, CR, p. 6-7, October, 1921*

I bear witness—and I know that the witness I bear is true— that the men and women who have been absolutely honest with God, who have paid their one-tenth, . . . God has given them wisdom whereby they have been able to utilize the remaining nine-tenths, and it has been of greater value to them, and they have accomplished more with it than they would if they had not been honest with the Lord.   *Heber J. Grant, CR, p. 30, April, 1912*

When the Latter-day Saints will pay an honest tithing unto the Lord there will be no need of talking about debts and of being in the bondage of debt. But the trouble is we do not do it.

—*Heber J. Grant, CR, p. 15, April, 1898*

Spiritual Benefits of Tithe Paying

If you desire the Spirit of God be honest in keeping the commandments of God. If you desire prosperity, and at the same time the testimony of the gospel, pay all your obligations to God and you shall have it. If you are not honest with God, you may prosper and you may be blessed with the things of this world,

but they will crowd out from your heart the spirit of the gospel; you will become covetous of your own means and lose the inspiration of Almighty God.
—Heber J. Grant, CR, p. 20, October, 1899

Prosperity comes to those who observe the law of tithing; and when I say prosperity I am not thinking of it in terms of dollars and cents alone, although as a rule the Latter-day Saints who are the best tithepayers are the most prosperous men, financially; but what I count as real prosperity, as the one thing of all others that is of great value to every man and woman living, is the growth in a knowledge of God, and in a testimony, and in the power to live the gospel and to inspire our families to do the same. That is prosperity of the truest kind.
—Heber J. Grant, CR, p. 10, April, 1925

Now, I believe that people are blessed in proportion to their liberality. I am not saying that they always make more dollars, perhaps, than the other man, but so far as an increase in the faith and in the testimony and the knowledge of the divinity of the work in which we are engaged, men that are honest with the Lord in the payment of their tithing grow as men never grow that are not honest; there is no question in my mind. Moreover, I am just foolish enough to believe that the Lord magnifies those who do pay their tithing and that they are more prosperous, on the average, than the men who do not. I believe that to those who are liberal the Lord gives ideas, and they grow in capacity and ability more rapidly than those that are stingy.
—Heber J. Grant, IE 44:9; 56, January, 1941

THE LORD WILL PROVIDE FOR THE OBEDIENT

If we do His will, He will take care of us as a people and as individuals. . . . I know, as well as I know I am standing before you today, that I have had money put into my trunk and into my pocket without the instrumentality of any man. This I know to a certainty.   *—Brigham Young, JD 2:128, April 17, 1853*

Of course there are some things I know and many that I do not; but I do know that Heber C. Kimball and myself used eighty-six dollars in board and other expenses while travelling on a mission, and that when we started we had but thirteen dollars, fifty cents. And I do know that I once took a five-dollar bill out of my pocket, when we were raising money for brother Joseph, and threw it in, and that the next day I had just as much as I had before I gave away the five dollars. I do know that when I went to pay some money that I owed, after giving some money to the poor, I had just as much when I came to pay my debts as I had before I gave any to the poor. I do know that I handed out a half-eagle to a poor man in my office and then found two half-eagles in my pocket that I never put there. And I also do know that I never hungered or thirsted for property.

—Brigham Young, JD 8:182, September 9, 1860

Three Reasons for Paying Tithing

First, that we may be entitled to the blessings, for it is a principle with promise, "Bring ye all the tithes into the storehouse, . . . and prove me now herewith, saith the Lord of Hosts, if I will not open you the windows of heaven, and pour you out a blessing, that there shall not be room enough to receive it. And I will rebuke the devourer for your sakes, and he shall not destroy the fruits of your ground; neither shall your vine cast her fruit before the time in the field, saith the Lord of Hosts." (Malachi 3:10, 11)

Second, we should fear the consequences of disobedience. It is written: "Behold, now it is called today (until the coming of the Son of man), and verily it is a day of sacrifice, and a day for the tithing of my people: for he that is tithed shall not be burned (at His coming)." O, say you, do you believe the Lord will burn the disobedient? Yes, I do. We are told that when God shall again cleanse the earth it shall be by fire, and it is evident that all who are not in harmony with the laws of God shall be consumed by the burning. . . . It is a precious promise that he who is tithed shall not be burned at His coming.

Third and this is the greatest reason, because God commands it, it is a duty to obey; and because it is good and right to obey. We are His children; we must be obedient to Him. He who promises and does not fulfill cuts himself off, but the obedient continue to be the sons of God.

—Joseph F. Smith, IE 2:783-784, August, 1899

A PROPHECY ON TITHE PAYING

Never but once in all my life have I stood up in a meeting and prophesied in the name of the Lord Jesus Christ, and that once was many, many years ago up in Idaho, at Paris. I was preaching that we should judge things not by the exception but by the general average and that the most prosperous, the most successful, the best financial men were those that were honest with God. And it seemed as though a voice said to me: "You lie, you lie. You will never live to pay your debts, although you have been an honest tithe-payer." If I had had a bucket of cold water poured over me, it could not have made a greater impression.

I stopped a moment, then I said, "I prophesy in the name of the Lord Jesus Christ that what I have said to you people is true, and that the Lord rewards us when we do our duty, and I prophesy that although I am a ruined man in the estimation of many men, I will yet live to pay my debts." And I was just $91,000 worse off than nothing, had two wives to support and the children of a dead wife. But from that very day my prophecy was fulfilled. The Lord blessed everything I touched, and in only three short years I was even with the world, financially speaking.   —*Heber J. Grant*, CR, p. 130, April, 1941

THE FAST OFFERING DONATION

The law to the Latter-day Saints, as understood by the authorities of the Church, is that food and drink are not to be partaken of for twenty-four hours, "from even to even," and that the Saints are to refrain from all bodily gratification and indulgences. Fast day being on the Sabbath, it follows, of course, that all labor is to be abstained from . . .

Now, while the law requires the Saints in all the world to fast from "even to even," and to abstain both from food and drink, it can easily be seen from the Scriptures and especially from the words of Jesus, that it is more important to obtain the true spirit of love for God and man, "purity of heart and simplicity of intention," than it is to carry out the cold letter of the law. . . . Many are subject to weakness, others are delicate in health, and others have nursing babies; of such it should not be required to fast. Neither should parents compel their little children to fast. . . . Better teach them the principle, and let them observe it when they are old enough to choose intelligently, than to so compel them.

—*Joseph F. Smith,* IE 6:148-149, December, 1902

We submit the equitable fast day plan of the Lord to the churches of the world as a wise and systematic way of providing for the poor. I say equitable, because it gives an opportunity for the contribution of much or little, according to the position and standing of those who contribute; and besides, helps both the giver and the receiver. If the churches would adopt the universal monthly fast day, as observed by the Latter-day Saints, and devote the means saved during the day to the alleviation, blessing and benefit of the poor, and with a view of helping them to help themselves, there would soon be no poor in the land.

—*Joseph F. Smith,* IE 10:832, August, 1907

CHAPTER XXXIII

The United Order or the Order of Enoch

WHAT IS THE UNITED ORDER?

O NE OF the first steps taken by the Prophet, after the establishment of headquarters in Kirtland, was the institution of what Latter-day Saints call the "United Order," a religio-social system, communal in its character, designed to abolish poverty, monopoly, and kindred evils, and to bring about unity and equality in temporal and spiritual things. It required the consecration to the Church by its members, of all their properties, and the subsequent distribution to those members, of what were termed "stewardships." Each holder of a stewardship—which might be the same farm, workshop, store, or factory that this same person had "consecrated"—was expected to manage it thereafter in the interest of the whole community; all his gains reverting to a common fund, from which he would derive a sufficient support for himself and those dependent upon him. The bishops, being the temporal officers of the Church, received the consecration of those properties and also assigned the stewardships; but they performed their duties under the direction of the First Presidency, who hold the keys of the Melchizedek Priesthood, to which the Aaronic or lesser priesthood is subject.

—*Joseph F. Smith*, MS 67:628, September, 1905

DISTINCTION BETWEEN TITHING AND THE UNITED ORDER

The law of consecration is in advance of the law of tithing and is a principle which, as sure as I am speaking, you and I will one day have to conform to. When that day comes we will be prepared to go to Zion.

—*Lorenzo Snow*, CR, p. 61-62, October, 1900

Zion can only be built up by the law that God revealed for that purpose, which is the law of consecration—not the law of tithing. The law of tithing was instituted because the people could not abide the greater law. If we could live up to the law of consecration, then there would be no necessity for the law of tithing, because it would be swallowed up in the greater law. The law of consecration requires all; the law of tithing only requires one-tenth of your increase annually.

—Joseph F. Smith, MS 56:386, October 29, 1893

So far as the law of tithing is concerned, there is about it something that is not of the same nature and character as the law of the United Order. It was added because the people were not willing to comply with this noble and high celestial law. . . .

Now this law (the United Order) should continue as long as salvation continues. It never has been repealed. The law of tithing could not repeal this law. The law of tithing is a lower law and was given of God. But the law of tithing does not forbid us obeying a higher law, the law of celestial union in earthly things. And the fact that we do not feel satisfied in simply obeying the law of tithing shows that it is a lesser law. Do you feel justified simply in obeying the law of tithing? Why, then, do you contribute to our temples and to bringing the people from the old countries, and to this object, and that, in thousands of ways, after you have properly and justly complied with the law of tithing? The fact that you do these things shows that you are not satisfied in merely obeying the law of tithing.

—Lorenzo Snow, JD 20:367-368, October 19, 1879

THE PURPOSE OF THE UNITED ORDER

The system of union, or the Order of Enoch, which God has taken so much pains to reveal and make manifest has been, and is, for the purpose of uniting the Latter-day Saints, the people of God, and preparing them for exaltation in His celestial kingdom.   *—Lorenzo Snow,* JD 19:342, April 21, 1878

When we consecrate our property to the Lord it is to administer to the wants of the poor and needy, for this is the law of God; it is not for the benefit of the rich, those who have no need. . . . Now for a man to consecrate his property, wife and children to the Lord is nothing more nor less than to feed the hungry, clothe the naked, visit the widow and fatherless, the

sick and afflicted, and do all he can to administer to their relief in their afflictions, and for him and his house to serve the Lord.
—*Joseph Smith, Jr.,* DHC 3:230-231, December, 1838

I cannot conceive of anything more beautiful and heavenly than a united brotherhood, . . . where our time, our property, our talents, our mental and bodily powers, are all exerted for the good of all; where no man grabs or takes advantage of another; where there is a common interest, a common purse, a common stock.
—*John Taylor,* JD 17:180, October 9, 1874

There are certain events awaiting the nations of the earth as well as Zion; and when these events overtake us we will be preserved if we take the counsel that is given us and unite our time, labor and means, and produce what we need for our own use; but without this we shall not be prepared to sustain ourselves and we shall suffer loss and inconvenience thereby.
—*Wilford Woodruff,* JD 17:70, May 8, 1874

THE UNITED ORDER IS THE ORDER OF HEAVEN

The Order of Enoch . . . is in reality the Order of Heaven. It was revealed to Enoch when he built up his city and gathered the people together and sanctified them, so that they became so holy and pure that they could not live among the rest of the people and the Lord took them away.
—*Brigham Young,* JD 13:2, April 7, 1869

Concerning the United Order, I wish you to understand that this is no new revelation; it is the order of the kingdom where God and Christ dwell; it has been from eternity and will be to eternity, without end. —*Brigham Young,* JD 17:154, August 9, 1874

I have looked upon the community of Latter-day Saints in vision and beheld them organized as one great family of heaven, each person performing his several duties in his line of industry, working for the good of the whole more than for individual aggrandizement; and in this I have beheld the most beautiful order that the mind of man can contemplate and the grandest results for the upbuilding of the kingdom of God and the spread of righteousness upon the earth. Will this people ever come to this order of things? Are they now prepared to live according to that patriarchal order that will be organized among the true and faithful before God receives His own? We all concede the point that when this mortality falls off, and with it its cares, anxieties, love of self, love of wealth, and love of power, and all the conflicting interests which pertain to this flesh, that then, when our spirits have returned to God who gave them, we will be subject to every requirement that He may make of us, that we shall then live together as one great family; our interest will be a general, a common interest. Why can we not so live in this world?

—*Brigham Young,* JD 12:153, January 12, 1868

No one supposes for one moment that in heaven the angels are . . . taking advantage one of another. . . . No Christian, no sectarian Christian, in the world believes this; they believe that the inhabitants of heaven live as a family, that their faith, interests and pursuits have one end in view—the glory of God and their own salvation. . . .

We will try to imitate in some small degree the family that lives in heaven and prepare ourselves for the society that will dwell upon the earth when it is purified and glorified and comes into the presence of the Father.

—*Brigham Young,* JD 17:117-118, June 28, 1874

CONCERNING THE ADMINISTRATION OF THE UNITED ORDER

I will say, first, that the Lord Almighty has not the least objection in the world to our entering into the Order of Enoch. I will stand between the people and all harm in this. He has not the least objection to any man, every man, all mankind on the face of the earth turning from evil and loving and serving Him with all their hearts. With regard to all those orders that the Lord has revealed, it depends upon the will and doings of the people, and we are at liberty from this conference, to go and build up a settlement, or we can join ourselves together in this city, do it legally—according to the laws of the land—and enter into covenant with each other by a firm agreement that we will live as a family, that we will put our property into the hands of a committee of trustees, who shall dictate the affairs of this society.   —*Brigham Young,* JD 16:8, April 7, 1873

The matter of consecration must be done by the mutual consent of both parties; for to give the bishop power to say how much every man shall have, and he be obliged to comply with the bishop's judgment, is giving to the bishop more power than a king has; and upon the other hand, to let every man say how much he needs, and the bishop be obliged to comply with his judgment, is to throw Zion into confusion and make a slave of the bishop. The fact is, there must be a balance or equilibrium of power between the bishop and the people, and thus harmony and good will may be preserved among you.
—*Joseph Smith Jr.*, DHC 1:364, June 25, 1833

A city of one hundred thousand or a million of people could be united into a perfect family and they would work together as beautifully as the different parts of the carding machine work together. Why, we could organize millions into a family under the Order of Enoch. —*Brigham Young*, JD 16:170, August 31, 1873

ECONOMIC BENEFITS UNDER THE ORDER OF ENOCH
I will tell you, Latter-day Saints, that unless we can enter into . . . the United Order with singleness of heart and pure motives, as the elders do when they go forth to preach the gospel, because it is God's command, your efforts will be of small avail. . . . But I will promise the Latter-day Saints that if they will go into these things allowing God to dictate in the interests of Israel and the building up of His Zion on the earth and take themselves and their individual interests out of the question, feeling they are acting for Him and His kingdom, they will become the wealthiest of all people, and God will bless them and pour out wealth and intelligence and all the blessings that earth can afford. —*John Taylor*, JD 20:163-164, March 2, 1879

When this people deed over their property, they understand what they are about; they know that they will eventually be exalted to possess all that is desirable—the land, the houses, the vineyards, the cattle, the gold, the silver, and all the riches of the heavens and of the earth. The Lord says, All these things are mine; and because of the willingness of my people, all will be restored back to me; and then I will put them in possession of all the riches of eternity. —*Lorenzo Snow*, JD 5:65, April 9, 1857

IMPORTANCE OF OBEDIENCE TO THE UNITED ORDER

Referring to the United Order, the Lord has given us to understand that whosoever refuses to comply with the requirements of that law, his name shall not be known in the records of the Church but shall be blotted out; neither shall his children have an inheritance in Zion. . . . If faith, repentance, and baptism and laying on of hands is right and true and demands our obedience, so does cooperation and the United Order.

Some may say, here such and such a man has been connected with the United Order and how foolishly he has acted, and others have gone into cooperation and made a failure of it. Yes, that may be all very true, but who is to blame? Shall we stop baptizing people and make no further efforts to establish the kingdom of God upon the earth because certain ones have acted foolishly and perhaps wickedly? Do the actions of such people render the principles of the gospel without effect or the doctrines we teach untrue? . . . Shall we then think of putting an end to these other principles because men have acted foolishly and selfishly and done wrong? No, I think not; I do not think we can choose one principle and reject another to suit ourselves. I think that all of these things, as we have received them, one after another, are equally binding upon us.
—*John Taylor,* JD 21:58-59, September 21, 1878

When the Church was established among the Nephites . . . this doctrine (United Order) was preached by them and practiced nearly two hundred years, resulting in peace, union, great prosperity, and miraculous blessings, greater than were ever experienced by any people of whom we have record. The most remarkable miracles were constantly wrought among them; their sick were healed, and in some instances their dead restored to life; these extraordinary manifestations of the approbation of God continued so long as they remained one in their temporal interest or were controlled in their financial matters according to the Order of Enoch.   —*Lorenzo Snow,* JD 16:274, October 7, 1873

THE UNITED ORDER AND THE CENTER STAKE
OF ZION

The principles of the United Order . . . are sacred and I assure you we will never go back to Jackson County, Missouri, there to build up the New Jerusalem of the Latter days, until there is a perfect willingness on our part to conform to its rules and principles.   —*Lorenzo Snow,* BFRLS, p. 375, April 5, 1877

The Lord has declared it to be His will that His people enter into covenant, even as Enoch and his people did, which of necessity must be before we shall have the privilege of building the Center Stake of Zion, for the power and glory of God will be there, and none but the pure in heart will be able to live and enjoy it.   —*Brigham Young,* JD 18:263, October 8,1876

If ever we build up a Zion here on this continent, and in case Zion ever comes down to us, and we expect it will, or that ours will go up to meet it, we have got to be governed by the same principles that they are governed by, or we can not be one; and if we ever get into the eternal worlds we shall have to be heirs of God and joint heirs with Jesus Christ.
          —*John Taylor,* JD 17:180 October 9,1874

The Saints. in Jackson County and other localities refused to comply with the order of consecration, consequently they were allowed to be driven from their inheritances; and should not return until they were better prepared to keep the law of God, by being more perfectly taught in reference to their duties and learn through experience the necessity of obedience. And I think we are not justified in anticipating the privilege of returning to build up the Center Stake of Zion, until we shall have shown obedience to the law of consecration.
          —*Lorenzo Snow,* JD 16:276, October 7, 1873

We have had a great deal said about the United Order and about our becoming one. And some people would wish—Oh, how they do wish, they could get around that principle, if they could! But you Latter-day Saints, you cannot get around it; you cannot dig around it; it will rise before you every step you take, for God is determined to carry out His purposes and to build up His Zion; and those who will not walk into line He will move out of the way and no place will be found for them in Israel. Hear it, you Latter-day Saints, for I say to you in the name of Israel's God that it is a revelation from the Most High, and you cannot get around it.   —*John Taylor,* JD 20:43, August 4, 1878

THE UNITED ORDER IS NOT A COMMUNISTIC ORDER

The Order of Enoch is not a communistic order after the manner of man, but a united order in which each man will be his own free agent. God will hold each man accountable for the use he makes of that agency and he will be rewarded according to the account which he renders. The Lord's plan is a righteous plan. The wise steward who is willing and industrious should not be made to sacrifice his time and substance to support the idle and shiftless.   —*Joseph F. Smith*, "Life Story of Brigham Young" by Gates and Widtsoe, p. 200

To our Church members we say: Communism is not the United Order and bears only the most superficial resemblance thereto; Communism is based upon intolerance and force, the United Order upon love and freedom of conscience and action: Communism involves forceful despoliation and confiscation, the United Order voluntary consecration and sacrifice.

Communists cannot establish the United Order, nor will Communism bring it about. The United Order will be established by the Lord in His own due time and in accordance with the regular prescribed order of the Church.

—*Heber J. Grant*, IE 39:488, August, 1936

CHAPTER XXXIV

The Holy Scriptures

THE SCRIPTURES ARE THE WORD OF GOD

THE Bible, Book of Mormon, Doctrine and Covenants, and Pearl of Great Price do not contain the wisdom of men alone, but of God. While they do not find their way into the homes of many people, they contain the word of the Lord. What mattereth it though we understand Homer and Shakespeare and Milton, and I might enumerate all the great writers of the world, if we have failed to read the Scriptures we have missed the better part of this world's literature.
—*George Albert Smith*, CR, p. 43, October, 1917

The Old and New Testaments, the Book of Mormon, and the book of Doctrine and Covenants . . . are like a lighthouse in the ocean or a finger-post which points out the road we should travel. Where do they point? To the fountain of light. . . . That is what these books are for. They are of God; they are valuable and necessary; by them we can establish the doctrine of Christ.
—*Brigham Young*, JD 8:129, July 22, 1860

When God speaks to the people, He does it in a manner to suit their circumstances and capacities. . . . Should the Lord Almighty send an angel to rewrite the Bible, it would in many places be very different from what it now is. And I will even venture to say that if the Book of Mormon were now to be re-written, in many instances it would materially differ from the present translation. According as people are willing to receive the things of God, so the heavens send forth their blessings.
—*Brigham Young*, JD 9:311, July 13, 1862

My mind reverts to the channels of communication from God to man. Here we have the Bible which gives a history and prophecy of the prophets from Adam down to our own day extending through a period of near 6,000 years. . . Then, again, we have the Book of Mormon, the stick of Joseph in the hands of Ephraim,

giving a history of the ancient inhabitants of this country from the time of their leaving the Tower of Babel to their disappearance from the land and of the visitation of Christ to them. We have these books from which to obtain knowledge. Then we have the book of Doctrine and Covenants, our testament, which contains the most glorious, godlike, solemn and eternal truths ever recorded within the lids of a book on the earth. All these records are the words of God to man; and though the heavens and earth pass away not one jot or tittle will ever fall unfulfilled.
—*Wilford Woodruff*, JD 22:331, October 8, 1881

We are called a peculiar people because, perchance, we thoroughly believe and obey the gospel of Jesus Christ. Our peculiarity lies very largely in the fact that we believe the Old and New Testaments actually contain the word of the Lord, as far as they have been translated correctly. We also firmly believe the Book of Mormon, which the world knows comparatively little of; and add to that unwavering belief in the Doctrine and Covenants and Pearl of Great Price. We regard the teachings contained therein as revelations of our Father in heaven to His children who dwell upon this earth.
—*George Albert Smith*, CR, p. 26, October, 1905

READ THE SCRIPTURES!

I admonish you, O Israel, search the Scriptures; read them in your homes; teach your families what the Lord has said; let us spend less of our time reading the unimportant and often harmful literature of the day and go to the fountain of truth and read the word of the Lord. . . .

We have the Old and the New Testaments, the Book of Mormon, and the Pearl of Great Price, also translated by the gift and power of God, in addition new revelations through the Prophet Joseph Smith. . . .

Will our Father hold us guiltless when we go home, if we have failed to teach our children the importance of these sacred records? I think not. He called His sons one by one, and they gave their lives that we might have the Old Testament. He sent His Only Begotten Son into the world, and His life was sacrificed in order that we might have the teachings of the New Testament. The prophets of God recorded in the Book of Mormon laid down their lives and sealed their testimonies with their blood, in order that the children of men might know what the Father desired of them. He sent the Prophet Joseph Smith, and he gave his life, together with his brother Hyrum, in order that we might have the truths contained in the sacred record known as the Doctrine and Covenants. Do you suppose that after the Lord has done all this for us, has given to this world the choicest and sweetest of men and women, whose lives have been dedicated to the blessing of mankind, many of them sealing their testimony with their blood, has placed within our reach the excellent teachings contained in these holy records, that He will consider us appreciative if we fail to teach them to our families and to impress them upon those with whom we come in contact?

—*George Albert Smith,* CR, p. 41; 43-44, October, 1917

The Bible, the Book of Mormon, the book of Doctrine and Covenants contain the words of eternal life unto this generation, and they will rise in judgment against those who reject them.

—*Wilford Woodruff,* JD 22:335, October 8, 1881

"WE BELIEVE THE BIBLE . . . AS FAR AS IT IS TRANSLATED CORRECTLY"

I believe the Bible as it read when it came from the pen of the original writers. Ignorant translators, careless transcribers, or designing and corrupt priests have committed many errors.

—*Joseph Smith, Jr.,* DHC 6:57, October 15, 1843

It has been proclaimed that there is a great difference between us and the Christian world. . . . The difference arises from the fact that we believe this Bible, wide open, from Genesis to Revelations. They believe it, sealed up, never to be opened again to the human family. They believe it shut, we believe it open; they believe it in silence, we believe it proclaimed on the house top.

—*Brigham Young,* JD 15:41, May 26, 1872

I have heard ministers of the gospel declare that they believed every word in the Bible was the word of God. I have said to them, "You believe more than I do." I believe the words of God are there; I believe the words of the devil are there; I believe that the words of men and the words of angels are there; and that is not all,—I believe that the words of a dumb brute

are there. I recollect one of the prophets riding and prophesying against Israel, and the animal he rode rebuked his madness.
                              —*Brigham Young*, JD 14:280, July 3, 1870

The Bible is true. It may not all have been translated aright,
and many precious things may have been rejected in the compilation and translation of the Bible; but we understand, from
the writings of one of the apostles, that if all the sayings and
doings of the Savior had been written, the world could not contain them. I will say that the world could not understand them.
They do not understand what we have on record, nor the character of the Savior, as delineated in the Scriptures; and yet it is
one of the simplest things in the world, and the Bible, when it
is understood, is one of the simplest books in the world for, as
far as it is translated correctly, it is nothing but truth, and in
truth there is no mystery save to the ignorant. The revelations of
the Lord to His creatures are adapted to the lowest capacity, and
they bring life and salvation to all who are willing to receive
them.   —*Brigham Young*, JD 14:135-136, May 21, 1871

We have testimony that the Bible is true, that the prophecies
contained in it are true, that Jesus is the Son of God and came
to redeem the world. Have the so-called Christian world this
kind of testimony? They have not. All the testimony they can
boast of is the testimony of eight men who lived nearly two
thousand years ago. The infidel world cannot receive their testimony, because they were parties concerned.
                              —*Brigham Young*, JD 12:208, May 10, 1868

Here is the Bible, the record of the Jews, given by the inspiration of the Lord through Moses and the ancient patriarchs
and prophets. Is it an imposture and as the infidels say, the work
of man? No, it is not in the power of any man who ever breathed
the breath of life to make such a book without the inspiration of
the Almighty.   —*Wilford Woodruff*, JD 16:35, April 7, 1873

THE GOSPEL PLAN IS CONTAINED IN THE BIBLE

In all my teachings, I have taught the gospel from the Old
and New Testaments. I found therein every doctrine and the
proof of every doctrine the Latter-day Saints believe in, as
far as I know, therefore I do not refer to the Book of Mormon

as often as I otherwise should. There may be some doctrines about which little is said in the Bible, but they are all couched therein, and I believe the doctrines because they are true, and I have taught them because they are calculated to save the children of men. —*Brigham Young*, JD 16:73-74, May 25, 1873

But I will say that the doctrines taught in the Old and New Testaments concerning the will of God towards His children here on the earth; the history of what He has done for their salvation; the ordinances which He has instituted for their redemption; the gift of His Son and His atonement—all these are true, and we, the Latter-day Saints, believe in them.
—*Brigham Young*, JD 13:174, May 29, 1870

We take this book, the Bible, which I expect to see voted out of the so-called Christian world very soon, they are coming to it as fast as possible, I say we take this book for our guide, for our rule of action; we take it as the foundation of our faith. It points the way to salvation like a fingerboard pointing to a city or a map which designates the locality of mountains, rivers, or the latitude and longitude of any place on the surface of the earth that we desire to find, and we have no better sense than to believe it; hence, I say that the Latter-day Saints have the most natural faith and belief of any people on the face of the earth. —*Brigham Young*, JD 13:236, February 20, 1870

THE BOOK OF MORMON—THE AMERICAN SCRIPTURE

The Book of Mormon is a record of the forefathers of our western tribes of Indians; having been found through the ministration of an holy angel and translated into our own language by the gift and power of God, after having been hid up in the earth for the last fourteen hundred years, containing the word of God which was delivered unto them. By it we learn that our western tribes of Indians are descendants from that Joseph who was sold into Egypt, and that the land of America is a promised land unto them, and unto it all the tribes of Israel will come, with as many of the Gentiles as shall comply with the requisitions of the new covenant.
—*Joseph Smith*, Jr., DHC 1:315, January 4, 1833

The Book of Mormon consists largely of the teachings of the prophets who, from age to age, taught the gospel to the people of ancient America.   —*George Albert Smith*, CR, p. 46, April, 1916

I read the Book of Mormon through, prayerfully, as a young man in my teens, and I became absolutely converted that it is exactly what it purports to be, namely, a record of the hand-dealings of God with many peoples that had located on the American continents before Columbus discovered America.
                    —*Heber J. Grant*, IE 39:660, November, 1936

This record [the Book of Mormon] contains an account of the ancient inhabitants of this continent and of the cities with which they overspread this land from sea to sea, the ruins of which still remain as standing monuments of the arts, science, power, and greatness of their founders. It also points out the establishing of this our own nation, with the conditions for its progress, and those predictions contained in the Book of Mormon—the stick of Joseph in the hand of Ephraim, will as truly be fulfilled as those contained in the Bible—the stick and record of Judah; and both these sticks or records contain prophecies of great import concerning the Gentile nations, and especially this land and nation, which are not yet fulfilled but must shortly come to pass: yea, their fulfillment is nigh, even at the doors.
                    —*Wilford Woodruff*, DHC 6:24, September, 1843

The Book of Mormon is the great, the grand, the most wonderful missionary that we have.
                    —*Heber J. Grant*, CR, p. 126, April, 1937

In the Book of Mormon, "The American volume of Scripture," the Lord has given to us information pertaining to this land upon which we dwell and called it a land favored above all other lands. I recommend that not only you Latter-day Saints read the Book of Mormon, but that our Father's other children read it. They will find that it contains, in addition to what the Bible has said about the world, what the Lord has said about this Western Hemisphere—that this should be a land of liberty unto the Gentiles and that no king should dwell upon this land, but that He, the God of heaven, would be our King and would fortify this land against all the nations, that this should be a land of peace and happiness, on condition that we would honor the God of this earth, the Father of us all. The factor controlling this promise is that we must keep the commandments of our Heavenly Father or it cannot be realized.

—George Albert Smith, CR, p. 108, October, 1940

There is not another nation under heaven but this, in whose midst the Book of Mormon could have been brought forth. The Lord has been operating for centuries to prepare the way for the coming forth of the contents of that Book from the bowels of the earth, to be published to the world, to show to the inhabitants thereof that He still lives and that He will, in the latter days, gather His elect from the four corners of the earth. It was the Lord who directed the discovery of this land to the nations of the Old World and its settlement, and the war for independence, and the final victory of the colonies, and the unprecedented prosperity of the American nation, up to the calling of Joseph the Prophet. The Lord has dictated and directed the whole of this, for the bringing forth and establishing of His kingdom in the last days.

—Brigham Young, JD 11:17, December 11, 1864

Let us take the Book of Mormon, which a man took and hid in his field, securing it by his faith, to spring up in the last days, or in due time; let us behold it coming forth out of the ground, which is indeed accounted the least of all seeds, but behold it branching forth, yea, even towering, with lofty branches, and Godlike majesty, until it, like the mustard seed, becomes the greatest of all herbs. And it is truth, and it has sprouted and come forth out of the earth, and righteousness begins to look down from heaven, and God is sending down His powers, gifts and angels, to lodge in the branches thereof.

—Joseph Smith, Jr., DHC 2:268, December, 1835

"WE . . . BELIEVE THE BOOK OF MORMON TO BE THE WORD OF GOD"

I told the brethren that the Book of Mormon was the most correct of any book on earth, and the keystone of our religion, and a man would get nearer to God by abiding by its precepts than by any other book.

—Joseph Smith, Jr., DHC 4:461, November 28, 1841

When the Book of Mormon came forth it was testified to by twelve witnesses, and who can dispute their testimony? No living person on the earth can do it; and besides the testimony of these twelve witnesses, hundreds and thousands have received a witness to themselves from the heavens, and who can dispute their testimony? No living person on the earth can do it.

—Brigham Young, JD 12:208, May 10, 1868

I do not believe that in any court of justice in the world if a man were being tried for murder and twelve reputable citizens testified of their knowledge of the circumstances leading to the murder, and there was no one who could testify against what they said, there would be a failure to convict the man. We have the testimony of Joseph Smith and the testimony of three witnesses to the effect that God gave them a knowledge regarding the Book of Mormon, that an angel of God declared from heaven that the book had been translated by the gift and power of God. These men were Oliver Cowdery, David Whitmer and Martin Harris. They left the Church, but to the day of their death they maintained their testimony regarding the declaration of the angel and that they were commanded to bear witness of the divinity of this book, and they did so. Eight men, some of whom were excommunicated from the Church, maintained their testimony that they had seen and handled the plates from which the Book of Mormon was translated, and they remained true to that testimony to the day of their death. The disbelief of all the world does not prove that those men did not tell the truth, because there are no witnesses on the other side.

It has been said that the Book of Mormon has fraud written upon every page of it. The Book of Mormon is in absolute harmony from start to finish with other sacred Scriptures. There is not a doctrine taught in it that does not harmonize with the teachings of Jesus Christ. There is not one single expression in the Book of Mormon that would wound in the slightest degree the sensitiveness of any individual. There is not a thing in it but what is for the benefit and uplift of mankind. It is in every way a true witness for God, and it sustains the Bible and is in harmony with the Bible. No group of men can write a book of six or seven hundred pages that is a fraud and have it in harmony in every particular with the Scriptures that were given to us by the prophets of God and by Jesus Christ and His apostles.

—Heber J. Grant, CR, p. 128-129, April, 1929

What did Oliver Cowdery (one of the three witnesses to the Book of Mormon) say, after he had been away from the Church years and years? He saw and conversed with the angel, who showed him the plates, and he handled them. He left the Church because he lost the love of the truth; and after he had traveled alone for years, a gentleman walked into his law office and said to him, "Mr. Cowdery, what do you think of the Book of Mormon now? Do you believe that it is true?" He replied, "No, sir, I do not." "Well," said the gentleman, "I thought as much; for I concluded that you had seen the folly of your ways and had resolved to renounce what you once declared to be true." "Sir, you mistake me: I do not *believe* that the Book of Mormon is true; I am past *belief* on that point, for I *know* that it is true, as well as I *know* that you now sit before me." "Do you still testify that you saw an angel?" "Yes, as much as I see you now; and I know the Book of Mormon to be true." Yet he forsook it. Every honest person who has fairly heard it knows that "Mormonism" is true, if they have had the testimony of it; but to practice it in our lives is another thing.

—Brigham Young, JD 7:55, June 27, 1858

I rejoice in the wonderful spirit of the Book of Mormon. I believe that it is one of the greatest missionaries in the hands of the elder that it is possible for him to have. I believe that no man can open that book and read it with a prayerful heart and ask God, in the name of Jesus Christ, for a testimony regarding its divinity, but what the Lord will manifest unto him by His Spirit the truth of the book. Now that is the promise made in the book itself, and God has performed it; He has done it in thousands of cases. There is a mark of divinity on this book; and I maintain that no man can read [it] . . . without receiving an impression of this kind. It is claimed by some that this book was written as a novel. I maintain that a man ought to have his head tapped for the simples who would undertake to say that any one would be idiotic enough to write a book like the Book of Mormon as a novel, hoping to sell it to the people.

—Heber J. Grant, CR, p. 57, April, 1908

I wish to mention here that the title page of the Book of Mormon is a literal translation, taken from the very last leaf on the left hand side of the collection or book of plates, which contained the record which has been translated, the language of the whole running the same as all Hebrew writing in general; and that said title page is not by any means a modern composition, either of mine or of any other man who has lived or does live in this generation.   —*Joseph Smith, Jr.*, DHC 1:71, 1830

THE BIBLE AND THE BOOK OF MORMON AGREE

No man can say that this book (laying his hand on the Bible) is true, is the word of the Lord, is the way, is the guideboard in the path, and a charter by which we may learn the will of God; and at the same time say that the Book of Mormon is untrue; if he has had the privilege of reading it, or of hearing it read, and learning its doctrines. There is not that person on the face of the earth who has had the privilege of learning the gospel of Jesus Christ from these two books, that can say that one is true and the other is false. No Latter-day Saint, no man or woman, can say the Book of Mormon is true and at the same time say that the Bible is untrue. If one be true, both are; and if one be false, both are false.
—*Brigham Young*, JD 1:38, July 11, 1852

The Book of Mormon in no case contradicts the Bible. It has many words like those in the Bible, and as a whole is a strong witness to the Bible. Revelations, when they have passed from God to man, and from man into his written and printed language, cannot be said to be entirely perfect, though they may be as perfect as possible under the circumstances; they are perfect enough to answer the purposes of heaven at this time.
—*Brigham Young*, JD 9:310, July 13, 1862

All my life I have been finding additional evidences that the Bible is the Book of books, and that the Book of Mormon is the greatest witness for the truth of the Bible that has ever been published.   —*Heber J. Grant*, IE 39:660, November, 1936

There is no clash in the principles revealed in the Bible, the Book of Mormon, and the Doctrine and Covenants; and there would be no clash between any of the doctrines taught by Joseph the Prophet and by the brethren now, if all would live in a way to be governed by the Spirit of the Lord. All do not live so as

to have the Spirit of the Lord with them all the time, and the result is that some get out of the way.
—*Brigham Young*, JD 5:329, October 7, 1857

The Book of Mormon is a history of the dealings of God with that people; the Bible is a history of the dealings of God with Judah and with the Jews and the twelve tribes of Israel: it contains in fact a short outline of the dealings of God with the Jaredites and Nephites from the building of the Tower of Babel down to the days of the Savior and after His resurrection. The Bible is the Stick of Judah in the hands of Judah, and the Book of Mormon the Stick of Joseph in the hands of Ephraim.

THE TRUTHS IN THE BOOK OF DOCTRINE AND COVENANTS

I consider that the Doctrine and Covenants, our testament, contains a code of the most solemn, the most Godlike proclamations ever made to the human family.
—*Wilford Woodruff*, JD 22:146, April 3, 1881

I say to my brethren that the book of Doctrine and Covenants contains some of the most glorious principles ever revealed to the world, some that have been revealed in greater fullness than they were ever revealed before to the world; and this, in fulfillment of the promise of the ancient prophets that in the latter times the Lord would reveal things to the world that had been kept hidden from the foundation thereof; and the Lord has revealed them through the Prophet Joseph Smith.
—*Joseph F. Smith*, CR, p. 9, October, 1913

In the last (conference) which was held at Brother Johnson's, in Hiram, after deliberate consideration, in consequence of the book of revelations, now to be printed, being the foundation of the Church in these last days and a benefit to the world, showing that the keys of the mysteries of the kingdom of our Savior are again entrusted to man, and the riches of eternity within the compass of those who are willing to live by every word that proceedeth out of the mouth of God, therefore the conference voted that they prize the revelations to be worth to the Church the riches of the whole earth, speaking temporally.
—*Joseph Smith, Jr.*, DHC 1:235, November, 1831

I wish that I had the ability to impress upon the Latter-day Saints the necessity of searching the commandments of God, the revelations from the Lord, the Creator of heaven and earth, as contained in the Doctrine and Covenants. If we as a people would live up to those wonderful revelations that have come to us, we would be a bright and shining light to all the wide world.

—Heber J. Grant, CR, p. 4, October, 1927

HOW TO STUDY THE SCRIPTURES

Do you read the Scriptures, my brethren and sisters, as though you were writing them a thousand, two thousand, or five thousand years ago? Do you read them as though you stood in the place of the men who wrote them? If you do not feel thus, it is your privilege to do so.

—Brigham Young, JD 7:333, October 8, 1859

Search the Scriptures—search the revelations which we publish and ask your Heavenly Father, in the name of His Son Jesus Christ, to manifest the truth unto you, and if you do it with an eye single to His glory, nothing doubting, He will answer you by the power of His Holy Spirit. You will then know for yourselves and not for another.

—Joseph Smith, Jr., DHC 1:282, August, 1832

Spend ten minutes in reading a chapter from the words of the Lord in the Bible, the Book of Mormon, the Doctrine and Covenants, before you retire or before you go to your daily toil. Feed your spiritual selves at home, as well as in public places.

—Joseph F. Smith, IE 7:135, December, 1903

That which characterizes above all else the inspiration and divinity of the Scriptures is the spirit in which they are written and the spiritual wealth they convey to those who faithfully and conscientiously read them. Our attitude, therefore, toward the Scriptures should be in harmony with the purposes for which they are written. They are intended to enlarge man's spiritual endowments and to reveal and intensify the bond of relationship between him and his God. The Bible, as all other books of Holy Writ, to be appreciated must be studied by those spiritually inclined and who are in quest of spiritual truths.

—Joseph F. Smith, JI 47:204, April, 1912

In our homes . . . it is our privilege, nay, it is our duty, to call our families together to be taught the truths of the Holy Scriptures. In every home children should be encouraged to read the word of the Lord, as it has been revealed to us in all dispensations. We should read the Bible, the Book of Mormon, the Doctrine and Covenants, and the Pearl of Great Price; not only read it in our homes, but explain it to our children, that they may understand the hand dealings of God with the peoples of the earth.   *—George Albert Smith,* CR, p. 12, April, 1914

WRITTEN SCRIPTURES NOT SUFFICIENT TO GUIDE THE CHURCH

With us the Bible is the first book, the Book of Mormon comes next, then the revelations in the book of Doctrine and Covenants, then the teachings of the living oracles.
—Brigham Young, JD 9:297, May 25, 1862

But in what part of the Bible do you find what we are to do this year or the next? This will be part of a new Bible, for when it takes place it will be written, and then that will be a Bible, and then the world will find that we shall have a "Mormon Bible."

Men have been opposed to the Book of Mormon because it was a new Bible. The poor fools did not know that wherever there was a true Church there was revelation, and that wherever there was revelation there was the word of God to man and materials to make Bibles of.   *—John Taylor,* JD 5:266, September 20, 1857

The Bible is good. . . . The Book of Mormon is good, and the book of Doctrine and Covenants, as land marks. . . . Those books are good for example, precedent, and investigation, and for developing certain laws and principles; but they do not, they cannot touch every case required to be adjudicated and set in order; we require a living tree—a living fountain—living intelligence, proceeding from the living priesthood in heaven, through the living priesthood on earth.
—John Taylor, MS 9:323, May 7, 1847

The Bible is all right, the Book of Mormon is all right, the Doctrine and Covenants is all right, and they proclaim the work

of God and the word of God in the earth in this day and generation until the coming of the Son of Man; but the Holy Priesthood is not confined particularly to those books, that is, it did
not cease when those books were made. It belongs to every
man that goes forth into the world, and these are our principles,
and these are our rights, and these are our duties, and these are
our gifts. The Holy Ghost is not confined to any one man, but
everyone should have it.

—*Wilford Woodruff,* CR, p. 18-19, October, 1897

On reading carefully the Old and New Testaments we can
discover that the majority of the revelations given to mankind
anciently were in regard to their daily duties; we follow in the
same path. The revelations contained in the Bible and the Book
of Mormon are examples to us, and the book of Doctrine and
Covenants contains direct revelation to this Church; they are
a guide to us, and we do not wish to do them away; we do not
wish them to become obsolete and to set them aside. We wish
to continue in the revelations of the Lord Jesus Christ day by
day and to have His Spirit with us continually. If we can do
this, we shall no more walk in darkness, but we shall walk in the
light of life.   —*Brigham Young,* JD 10:284, November 6, 1863

He [the Lord] will continue to feed us the bread of life
as we need it from time to time, if we will but live in accordance
with the teachings we have already received.

—*George Albert Smith,* CR, p. 118, October, 1912

CHAPTER XXXV

Keeping the Sabbath Day Holy

THE SABBATH WAS MADE FOR MAN

THE Lord has directed His people to rest one-seventh part of the time, and we take the first day of the week and call it our Sabbath. This is according to the order of the Christians. We should observe this for our own temporal good and spiritual welfare. When we see a farmer in such a hurry that he has to attend to his harvest and to haying, fence-making, or to gathering his cattle on the Sabbath day, as far as I am concerned, I count him weak in the faith. He has lost the spirit of his religion, more or less. Six days are enough for us to work, and if we wish to play, play within the six days; if we wish to go on excursions, take one of those six days, but on the seventh day come to the place of worship, attend to the Sacrament, confess your faults one to another and to our God, and pay attention to the ordinances of the House of God.

—Brigham Young, JD 15:81, June 2, 1872

God made or designated the Sabbath day for a day of rest, a day of worship, a day for goodly deeds, and for humility and penitence and the worship of the Almighty in spirit and in truth.

—Joseph F. Smith, CR, p. 10, April, 1915

To serve the Lord is one of the great objects of our existence; and I appreciate as a great privilege the opportunity we enjoy of worshiping God on the Sabbath day. And when we do meet to worship God, I like to see us worship Him with all our hearts. I think it altogether out of place on such occasions to hear people talk about secular things; these are times, above all others, when our feelings and affections should be drawn out towards God. If we sing praises to God, let us do it in the proper spirit; if we pray, let every soul be engaged in prayer, doing it with all our hearts, that through our union our spirits may be blended in one, that our prayers and our worship may be available with God, whose Spirit permeates all things and is always present in the assemblies of good and faithful Saints.

—*John Taylor*, JD 22:226, June 26, 1881

The Sabbath is a day of rest and of worship, designated and set apart by special commandment of the Lord to the Church of Jesus Christ of Latter-day Saints, and we should honor and keep it holy. We should also teach our children this principle.

—*Joseph F. Smith*, CR, p. 1-2, October, 1901

If I had my own mind, I would devote the time for meetings like this within the measure of the six days and on the seventh rest from all my labors, for the express purpose of renewing the mental and physical powers of man. They require it, as the Lord well knew; hence He established a day of rest.

—*Brigham Young*, JD 8:58, May 20, 1860

We should remember to preserve holy one day in the week as a day of rest—as a memorial of the rest of the Lord and the rest of the Saints; also for our temporal advantage, for it is instituted for the express purpose of benefiting man. It is written in this book, the Bible, that the Sabbath was made for man, and not man for the Sabbath. It is a blessing to him. As little labor as possible should be done upon that day: it should be set apart as a day of rest, to assemble together in the place appointed, according to the revelation, confessing our sins, bringing our tithes and offerings, and presenting ourselves before the Lord, there to commemorate the death and sufferings of our Lord Jesus Christ.   —*Brigham Young*, JD 6:277-278, August 29, 1852

THE SABBATH A DAY FOR REST AND WORSHIP

Persons professing to be Saints should assemble themselves together on the Lord's day, except those who may be necessarily detained at home to keep the house, take care of the children, or to perform some work of necessity and mercy; the rest should assemble in the place appointed for worship and the offering up of our sacraments.

—*Brigham Young*, JD 10:284, November 6, 1863

My belief is that it is the duty of Latter-day Saints to honor the Sabbath day and keep it holy, just as the Lord has commanded us to do. Go to the house of prayer. Listen to instructions. Bear your testimony to the truth. Drink at the fountain of knowledge and of instruction, as it may be opened for us from those who are inspired to give us instructions. When we go home get the family together. Let us sing a few songs. Let us read a chapter or two in the Bible, or in the Book of Mormon, or in the book of Doctrine and Covenants. Let us discuss the principles of the gospel which pertain to advancement in the school of divine knowledge, and in this way occupy one day in seven. I think it would be profitable for us to do this.

—*Joseph F. Smith*, IE 19:862, August, 1916

And on the Sabbath days . . . between the hours of service, I would love to . . . get acquainted with my children, keep in touch with them, and to keep in touch with the Scriptures, and to think of something besides fun and jokes and laughter and merriment and such things as these.

—*Joseph F. Smith*, YWJ 27:457, June 11, 1916

What are we required to do on the Sabbath day? . . . Here are some of the simple requirements:

The Sabbath is appointed unto you to rest from your labors.

The Sabbath is a special day for you to worship, to pray and to show zeal and ardor in your religious faith and duty—to pay devotions to the Most High.

The Sabbath is a day when you are required to offer your time and attention in worship of the Lord; whether in meeting, in the home, or wherever you may be—that is the thought that should occupy your mind.

The Sabbath day is a day when, with your brethren and sisters, you should attend the meetings of the Saints prepared to partake of the Sacrament of the Lord's Supper; having first confessed your sins before the Lord and your brethren and sisters and forgiven your fellows as you expect the Lord to forgive you.

On the Sabbath day you are to do no other thing than to prepare your food with singleness of heart, that your fasting may be perfect and your joy may be full. This is what the Lord calls fasting and prayer.

The reason for this required course upon the Sabbath day is . . . that one may more fully keep himself unspotted from the world; and to this end, also, the Saints are required to go to the house of prayer and offer up their sacraments on the Sabbath day.

—*Joseph F. Smith*, IE 13:842-843, July, 1910

This people called Latter-day Saints are required by the revelations that the Lord has given to assemble themselves together on this day. . . . In this commandment we are required to come together and repent of our sins and confess our sins and partake of the bread and of the wine, or water, in commemoration of the death and sufferings of our Lord and Savior.

—*Brigham Young,* JD 16:168, August 31, 1873

In meeting together on Sabbath days we assemble generally for the purpose of renewing our spiritual strength by partaking of the emblems of the broken body and shed blood of our Lord and Savior Jesus Christ, communing with our own hearts and reflecting upon things pertaining to the kingdom of God, and of speaking and listening to those things that have a tendency to enlighten our minds and establish us in the faith, to increase and confirm our hopes, and to enable us to press onward with avidity, confidence, and renewed determination in the path which the Lord has marked out for us to travel in.

—*John Taylor,* JD 18:278, November 5, 1876

THE RESULTS OF BREAKING THE SABBATH

This very day upon which we meet here to worship, viz., the Sabbath, has become the play-day of this great nation—the day set apart by thousands to violate the commandment that God gave long, long ago, and I am persuaded that much of the sorrow and distress that is afflicting and will continue to inflict mankind is traceable to the fact that they have ignored His admonition to keep the Sabbath day holy.

—*George Albert Smith,* CR, p. 120, October, 1935

"Thou shalt honor the Sabbath day and keep it holy." Do we do it? Is it necessary to do it? It is absolutely necessary to do so in order that we may be in harmony with God's law and commandments; and whenever we transgress that law or that commandment we are guilty of transgressing the law of God. And what will be the result, if we continue? Our children will follow in our footsteps; they will dishonor the command of God to keep one day holy in seven and will lose the spirit of obedience to the laws of God and His requirements, just as the father will lose it if he continues to violate the commandments.

—*Joseph F. Smith,* CR, p. 9-10, October, 1912

We have no right to break the Sabbath. We have no right to neglect our meetings to attend to our labors. I do not believe that any man who has ever belonged to this Church and kingdom, since its organization, has made anything by attending to his farm on the Sabbath: but if your ox falls into a pit, get him out; to work in that way is all just and right, but for us to go farming to the neglect of our meetings and other duties devolving upon us is something we have no right to do. The Spirit of God does not like it, it withdraws itself from us, and we make no money by it. We should keep the Sabbath holy. We should attend our meetings.   —*Wilford Woodruff*, JD 21:191, July 3, 1880

There are some who say they will not go to meeting because they know just who will talk and what they will say. I realize that such persons are becoming indifferent to the spiritual things of the kingdom. I know people, who, in the old world, would go many miles to a meeting because they were in love with the gospel. They will not cross the street now because they have lost that love. Just as surely as failing to eat will cause our physical frames to shrink and die, just so sure neglect to supply our spiritual natures will bring death to them.
     —*Heber J. Grant*, Journal History, p. 2, September, 1888

I have seen men in high places start in by drinking tea and coffee, saying, "That doesn't amount to anything," then next using liquor, then next finding fault with the authorities of the Church, and the first thing I knew they left the Church; but I have never known a person, man or woman, who attended his meetings and partook of the spirit and inspiration that are present in the meetings of true, faithful Latter-day Saints, who has ever apostatized.   —*Heber J. Grant*, DNCS, April 10, 1937

I call upon you, ye Latter-day Saints, to repent of your iniquities and keep the Sabbath day holy, set it aside as a day of rest, a day to meet together to perform your sacraments and listen to the words of life and thus be found keeping the commandments and setting a good example before your children. . . . If we do not these things, His Spirit will depart from us, and we will be left to ourselves. God will not be mocked; . . . we shall reap the reward of our doings.
     —*John Taylor*, JD 20:24, July 7, 1878

PROVIDE FOR AMUSEMENTS DURING THE WEEK

It is incumbent on members of the Church to so plan their work that there shall be no excuse for robbing the Lord's day of its sanctity. To this end let the boys and girls have a half holiday during the week, which may be profitably used for recreations, leaving the Sabbath for spiritual culture and worship. It is equally obligatory that we so plan our amusements that these shall not interfere with our worship. Let therefore some other night than Saturday be provided for the purpose. The Lord has commanded His people to observe the Sabbath day to keep it holy and on that day to go to the house of prayer and offer up their sacraments in righteousness with willing hearts and penitent spirits.   —*Joseph F. Smith*, IE 12:315, February, 1909

Let us play and take recreation to our hearts' content during other days, but on the Sabbath let us rest, worship, go to the house of prayer, partake of the sacrament, eat our food with singleness of heart, and pay our devotions to God, that the fullness of the earth may be ours and that we may have peace in this world and eternal life in the world to come.

"But," says one, "in our settlement we have no other day for amusement and sports, excursions and outings, ball games and races."

Then demand one.

Is it possible that parents, in the face of the promises of the Lord, will deny a day in the week when their children may have recreation and so force them to spend the Sabbath in sports!

One prominent man, in one of the northern stakes, where ball games and other sports are said to be the rule on Sunday, asked what could be done to remedy the evil. He was told to try a half holiday on one of the week days.

"Then," he replied, "we can have no change nor remedy. Here are hundreds of acres of hay and ripening fields crying for workmen, and we cannot spare our boys for play."

The best reply to such an argument is the question; "Which is best, to let the hay go to ruin, or the boy?" Let the hay go; save the boy. He is worth more than all your material possessions. Save him in the spirit of the gospel,—protect him from Sabbath breaking,—by offering a little temporal sacrifice, and the Lord will keep His promises to you. Get together in your

ward, unitedly select a day for play and recreation and, like faithful Saints, demand that the Sabbath day, as far as you and yours are concerned, shall be devoted to the Lord our God!
—Joseph F. Smith, IE 13:844, July, 1910

"We stand for a sacred Sabbath and a weekly half holiday." A sacred Sabbath is not automobile riding to the canyons on Sunday. A sacred Sabbath is not going out on excursions on Sunday. A sacred Sabbath is to attend to our meetings and to read the Scriptures, to supplicate God, and to have our minds set upon the things that are calculated to save us in this life and in the life to come. *—Heber J. Grant, IE 24:874, June 12, 1921*

THE NEED FOR A SUNDAY LAW

I am decidedly and emphatically in favor of a Sunday law which will not only prevent the playing of baseball but will also provide for the closing of theatres and other places of amusement.
—Heber J. Grant, IE 16:262-263, January, 1913

I am opposed to Sabbath breaking. It is wrong. It is contrary to the law of God. It is a transgression of the commandment of the Lord. I am opposed to men, women and children going to pleasure resorts on the Sabbath day.
—Joseph F. Smith, MS 56:710, August 22, 1897

I feel that it is a reproach to the Latter-day Saints that we should have amusements in our towns and cities on the day of the Lord. As the years come and go, and young men and young women go to their ruin because of losing their respect for the Sabbath and the sacredness of the day, I feel that the men who have sat in the legislature, and who have failed to protect us against the evil, will have much to answer for.
—Heber J. Grant, IE 39:660, November, 1936

CHAPTER XXXVI

The Sacrament of the Lord's Supper

THE ORDINANCE OF THE SACRAMENT

THE Sacrament of the Lord's Supper is a very important and sacred ordinance; however simple it may appear to our minds, it is one which will add to our acceptance before God or to our condemnation.

—*Joseph F. Smith*, JD 15:324, February 9, 1873

I look upon the sacrament as an ordinance of great importance to us; in fact, from the days of Adam down to the days of Jesus Christ, there were sacrifices offered; not only by Adam but by his posterity, by Moses and the House of Israel, and all the generations of people who were led by the Lord—sacrifices were offered as a type of the great sacrifice to be made by the Messiah. They offered the blood of bulls, rams and doves as a type of the great and last sacrifice and death of the Messiah, whose blood was shed for the redemption of the world. Prior to the death of the Savior, the Sacrament of the Lord's Supper was administered to His disciples, and they were informed that they were to partake of the bread as an emblem of the broken body of the Lord, and of the wine—or whatever is made use of as a substitute—in token of the shed blood of the Lord Jesus Christ.

—*Wilford Woodruff*, JD 22:169, June 12, 1881

The sacrament is of great importance. The Lord Himself ordained that we partake of these emblems. There are many people who believe it is necessary to be baptized and to have other ordinances of the gospel performed in their behalf, and yet they become indifferent and careless regarding the Sacrament of the Lord's Supper. It was regarded of such importance by our Father in heaven that, through His beloved Son and the apostles and prophets, as recorded in the Scriptures, the Saints were admonished to partake of it regularly. . . . Our Father in heaven does not give us commandments or advice that are not of importance.

—*George Albert Smith*, CR, p. 35, April, 1908

I would exhort my brethren and sisters to receive this ordinance every Sabbath, when they meet together, as is our practice; not following the customs of others, for with some denominations this is administered once a month, with others once in three months, with others never, they not believing in outward ordinances. . . .

We are in the habit of partaking of the contents of the cup each Sabbath when we meet together, and I do pray you, my brethren and sisters, to contemplate this ordinance thoroughly and seek unto the Lord with all your hearts that you may obtain the promised blessings by obedience to it. Teach its observance to your children; impress upon them its necessity. Its observance is as necessary to our salvation as any other of the ordinances and commandments that have been instituted in order that the people may be sanctified, that Jesus may bless them and give unto them His spirit, and guide and direct them that they may secure unto themselves life eternal. Impress the sacredness of this important ordinance upon the minds of your children.

—*Brigham Young*, JD 19:91-92, August 19, 1877

This ceremony has been attended to throughout generations that are past and still it is attended to. Jesus said also, "Do this until I come again." . . . This ordinance has been renewed to us and is part and parcel of the new covenant God has made with His people in the latter days. It was practiced among the ancient Saints who resided upon this continent, long before it was discovered by Columbus, as well as upon the continent of Asia among the Saints that lived there. When we attend to this ordinance we do it upon the same principle that they did anciently, whether among the Saints of God on the Asiatic continent or among the Saints on the American continent.

—*John Taylor*, JD 10:113, February 22, 1863

In what consists the benefit we derive from this ordinance? It is in obeying the commands of the Lord. When we obey the commandments of our Heavenly Father, if we have a correct understanding of the ordinances of the house of God, we receive all the promises attached to the obedience rendered to His commandments. —*Brigham Young*, JD 2:3, October 23, 1853

THE PURPOSE OF THE SACRAMENT

When Jesus came and suffered, "the just for the unjust," . . . the law of sacrifice was fulfilled, and instead thereof He

gave another law, which we call the "Sacrament of the Lord's Supper," by which His life and mission, His death and resurrection, the great sacrifice He had offered for the redemption of man, should be kept in everlasting remembrance. . . . Therefore, this law is to us what the law of sacrifice was to those who lived prior to the first coming of the Son of Man, until He shall come again. Therefore, we must honor and keep it sacredly.
                              —*Joseph F. Smith,* JD 15:324; 327, February 9, 1873

The Sacrament of the Lord's Supper . . . is an ordinance of the gospel, one as necessary to be observed by all believers as any other ordinance of the gospel. What is the object of it? It is that we may keep in mind continually the Son of God who has redeemed us from eternal death and brought us to life again through the power of the gospel. . . . It is necessary to partake of the sacrament, as a witness to Him that we do remember Him, are willing to keep the commandments He has given us, that we may have His Spirit to be with us always—even to the end, and also that we may continue in the forgiveness of sins.
                              —*Joseph F. Smith,* JD 19:192, September 30, 1877

We do this in remembrance of the death of our Savior; it is required of His disciples until He comes again, no matter how long that may be. No matter how many generations come and go, believers in Him are required to eat bread and drink wine in remembrance of His death and sufferings until He comes again. Why are they required to do this? To witness unto the Father, to Jesus and to the angels that they are believers in and desire to follow Him in the regeneration, keep His commandments, build up His kingdom, revere His name and serve Him with an undivided heart, that they may be worthy to eat and drink with Him in His Father's kingdom. This is why the Latter-day Saints partake of the ordinance of the Lord's Supper.
                              —*Brigham Young,* JD 13:139-140, July 11, 1869

In partaking of the sacrament we not only commemorate the death and sufferings of our Lord and Savior Jesus Christ, but we also shadow forth the time when He will come again and when we shall meet and eat bread with Him in the kingdom of God.   —*John Taylor,* JD 14:185, March 20, 1870

It is one of the greatest blessings we could enjoy, to come before the Lord and before the angels and before each other, to witness that we remember that the Lord Jesus Christ has died for us. This proves to the Father that we remember our covenants, that we love His gospel, that we love to keep His commandments and to honor the name of the Lord Jesus upon the earth.
  —*Brigham Young*, JD 6:277, August 29, 1852

It would seem that the coming of the Savior to the world, His suffering, death, resurrection and ascension to the position He occupies in the eternal world before His Heavenly Father, has a great deal to do with our interests and happiness; and hence this continued memorial that we partake of every Sabbath. This sacrament is the fulfillment of the last request of Jesus Christ to His disciples. "For as often as ye eat this bread, and drink this cup, ye do shew the Lord's death till He come." (1 Corinthians 11:26) Faith in this ordinance would necessarily imply that we have faith in Jesus Christ, that He is the Only Begotten of the Father, that He came from the heavens to the earth to accomplish a certain purpose which God had designed—even to secure the salvation and exaltation of the human family. All this has a great deal to do with our welfare and happiness here and hereafter. The death of Jesus Christ would not have taken place had it not been necessary. That this ceremony should be instituted to keep that circumstance before the minds of His people bespeaks its importance as embracing certain unexplained purposes and mysterious designs of God.
  —*John Taylor*, JD 10:114, February 22, 1863

THE USE OF BREAD AND WINE IN THE SACRAMENT

Brother Clements inquired why we used bread and wine in the ordinance of the Lord's supper. . . . Bread is the staff of life. . . . You bless it and partake of it as the staff of life that Jesus Christ has given you and emblematical of His broken body. . . . He poured out His blood freely to redeem a fallen world— the wine answering to the blood which Jesus spilled, if you partake of it in faith; for it is the faith that brings the blessing of life to you. It is through obedience to the ordinance that God bestows renewed life upon you. By this means the children of God have life within them to live and not die.

The wine answers to the blood of Christ and the bread to His body. His blood was poured out as we pour out wine, and His body was broken as we break bread, to redeem a fallen world and all things pertaining to it, so far as the curse had fallen.   —*Brigham Young*, JD 7:163, June 5, 1859

I know that in the Christian world sermon after sermon is preached on this subject; yet people there differ in their belief concerning these emblems. The Mother Church of the Christian world believes that the bread becomes the actual flesh of Jesus, and that the wine becomes His blood; this is preposterous to me. It is bread, and it is wine; but both are blessed to the souls of those who partake thereof. But to be followers of the Lord Jesus more is required than merely to partake of the bread and wine—the emblems of His death and suffering—it is necessary that strict obedience be rendered to His requirements.
                          —*Brigham Young*, JD 13:140, July 11, 1869

We believe that the sacrament is not the literal body and blood of our Lord; in other words, we do not believe in the doctrine of Transubstantiation.
                          —*George Albert Smith*, CR, p. 36, April, 1908

ON ADMINISTERING TO AND RECEIVING THE SACRAMENT

I admonish you, my brethren, that when we officiate in administering the sacrament we repeat, if possible, the exact words given by revelation, and that we do so with the Spirit of the Lord. When we repeat these prayers, we should feel the sentiments expressed by the words that we speak. Then I say also to those who partake of the sacrament, we should consider seriously the covenants we make with our Father. Let us pay strict attention to those covenants and let us see to it that we eat and drink worthily, for the blessings of our souls and for the increase of our spiritual strength.   —*George Albert Smith*, CR, p. 37, April, 1908

The Lord has indicated the importance of the sacrament in another way. There are certain of the priesthood who are not permitted to officiate in this ordinance. The deacon or teacher may not administer the sacrament, and those who bear no priesthood cannot act in this capacity. The Lord has certainly emphasized its importance by designating those who may officiate. Our people have been taught to take the sacrament with the right hand; we believe that is appropriate, and proper, and acceptable to our Father. The sacrament should not be accepted with a gloved hand; nobody should receive it in that irreverent manner. We should partake of it in humility, with preparation of clean hands and pure hearts, and with a desire to be acceptable to our Father; then we will receive it worthily and rejoice in the blessing that comes to us by reason of it.

—*George Albert Smith,* CR, p. 36, April, 1908

Before partaking of this sacrament, our hearts should be pure; our hands should be clean; we should be divested of all enmity toward our associates; we should be at peace with our fellow men; and we should have in our hearts a desire to do the will of our Father and to keep all of His commandments. If we do this, partaking of the sacrament will be a blessing to us and will renew our spiritual strength.

—*Heber J. Grant,* Journal History, p. 2, September 9, 1888

People wonder sometimes why we have sickness amongst us. The Apostle Paul in writing to the Corinthians, in referring to divisions that existed among them, together with their unworthiness when partaking of the Lord's supper, says, "For this cause many are weak and sickly among you, and many sleep." Do you believe a principle of that kind? I do. Let us fear God then, honor Him, and keep His commandments.

—*John Taylor,* JD 20:360, November 30, 1879

How long do you suppose a man may partake of this ordinance unworthily and the Lord not withdraw His Spirit from him? How long will he thus trifle with sacred things and the Lord not give him over to the buffetings of Satan until the day of redemption! The Church should know if they are unworthy from time to time to partake, lest the servants of God be forbidden to administer it. Therefore our hearts ought to be humble and we to repent of our sins and put away evil from among us. —*Joseph Smith, Jr.,* DHC 2:204, March 1, 1835

CHILDREN TO RECEIVE THE SACRAMENT

The practice of administering the Sacrament of the Lord's Supper to the children of the Sabbath Schools is generally observed throughout the entire Church. The children are entitled to the sacrament by reason of the fact that they have not reached the years of accountability and are not, therefore, under the same divine responsibility that falls upon them when they have attained the eighth year of their age.

—Joseph F. Smith, JI 37:432, July, 1902

Many years ago, in the midst of a blind and pernicious religious sentiment that condemned unbaptized infants to endless perdition, the Prophet Joseph Smith revealed the truth that "Little children are alive in Christ, even from the foundation of the world," and that if parents will repent and be baptized "and humble themselves as a little child, they shall all be saved with their little children." In harmony with this truth, Sunday School officers and teachers have been instructed to give to each enrolled child, according to his age and understanding, every privilege of participation in the benefits of the principles and ordinances of the gospel, including the partaking of the Sacrament of the Lord's Supper. Whether the child was born in the Church or not makes no difference. He is worthy, through the atonement of Jesus Christ, to partake of the sacrament.

—Joseph F. Smith, MS 75:346, May, 1913

CHAPTER XXXVII

The Power of Prayer

LATTER-DAY SAINT BELIEF IN THE EFFICACY OF PRAYER

W E . . . accept without any question the doctrines we have been taught by the Prophet Joseph Smith and by the Son of God Himself, that we pray to God, the Eternal Father, in the name of His Only Begotten Son, to whom also our father Adam and his posterity have prayed from the beginning.
—*Joseph F. Smith, CR, p. 6, October, 1916*

Although the Christian religion, under whatever form it may be practiced, teaches mankind to pray unto God in the name of the Lord Jesus Christ, yet it is very few who suppose that their prayers amount to anything, that God will listen to their supplications, or that they will prove of any special benefit. A feeling of this kind tends more or less to unbelief instead of faith in God, and hence we find very few men in our day who act as men of God did in former days, that is, seek unto Him for guidance and direction in the affairs of life.
—*John Taylor, JD 14:357, March 17, 1872*

There is no more prayerful people on earth than the Latter-day Saints. There is not another people who are nearer to God their Father than are the Latter-day Saints; for they have the right to go to Him in their secret chamber, at the altar of prayer in their own homes; they can bow down and get very near unto the Lord, nearer, I think, than any other people. I do not say it boastfully either; I say it as I believe it to be a simple truth. Does it not stand to reason that a man who has received the gift of the Holy Ghost by the laying on of hands, a man that has been born again of the water and of the Spirit, in accordance with the plan that God has instituted by which he may come into His fold, can get nearer to God than those that have not been born again or those who have not been endowed with the Spirit of the Lord? Of course, it stands to reason, and it is consistent to claim that much for the Latter-day Saints.

—*Joseph F. Smith*, CR, p. 6-7, April, 1912

When you have labored faithfully for years, you will learn this simple fact—that if your hearts are aright and you still continue to be obedient, continue to serve God, continue to pray, the Spirit of revelation will be in you like a well of water springing up to everlasting life. Let no person give up prayer because he has not the spirit of prayer, neither let any earthly circumstance hurry you while in the performance of this important duty. By bowing down before the Lord to ask Him to bless you, you will simply find this result—God will multiply blessings on you temporally and spiritually. Let a merchant, a farmer, a mechanic, any person in business live his religion faithfully, and he need never lose one minute's sleep by thinking about his business; he need not worry in the least, but trust in God, go to sleep and rest. I say to this people—pray, and if you cannot do anything else, read a prayer aloud that your family may hear it, until you get a worshiping spirit and are full of the riches of eternity, then you will be prepared at any time to lay hands on the sick or to officiate in any of the ordinances of this religion.

—*Brigham Young*, JD 12:103, November 17, 1867

SEEK TO KNOW GOD

We would say to the brethren, seek to know God in your closets, call upon Him in the fields. Follow the directions of the Book of Mormon and pray over, and for your families, your cattle, your flocks, your herds, your corn, and all things that you possess; ask the blessing of God upon all your labors and everything that you engage in.   —*Joseph Smith, Jr.*, DHC 5:31, June 15, 1842

The minute a man stops supplicating God for His Spirit and direction, just so soon he starts out to become a stranger to Him and His works. When men stop praying for God's Spirit, they place confidence in their own unaided reason, and they gradually lose the Spirit of God, just the same as near and dear friends, by never writing to or visiting with each other, will become strangers.   —*Heber J. Grant*, IE 47:481, August, 1944

It matters not whether you or I feel like praying, when the time comes to pray, *pray*. If we do not feel like it, we should pray till we *do*. . . . You will find that those who wait till the Spirit bids them pray will never pray much on this earth.
—*Brigham Young*, JD 13:155, November 14, 1869

Let all persons be fervent in prayer, until they know the things of God for themselves and become certain that they are walking in the path that leads to everlasting life; then will envy, the child of ignorance, vanish, and there will be no disposition in any man to place himself above another; for such a feeling meets no countenance in the order of heaven.
—*Brigham Young*, JD 9:150, January 12, 1862

You should enter your secret closets and call upon the name of the Lord. Many of you have learned how to pray; then fail not to let your prayers ascend up into the ears of the God of Sabaoth; and He will hear you. I think sometimes that we do not fully comprehend the power that we have with God in knowing how to approach Him acceptably. All that these men holding the priesthood and all that our sisters need do is to live near to God and call upon Him, pouring out their soul's desires in behalf of Israel, and their power will be felt, and their confidence in God will be strengthened.
—*Wilford Woodruff*, JD 24:55, January 27, 1883

If we draw near to Him, He will draw near to us; if we seek Him early, we shall find Him; if we apply our minds faithfully and diligently, day by day, to know and understand the mind and will of God, it is as easy as, yes, I will say easier than it is to know the minds of each other, for to know and understand ourselves and our own being is to know and understand God and His being.
—*Brigham Young*, JD 13:312, April 17, 1870

THE PURPOSE OF PRAYER

One of the requirements made of the Latter-day Saints is that they shall be faithful in attending to their prayers, both their secret and family prayers. The object that our Heavenly Father has in requiring this is that we may be in communication with Him and that we may have a channel open between us and the heavens whereby we can bring down upon ourselves blessings

from above. No individual who is humble and prayerful before
God and supplicates Him every day for the light and inspiration
of His Holy Spirit will ever become lifted up in the pride of his
heart or feel that the intelligence and the wisdom that he possesses are all sufficient for him.

The prayerful and humble man will always realize and feel
that he is dependent upon the Lord for every blessing that he
enjoys, and in praying to God he will not only pray for the light
and the inspiration of His Holy Spirit to guide him, but he will
feel to thank Him for the blessings that he receives, realizing
that life, that health, that strength, and that all the intelligence
which he possesses come from God, who is the Author of his
existence.

If we do not keep this channel of communication open between us and our Heavenly Father, then are we robbed of the
light and inspiration of His Spirit and of that feeling of gratitude
and thanksgiving that fills our hearts and that desire to praise
God for His goodness and mercy to us.
                              —*Heber J. Grant*, IE 45:779, December, 1942

I am convinced that one of the greatest and one of the best
things in all the world to keep a man true and faithful in the gospel of the Lord Jesus Christ is to supplicate God secretly in the
name of Jesus Christ, for the guidance of His Holy Spirit. I am
convinced that one of the greatest things that can come into
any home to cause the boys and girls in that home to grow up
in a love of God and in a love of the gospel of Jesus Christ is
to have family prayer; not for the father of the family alone to
pray, but for the mother and for the children to do so also, that
they may partake of the spirit of prayer and be in harmony, be
in tune, to have the radio, so to speak, in communication with the
Spirit of the Lord. I believe that there are very few who go
astray, that very few lose their faith, who have once had a knowledge of the gospel, and who never neglect their prayers in their
families and their secret supplications to God.
                              —*Heber J. Grant*, CR, p. 7-8, October, 1923

The Lord says, I will be sought unto by my people for the
blessings that they need. And instead of our classing prayer
among the duties devolving upon us as Latter-day Saints, we
should live so as to deem it one of the greatest privileges ac-

corded to us; for were it not for the efficacy of prayer what would have become of us both as a people and as individuals?
—*Brigham Young,* JD 19:222, April 22, 1877

It is the commandment of the Lord that we shall remember God morning and evening and, as the Book of Mormon tells us, "at all times." We should carry with us the spirit of prayer throughout every duty that we have to perform in life. Why should we? One of the simple reasons that appeals to my mind with great force is that man is so utterly dependent upon God!
—*Joseph F. Smith,* CR, p. 6, October, 1914

WHY PRAY?

The Lord has called upon us to pray with our families and in secret that we may not forget God. If we neglect this, we lose the inspiration and power from heaven; we become indifferent, lose our testimony, and go down into darkness.
—*Heber J. Grant,* JH, p. 2, September 9, 1888

I fear, as a people, we do not pray enough, in faith. We should call upon the Lord in mighty prayer and make all our wants known unto Him. For if He does not protect and deliver us and save us, no other power will. Therefore our trust is entirely in Him. Therefore our prayers should ascend into the ears of our Heavenly Father day and night.
—*Wilford Woodruff,* MS 48:806, October 26, 1886

I have more faith in prayer before the Lord than almost any other principle on earth. If we have no faith in prayer to God, we have not much in either Him or the gospel. We should pray unto the Lord, asking Him for what we want. Let the prayers of this people ascend before the Lord continually in the season thereof, and the Lord will not turn them away, but they will be heard and answered, and the kingdom and Zion of God will rise and shine, she will put on her beautiful garments and be clothed with the glory of her God and fulfill the object of her organization here upon the earth.
—*Wilford Woodruff,* JD 17:249, October 9, 1874

And do not forget to call upon the Lord in your family circles, dedicating yourselves and all you have to God every day of your lives; and seek to do right and cultivate the spirit

of union and love, and the peace and blessing of the living God
will be with us, and He will lead us in the paths of life; and we
shall be sustained and upheld by all the holy angels and the
ancient patriarchs and men of God, and the veil will become
thinner between us and our God, and we will approach nearer
to Him, and our souls will magnify the Lord of hosts.
                          —*John Taylor,* JD 20:361, November 30, 1879

If faithful, we have a right to claim the blessings of the Lord
upon the labor of our hands, our temporal labors. The farmer
has a right to ask the Lord for blessings upon his farm, upon the
labor that he bestows upon it. . . . It is our privilege to ask God
to remove the curse from the earth and to make it fruitful. . . .
It is our privilege to ask God to bless the elements that surround
us and to temper them for our good, and we know He will hear
and answer the prayers of His people, according to their faith.
                          —*Joseph F. Smith,* CR, p. 10, April, 1898

We should pray for the blessings of the Lord upon our families, our farms, our flocks, our herds, our business and everything
that we possess in the world. Do not forget to pray. Don't suppose for a moment that you are as safe and secure in the favor
of the Lord when you feel independent of Him as you will be
if you feel your dependence upon Him all the day long.
                          —*Joseph F. Smith,* CR, p. 140, April, 1915

Whenever you are in doubt about any duty or work which
you have to perform never proceed to do anything until you go
and labor in prayer and get the Holy Spirit. Wherever the Spirit
dictates you to go or to do, that will be right; and, by following
its dictates, you will come out right.
                          —*Wilford Woodruff,* JD 5:85, April 9, 1857

Men and women who neglect to keep a radio communication
with God are destroying, to a certain extent, their opportunities
to grow in the knowledge and testimony of the divinity of this
work. The Lord has said that it is our duty to supplicate Him,
and if we fail to do it we shall fail to grow as we otherwise
would. . . . I say to you that of all my acquaintances I have never
known of one who, having fulfilled the law, kept the commandments of God and supplicated Him for His guidance, has ever
lost the faith or the testimony of the divinity of this work in
which we are engaged.   —*Heber J. Grant,* IE 28:931, June 7, 1925

HOW TO PRAY

Prayer does not consist of words, altogether. True, faithful, earnest prayer consists more in the feeling that rises from the heart and from the inward desire of our spirits to supplicate the Lord in humility and in faith, that we may receive His blessings. It matters not how simple the words may be, if our desires are genuine and we come before the Lord with a broken heart and contrite spirit to ask Him for that which we need.
—*Joseph F. Smith*, CR, p. 69, October, 1899

When we pray we should call upon Him [God] in a consistent and reasonable way. We should not ask the Lord for that which is unnecessary or which would not be beneficial to us. We should ask for that which we need. . . . But when we ask of God for blessings let us ask in the faith of the gospel, in that faith that He has promised to give to those who believe in Him and obey His commandments.   —*Joseph F. Smith*, CR, p. 7, October, 1914

We do not have to weary Him with long prayers. What we do need and what we should do as Latter-day Saints, for our own good, is to go before Him often, to witness unto Him that we remember Him and that we are willing to take upon us His name, keep His commandments, work righteousness; and that we desire His Spirit to help us. Then, if we are in trouble, let us go to the Lord and ask Him directly and specifically to help us out of the trouble that we are in; and let the prayer come from the heart, let it not be in words that are worn into ruts in the beaten tracks of common use, without thought or feeling in the use of those words.   —*Joseph F. Smith*, IE 11:730, June 14, 1908

One of the greatest prayers that a man can offer . . . is that, when an elder of Israel stands before the people, he may communicate and tell some thoughts to do the people good and build them up in the principles of truth and salvation. Prayers of this kind are as agreeable in the ears of the Lord as any prayers that an elder of Israel can possibly offer, for when an elder stands before the people he should do so realizing that he stands before them for the purpose of communicating knowledge, that they may receive truth in their souls and be built up in righteousness by receiving further light, progressing in their education in the principles of holiness.   —*Lorenzo Snow*, JD 4:182, January 18, 1857

It is not good for us to pray by rote, to kneel down and repeat the Lord's prayer continually. I think that one of the greatest follies I have ever witnessed is the foolish custom of men repeating the Lord's prayer continually without considering its meaning. . . . It thus becomes only a form; there is no power in it; neither is it acceptable, because it is not offered from the heart, nor with the understanding; and I think that it is desirable for us to look well to our words when we call upon the Lord. . . . Let us speak the simple words, expressing our need, that will appeal most truly to the Giver of every good and perfect gift. He can hear us in secret; and He knows the desires of our hearts before we ask, but He has made it obligatory and a duty that we shall call upon His name.
—*Joseph F. Smith,* IE 11:730-731, June 14, 1908

Do you have prayers in your family? . . . And when you do, do you go through the operation like the guiding of a piece of machinery, or do you bow in meekness and with a sincere desire to seek the blessing of God upon you and your household? That is the way that we ought to do and cultivate a spirit of devotion and trust in God, dedicating ourselves to Him, and seeking His blessings.   —*John Taylor,* JD 21:118, November 28, 1879

You can obtain knowledge through repentance, humility, and seeking the Lord with full purpose of heart until you find Him, He is not afar off. It is not difficult to approach Him, if we will only do it with a broken heart and a contrite spirit.
—*Joseph F. Smith,* CR, p. 71, October, 1899

I say to my brethren, when they are fasting and praying for the sick and for those who need faith and prayer, do not go beyond what is wise and prudent in fasting and prayer. The Lord can hear a simple prayer offered in faith, in half a dozen words, and He will recognize fasting that may not continue more than twenty-four hours just as readily and as effectually as He will answer a prayer of a thousand words and fasting for a month.
—*Joseph F. Smith,* CR, p. 133-134, October, 1912

Jesus Christ is the medium through whom we are to approach the Father, calling upon Him in the name of Jesus; for there is no name given under heaven, nor known among men, whereby we can be saved but the name of Jesus Christ.
—*John Taylor,* JD 20:175, April 8, 1879

THE ORDER OF PRAYER

Heads of families should always take the charge of family worship and call their family together at a seasonable hour, and not wait for every person to get through with all they may have to say or do. If it were my prerogative to adopt a plan for family prayer, it would be the following: Call your family or household together every morning and evening, previous to coming to the table, and bow before the Lord to offer up your thanksgiving for His mercies and providential care of you. Let the head of the family dictate; I mean the man, not the woman. If an elder should happen to be present the head of the house can call upon him, if he chooses so to do, and not wait for a stranger to take the lead at such times; by so doing we shall obtain the favor of our Heavenly Father, and it will have a tendency to teach our children to walk in the way they should go.
—*Brigham Young*, DHC 4:309, March 10, 1840

Again, suppose a family wish to assemble for prayer, what would be orderly and proper? For the head of the family to call together his wife . . . and children, except the children who are too small to be kept quiet, and when he prays aloud all present, who are old enough to understand, should mentally repeat the words as they fall from his lips; and why so? That all may be one.   —*Brigham Young*, JD 3:53, July 13, 1855

It is the duty of fathers and mothers to call their families together and instruct them. It is our duty to bow before the Lord in prayer in our homes. It is our duty to ask the blessing upon the food that we partake of and to thank Him who gives us all these things.   —*George Albert Smith*, CR, p. 32, April, 1929

Say your prayers always before going to work. Never forget that. A father—the head of the family—should never miss calling his family together and dedicating himself and them to the Lord of Hosts, asking the guidance and direction of His Holy Spirit to lead them through the day—that very day. Lead us this day, guide us this day, preserve us this day, save us from sinning against Thee or any being in heaven or on earth this day! If we do this every day, the last day we live we will be prepared to enjoy a higher glory.   —*Brigham Young*, JD 12:261, August 9, 1868

DOES GOD HEAR AND ANSWER PRAYERS?

If man can communicate across the continent by means of a telephone without wires—by means of human invention, by reason of the wisdom of man, is there any one who doubts the ability of God to hear the earnest, honest supplication of the soul? . . . When you can communicate to some one in the midst of the ocean from your home, far inland from the ocean—do not for a moment doubt that the Lord understands all these means of communication and that He has means of hearing and understanding your innermost, exact thoughts.
                    —*Joseph F. Smith,* GD, p. 216, Novmber 25, 1917

The Lord will hear and answer the prayers we offer to Him and give us success if it is for our best good. He never will and never has forsaken those who serve Him with full purpose of heart; and the temptations that come from below, although strong, never are successful if we are faithful. But we must always be prepared to say "Father, thy will be done," and leave the time and the manner and the nature of our blessings to God in His wisdom.   —*Heber J. Grant,* IE 48:67, February, 1945

We are told in relation to these matters that the hairs of our heads are numbered; that even a sparrow cannot fall to the ground without our Heavenly Father's notice; and predicated upon some of these principles are some things taught by Jesus, where He tells men to ask and they shall receive. What! the millions that live upon the earth? Yes, the millions of people, no matter how many there are. Can He hear and answer all? Can He attend to all these things? Yes.
                    —*John Taylor,* JD 26:31, December 14, 1884

The Lord is no respecter of persons, and to all who are willing to seek in prayer, with preparation, and work, having a desire in their hearts for spiritual light and understanding, He will grant abundantly without reproach. But no light will come to the unwilling, for they will not ask. The promise that they shall receive is made only to those who ask; and that they shall find, only to those who seek.
                    —*Joseph F. Smith,* IE 19:173, December, 1915

I have had my prayers answered time and time again, and not only have I had my prayers answered but I know as I know that I live that God hears and answers the prayers of honest people.   —*Heber J. Grant,* CR, p. 12, October, 1941

CHAPTER XXXVIII

Missionary Work

"GO, YE MESSENGERS OF HEAVEN"

Go, ye messengers of heaven,
Chosen by divine command;
Go and publish free salvation
To a dark, benighted land.

Go to island, vale, and mountain,
To fulfill the great command;
Gather out the sons of Jacob;
To possess the promised land.

When your thousands all are gathered,
And their pray'rs for you ascend,
And the Lord has crown'd with blessings
All the labors on your hand,

Then the song of joy and transport
Will from ev'ry land resound;
Then the heathen, long in darkness,
By the Savior will be crown'd.
                    —John Taylor, Gospel Kingdom, p. 383

THE IMPORTANCE OF MISSIONARY WORK

The missionary work of the Latter-day Saints is the greatest of all the great works in all the world.
                    —Heber J. Grant, CR, p. 5, October, 1921

My understanding is that the most important mission that I have in this life is: first, to keep the commandments of God, as they have been taught to me; and next, to teach them to my Father's children who do not understand them.
                    —George Albert Smith, CR, p. 50, October, 1916

There can be no greater or more important calling for man
than that in which the elders of the Church of Jesus Christ of
Latter-day Saints are engaged when in the discharge of their
duties as missionaries to the world. They stand as teachers,
counselors and leaders to the people. They are commissioned
with the word of life and "the power of God unto salvation,"
to minister unto this proud, conceited, self-righteous, but benighted and degenerate world.
                              —*Joseph F. Smith,* MS 37:408, June 28, 1875

It is necessary that all have the privilege of receiving or
rejecting eternal truth, that they may be prepared to be saved
or be prepared to be damned.
                              —*Brigham Young,* JD 7:139, December 18, 1859

Do we realize that every man is in the image of God and is
a son of God and every woman His daughter? No matter where
they may be, they are His children, and He loves them and desires
their salvation. Surely as members of this Church we cannot
sit idly by. We cannot receive the beneficent favor of our
Heavenly Father that is bestowed upon us, the knowledge of
eternal life, and selfishly retain it, thinking that we may be
blessed thereby. It is not what we receive that enriches our
lives, it is what we give.
                              —*George Albert Smith,* CR, p. 46, April, 1935

I remember that in revelation after revelation given just
before the Church was organized, and in its early day, that
men came to the man whom God had chosen as His prophet and
asked that he inquire of the Lord what was the most important
labor for them to perform. Uniformly, the answer came that
the greatest and most profitable labor in which they could engage was to bring souls to a knowledge of the gospel.
                              —*George Albert Smith,* CR, p. 32, October, 1916

I want to emphasize that we as a people have one supreme
thing to do and that is to call upon the world to repent of sin,
to come to God. And it is our duty above all others to go forth
and proclaim the gospel of the Lord Jesus Christ, the restoration
again to the earth of the plan of life and salvation. . . . We have
in very deed the pearl of great price. We have that which is of

more value than all the wealth and scientific information which the world possesses. We have the plan of life and salvation. The first great commandment was to love the Lord our God with all our hearts, might, mind and strength; and the second was like unto it, to love our neighbors as ourselves. And the best way in the world to show our love for our neighbor is to go forth and proclaim the gospel of the Lord Jesus Christ, of which He has given us an absolute knowledge concerning its divinity.
—Heber J. Grant, CR, p. 175-176, April, 1927

Our most important obligation . . . is to divide with our Father's children all those fundamental truths, all His rules and regulations which prepare us for eternal life, known as the gospel of Jesus Christ. Until we have done that to the full limit of our power, we will not receive all the blessings which we might otherwise have.   *—George Albert Smith*, CR, p. 119, October, 1945

We will attain our exaltation in the celestial kingdom only on the condition that we divide with our Father's other children the blessings of the gospel of our Lord and observe the commandments that will enrich our lives here and hereafter.
—George Albert Smith, CR, p. 31, October, 1938

We ought to be full of light and life and the power and spirit of the living God and feel that we are messengers to the nations of the earth; we ought to feel the word of God burning like fire in our bones, feeling desirous to go and snatch men from the powers of darkness and the chains of corruption with which they are bound and lead them in the paths of life. We ought to be prepared to go forth weeping, bearing precious seed that we might come back again rejoicing bringing our sheaves with us.
—John Taylor, JD 20:228, December 15, 1878

I would rather have a son in the vineyard, saving the souls of men, than to have him heaping up gold at home and becoming a millionaire.   *—Wilford Woodruff*, MS 83:321, July, 1884

The day will come when the gospel will be presented to the kings and queens and great ones of the earth; but it will be presented with a different influence from that with which it has been presented to the poor, but it will be the same gospel. We shall not present any other gospel; it is the same from everlasting to everlasting.   *—Brigham Young*, JD 13:150, July 11, 1869

The Lord hates a quitter, and there should be no such thing
as quitting when we put our hands to the plow to save men.
                    —*Joseph F. Smith,* IE 13:1055, October, 1910

A few words now, with regard to preaching. The greatest
and loudest sermon that can be preached, or that ever was
preached on the face of the earth, is practice. No other is equal
to it.   —*Brigham Young,* JD 12:271, August 16, 1868

THE SACRED RESPONSIBILITY OF PROCLAIMING
THE GOSPEL

There never was a set of men since God made the world
under a stronger responsibility to warn this generation, to lift up
our voices long and loud, day and night so far as we have the
opportunity and declare the words of God unto this generation.
We are required to do this. This is our calling. It is our duty.
It is our business.   —*Wilford Woodruff,* JD 21:122, June 6, 1880

To my brethren in the priesthood I beg to offer a few words
of counsel, instruction, and exhortation. Upon you rest high
and sacred responsibilities, which relate not only to the salvation
of this generation, but of many past generations and many to
come. The glorious ensign of Emanuel's kingdom once again
established in the world must be unfurled in every nation, kingdom, and empire; the voice of warning, the voice of the bridegroom, "prepare ye, prepare ye, the way of the Lord" must be
carried forth unto all people; you are the ones whom the Lord
has selected for this purpose.
            —*Lorenzo Snow,* MS 13:362, December 1, 1851

Upon us, as elders in this Church, has been laid the obligation to go into all the world and preach the gospel unto every
creature. We have received a wonderful gift, but with that gift
comes a great responsibility. We have been blessed of the Lord
with a knowledge beyond our fellows, and with that knowledge
comes the requirement that we divide it with His children,
wherever they may be. —*George Albert Smith,* CR, p. 53, April, 1922

The Lord said to Ezekiel, "I have made thee a watchman
unto the House of Israel. When I say unto the wicked, Thou

shalt surely die; and thou givest him not warning, nor speakest to warn the wicked from his wicked way, to save his life; the same wicked man shall die in his iniquity; but his blood will I require at thine hand. Yet if thou warn the wicked, and he turn not from his wickedness, nor from his wicked way, he shall die in his iniquity; but thou hast delivered thy soul." This is precisely our condition today. As apostles, seventies, high priests and elders, we and all men who bear any portion of the Holy Priesthood, are watchmen upon the walls of Zion and messengers to all the inhabitants of the earth, and all of us will be held responsible if we do not improve our time and lift the warning voice, as far as we have opportunity, and warn this generation of the judgments of God which await them.

—Wilford Woodruff, MS 48:803, October 26, 1886

I tell you, my brethren, in the name of God, that right among the nations of Europe, where many of you have come from, there will be some of the bloodiest scenes that you ever read of; and God expects you to assist in warning the nations and in gathering the honest in heart. Then when you come back, having accomplished a good mission, you can say, "My garments are clean from the blood of this generation." Many of you cannot say that now, therefore I wish to remind you of these things, that you may reflect upon them and prepare yourselves for the work that is before you.

—John Taylor, JD 20:47, August 4, 1878

I will say as Paul did, "Woe be unto me if I preach not the gospel." I will say the same for the apostles, the high priests, the seventies, and the elders, so far as they are called to declare the words of life and salvation to this generation; the judgments of God will rest upon us if we do not do it. You may ask why. I answer, because a dispensation of the gospel of Jesus Christ has never been given to man in ancient days or in this age, for any other purpose than for the salvation of the human family.

—Wilford Woodruff, JD 22:204, January 9, 1881

I further wish to state to the twelve and to the seventies, and to the elders that they are not responsible for the reception or the rejection by the world of that word which God has given to them to communicate. It is proper for them to use all necessary diligence and fidelity, and plainly and intelligently, and with prayer and faith to go forth as messengers to the nations, as the legates of the skies, clothed upon with authority from the God of heaven, even the authority of the Holy Priesthood, . . . and when they have performed their labors and fulfilled their duties, their garments are free from the blood of this generation, and the people are then left in the hands of God their Heavenly Father. For the people . . . will be responsible to God for their rejection of the gospel and not to us.

—John Taylor, JD 24:289, Ocober 7, 1883

HOME MISSIONARY WORK

Do you realize, brethren and sisters, that in this city, the headquarters of the Church, there are approximately fifty thousand people who know very little about the gospel of Jesus Christ? They are our neighbors, they are our Father's children, they are identified with the other churches, or else they do not belong to any church, but I think I am safe in saying that ninety per cent of them have no idea what the gospel of Jesus Christ really is. I believe that the greatest mission field in all the world is in the valleys of these great mountains. . . .

It is not necessary for you to be called to go into the mission field in order to proclaim the truth. Begin on the man who lives next door by inspiring confidence in him, by inspiring love in him for you because of your righteousness, and your missionary work has already begun.

—George Albert Smith, CR, p. 48-49; 51, October, 1916

Within the last year, I have had the privilege of meeting and conversing on the gospel with some men who live in this community, not members of our Church. . . .

I might say, with reference to . . . one man, that after talking to him a couple of hours on the train, "Why," he said to me, "Mr. Smith, that is beautiful to me. I think you ought to send your missionaries to such men as I am, right here in Salt Lake City. There are hundreds of men here who would like to hear what you have told me tonight, and we would be better men for the teaching." He told me he employed members of our Church, some returned missionaries, and none of them had ever spoken to him about the gospel. I said, "You would not expect a man

to ask you to give him time in your office to teach you 'Mormonism.' If you were to invite him to come in, he would be glad to explain his views." Then he said, "Do your missionaries who are in the world go only to the homes where they are invited?" That awakened a thought in my mind, are you doing your duty? are we performing the labor that the Lord has entrusted to our care? do we sense the responsibility that is upon us? or are we idly floating down stream, going with the tide taking it for granted that in the last day, we will be redeemed?
—*George Albert Smith*, CR, p. 49, October, 1916

It is my firm conviction . . . that unless we stir ourselves more than we are doing, that when we go to the other side of the veil we will meet there men and women who have been our neighbors and associates and lived among us that will condemn us because we have been so inconsiderate of them in not telling them of the truth of the gospel of our Lord.
—*George Albert Smith*, CR, p. 49, October, 1916

I know that there is no other name under heaven whereby we may hope to gain exaltation, but the name of Jesus Christ, our Savior. There is no other gospel of salvation and we, my brethren who bear the Holy Priesthood, have the responsibility of carrying that message, not only to the nations of the earth, but of exemplifying it in our lives and teaching it to those who are our neighbors, not of our faith. I warn you this day that the Lord holds us responsible to call His children to repentance and for the promulgation of His truth. If we fail to take advantage of our opportunities to teach the sons and daughters of God, who are not of our faith, who dwell in our midst, this gospel of our Lord, He will require at our hands on the other side of the veil what we have failed to do, so let us not be recreant.
—*George Albert Smith*, CR, p. 48, April, 1916

WHO SHOULD PREACH?

Our duty is to preach the gospel to all men. Who, the First Presidency? Yes, if there is nobody else. The Twelve? Yes, it is their special calling to preach it themselves or see that it is preached to all the world. And, then, the seventies, it is their duty to go forth at the drop of the hat, as minute men, to preach

the gospel to all nations, under the guidance of the Twelve. And, then, it is for those who are in Zion, the high priests and others, to go and preach the gospel.
                    —*John Taylor,* JD 26:110, October 20, 1881

No person but the President of the Church has the authority to call missionaries to preach the gospel; others may suggest or recommend, but they do so to him, and he issues the call.
                    —*Joseph F. Smith,* JI 37:82, February, 1902

Men cannot legally and authoritatively go forth to preach the gospel until they are sent; and men cannot hear the word and be converted by the same unless they hear it through the mouth of a preacher who is sent, and who has power to administer in the ordinances of the gospel.
                    —*Wilford Woodruff,* JD 23:78, March 26, 1882

We send our elders to preach the gospel. Who sends them? President Woodruff? In one sense, no. The God of Israel sends them. It is His work. There is no mortal man that is so much interested in the success of an elder when he is preaching the gospel as the Lord that sent him to preach to the people who are the Lord's children.   —*Lorenzo Snow,* MS 56:451, April 7, 1894

In accordance with the present regulations of the First Presidency, brethren are not now sent on missions who have not themselves a testimony of the truth of the work of the Lord. It is deemed inconsistent to send men out into the world to promise to others through obedience to the gospel that which they have not themselves received. Neither is it considered proper to send men out to reform them. Let them first reform at home if they have not been strictly keeping the commandments of God.
                    —*Joseph F. Smith,* JI 37:83, February, 1902

CHARACTERISTICS OF A GOOD MISSIONARY

There are many excellent men but very few really good missionaries. The characteristics of a good missionary are: A man who has sociability—whose friendship is permanent and sparkling —who can ingratiate himself into the confidence and favor of men who are in darkness.   —*Joseph F. Smith,* GD, p. 356, a. 1904

The kind of men we want as bearers of this gospel message are men who have faith in God; men who have faith in their religion; men who honor their priesthood; men in whom the people who know them have faith and in whom God has confidence, and not some poor unfortunate beings who are wanted to leave a place because they cannot live in it; but we want men full of the Holy Ghost and the power of God that they may go forth weeping, bearing precious seed and sowing the seeds of eternal life, and then returning with gladness, bringing their sheaves with them. . . . Men who bear the words of life among the nations ought to be men of honor, integrity, virtue and purity; and this being the command of God to us, we shall try and carry it out.
—John Taylor, JD 21:375, October 7, 1879

We want men to preach the gospel who are honorable and upright men and full of the Holy Ghost.
—John Taylor, JD 20:178, April 8, 1879

All the messengers in the vineyard should be righteous and holy men and call upon the Lord in mighty prayer, in order to prevail. It is the privilege of every elder in Israel, who is laboring in the vineyard, if he will live up to his privileges, to have dreams, visions and revelations, and the Holy Ghost as a constant companion, that he may be able thoroughly to gather out the blood of Israel and the meek of the earth and bring them into the fold of Christ.
—*Wilford Woodruff*, MS 48:804-805, October 26, 1886

Get into your hearts, young people, to prepare yourselves to go out into the world where you can get on your knees and draw nearer to the Lord than in any other labor.
—*Heber J. Grant*, IE 39:396, July, 1936

When a man is called to go on a mission and a field of labor is assigned him, he should, I think, say in his heart, not my will be done, but thine, O Lord. We find it a little difficult sometimes to get the right men to go to certain distant lands to preach the gospel. . . . We expect every man to be on hand to go wherever he may be called, and then he may expect the blessing of the Lord to attend him in his labors.
—*Joseph F. Smith*, JD 25:100, April 6, 1884

THE SPIRIT OF THE WORK NECESSARY FOR SUCCESS

I had only traveled a short time to testify to the people, before I learned this one fact, that you might prove doctrine from the Bible till doomsday, and it would merely convince a people but would not convert them. You might read the Bible from Genesis to Revelation and prove every iota that you advance, and that alone would have no converting influence upon the people. Nothing short of a testimony by the power of the Holy Ghost would bring light and knowledge to them—bring them in their hearts to repentance. Nothing short of that would ever do. —*Brigham Young,* JD 5:327, October 7, 1857

We may know all about the philosophy of the ages and the history of the nations of the earth; we may study the wisdom and knowledge of man and get all the information that we can acquire in a lifetime of research and study, but all of it put together will never qualify any one to become a minister of the gospel unless he has the knowledge and spirit of the first principles of the gospel of Jesus Christ.
—*Joseph F. Smith,* CR, p. 138, April, 1915

An elder of Israel may preach the principles of the gospel, from first to last, as they are taught to him, to a congregation ignorant of them; but if he does not do it under the influence of the Spirit of the Lord, he cannot enlighten that congregation on those principles; it is impossible.
—*Brigham Young,* JD 1:3, January 16, 1853

If those who are going to preach do not go with that faith that pertains to eternal life and that spirit that is like a well of water, springing up into everlasting life, their labors will be vain. They may be the best theoretical theologians in the world —may be able to preach a Bible and a half in a sermon, to read history without a book, and understand all the dealings with men from the days of Adam till now; and, without the Spirit of the living God to guide them, they will not be able to accomplish anything to their credit towards building up His kingdom. They must realize that success in preaching the gospel springs not from the wisdom of this world. They must so live as to enjoy the power of God. —*Brigham Young,* JD 8:70-71, April 22, 1860

The Spirit of the Lord accompanies the elders. God blesses those who go forth to preach this gospel. If this gospel were not the truth, honest, prayerful, diligent, humble men would discover that fact, but I have yet to hear of one man in all the . . . years that this gospel has been preached, who has gone forth to proclaim it and who has been a diligent, faithful man, who has returned and announced that he has discovered that they have the gospel of Christ in some other land or some other clime. But I have heard of thousands who have studied other gospels, tens of thousands; I have known many who have been members of many different denominations, who never found peace and joy and perfect contentment until they embraced the gospel of Jesus Christ.   —*Heber J. Grant,* CR, p. 49, October, 1912

THE CORRECT PROCEDURE OF MISSIONARY WORK

Seek to help save souls, not to destroy them: for verily you know, that "there is more joy in heaven, over one sinner that repents, than there is over ninety and nine just persons that need no repentance." Strive not about the mysteries of the kingdom; cast not your pearls before swine, give not the bread of the children to dogs, lest you and the children should suffer, and you thereby offend your righteous Judge.
                              —*Joseph Smith, Jr.,* DHC 2:230, June, 1835

Avoid contentions and vain disputes with men of corrupt minds, who do not desire to know the truth. Remember that "it is a day of warning, and not a day of many words." If they receive not your testimony in one place, flee to another, remembering to cast no reflections, nor throw out any bitter sayings. If you do your duty, it will be just as well with you, as though all men embraced the gospel.
                              —*Joseph Smith, Jr.,* DHC 1:468, December 19, 1833

First, it becomes an elder when he is traveling through the world, warning the inhabitants of the earth to gather together that they may build up an holy city unto the Lord—instead of commencing with children, . . . they should commence their labors with parents, or guardians; and their teachings should be such as are calculated to turn the hearts of the fathers to the children, and the hearts of the children to the fathers; and no influence should be used with children, contrary to the consent of their parents or guardians. . . . And if children embrace the gospel, and their parents or guardians are unbelievers, teach them to stay at home and be obedient to their parents or guardians, if they require it; but if they consent to let them gather with the people of God, let them do so, and there shall be no wrong; and let all things be done carefully and righteously and God will extend to all such His guardian care.

And secondly, it is the duty of elders, when they enter into any house, to let their labors and warning voice be unto the master of that house; and if he receive the gospel, then he may extend his influence to his wife also, with consent, that peradventure she may receive the gospel: but if a man receive not the gospel, but gives his consent that his wife may receive it and she believes, then let her receive it. But if a man forbid his wife, or his children, before they are of age, to receive the gospel, then it should be the duty of the elder to go his way and use no influence against him and let the responsibility be upon his head; shake off the dust of thy feet as a testimony against him, and thy skirts shall then be clear of their souls. . . .

Thirdly, it should be the duty of an elder, when he enters into a house, to salute the master of that house, and if he gain his consent, then he may preach to all that are in that house; but if he gain not his consent, let him not go unto his slaves, or servants, but let the responsibility be upon the head of the master of that house, and the consequences thereof.

—*Joseph Smith, Jr.,* DHC 2:262-263, November, 1835

As each missionary goes forth it is strictly required of him that he shall not baptize a child without its parents' consent nor a wife without her husband's consent. This is binding upon him, and should any ask for baptism of him under such circumstances it is his duty to advise against and decline to do it. Duty is first with us—duty to God, duty to the Church, duty to the home and duty to our country.   —*Joseph F. Smith,* MS 73:403, June, 1911

And when you are called . . . to preach the gospel on foreign missions, . . . take a course to save every person. There is no man or woman within the pale of saving grace but that is worth saving. There is no intelligent being, except those who have

sinned against the Holy Ghost, but that is worth, I may say, all the life of an elder to save in the kingdom of God.
—Brigham Young, JD 9:124, February 17, 1861

EDUCATIONAL FEATURES OF MISSIONARY WORK

I would like to impress upon the minds of the brethren, that he who goes forth in the name of the Lord, trusting in Him with all his heart, will never want for wisdom to answer any question that is asked him, or to give any counsel that may be required to lead the people in the way of life and salvation, and he will never be confounded worlds without end. . . . Go in the name of the Lord, trust in the name of the Lord, lean upon the Lord, and call upon the Lord fervently and without ceasing, and pay no attention to the world. You will see plenty of the world— it will be before you all the time—but if you live so as to possess the Holy Ghost you will be able to understand more in relation to it in one day than you could in a dozen days without it, and you will at once see the difference between the wisdom of men and the wisdom of God, and you can weigh things in the balance and estimate them at their true worth.
—Brigham Young, JD 12:34, April 14, 1867

These missionaries are now going to school to teach others, and in teaching others they themselves will be instructed, and when they rise to speak in the name of Israel's God, if they live in purity and holiness before Him, He will give them words and ideas of which they never dreamed before. I have traveled hundreds and thousands of miles to preach this gospel among all grades and conditions of men, and there is one thing that always gave me satisfaction— I never yet found a man in any part of the world who could overturn one principle that has been communicated to us; they will attempt it, but error is a very singular weapon with which to combat truth; it never can vanquish it. When men go forth in the name of Israel's God there is no power on earth that can overturn the truths they advocate. . . . they have the light of revelation, the fire of the Holy Ghost, and the power of the priesthood within them.
—John Taylor, JD 12:21-22, April 14, 1867

LATTER-DAY SAINT MISSIONARIES RECEIVE
NO SALARY

Our missionaries go out at the call of the Church. They are not paid salaries; the Church does not even pay their way or their expenses while they are gone. The burden is upon themselves or upon their families, and it is only when their mission is ended that the Church bears any expense—it pays their way home.   *—Joseph F. Smith,* MS 73:403, June, 1911

I would say to these brethren—let it be your study to fulfill your mission. Never mind the world, never mind the dollars and cents, the pounds, shillings, and pence. You cleave to God, live your religion, magnify your callings, humble yourselves before God, call upon Him in secret, and He will open your path before you, and you shall have food and clothing, and your every want will be supplied, and you will be able to accomplish a good work and return to Zion in peace and safety. These are my feelings.   *—John Taylor,* JD 12:22, April 14, 1867

THE REWARDS OF MISSIONARY SERVICE

It is not an easy task; it is not a pleasant thing, perhaps, to be called out into the world, to leave our dear ones, but I say to you it will purchase for those who are faithful, for those who discharge that obligation as they may be required, peace and happiness beyond all understanding, and will prepare them that, in due time, when life's labor is complete, they will stand in the presence of their Maker, accepted of Him because of what they have done.

—George Albert Smith, CR, p. 53, April, 1922

We spend most of our time, many of us, seeking the things of this life that we will be compelled to leave when we go from here, yet there are the immortal souls around us whom, if we would, we could teach and inspire to investigate the truth and implant in their hearts a knowledge that God lives. What treasure in all the world could be so precious to us, for we would have their gratitude here and their everlasting and eternal appreciation in the world to come.

—George Albert Smith, CR, p. 49-50, October, 1916

I feel sorry for the man or the woman who has never experienced the sweet joy which comes to the missionary who proclaims the gospel of Jesus Christ, who brings honest souls to a knowledge of the truth, and who hears the expressions of gratitude and thanksgiving that come from the hearts of those who have been brought by his labor to a comprehension of life eternal.

—Heber J. Grant, CR, p. 23, October, 1907

Chapter XXXIX

Education: Searching for Eternal Truths

THE VALUE OF TRUTH

I ONCE READ a man's view of education—he was not a Mormon, but a man of the world—who said, "No man is fully educated unless he can tell where he came from, why he is here, and where he is going to." That being the case, I thought there were few fully educated in the world.
—*Wilford Woodruff*, JD 22:209, January 9, 1881

There is not a man born into the world but has a portion of the Spirit of God, and it is that Spirit of God which gives to his spirit understanding. Without this, he would be but an animal like the rest of the brute creation, without understanding, without judgment, without skill, without ability, except to eat and to drink like the brute beast. But inasmuch as the Spirit of God giveth all men understanding, he is enlightened above the brute beast. He is made in the image of God Himself, so that he can reason, reflect, pray, exercise faith; he can use his energies for the accomplishment of the desires of his heart, and inasmuch as he puts forth his efforts in the proper direction, then he is entitled to an increased portion of the Spirit of the Almighty to inspire him to increased intelligence, to increased prosperity and happiness in the world; but in proportion as he prostitutes his energies for evil, the inspiration of the Almighty is withdrawn from him, until he becomes so dark and so benighted, that so far as his knowledge of God is concerned, so far as the future or hopes of eternal life are concerned, he is quite as ignorant as a dumb brute.　　　　—*Joseph F. Smith*, JD 25:54, February 17, 1884

Seek first the kingdom of God and His righteousness, and all else that is desirable, including the knowledge for which you yearn, shall be given unto you.
—*Joseph F. Smith*, JI 38:627, October 15, 1903

He that makes a pin does more than he who commands armies; and he that invents a new thing for the benefit of man should be honored more than a king. Wisdom is better than wealth. To be great, be good; to be rich, be contented; and to be respected, respect yourself.
                    —*John Taylor,* "Nauvoo Neighbor," August 21, 1844

The child grows from childhood to boyhood, and from boyhood to manhood, with a constant and steady growth; but he cannot tell how or when the growth occurs. He does not realize that he is growing; but by observing the laws of health and being prudent in his course he eventually arrives at manhood. So in reference to ourselves as Latter-day Saints. We grow and increase. We are not aware of it at the moment; but after a year or so we discover that we are, so to speak, away up the hill, nearing the mountain top.   —*Lorenzo Snow,* CR, p. 2, April, 1899

We hear much of men who are specially gifted, of geniuses in the world's affairs; and many of us force ourselves to think that we are capable of little and therefore may as well take life easy since we do not belong to that favored class. True, not all are endowed with the same gifts, nor is everyone imbued with the strength of a giant; yet every son and every daughter of God has received some talent, and each will be held to strict account for the use or misuse to which it is put. The spirit of genius is the spirit of hard work, plodding toil, whole-souled devotion to the labor of the day.   —*Joseph F. Smith,* JI 38:689, 1903

I long for the time that a point of a finger, or motion of the hand, will express every idea without utterance. When a man is full of the light of eternity, then the eye is not the only medium through which he sees, his ear is not the only medium by which he hears, nor the brain the only means by which he understands. When the whole body is full of the Holy Ghost, he can see behind him with as much ease, without turning his head, as he can see before him. If you have not that experience, you ought to have. It is not the optic nerve alone that gives the knowledge of surrounding objects to the mind, but it is that which God has placed in man—a system of intelligence that attracts knowledge, as light cleaves to light, intelligence to intelligence,

and truth to truth. It is this which lays in man a proper foundation for all education. I shall yet see the time that I can converse
with this people and not speak to them, but the expression of my
countenance will tell the congregation what I wish to convey,
without opening my mouth.

—*Brigham Young*, JD 6:317, April 7, 1852

GOD IS THE SOURCE OF ALL INTELLIGENCE

God is the source, the fountain of all intelligence, no matter
who possesses it, whether man upon the earth, the spirits in the
spirit world, the angels that dwell in the eternities of the Gods,
or the most inferior intelligence among the devils in hell. All
have derived what intelligence, light, power, and existence they
have from God—from the same source from which we have received ours.   —*Brigham Young*, JD 8:205, October 14, 1860

All truth cometh from the Lord. He is the fountain of truth;
or in other words, He is the everlasting spring of life and truth,
and from Him cometh all knowledge, all wisdom, all virtue and
all power. . . . God knew the truth before any heathen philos-
opher. No man has received intelligence but has had to come to
the Fountain Head.   —*Joseph F. Smith*, YWJ 18:314, June 7, 1907

The Father, Son and Holy Ghost, as one God, are the fountain of truth. From this fountain all the ancient learned philosophers have received their inspiration and wisdom—from it they
have received all their knowledge. If we find truth in broken
fragments through the ages, it may be set down as an incon-
trovertible fact that it originated at the fountain and was given
to philosophers, inventors, patriots, reformers, and prophets by
the inspiration of God. It came from Him through His Son Jesus
Christ and the Holy Ghost, in the first place, and from no other
source. It is eternal.   —*Joseph F. Smith*, IE 10:629, June, 1907

I believe that the Lord has revealed to the children of men
all that they know. I do not believe that any man has discovered
any principle in science, or art, in mechanism, or mathematics, or
anything else, that God did not know before he did. Man is indebted to the Source of all intelligence and truth, for the knowl-

edge that he possesses; and all who will yield obedience to the promptings of the Spirit . . . will get a clearer, a more expansive, and a more direct and conclusive knowledge of God's truths than anyone else can do.   *—Joseph F. Smith,* CR, p. 85-86, April, 1902

All the intelligence which men possess on the earth, whether religious, scientific or political—proceeds from God—every good and perfect gift proceeds from Him, the fountain of light and truth, wherein there is no variableness nor shadow of turning. The knowledge of the human system has proceeded from the human system itself, which God has organized.
    —John Taylor, JD 10:275, October 25, 1863

Who controls the heavens and the earth? The Gods in the eternal worlds. Who has implanted certain principles in matter and in all creation? God has done it. All things are subject to these laws; and if men can place themselves under His guidance and find the way to approach the great Elohim, they will know more in a short time than all this world together know in all their lives and more than all the combined intelligence of the world, for God is the foundation of all wisdom and the source of all intelligence and knowledge.
    —John Taylor, JD 25:215, June 29, 1884

In knowledge there is power. God has more power than all other beings, because He has greater knowledge; and hence He knows how to subject all other beings to Him. He has power over all.   *—Joseph Smith, Jr.,* DHC 5:340, April 8, 1843

THE GOSPEL EMBRACES ALL TRUTH

Every art and science known and studied by the children of men is comprised within the gospel.
    —Brigham Young, JD 12:257, August 9, 1868

In regard to our religion, I will say that it embraces every principle of truth and intelligence pertaining to us as moral, intellectual, mortal and immortal beings, pertaining to this world and the world that is to come. We are open to truth of every kind, no matter whence it comes, where it originates, or who believes in it. Truth, when preceded by the little word "all," comprises everything that has ever existed or that ever will exist and be known by and among men in time and through the endless ages of eternity.   *—John Taylor,* JD 16:369, February 1, 1874

If there is anything good and praiseworthy in morals, religion, science, or anything calculated to exalt and ennoble man, we are after it. But with all our getting, we want to get understanding, and that understanding which flows from God.

—John Taylor, JD 20:48, August 4, 1878

We believe in all truth, no matter to what subject it may refer. No sect or religious denomination in the world possesses a single principle of truth that we do not accept or that we will reject. We are willing to receive all truth, from whatever source it may come; for truth will stand, truth will endure.

—Joseph F. Smith, CR, p. 7, April, 1909

MAN CANNOT BE SAVED IN IGNORANCE

As far as we degenerate from God, we descend to the devil and lose knowledge, and without knowledge we cannot be saved, and while our hearts are filled with evil, and we are studying evil, there is no room in our hearts for good, or studying good. . . .

A man is saved no faster than he gets knowledge, for if he does not get knowledge, he will be brought into captivity by some evil power in the other world, as evil spirits will have more knowledge and consequently more power than many men who are on the earth. Hence it needs revelation to assist us and give us knowledge of the things of God.

—Joseph Smith, Jr., DHC 4:588, April 10, 1842

It is not wisdom that we should have all knowledge at once presented before us; but that we should have a little at a time; then we can comprehend it. . . .

Add to your faith knowledge, etc. The principle of knowledge is the principle of salvation. This principle can be comprehended by the faithful and diligent; and every one that does not obtain knowledge sufficient to be saved will be condemned. The principle of salvation is given us through the knowledge of Jesus Christ. *—Joseph Smith, Jr.*, DHC 5:387, May 14, 1843

Our hope of salvation must be founded upon the truth, the whole truth, and nothing but the truth, for we cannot build upon error and ascend into the courts of eternal truth and enjoy the glory and exaltation of the kingdom of our God. That cannot be done. *—Joseph F. Smith*, CR, p. 3, October, 1917

We need constant instruction, and our great heavenly Teacher requires of us to be diligent pupils in His school, that we may in time reach His glorified presence. If we will not lay to heart the rules of education which our Teacher gives us to study, and continue to advance from one branch of learning to another, we never can be scholars of the first class and become endowed with the science, power, excellency, brightness and glory of the heavenly hosts; and unless we are educated as they are, we cannot associate with them.

—Brigham Young, JD 10:266, October 6, 1863

If this language that I have just quoted (James 11:14-19) is correct, the devils believe in God. When Jesus cast devils out, they cried out and testified that He was the Son of God. Did that knowledge save them? Will the knowledge that you and I have save us? The more abundantly we have been blessed of God, the more testimonies we have received of the divinity of the mission of the Prophet Joseph Smith, the oftener we have seen the sick healed, the oftener we have seen the manifestations of the gift of tongues and the gift of prophecy, the greater is our responsibility to labor for the onward advancement of the work of God. Of those to whom much is given, much is expected. As we grow and increase in knowledge and in the testimony of the Spirit of God, we must also grow and increase in labor and effort for the advancement of the work of God or we will lose the Spirit of God. It is not a knowledge that God lives that will save us, it is keeping the commandments of God.

—Heber J. Grant, MS 59:133, November 22, 1896

DISTINCTION BETWEEN KNOWLEDGE AND INTELLIGENCE

There is a difference between knowledge and pure intelligence. Satan possesses knowledge, far more than we have, but he has not intelligence or he would render obedience to the principles of truth and right. I know men who have knowledge, who understand the principles of the gospel, perhaps as well as you do, who are brilliant, but who lack the essential qualification of pure intelligence. They will not accept and render obedience thereto. *Pure intelligence comprises not only knowledge, but also the power to properly apply that knowledge.*

—Joseph F. Smith, GD, p. 58, a. 1913

The mere stuffing of the mind with a knowledge of facts is not education. The mind must not only possess a knowledge of the truth, but the soul must revere it, cherish it, love it as a priceless gem; and this human life must be guided and shaped by it in order to fulfill its destiny. The mind should not only be charged with intelligence, but the soul should be filled with admiration and desire for pure intelligence which comes of a knowledge of the truth. The truth can only make him free who hath it and will continue in it. And the word of God is truth, and it will endure forever.

Educate yourself not only for time, but also for eternity.
                    —Joseph F. Smith, "The Contributor" 16:570, June 5, 1895

IMPART KNOWLEDGE TO OTHERS

A man who wishes to receive light and knowledge, to increase in the faith of the Holy Gospel, and to grow in the knowledge of the truth as it is in Jesus Christ, will find that when he imparts knowledge to others he will also grow and increase. Be not miserly in your feelings, but get knowledge and understanding by freely imparting it to others.
                              —Brigham Young, JD 2:267, April 8, 1855

When a person receives intelligence from the Lord, and is willing to communicate that for the benefit of the people, he will receive continual additions to that intelligence; and there is no end to his increase so long as he will hold fast to the faith of the Lord Jesus Christ.
                                —Lorenzo Snow, JD 5:64, April 9, 1857

Education is a good thing, and blessed is the man who has it and can use it for the dissemination of the gospel without being puffed up with pride.
                            —Brigham Young, JD 11:214, April 29, 1866

I would urge upon the young men to do nothing for show, but to do their best to obtain knowledge and then strive to put the knowledge obtained to practical use. I am acquainted with some people who are regular encyclopedias of knowledge, but so far as their knowledge being utilized for the benefiting of their fellow men, they might just as well not possess it or be deaf, dumb, and blind; this is all wrong.
                              —Heber J. Grant, IE 3:304, February, 1900

It is not what you eat that benefits you, but what you digest. What you hear today is of no use to you unless you put it into practice. Somebody has said, and I have often repeated it: "Knowledge without practice is like a glass eye—all for show and nothing for use." . . .

Knowledge is of no value unless you put it into practice. All the teachings in the world, unless the individual is living that which he teaches, will not carry the spirit of right action. It does not carry with it the weight; it does not really touch the hearts of those who listen.

—Heber J. Grant, IE 36:224, February, 1933

All the knowledge in the world would not amount to anything unless we put that knowledge into actual practice. We are the architects and builders of our lives, and if we fail to put our knowledge into actual practice and do the duties that devolve upon us we are making a failure of life.

—Heber J. Grant, IE 42:329, June, 1939

CONCERNING THE TRAINING OF CHILDREN

Train your children to be intelligent and industrious. First teach them the value of healthful bodies and how to preserve them in soundness and vigor; teach them to entertain the highest record for virtue and chastity, and likewise encourage them to develop the intellectual faculties with which they are endowed. They should also be taught regarding the earth on which they live, its properties, and the laws that govern it; and they ought to be instructed concerning God, who made the earth, and His designs and purposes in its creation, and the placing of man upon it. They should know how to cultivate the soil in the best possible manner; they should know how to raise the best kind of fruits adapted to the soil and climate; they should be induced to raise the best kinds of stock, and to care for them properly when they come into their possession. And whatever labor they pursue they should be taught to do so intelligently; and every incentive, at the command of parents to induce children to labor intelligently should be held out to them. *—John Taylor, JD 24:167, May 19, 1883*

See that your children are properly educated in the rudiments of their mother tongue, and then let them proceed to higher branches of learning; let them become more informed in every department of true and useful learning than their fathers are. When they have become well acquainted with their language, let them study other languages, and make themselves fully acquainted with the manners, customs, laws, governments, and literature of other nations, peoples, and tongues. Let them also learn all the truth pertaining to the arts and sciences and how to apply the same to their temporal wants. Let them study things that are upon the earth, that are in the earth, and that are in the heavens.   —*Brigham Young*, JD 8:9, March 4, 1860

In regard to schools and the education of the young. . . . We have committed to our care pearls of great price; we have become the fathers and mothers of lives, and the Gods and the Holy Priesthood in the eternal worlds have been watching us and our movements in relation to these things. We do not want a posterity to grow up that will be ignorant, depraved, corrupt, and fallen, that will depart from every principle of right; but one that will be intelligent and wise, possessing literary and scientific attainments, and a knowledge of everything that is good, praiseworthy, intellectual and beneficial in the world. . . . And above all other things, teach our children the fear of God. . . . Teach them how to approach God, that they may call upon Him and He will hear them.
—*John Taylor*, JD 20:60, September 22, 1878

THE PURPOSE OF CHURCH SCHOOLS

I remember speaking, upon one occasion, in one of our great Church schools, and I said that I hoped it would never be forgotten that the one and only reason why there was any necessity for a Church school was to make Latter-day Saints. If it were only for the purpose of gaining secular knowledge or improving in art, literature, science and invention, so far as our information was concerned, and adding to it on these subjects, that there was no need of Church schools, because we could gain these things from our secular schools supported by the taxation of the people; and that we had an abundance of uses for all the means that the Church possesses, all the tithing that might come into our hands, without expending vast sums of money upon Church schools. But if we kept in our minds the one central thing, namely, the making of Latter-day Saints in our schools, then they would be fulfilling the object of their existence. The amount of money expended would cut no figure at all, because we cannot value in dollars and cents the saving of a single soul.

—Heber J. Grant, IE 24:866, August, 1921

The specific purpose of the Church school system is to make Latter-day Saints. *—Heber J. Grant,* IE 26:1091, October 18, 1922

There are a great many branches of education: some go to college to learn languages, some to study law, some to study physics, and some to study astronomy, and various other branches of science. We want every branch of science taught in this place that is taught in the world. But our favorite study is that branch which particularly belongs to the elders of Israel—namely, theology. Every elder should become a profound theologian— should understand this branch better than all the world.

—Brigham Young, JD 6:317, April 7, 1852

WILL A PERSON EVER CEASE TO LEARN?

I shall not cease learning while I live, nor when I arrive in the spirit world; but shall there learn with greater facility; and when I again receive my body, I shall learn a thousand times more in a thousand times less time; and then I do not mean to cease learning, but shall still continue my researches.

—Brigham Young, JD 8:10, March 4, 1860

Can we know anything here that we did not know before we came? Are not the means of knowledge in the first estate equal to those of this? I think the spirit, before and after this probation, possesses greater facilities, aye, manifold greater, for the acquisition of knowledge, than while manacled and shut up in the prison-house of mortality.

—Joseph F. Smith, "The Contributor" 4:114, a. 1883

If we continue to learn all that we can pertaining to the salvation which is purchased and presented to us through the Son of God, is there a time when a person will cease to learn? Yes, when he has sinned against God the Father, Jesus Christ the Son, and the Holy Ghost—God's minister; when he has denied the Lord, defied Him and committed the sin that in the Bible is termed the unpardonable sin—the sin against the Holy Ghost. That is the time when a person will cease to learn, and from that time forth will descend in ignorance, forgetting that which they formerly knew. . . . They will cease to increase, but must decrease. . . These are the only characters who will ever cease to learn, both in time and eternity.

—*Brigham Young*, JD 3:203, February 17, 1856

Index

A

AARONIC PRIESTHOOD (see also Priesthood)—restored by John the Baptist, 106, 185-186, 191-192; has charge of temporal affairs, 189, 192-193; powers of, 195.

ABRAHAM—received promise of eternal increase, 75; was foreordained, 151; tithing in day of, 324.

ACCOUNTABLE—man held, for his influence and conduct, 55; kings, for actions, 55.

ACTS—man to be held accountable for his, 55; our, are recorded, 59.

ADAM—priesthood first given to, 186; his part in the creation, 266-267; not made of dust of this earth, 267; marriage of, and Eve, 301; tithing practiced in day of, 324.

ADAMIC DISPENSATION—also called patriarchal, 162-164.

ADMINISTERED—how tithing is to be, 327-328.

ADMINISTERING TO THE SICK—correct order of, 175-176.

ADVICE—to young L.D.S. members, 306-307.

AGENCY, FREE (see Free Agency)

ALMIGHTY (see God)

AMERICAN CONTINENT—Zion to be on, 245-246.

AMUSEMENT — provide for, during week, 362-363.

ANGELS — distinction between, and gods, 77; definition of, 77; of destruction, 125, 233.

APOSTLE (see also Twelve Apostles)—prophet not so great as an, 290.

APOSTLESHIP—powers of, 196.

ASCEND—Latter-day Zion to, 250.

ATONEMENT—necessary for exaltation, 73; repentance necessary for full efficacy of, 101; Latter-day Saint concept of, 144; need of, 144-146; purpose of, 146-147; effect of, 147-148; to whom does the, extend?, 148-149.

AUTHORITY (see also Priesthood) — priesthood, necessary to baptize, 106; necessary to confer Gift of Holy Ghost, 116; bestowed only by laying on of hands, 117; priesthood is, of God, 194; no ordinance can be performed without, 196; correct line of, 213-214; necessary to preach gospel, 388.

AUXILIARY ORGANIZATIONS — are dependent upon priesthood, 215-216; partial list of, 216.

B

BAPTISM—no, in spirit world, 31, 111; necessary to enter celestial kingdom, 64; definition of, 104-105; faith and repentance should precede, 105-106; authority necessary to perform, 106; necessary to enter kingdom of God, 107-108; a sign ordained of God, 107-108; should be by immersion, 108-109; for the remission of sins, 109-110; of children not scriptural, 110-111.

BAPTISM FOR THE DEAD (see also Baptism)—Latter-day Saint belief in, 111-112; doctrine of, in New Testament, 112; general characteristics of, 112-113; to be performed in a temple, 113.

BAPTIZE—do not, children without parents' consent, 392.

BAR OF GOD—every man to stand before, 50-51, 53.

BEARER OF PRIESTHOOD (see Priesthood Bearer)

BELIEF—distinction between faith and, 98-99.

BENEFITS—derived by worthy priesthood bearers, 203-204.

BIBLE—authority not derived from, 195; the word of God, 343-344; we believe the, as far as it is translated correctly, 345-346; gospel plan contained in, 346-347; Book of Mormon and, agree, 352-353.

BIRTH CONTROL—is a crime, 308.

BIRTHRIGHT—preserve your, 160-161.

BISHOP—selection, calling and appointment of, 193, 206, 211; trial of, 193; duties of, 210-211; position of, in Church government, 211-213.

BLESSINGS—of living a worthy life, 18-19; predicated upon law, 54.

BLOOD—to be replaced by spiritual matter in the resurrection, 44; of Jesus atones for our sins, 149; once circulated in God's viens, 275.

BODIES—distinction between translated and resurrected, 47-49.

BODY—importance of obtaining a, 13-15; identical, of Jesus Christ resurrected, 38; not perfect without the spirit, 41; resurrection of the, 42-44; develops after the resurrection, 44-46; actual, is resurrected, 48; resurrected, necessary to enter celestial kingdom, 66; God has, of flesh and bone, 273-275.

BOOK OF LIFE, THE LAMB'S — all names written there, 143.

BOOK OF MORMON — the word of God, 343-344; stick of Joseph, 343-344, 348, 353; the American scripture, 347-349; we believe, to be word of God, 349-352; title page of, literal translation, 351-352; Bible and, agree, 352-353.

BREAD AND WINE—use of, in sacrament, 367-368.

BURIAL—the, of the body, 48-49.

C

CALAMITIES—to come, 223-225.

CALLINGS—priesthood same but, are different, 196-197.

CELESTIAL GLORY—compared to the sun, 62.

CELESTIALIZED EARTH (see also Earth) — residence for celestial beings, 268-269; to shine like sun, 269-270.

CELESTIAL KINGDOM—entrance requirements of, 63-66, 383; resurrected body necessary to enter, 66; consent of Joseph Smith necessary to enter, 66; few will achieve, 66; conditions of the, 66-68; heirs of the, 67; to be on this earth, 68, 268-269; the family unit in the, 69-70; temple ordinances necessary to enter, 121; Holy Priesthood belongs to, 187; entrance necessary to have spirit children, 303.

CELESTIAL LAW — only celestial beings can live, 67.

CELESTIAL MARRIAGE (see also Marriage)—nature of, 301-302; not necessarily plural marriage, 301.

CHASTITY—teach children value of, 403.

CHILDREN—are offspring of God, 5, 275-278; the resurrection of, 44-46; are redeemed by Christ, 45-46; are saved in the celestial kingdom, 67; baptism of, not scriptural, 110-111; to live to see Christ, 255; to receive Sacrament, 370; the training of, 403-404.

CHRIST (see Jesus Christ)

CHURCH GOVERNMENT—chapter on, 207-219; order of, 211-213; line of

authority in, 213-214; priesthood organization necessary in, 215-216; sustaining of Church officers, 216-218; settlement of disputes, 218-219; payment of Church officers, 327-328.

CHURCH MEMBERS (see Latter-day Saints)

CHURCH OFFICES (see also Church Government)—a synopsis of 208-211.

CHURCH OF JESUS CHRIST OF LATTER-DAY SAINTS (see also Latter-day Saints)—will not be destroyed, 168; only Church with divine authority, 195; not a sect, 195; office holding in, 207-208; is patriarchal in nature, 207; to fill the world, 255.

CIGARETTES (see Tobacco)

CITY OF ENOCH (see also Zion)—to descend from heaven, 250.

CITY OF ZION (see Zion)

CIVIL MARRIAGE (see also Marriage)—for time only, 305; may be performed by priesthood, 308-309.

COFFEE (see Hot Drinks)

COMFORTER (see Holy Ghost and Holy Spirit)

COMMANDMENT—Word of Wisdom is a, of God, 311-312; tithe payment is a, with promise of blessing, 329.

COMMUNICATION BETWEEN GOD AND MAN (see Revelation and Prayer)

COMMUNISM—is not the United Order, 342.

CONDUCT — man held accountable for, 55.

CONFESS—your sins, 99.

CONSECRATION, PRINCIPLE OF (see United Order)

CONSTITUTION OF THE UNITED STATES—to hang by a thread, 230-231; "Mormon" elders to save, 230-231.

CORNELIUS — received Holy Ghost before baptism, 118.

COUNCIL IN HEAVEN—the great, 5-6.

COUNCIL OF THE SEVENTY — the position of, in Church government, 197, 210-211; a traveling council, 210; mission of, 210; line of authority of, 213-214.

COVENANTS — broken, must be atoned for, 51; with God, 126-127; of the Sacrament, 368-369.

COWDERY, OLIVER—Aaronic Priesthood restored to, 106; statement on Book of Mormon, 351.

CREATION—of the earth, 266-268.

D

DAWNING—the millennium is, 259.

DEACON—position of, in Church government, 211-213.

DEAD—work for, should not be neglected, 121; not perfect without the living, 122, 129; identification of, necessary for temple work, 131-132.

DEATH — transition from, into spirit world, 28; is separation of spirit and body, 28; on, and burial, 48-49; does not destroy body, 48; preferred to apostasy, 88.

DEATHBED — repentance on, is not scriptural, 102-103.

DECEIVED—God is not, 99; elect may be, 231.

DECREES OF GOD—some are fixed and immovable, 107-108.

DEEDS—every man must answer for, 50-51, 53-55.

DEFORMITIES—to be removed after the resurrection, 43.

DESTINY OF MAN (see Godhood)

DEVELOPS—the body, after the resurrection, 44-46.

DEVIL (see Satan)

DISEASE—a result of the Fall, 173-174; to be banished from celestialized earth, 268.

DISPENSATION OF FULLNESS OF TIMES — preparation for, 164-166; Joseph Smith, Jr. head of, 165; work of, 166-168; was foreordained to survive, 168; a vision concerning, 169.

DISPENSATIONS—the series of, 162-163; the Gospel, 162-169; the Gospel before Christ, 163; preparation for last dispensation, 164; dispensation of fullness of times, 164-166; work of last dispensation, 166-168.

DISPUTES — settlement of, among Church members, 218-219; avoid contentions and, 391.

DISTRESS—world to be in, 249.

DIVINE CONCEPTION OF CHRIST—statements concerning, 280-281.

DIVINE DEBT (see The Fall and Atonement)

DIVORCE—Church stand against, 307.

DOCTRINE AND COVENANTS — the word of God, 343-344; L.D.S. testament, 343-344, 353; truths in, 353-354; guides to Church, 356.

DREAMS—and visions, 178-179.

E

EARTH—requisite that an, be organized for mortals, 15; spirit world is on the, 26; Christ to reign on, 252-253, 263-264; story of the, 265-270; its position in the great plan, 265-266; the creation of, 266-268; to be celestialized, 268-269.

EARTHQUAKES — numerous in last days, 223-225.

EARTHS — space for many, in the heavens, 128.

EATING—be temperate in, habits, 321.

ECONOMIC THEORY, OF MORMONISM (see Tithing and United Order)

EDUCATION — temples to introduce higher branches of, 134-135; a man's view of, 392; is a good thing, 402-403.

ELDER BROTHER—Jesus Christ is our, 281-282.

ELDERS — have authority to confer Gift of Holy Ghost, 116; powers of, 194, 197; position of, in Church government, 211-213; to preach Gospel, 384-386.

ELECT—very, may be deceived, 231.

ELEMENT—is eternal in nature, 43.

ELIAS—spirit of, is first, 132.

ELIJAH—the mission of, 132; restored keys of priesthood, 191.

ELOHIM—knows the thoughts of men, 53, 279; no respecter of persons, 120; a distinct personage, 273-275, 277; is our Father, 275-276, 279; man formed in image of, 276-278; once as we are now, 71-73, 277; has a body of flesh and bone, 278-279; what God does, 279-280; is literal Father of Jesus Christ, 280-281.

EMBRYO—men are gods in, 73-75.

ENDOWMENT, HOLY OR TEMPLE—definition, purpose, and nature of, 124.

ETERNAL DESTINY — depends upon actions in mortality, 15, 19.

ETERNAL INCREASE — celestial beings to have, 69; promised to the faithful, 75-76.

ETERNAL LIFE—obedience necessary to obtain, 19; the greatest gift of God, 37, 84.

ETERNAL LIVES—blessing of, 303-304.

ETERNAL MARRIAGE (see Celestial Marriage)

ETERNAL PROGRESSION—the plan of, 7-10; belief of Latter-day Saints on, 30; is the law of heaven, 78-79.

EVANGELIST (see Patriarch)

EVIL—satan the cause of, 19-22, 161; knowledge of, necessary, 22; how to distinguish, 24-25.

EXALTATION—depends upon actions, 19; knowledge of good and evil necessary for, 22-24; baptism necessary for, 107-108; ordinances necessary to achieve, 123; free agency needed to obtain, 158; sufferings of Jesus necessary for His, 283-284.

EXAMPLE—teach by, 384.

EXCOMMUNICATION — priesthood taken away by, 205-206.

EXPECTED — where much is given, much is, 59-60.

EXPERIENCE, NEED OF — necessary for exaltation, 19.

EZEKIEL—statement of the Lord to, 384-385.

F

FAITH—is first principle of Gospel, 95-96; how, may be acquired, 96-97; without works is dead, 97; is a gift of God, 97; the power of, 97-98; is wanting, 97-98; distinction between, and belief, 98-99; tithing is a test of, 328-329.

FAITHFUL—to become gods, 76.

FALL, THE—divine debt was contracted, 145; diseases are a result of, 173-174.

FALSE GIFTS—concerning, 180.

FAMILY — organization to continue after resurrection, 69, 70, 304.

FAMILY LIFE—statements concerning, 307-308.

FAMINE—predictions concerning, 223-225.

FAST DAY—plan for taking care of poor, 333-334.

FASTING—definition of, on fast day, 333-334; be temperate in, 378.

FAST OFFERING DONATION—statements on, 333-334.

FATHER, DUTIES OF—to administer to the sick, 176; to confer patriarchal blessings, 196; highest authority in home, 308; to lead in prayer, 379.

FINANCIAL REWARDS — of obeying Word of Wisdom, 319-320; of tithe paying, 329-330.

FIRST AND SECOND RESURRECTION —a vision concerning the, 37-38.

FIRST ESTATE (see also Pre-existence)—all mortals kept their, 7.

FIRST PRESIDENCY—office of presidency, 208-209; relationship to Twelve Apostles, 213-214; question of succession to, 214-215; to call missionaries, 387-388.

FIRST PRINCIPLES , OF GOSPEL— necessary for salvation, 141.

FLESH AND BLOOD — cannot enter spirit world, 27.

FLESH OF BEAST AND BIRDS—to be eaten sparingly, 317-318.

FOREORDAINED — man, to become like God, 72; holy men, before their birth, 151; who was, ?, 152-154.

FOREORDINATION—principle of, 151; is not predestination, 151-152.

FREE AGENCY—free will a correct principle, 152; the principle of, 155-156; is an eternal principle, 156-157, 264; necessary for fair judgment, 157; necessary for exaltation, 158.

FREEDOM OF WORSHIP—Latter-day Saint belief in, 158-159; to prevail during Millennium, 261-262.

G

GARDEN OF EDEN—gospel principles unchanged since, 91.

GARMENTS OF HOLY PRIESTHOOD— do not mutilate, 126-127.

GATHERING — principle of, 238-239, 241-243; to American Zion, 241-243.

GATHERING OF ISRAEL—chapter on, 237-244; Israel to gather home, 237-238; purpose of, 238-239.

GENEALOGIES — Latter-day Saints should trace, 126.

GENERAL AUTHORITIES (see Church Offices)

GENERATION—this, would put Jesus to death, 224; shall not pass away . . . before Christ comes, 253.

GENIUS—spirit of, is hard work, 397.

GIFT OF HOLY GHOST—the greatest gift to man, 113; a principle of revelation, 115; conferred only by laying on of hands, 116-117; repentance must precede, 116; authority necessary to confer, 116; distinction between Holy Ghost and, 117-118; God confers, through proper authority, 288.

GIFTS OF SPIRIT—imparted by laying on of hands, 116-117, 171; the gifts enumerated, 170-180; Latter-day Saint belief in, 170-171; how these, are made manifest, 171-172; only for faithful, 172-173; gift of healing, 173-174; gift of tongues,

J

JACKSON COUNTY, MISSOURI—center stake of Zion in, 246-247, 340-341.

JACOB—was foreordained, 151.

JAREDITES (see Book of Mormon)

JEHOVAH (see Jesus Christ)

JERUSALEM—to be rebuilt, 237, 239-241, 245, 255-256.

JESUS CHRIST — preaching in the spirit world, 33-34; the pattern of the resurrection, 38-39; the literal son of Elohim, 74, 280-281; Saints baptized in name of, 104; the atonement of, 144-150; was foreordained, 151-152; healed the sick, 173-174; second coming of, 252-258; future mission of, 257-258; few will be prepared to meet, 258; to rule over the earth, 263-264; divine conception of, 280-281; is our Elder Brother, 281-282; mission of, 282-283; sufferings of, necessary for exaltation, 283-284; Sacrament in remembrance of, 366-367; prayers offered in name of, 378.

JEWS (see also Israel) — return of, to Jerusalem, 239-241; gospel to be preached to, 240-241; gathering of, to precede second coming, 256; Bible the record of, 346, 353.

JOHN THE BAPTIST — restored Aaronic Priesthood, 106, 185-186, 191-192; Gospel known before time of, 163.

JUDGE—who will, ?, 56; man to help, himself, 56-57; not your fellow mortals, 58-59.

JUDGMENT—the, extends to all, 50-51; God's, is just, 51-52; based on thoughts and actions, 53-55; determined by knowledge, 59-60; free agency necessary for fair, 157.

JUSTICE—satisfied by atonement of Christ, 148.

K

KEYS OF PRIESTHOOD — definition of, 190-191; restoration of, to Joseph Smith, 191-192.

KINGDOM OF GOD—authority necessary to organize, 194; the establishment of, 232; seek first, 396

KINGS—to give an account before God, 55; to visit Zion, 247.

KNEE—every, shall bow and tongue confess, 261-262.

KNOWLEDGE — satan possesses great, 20-22, 401; of good and evil

necessary, 22-24; in, there is power, 399; distinction between intelligence and, 401-402; impart, to others 402-403; without practice is useless, 402-403.

L

LAMANITES — to receive the priesthood, 205; numbered with Israel, 237; are descendants of Joseph, 347; Book of Mormon partial record of, 347-348.

LAMPS—seven golden, set in heavens, 233-234.

LAND OF ZION (see Zion)

LANGUAGES—study other, 404, 405.

LAST DAYS—book on 221; conditions existing in, 223-225; Spirit of God to withdraw, 224, 227, 228; wars and rumors of war, 226-227; wickedness to increase, 228-229; how to escape judgments of, 235-236.

LAST DISPENSATION (see Dispensation of Fullness of Times)

LATTER-DAY SAINT CHURCH (see also Church Government)—will not be destroyed, 168; founded on revelation, 293-294.

LATTER-DAY SAINTS — should trace genealogies, 126; to become saviors on Mount Zion, 130-131; are entitled to revelation, 296-297; advice to young, 306-307; all, should pay tithing, 325; should honor Sabbath day, 358-360.

LAW—all things governed by, 61.

LAW OF CONSECRATION (see United Order)

LAW OF REVENUE (see Tithing)

LAYING ON OF HANDS FOR THE GIFT OF THE HOLY GHOST. (see also Gift of Holy Ghost)—an ordinance of the gospel, 113-115; purpose of, 115; repentance must precede, 116; authority necessary to perform, 116.

LEARN—will a person ever cease to, ?, 405-406.

LEAVEN—gospel works like, 88.

LESSER PRIESTHOOD (see Priesthood)

LEVITICAL PRIESTHOOD (see Priesthood)

LIQUOR—is not good for man, 314-316; evils of, 315; on whisky makers, 316.

LIVING—not perfect without the dead, 122, 129; must perform ordinances for dead, 129.

354-355; written, not sufficient to guide Church, 355-356.

SEA—to engulf mighty cities, 223.

SEALING, THE ORDINANCE OF — need of, 125; must be performed on earth, 125; priesthood necessary to perform, 125, 305; genealogy work in connection with, 126; to be performed in temple, 135.

SEALS—are about to be opened, 224, 234.

SECOND COMING OF CHRIST — Jesus to return to Jews, 240; Christ to reign on earth, 252-253; time of, 253-255; Latter-day Saint belief concerning, 252-258; events to precede, 255-257; few will be prepared to witness, 258.

SELF-REGISTERING MACHINE—man a, 56-58.

SEVENTY (see also Council of the Seventy)—powers of, 197; duties of, 210; position of, 211-212; to preach gospel, 384-386.

SICK—order of administering to, 175-176.

SIGNS — follow the Latter-day believer, 170-173.

SIN—is co-eternal with righteousness, 23; is upon all earths, 22; confess your, 99; no man saved in, 101; the unpardonable, 130; man cannot forgive own, 146-147; necessity to repent of, 150.

SMITH, JOSEPH, JR.—consent of, necessary to enter celestial kingdom, 66; was foreordained, 153-154; head of last dispensation, 165, 260; priesthood restored to, 185-186; restoration of keys of priesthood to, 191-192; keys of gathering committed to, 242; origin of Word of Wisdom, 311.

SONS OF GOD—men are, 73-75.

SONS OF PERDITION — all to be saved except, 142; have their free agency abridged, 160.

SOUL—composed of spirit and body, 18; must bear own sins, 51.

SPIRIT BEINGS—differences between, 27-28; are familiar with each other, 30; composed of refined matter, 30; watch over mortals, 31-32; taught Gospel plan of salvation, 33.

SPIRIT OF GOD — to be withdrawn from the earth, 224, 227, 228; distinction between, and Holy Ghost, 287-288; gives man's spirit understanding, 396.

SPIRIT OF MAN—is eternal, 3.

SPIRITUAL BENEFITS—of tithe paying, 330-331.

SPIRIT WORLD—is on the earth, 26; beings in the, 26-28; conditions of the, 29-31; vision concerning the, 32-34; missionary work in the, 33, 34-35; resurrected beings officiate in, 47; no baptisms performed in, 111-112, 120; no marriages performed in, 111.

SPRINKLING — baptism by, not acceptable, 108-109.

STAKES—Presidents of Stakes presides over, 218-219.

STANDARD CHURCH WORKS (see Scriptures)

STEWARDSHIPS (see United Order)

STICK OF JOSEPH (see Book of Mormon)

STRONG DRINKS (see Liquor)

SUCCESSION — question of, to the Presidency, 214-215.

SUFFERINGS—of Jesus necessary for His exaltation, 283-284.

SUN—to be darkened, 233-234, 256; earth to shine like' the, 269-270.

SUNDAY (see also Sabbath)—need for a, law, 363.

SUSTAINING CHURCH OFFICERS—statements on, 216-218.

SWORD—he who will not take up, must flee to Zion, 249-250.

T

TABERNACLE—mortal, necessary for salvation, 138.

TEA (see Hot Drinks)

TEACHERS—position of, in Church government, 211-213.

TEACHING—must precede baptism, 105.

TEMPERATE—in all things be, 321-322.

TEMPLE MARRIAGE (see also Celestial and Eternal Marriage)—benefits of, 302-304; priesthood authority necessary to perform, 305-306.

TEMPLE ORDINANCES—baptism for the dead, 111-113; need for, 120; purpose of, 121-122; same for living and dead, 122-124; the Holy Endowment, 124; the sealing ordinance, 125-126; covenants with God, 126-127; rules regulating, 131-132.

TEMPLES, LATTER-DAY SAINT—need of, 120, 134-135; many to be built, 121, 134, 261; vision concerning, 136.

ISBN 0-88494-012-8
SKU 1673150
$10.95